# SWIMMING UP NIAGARA FALLS!

The Battle to Get Disability Rights Added to the *Canadian Charter of Rights and Freedoms*

# SWIMMING UP NIAGARA FALLS!

The Battle to Get Disability Rights Added to the *Canadian Charter of Rights and Freedoms*

**M. David Lepofsky**

CNIB BEYOND PRINT

Typeset and design by Edwin Wong. Front cover photo by Yinan Chen. Back cover still taken from AODA Alliance, "David Lepofsky bears witness to Parliament on March 19, 2024 (long version with Q&A, 39 minutes)," Ottawa, ON. *YouTube*: <https://www.youtube.com/watch?v=T5EV5zJTDDI>.

CNIB Beyond Print is producing accessible and commercial formats of M. David Lepofsky's book with permission to help make it available to readers with print disabilities and the general market.

This work was initially published by *The Windsor Yearbook of Access to Justice* on April 12, 2024 as follows: Lepofsky, M. David "Swimming Up Niagara Falls! The Battle to Get Disability Rights Added to the Canadian Charter of Rights and Freedoms" (2023) 39 Wind YB Access Just at 169. Online: <https://wyaj.uwindsor.ca/index.php/wyaj/index> DOI: <https://doi.org/10.22329/wyaj.v39.8579>.

Library and Archives Canada Cataloguing in Publication

Title: Swimming up Niagara Falls! : the battle to get disability rights added to the Canadian Charter of Rights and Freedoms / M. David Lepofsky.

Names: Lepofsky, M. David, author.

Description: Includes bibliographical references.

Identifiers: Canadiana (print) 20240459547 | Canadiana (ebook) 20240459601 | ISBN 9781007000118 (softcover) | ISBN 9781007000149 (hardcover) | ISBN 9781007000125 (EPUB) | ISBN 9781007000132 (Kindle)

Subjects: LCSH: People with disabilities—Civil rights—Canada—History—20th century. | LCSH: People with disabilities—Legal status, laws, etc.—Canada—History—20th century. | LCSH: Canada. Canadian Charter of Rights and Freedoms. | LCSH: Lepofsky, M. David. | LCSH: Blind lawyers—Canada—Biography. | LCSH: Lawyers—Canada—Biography. | LCSH: Blind—Canada—Biography. | LCGFT: Autobiographies.

Classification: LCC HV1559.C3 L37 2024 | DDC 323.3/70971—dc23

CNIB Beyond Print
1929 Bayview Avenue. Toronto, Ontario M4G 3E8
beyondprint@cnib.ca
https://cnib-beyondprint.ca

# FOREWORD

This generation will be remembered as the generation that watched rights graduate from legal adolescence into constitutional maturity. One by one, we came increasingly to recognize the discriminatory social, economic, and political impact people experienced based on race, gender, colour, religion, age, or national and ethnic origin. What we had not yet fully appreciated was that people with disabilities were no less entitled to protection and redress for the inhibiting barriers that their disabilities confronted.

Along came David Lepofsky, a scrappy and brilliant blind law student who could not understand — and refused to accept — why protection for equality in section 15 of the newly proposed *Canadian Charter of Rights and Freedoms* excluded people with disabilities. He researched, he cajoled, he advocated, and he, as well as other important disability rights advocates, did not stop until they persuaded. The rest is history.

This book is the story of his personal and professional awakening and how he used the realities of his own life and experiences to figure out how to spread hope, optimism, resilience, and courage among those who had been ignored in the wake of better understood social inequalities. And after he and the other great disability advocates together got recognition in section 15 that it was unconstitutional to discriminate on the basis of disability, he has spent the rest of his life dedicated to making sure that the rest of us understand the multiple impacts that disability and discrimination have on ongoing relationships.

All this is explained in classic Lepofsky style — wry, funny, pungent, poignant, fearless, modest, generous, and proudly different. Ultimately, the story that emerges is the story of a hero and his heroic passion for justice. It was an honour to watch and cheer from a front row seat as all of this unfolded. And it is an even greater honour to be his friend.

Rosalie Silberman Abella
April 2023

# ACKNOWLEDGEMENTS AND DEDICATION

I acknowledge with incredible gratitude my friends who encouraged me for so long to write this account. Thank you for persisting, despite my reluctance. I thank my friends who generously provided wise feedback on drafts and who helped me excavate and review key records of these events from my garage. I am especially indebted to my superb, dedicated, unflappable, thorough, patient, and dependable research assistant, Shirelle Cogan, then a student at the Osgoode Hall Law School, who devoted an incredible number of hours to help make this project come to fruition.

I am deeply grateful to the Canadian National Institute for the Blind for entrusting me with the opportunity to speak for them in 1980 and 1981 on the need for the disability amendment.

Finally, I cannot put into words how lucky I am to have the magnificent Dr. Jill Bee Rich as my wife. She provided entirely candid and unflinching feedback on the final draft, which led to desperately needed and much appreciated improvements.

I bear the sole responsibility for any deficiencies in this text.


I dedicate this retrospective to the memory of my beloved mother Joan Lepofsky, who, by her incredible example, taught me the meaning and importance of "tenacity."

# TABLE OF CONTENTS

# I. INTRODUCTION

## A. The Opening Overture

How did an exhausted, untested, inexperienced, nervous, blind 23-year-old law student find himself in front of an august committee of senators and members of parliament who were holding nationally televised public hearings in December 1980? How did he end up delivering a hastily prepared argument on why equality rights for people with disabilities should be added to the proposed new charter of rights that was to be included in Canada's Constitution?

36 hours earlier, the phone unexpectedly rang in the kitchen of my family's suburban Toronto home. It was dinnertime on a cold December evening. I had just returned home to have dinner with my parents. I had just left an historic afternoon at the Ontario legislature, where I watched with eager anticipation as a provincial bill passed second reading, which, for the first time, would ban discrimination based on disability in employment, housing, goods, and services. I was part of a team of disability rights advocates who had slogged long and hard to reach that interim legislative milestone. After dinner, I planned to get back to cramming for my next exam in a seemingly endless parade of tedious Ontario bar admissions examinations, having cavalierly played hooky that day from studying.

I picked up the phone. My jaw plummeted to the floor. An official from Canada's Parliament was officially inviting the Canadian National Institute for the Blind [CNIB] to make a presentation in Ottawa a scant 36 hours later at the nationally televised public hearings being conducted by the Special Joint Committee of the Senate and the House of Commons on the Constitution of Canada (Joint Committee). I was the one who would have to prepare and deliver that presentation. Two months earlier, I had struggled to talk the CNIB into joining in the public battle over the shape of Canada's reformed Constitution and to let me be its official spokesperson. The time slot we were offered at the Joint Committee was an immediate "take it or leave it" invitation. No, we could not defer this to the following week to give me some hope of properly preparing. I had no speech prepared, no research in progress, no experience appearing before a parliamentary committee, and no training while at law school on basic legal concepts like equality, human rights, or discrimination. I also had no authority to unilaterally accept this invitation. That did not stop me from instantly accepting it.

Two months earlier, in October 1980, Canada's prime minister, Pierre Trudeau, announced that the federal government was going to call on the United Kingdom's Parliament to patriate Canada's Constitution. For the previous 113 years, Canada's Constitution had been a UK statute that only the British Parliament could amend. To "patriate" the Constitution, the British Parliament would transform it into a Canadian law that only Canada could amend. Trudeau had also announced at that time that a new charter of rights would be added to the Constitution. Up to then, our Constitution had included nothing akin to the US *Bill of Rights*, about which Canadians heard so much from American television programs.[1] Trudeau could get only two of Canada's 10 provincial governments to buy into this plan, so he decided to proceed over the objection of the eight hold-out provincial premiers.

It was great that Trudeau's proposed *Charter* would include section 15, a new constitutional right to equality. However, the proposed wording of section 15 would not make it unconstitutional to discriminate because of disability. It banned discrimination based only on race, national or ethnic origin, colour, religion, age, or sex. When I learned of that proposed wording that autumn, I was not happy! Nor were a number of others in the disability community who had learned of it. A number of people with disabilities separately sprang into action. It was realized that we needed an amendment to section 15 of the proposed Charter to add disability to its list of grounds of forbidden discrimination. In this retrospective, I call this the "disability amendment."

In 1980, there was far too little coordination of efforts among those campaigning for the disability amendment. For my part, I knew only a little about a few of the individuals who worked on this goal. I was oblivious to much, if not most, of their efforts. There was very little time to act. Trudeau was on a tear to race his constitutional reform package through Parliament as quickly as possible. We did not have the benefit of vital technology that disability rights advocates now regularly use, such as the Internet and social media. This was not just an uphill battle. It was akin to swimming up Niagara Falls. The chances of winning this one hovered close to zero. However, through a series of events that no one could have predicted in

---

1 *Bill of Rights*, 1791, *General Records of the United States Government*, RG 11, National Archives.

advance, we collectively won. In the following pages, I give my perspective on this saga.

## B. Why this Retrospective?

The little-known saga of the disability amendment is a compelling one. Equality for people with disabilities was the only constitutional right added to the *Canadian Charter of Rights and Freedoms* during the widely publicized 18-month epic battle over the patriation of Canada's Constitution, which lasted from October 1980 to April 1982.[2] It was won without any of the grassroots-organizing experience or the major technological tools that are today an indispensable part of the community organizer's and disability advocate's toolkit.

The disability amendment stands in dramatic contrast to the rest of the *Charter*. The *Charter* as a whole was a top-down idea. It was handed to the public by Canada's political leaders. Before 1980, there was no mass grassroots movement demanding that a charter of rights be added to Canada's Constitution. The 1980–1981 constitutional patriation battle was overwhelmingly a verbal tennis match between federal and provincial politicians and public servants, adorned in their business attire. The public for the most part looked on from the sidelines, as curious or bored spectators, if they were looking at all. In contrast, the disability amendment was a bottom-up phenomenon. The idea of it and the pressure for it came from the public. Admittedly, these were small, barely publicized corners of the public, but their efforts nevertheless won the day.

Sadly, very few know anything about the story of the disability amendment to section 15 of the *Canadian Charter of Rights and Freedoms*. I suspect that, over the past four decades, many who delivered law school courses in Canadian constitutional law did not teach their students that disability was intentionally left out of the original text of the *Charter*'s equality rights guarantee and that we successfully fought to get it added. I question how often, if at all, their students have learned that, during the 18 months of Canada's 1980–1981 constitutional patriation marathon, only one new constitutional right was added to the *Charter* — namely, disability equality. I suspect that many people with disabilities, disability rights

---

2 *Canadian Charter of Rights and Freedoms*, Part 1 of the *Constitution Act, 1982*, being Schedule B to the *Canada Act 1982* (UK), 1982, c 11.

advocates, and disability organizations do not know much, if anything, about these events. People and organizations who today try to get governments and private organizations to take action to remove and prevent disability barriers could benefit from knowing about the fight that disability advocates collectively won in 1980 and 1981 as well as the lessons we learned along the way.

Up to now, extremely little has been written about the battle for the disability amendment. With the help of an able research assistant, all we could find was one book chapter, authored by my friend and disability rights colleague Yvonne Peters (who was also a participant in these events). This retrospective incorporates information that she documented and that I learned from her account. My aim is to record what I recall and what I could document of the major events that took place four decades ago and to help others learn from them, as have I throughout the ensuing years. This is an unusual stew. I ladle into it historic events, an analysis of arguments made, tactical reflections, tips on effective community organizing and law reform advocacy, and a look at how this has influenced disability rights over the following four decades. For good measure, I stirred in a heaping helping of my own personal story as it blended with these other ingredients. The result is part historical account, part legal/constitutional analysis, part autobiography/personal memoir, and part a political activist's handbook on advocacy strategies. Sometimes, these ingredients are neatly separated from each other. At other points, they are blended.

This retrospective draws heavily upon public historical records that I could easily find (mainly the official transcripts or "Hansard" of proceedings in Canada's Parliament), my prodigious personal recollections, and a bundle of internal documents from the CNIB that I have retained for 43 years. I dug those up from a mountain of boxes in my garage in preparation for this retrospective. There turns out to be some benefit in my deep-rooted resistance to throwing anything out!

## C. For Whom this Retrospective is Written

This account is aimed at anyone interested in Canadian political or legal history, people who want to learn about social justice advocacy, and, of course, those interested in Canadian constitutional law. I have an enormous soft spot in my heart for anyone who wants to learn about advocacy on disability issues and, especially, for the next generations of disability rights advocates. I am eager to share insights on strategies, tactics, wins, and losses that could interest anyone who has a hankering for equity, human rights, and social justice. I hope it is also a good read for people who thirst for none of that but who might enjoy an interesting saga.

I hope my contrasting of 1980 tactics with those we use today will be enlightening and even a tad amusing. Writing this, it feels at times like the apocryphal stories of a grandparent telling their grandchild about the olden days when they had to slog on foot through the snow or swamps for hours each morning just to get to school, long before there were school buses. This story can ultimately interest anyone. The disability amendment to the *Charter* is part of Canada's history. I wish it could become part of our collective consciousness. You do not need to know any Canadian constitutional law, or law of any sort, to read this retrospective. At the same time, and perhaps paradoxically, I have endeavoured to make it informative for constitutional law and human rights aficionados. I encourage anyone teaching courses on human rights, discrimination, and equity law, Canadian history, political science, or anything to do with social justice or equity to consider using this retrospective in their curricula.

## D. What You Will Find in these Pages

Here is a quick tour of what lies in the pages ahead. Chapter II sets the stage. It introduces the saga by describing Prime Minister Pierre Trudeau's 1980 proposal to patriate Canada's Constitution. It explains how the proposed new *Charter* left people with disabilities out of the proposed new constitutional right to equality, triggering the need for the disability amendment. Chapter III introduces me into this story. It describes who I was as of 1980, how I became totally blind, and what led me to become interested in advocating for disability rights. Stay tuned for a subway ride in 1974 that changed my life. Chapter IV paints a picture of the advocacy backdrop in 1980. It describes what the world of disability advocacy was like back then, contrasted to the current milieu.

Chapter V explains what I was trying to achieve through my advocacy for the disability amendment. The answer turns out not to be as obvious as it might at first have seemed. Chapter VI tells how I got started in the campaign for the disability amendment, why I chose the CNIB as my soapbox or platform for this advocacy, and how I got the CNIB on board. I also explain what I did to start advocating for the disability amendment. Chapter VII is where I outline the important things that I did not do in 1980 but should have done when advocating for something like the disability amendment. I now have the benefit of many years of voluntary disability rights advocacy efforts, a great deal of new technology, and wins and losses from which I have learned. Chapter VIII digs into the question that pervades this retrospective: why did the Trudeau government decide not to include protection for people with disabilities in section 15 of the *Charter* in the first place? I describe what I thought back in 1980 and what I have cobbled together since then. Chapter IX recounts the story of the vital first round in the campaign for the disability amendment. It was unexpectedly waged at the House of Commons Special Committee on the Disabled and Handicapped, even before the Joint Committee got its hands on the Trudeau patriation package.

Chapter X takes a close look at the arguments presented to Parliament in support of the disability amendment by the two other major disability organizations that were invited to the Joint Committee's public hearings on the constitutional patriation package. Those are the Canadian Organization of Provincial Organizations of the Handicapped [COPOH], which is now called the Council of Canadians with Disabilities, and the Canadian Association for the Mentally Retarded [CAMR], which is now called Inclusion Canada. Chapter XI describes three harmful arguments that were presented by others to Parliament's public hearings, which, if accepted, would have worked against full protection of equality rights for people with disabilities. In this little-known part of our history, those arguments came from other equality-seeking organizations. Chapter XII returns to that unexpected phone call I got on that cold December evening, inviting CNIB to make a presentation to the Joint Committee's public hearings on the proposed reforms to Canada's Constitution. Join me during the following frantic 36 hours of preparation to make that presentation. Chapter XIII is devoted to a close look at the presentation that I made to the Joint Committee hearings on 12 December 1980. Appendix 1 is a transcript of that presentation. Chapter XIV dives into the Joint Committee's clause-by-clause debate over the patriation bill, as it pertains to the disability amendment. It culminates with the Joint Committee passing the disability amendment on 28 January 1981 and rare media coverage of that issue on the CBC national radio the next morning.

In Chapter XV, I do my best to figure out why people with disabilities ended up winning the disability amendment. This question remains an open one. The saga did not end there. Chapter XVI discusses the events in the fall of 1981 in which people with disabilities lost ground. This is because of the last-minute addition to the Charter of the infamous "notwithstanding clause." That clause lets Parliament and provincial legislatures override some constitutional rights with impunity, including our constitutional right to protection against discrimination because of mental or physical disability that we had won earlier that year. I wrap up this retrospective with three concluding chapters. In Chapter XVII, I offer a brief evaluation of the role that the news media played, or should have played, during the campaign for the disability amendment. Chapter XVIII looks at the disability amendment's impact on people with disabilities over the past four decades. Finally, the disability amendment's impact on my own life is explored in Chapter XIX.

Most of the source documents on which I rely would be hard, if not impossible, for you the reader to dig up yourself. As a result, at key points, I include key quotations from them that you can read, skim, or skip, as you like.

## E. The Warning Label!

Here is this retrospective's official warning label. It thankfully has no fine print, writes this blind author! This retrospective is absolutely not a comprehensive objective history of the events that led to the passage of the disability amendment. As a participant in some of these events, I cannot pretend to approximate the role of an objective historian. I attempt to do three things. First, I describe the public events about which I know or about which reliable research can document, such as the record of what was said in Parliament. Second, I tell my own story and record my recollections. Third, I use those events as a platform to help others learn about advocating for disability rights or any other kind of social justice advocacy.

When these events were unfolding, I, in truth, had virtually no idea what I was doing. I learned so much as I stumbled through these events. Looking back on them has taught me even more. I am eager to share what I learned along the way. I want to be sure not to in any way exaggerate my role in the events leading to the disability amendment. I was unbelievably lucky that, so early in my career, circumstances converged to give me a chance to take part in this campaign. I am forever thankful for having had that opportunity.

As I say in every speech that I have given about these events, I was but one of many people whose collective efforts combined to produce a happy result. I have been flummoxed, embarrassed, and uncomfortable on occasions when a well-meaning person over-inflates my role in the campaign to win the disability amendment. This has happened a few times when a person lavishes excessive praise on me while introducing me to an audience before I give a speech. I feel it is very important to correct any such introduction of me. Of necessity, this account focuses on what I did during the battle for the disability amendment. This is because this retrospective is in a significant way akin to a memoir. I wish that I could have unearthed and documented all the efforts of the other people who helped win the disability amendment. I wish as well that we could identify and name them all. I hope this retrospective inspires others to find out more about this history and publish what they discover.

Sadly, several key players are no longer alive. I would not even know how to start to dig up the relevant paper trail if it could be found, beyond what was buried in my garage. I recall that, years ago, a video oral history was recorded with a number of the key players, such as David Smith, the Liberal member of parliament who played a critical role advocating to his Caucus behind closed doors. So far, no one has been able to track down this potential priceless piece of history. I do not recall if I was interviewed for that video oral history. It was online many years ago. It has vanished from the Internet since then. The organization that I thought had created it, the Canadian Disability Rights Council has since dissolved and folded into the Council of Canadians with Disabilities.

After I do an interview, argue a court case, or present to a legislative committee, I always try to critique myself and decide what I could have done better. In these pages, I try to do the same with my advocacy efforts in support of the disability amendment. You are the ultimate judge! The fact that we collectively won the day in 1981 does not mean that every step we each took was the right one. As this account shows, there are things that, in hindsight, I wish I had done differently. That things turned out well in the end does not diminish the importance of learning from errors and oversights.

## F. Spoiler Alert: Five Lessons Lepofsky Learned

So many of the lessons I learned during the *Charter* disability amendment campaign have stuck with me through decades of advocacy since then. Before I start to tell the disability amendment's story, I offer some reflections on what I learned from experiencing it. You can read them now or save them to the end. In any event, this introductory chapter already gave away the big spoiler on the first page. Yes, we did eventually win the disability amendment!

The first lesson I learned from these events is one that I have shared over and over with first-year law students and anyone else interested in learning to do disability rights advocacy. No matter how little knowledge and experience you have when you are just starting out, you still can make a real difference! Do not wait to try until later in your career! Young lawyers are often racked with a distressing sense that they have no idea what they are doing. They are intimidated by senior lawyers who radiate confidence, experience, and tactical sophistication. They fear they must wait for many years until they accumulate much more knowledge, skills, and confidence. I certainly remember being overwhelmed by that early wave of trepidation in my law practice.

Entirely contradicting this, however, is the compelling fact that among the biggest collective "wins" in which I have taken part in over four decades of volunteer disability advocacy was my experience in the fight for the disability amendment. That took place at the very start of my career, months before I even got my ticket to call myself a lawyer! I encourage law students that, when they seek to admit themselves to the bar of justice, they should also admit themselves to the bar of social justice. Grab each chance to make a difference. Sometimes, the most amazing opportunities come at the most unlikely times. The same, I should add, goes for anyone who wants to do social justice advocacy, whether as a lawyer, social worker, politician, public servant, or private individual, whether they are acting as part of a larger organization or venturing into the arena on their own.

Second, I learned from the disability amendment campaign not to be deterred by the fact that a social justice goal appears manifestly impossible to achieve, like swimming up Niagara Falls. In the fall of 1980, it was obvious to me that our chances of winning the disability amendment were, at best, around zero. Equality for people with disabilities was not on the agenda or radar of any political parties. I had no connections within government. The media did not know a thing about this issue. Reporters and pundits were preoccupied with the fight between the federal government and the provinces over the issue of how many provinces needed to agree to the Constitution's patriation. There was scant public discussion of the specific contents of the *Charter*.

Months after we collectively won the disability amendment, I wrote the CNIB a reflective memo on 4 January 1982, summarizing what we gained and the lessons learned. Among these, I concluded that, when it comes to this kind of disability advocacy, "foolish, unrealistic optimism must be the order of the day."[3] I concluded just after these events: "One can never predict how a government decision will be made, since the ebbs and flows of political waters are both easily changed, and hard to understand."[4] Disability advocacy, I have learned, requires an enduring capacity to suspend disbelief. Fortunately, I am a huge fan of the *Star Trek* television series, as these pages reveal at several points. I am used to suspending disbelief, driven by an optimistic view of the future even when the present may seem bleak.

Shortly after the events recounted in this retrospective, my advocacy DNA was permanently rewritten. Since then, I have not been deterred by the fact that an advocacy goal we seek appears to obviously be impossible to achieve. Any number of times, reporters have told me that a goal we are trying to achieve is politically impossible. They skeptically ask how I stay so optimistic. I respond: "Uphill is where we live." I have often been asked: "Don't you get frustrated? Doesn't all that resistance you face just get you down?" My answer is amply fuelled by our experience battling for the disability amendment. You do not do social justice advocacy because it is easy. If it were easy, we would not have to fight for such basic needs and rights. Asking me this question, I explain, is like asking a career swimmer if they mind getting wet! This attitude of unflappable optimism, obvious reality notwithstanding, has become a helpful weapon in our ongoing disability rights advocacy. I want us to be known as people who do not give up. "Tenacity is our middle name," I have tweeted many times.

Third, as this account illustrates, it is important to immediately jump on any advocacy opportunity that unexpectedly drops in your lap, no matter how little potential it appears to offer. You never know when these long-shot efforts may help the cause. When a federal cabinet minister appears on CBC Radio's national call-in program, interrupt studying for bar exams and keep dialing until you get through! Confront the cabinet minister on the air when they least expect it with a question about the disability amendment! When a low-profile powerless Select Parliamentary Committee holds hearings on disability issues that are obviously a superficial public relations exercise, exploit that opportunity to press for progress and build connections with politicians.

---

3 M David Lepofsky, *A Final Report on CNIB Lobbying Work in the Human Rights Area, with a View to Future Advocacy Endeavors* (4 January 1982) at 13.

4 *Ibid* at 13–14.

Fourth, never be deterred by an absence of a grassroots surge in support of your cause. In the fall of 1980, there was no groundswell of grassroots activism pressuring for the disability amendment. Few people with disabilities likely even knew that they were left out of section 15 of the *Charter* or that the *Charter* even had a section 15, or that some people were campaigning for the disability amendment. One of our biggest collective wins in my lifetime was achieved despite all of that.

Finally, the campaign for the disability amendment is an excellent example of a pattern I have discovered time and again in my years as a volunteer disability rights advocate. Most legislation and new government programs do not originate from a grassroots community effort. They instead emerge top-down from the boring platforms of political parties or the dreary offices of unidentified government policy experts, buried in the bureaucracy. I earlier described the proposed *Charter* as one of these. In stunning contrast, some of the most important initiatives to expand the rights of people with disabilities have a "bottom-up" origin. The disability amendment to section 15 of the *Charter*, the 2005 *Accessibility for Ontarians with Disabilities Act*, and the federal 2019 *Accessible Canada Act*, are leading illustrations of these efforts.[5] It has been an honour and a privilege to be part of the campaigns that led to their enactment and that try to get them effectively implemented.

---

5 *Accessibility for Ontarians with Disabilities Act*, SO 2005, c 11; *Accessible Canada Act*, SC 2019, c 10.

# II. SETTING THE STAGE FOR THIS STORY: WHAT WAS PRIME MINISTER PIERRE TRUDEAU'S PROPOSAL TO PATRIATE CANADA'S CONSTITUTION?

## A. Constitution? What Constitution?

The saga that I recount here was spawned by Prime Minister Pierre Trudeau's announcement on 2 October 1980 — namely, that the federal government would call on the British Parliament to patriate Canada's Constitution while adding to it a brand-new *Canadian Charter of Rights and Freedoms*.[1] Shall we set the stage? Let us take a quick jaunt back to the second half of the 19th century. When Canada was established as a country or "dominion" in 1867, its Constitution was very different from the American Constitution. The US Constitution, a single document, was an organic creation of the American colonies after they declared their independence from Great Britain in 1776, clobbered the British in the American Revolution, and started building their new republic. A cadre of US leaders hunkered down in Philadelphia over the summer of 1787 to negotiate a new constitution. They then campaigned around the young country to get each of the states to eventually sign on.

The Canadian constitutional story was oh so different. In 1867, a group of British colonies north of the United States were collectively called British North America. Their own cadre of political leaders got together in Charlottetown, Prince Edward Island. They then met in Quebec City and, finally, in London, England, to hash out the terms of the new union. Canada's so-called "Fathers of Confederation" (yes, all male) decided to join several of the British colonies together as "Canada," driven by fear that the United States might invade British North America. Canada has often inaccurately called itself a "Confederation." It is actually a federation, not a confederation. Government power in a confederation is much more decentralized than in a federation like Canada's.

---

1 *Canadian Charter of Rights and Freedoms*, Part 1 of the *Constitution Act, 1982*, being Schedule B to the *Canada Act 1982* (UK), 1982, c 11 [*Charter*].

Unlike the rebellious United States, this new Canadian political entity remained part of the British Empire, later the British Commonwealth, ultimately under the British Crown. Before 1867, the UK Parliament had authority over British North America. In this new 1867 arrangement, several of Canada's colonies became "provinces." Each had its own provincial legislature and government. A new federal government was created. Canada went on to incorporate lands from the Hudson's Bay Company. Much of that turf later became additional provinces. The rest remain territories within Canada. The United Kingdom retained authority over Canada's foreign affairs for several more decades.

This new arrangement was spelled out in a statute that the UK Parliament passed called the *British North America Act, 1867*.[2] Canadian constitutional law buffs called it the *BNA Act*. The *BNA Act*, along with several other entirely unexciting and lesser-known British statutes, combined to make up Canada's Constitution.[3] The UK Parliament's ultimate control over Canada continued even after 1867. It was not until 1931 that Canada secured ultimate sovereignty over all its laws, except for those British laws that had created Canada's Constitution. If Canada wanted to alter that Constitution, it could not do so itself. It had to ask the UK Parliament to amend the *BNA Act* — an intermittent dry topic of conversation over the next century but likely not by very many people.

In 1977, when I studied constitutional law in law school, what we studied was the *BNA Act*. We read arcane cases interpreting it. Those court decisions explored which kinds of laws the provincial legislatures could pass and which ones Canada's Parliament could enact (federalism cases). Off and on during the 1970s, there were inconclusive discussions between the federal government and the provinces over the idea of patriating Canada's Constitution. If Canada asked, the UK Parliament would give up any authority to amend Canada's Constitution. Once patriated, Canada's Constitution would become an organic Canadian law, along the same lines as the US Constitution.

By 1980, Canada's politicians were embroiled in a seemingly endless spat over how many provinces must support a change to Canada's Constitution before the UK Parliament could or should pass a British law to

---

2 *British North America Act, 1867* (UK), 30–31 Vict, c 3.

3 Donald F Bur, *Laws of the Constitution: Consolidated* (Edmonton: University of Alberta Press, 2021).

amend it. Before we could patriate our Constitution, the federal government and provinces first had to figure out what the rules would be for amending the Constitution once patriated. That was referred to as the Constitution's "amending formula." This new amending formula would have to be written into the new patriated Constitution. The bun fights among politicians and between senior public servants went on and on. Canada's provinces and the federal government squabbled and postured in public and private.[4] Some wanted to shift the balance of power between the federal government and the provinces, making one level of government or the other stronger. A patriation package could adjust this debate.

Also on the squabbling table over the 1970s was a proposal to add a charter of rights to Canada's Constitution. A charter of rights could list a series of fundamental constitutional rights, rights that no laws or government action could ever violate — well, subject to exceptions, of course! They hurled pastry projectiles over that too! Prime Minister Pierre Trudeau was a passionate proponent of "entrenching" (including in the Constitution) a charter of rights. Some provincial premiers were dead set against it. The public was, for the most part, a bystander to all of this, when it should have been a central participant in the discussion. After all, were they not our rights that were on the bargaining table?

By 1980, the US *Bill of Rights* had been part of the US Constitution for around two centuries.[5] In contrast, Canada's Constitution had no bill or charter of constitutional rights at all. In some fleeting Canadian case law, some judges suggested that there might be an implied bill of rights in Canada's Constitution. Those judges considered reading some basic rights, like the freedom of expression, into Canada's Constitution, as an unwritten bill of rights.[6] That viewpoint never commanded a majority view in the

---

4 Robert Sheppard & Michael Valpy, *The National Deal: The Fight for a Canadian Constitution* (Toronto: Fleet Books, 1982) at 38–64, 65–77.

5 *Bill of Rights*, 1791, *General Records of the United States Government*, RG 11, National Archives.

6 See e.g. *Boucher v The King*, [1951] SCR 265, [1950] 1 DLR 657; *Saumur v City of Quebec*, [1953] 2 SCR 299, [1953] SCJ No 49 (QL); *Switzman v Elbling and Attorney General of Quebec*, [1957] SCR 285, 7 DLR (2d) 337; *McKay et al v The Queen*, [1965] SCR 798, 53 DLR (2d) 532; *Nova Scotia Board of Censors v McNeil*, [1978] 2 SCR 662, [1978] SCJ No 25 (QL); *Dupond v City of Montreal et al*, [1978] 2 SCR 770, [1978] SCJ No 33 (QL); *Attorney General of Canada v Law Society of British Columbia*, [1982] 2 SCR 307, [1982] SCJ No 70 (QL).

Supreme Court of Canada. By 1980, it was clear that Canadian courts would not invent and vigorously enforce their own unwritten constitutional bill of rights. It was up to legislators to entrench a bill or charter of constitutional rights in our Constitution.

"But what about the *Canadian Bill of Rights* that Canada's Parliament enacted in 1960?"[7] By 1980, the *Canadian Bill of Rights* two decades on the law books had turned out to be an abysmal flop. It was just an ordinary federal statute, not a list of rights that were entrenched in the Constitution. It applied only to the federal government and not to the actions of the provincial legislature or municipal governments. The Supreme Court of Canada had interpreted it so narrowly that it was toothless and ineffective.[8] This was another unsubtle judicial signal that, if Canada wanted fundamental rights to be taken seriously and given full judicial force, they needed to be entrenched as constitutional rights.

## B. Trudeau's Decision to Go it Alone in October 1980

As the summer of 1980 unfolded, things heated up in Ottawa on this not-so-hot topic. No agreement had been reached between federal and provincial politicians over the patriation of Canada's Constitution, the amending formula to be added to it, or the possibility of entrenching a charter of rights.[9] Hanging over the political leaders and the country was an additional constitutional burning question for maybe a dozen or so Canadians to angrily argue about at their breakfast tables: how much support did a patriation package need before the UK Parliament could pass it? Could the federal government go it alone and ask the UK Parliament with none of the provinces supporting it? If some provinces were needed to endorse the federal government's request of London, then how many supportive provinces was the mandatory minimum?

---

7 *Canadian Bill of Rights*, SC 1960, c 44.

8 See generally Walter Surma Tarnopolsky, *The Canadian Bill of Rights*, 2nd rev ed (Toronto: McClelland & Stewart, 1975).

9 See Sheppard & Valpy, *supra* note 4 at 38–64, 65–77.

By September 1980, it was clear that no patriation deal was going to be reached through federal-provincial negotiation. On 2 October 1980, Prime Minister Trudeau announced that, because no agreement was reached through negotiation, his federal government would unilaterally ask the UK Parliament to patriate the Constitution.[10] His package included a new charter of rights and a constitutional amending formula.

## C. What Did Trudeau Propose in His *Canadian Charter of Rights and Freedoms*?

The *Canadian Charter of Rights and Freedoms* that Trudeau placed before Canada's Parliament in October 1980 included fundamental freedoms like freedom of expression and religion (section 2), democratic rights to vote in and run for federal or provincial elections (section 3), mobility rights to enter and leave Canada or travel freely from province to province (section 6), legal rights like the right to a fair trial for accused persons (sections 8–14), and minority language educational rights for French and English linguistic minorities across Canada (section 23).[11] Most important of all for this saga, it included a new constitutional guarantee of the right to equality in section 15.

Section 15 of the *Charter*, as initially proposed in October 1980, read as follows:

> Non Discrimination Rights
>
> 15. (1) Everyone has the right to equality before the law and to the equal protection of the law without discrimination because of race, national or ethnic origin, colour, religion, age or sex.
>
> Affirmative action programs
>
> (2) This section does not preclude any law, program or activity that has as its object the amelioration of conditions of disadvantaged persons or groups.

The constitutional rights in this draft of the *Charter* were not designed to be absolute. Section 1 of the original text of the *Charter* in October 1980 created this massive loophole:

---

10 *Ibid* at 78–79.

11 *Charter*, *supra* note 1.

Guarantee of Rights and Freedoms

1. The *Canadian Charter of Rights and Freedoms* guarantees the rights and freedoms set out in it subject only to such reasonable limits as are generally accepted in a free and democratic society with a parliamentary system of government.

## D. Our Problem: Equality for People with Disabilities was Left Out!

Sometime in the fall of 1980, I first read the wording of the proposed section 15 of the *Charter*. It was instantly clear to me beyond any doubt that it categorically left out equality for people with disabilities. The only grounds of discrimination that it forbade were those that it listed. Disability was nowhere to be found! I was livid but hardly surprised. In situation after situation, people with disabilities are so often simply left out. What was I to do about it? We needed Parliament to amend this proposed *Charter*, to add disability to the list of grounds on which discrimination was to be forbidden. To economize the number of words that I use to describe this (which is not usually in my nature), I call it "the disability amendment." What did I do about it? What did others do? That is the story that lies ahead.

## E. The National Fight Begins Over the Trudeau Plan

The federal opposition parties had to quickly figure out where they stood on Trudeau's entire constitutional reform strategy.[12] By the end of October 1980, the opposition federal New Democratic Party, Canada's national social democratic party, went on the record supporting the patriation package.[13] So were the governments of Ontario and New Brunswick. The other provinces were opposed. Joining them in opposition to Trudeau was the federal Progressive Conservative Party.[14] The battle lines were drawn. Let the political slugfest begin! On 23 October 1980, Trudeau's Liberal government used its majority in the House of Commons to impose "closure."[15] That ended the first round of debates on the floor of the House of Commons on the

---

12 See Sheppard & Valpy, *supra* note 4 at 78–109, 110–134.

13 *Ibid* at 115–118.

14 *Ibid* at 50, 78–109.

15 Canada, Parliament, *House of Commons Debates*, 32nd Parl, 1st Sess, Vol IV (23 October 1980) at 3978.

patriation package and punted it to a parliamentary committee to study the bill. Normally, that would be a committee of the House of Commons. Later, after the House passed the bill, it would be expected to go to Canada's Senate (whose members are appointed and not elected to office) for debates and vote. The Senate too could set up a committee to study the bill.

To move things along more quickly, the Trudeau government decided that the bill would go instead to a Special Joint Committee of the Senate and the House of Commons, an exceptional procedure.[16] That committee would include some members of parliament (that is, elected members of the House of Commons) as well as some appointed senators. Canada's two Houses of Parliament, the appointed Senate, and the elected House of Commons could move this all along more quickly, and avoid duplication of effort, by holding one set of public hearings in this Joint Committee. Otherwise, there could have been one set of public hearings before the House of Commons and later another set of duplicative public hearings before the Senate.

The committee was called the Special Joint Committee of the Senate and the House of Commons on the Constitution of Canada [Joint Committee]. It was that Joint Committee before which I appeared on 12 December 1980 to press for the disability amendment. The Joint Committee started its work on 6 November 1980. It immediately got tied up in procedural wrangling.[17] 1 week later, on 13 November 1980, the Trudeau government agreed that the Joint Committee would televise its proceedings.[18] The opposition had pressed for this decision, which turned out to have been very good for the government and for those of us pressing for the disability amendment. The House of Commons had begun to allow television cameras to record and broadcast debates on the floor of the House a mere 3 years earlier. It had never before televised any parliamentary committee.

Initially, the Joint Committee had ridiculously short timelines to hold public hearings, to debate the bill's details, and to vote on possible amendments. On 2 December 1980, again responding to opposition pressure, the government allowed the Joint Committee an additional 2 months to do its work, ending on 6 February 1981.[19] Had they not granted that extension,

---

16 Sheppard & Valpy, *supra* note 4 at 343.

17 *Ibid* at 343.

18 *Ibid*.

19 *Ibid*.

I would never have had the chance to appear before the Joint Committee. The Joint Committee finished its work and reported the bill back to Parliament on 13 February 1981.[20] From there, the House of Commons and Senate could give the bill its final consideration.

[20] Canada, Senate and House of Commons, *Minutes of Proceedings and Evidence of the Special Joint Committee of the Senate and of the House of Commons on the Constitution of Canada*, Report to Parliament, No 57 (13 February 1981), online: <primarydocuments.ca/wp-content/uploads/2018/04/SpecJointComConstitution571981Feb13.pdf>.

# III. WHO WAS DAVID LEPOFSKY IN 1980?

## A. My Long and Winding Road Leading to Total Blindness

What circuitous path led me to end up as a 23 year old in front of a daunting assembly of members of Canada's House of Commons and Senate on the morning of 12 December 1980, with 45 minutes to try to convince them to make an unprecedented, unexplored, lasting change to Canada's Constitution for the benefit of people with disabilities? The David Lepofsky of 2023, writing this, is light years away from the David Lepofsky in the fall of 1980. I am eager to illuminate some of the decisive events in my young life that made me tick back then.

When I was born in Toronto on 6 June 1957, I had no eyesight in my right eye. My left eye had limited but quite useful near vision. I was born with a weird combination of eye problems. In my early teens, I asked my world-renowned ophthalmologist Dr. Michael Shae what my eye condition was called. He pondered longer than I had expected and then declared: "Lepofsky syndrome." My eyes' strange brew of birth malformations made me ophthalmologically unusual. When I was a child and early teen, I thought of myself as a sighted person, albeit one with partial or low vision. I did not then refer to myself as "blind." I was very, very near-sighted. My good eye, the left one, could see clearly with rich detail when people or objects were within a few meters. With that eye, I had to be 20 feet away to see what a normally functioning eye could see from 400 feet away.

I visually recognized people when they were within a few feet of me. If they were 10 or 15 feet away, I could tell there were people there and might, depending on the lighting, be able to discern the colour of their clothes, but I could not visually tell who they were. I wore glasses, but they did not really help. Glasses could not fix this vision limitation. It amazed me just how many strangers over the years asked my mother Joan Lepofsky and me why we did not get stronger glasses. When they would offer my mother and me this sage and unsolicited advice, I would sarcastically think to myself: "Shucks, why the heck didn't we ever think of that clever idea?"

I could read a print book if I held it a few inches from my nose. Ever since I was a little kid, I was a voracious reader of books, novels, comic magazines, newspapers, and anything else I could grab. Superhero comic magazines — Marvel but, of course, never DC — were a favourite. My mother caught me one morning when I falsely claimed that I had not been up all night reading comic magazines. She did not let me know until I was much older that, as I shamelessly fibbed to her, I had a telltale big black ink dot on my nose and chin from holding the comic magazines so close to my face.

Like my friends, I watched television endlessly as a child and teen. I had to sit within a few feet of the screen to see it clearly. An expensive huge television might be as large as 20 inches back then. If only we could have had the much larger screens of today! I typically watched black and white television. My mother was concerned about radiation exposure from sitting too close to a colour television, a supposed side effect indicated by some news reports. Who knew? Later, I got a high magnification "monocular" to help me sit further away while watching television. It was half of a pair of binoculars, mounted in frames of eyeglasses, a clever new visual aid in the 1960s. It felt like quite a weight on my nose. It let me watch colour television while sitting a few feet away from that radiation we feared.

I had no depth perception because I was blind in one eye. Friends enjoyed ribbing me about my "lack of depth." I discerned distance by the size of objects in the configuration of their shadows. I suppose that is how sighted people with stereoscopic vision perceive depth when they watch a two-dimensional surface image, such as a movie on a movie screen or a flat screen television or computer monitor. I could ride a bike during the day but not safely at night. During the latter years of elementary school, I regularly rode a bike to and from school. My parents never knew how often I slipped out to ride at night despite this prohibition! Somehow, I was never injured.

Looking at me from a distance, you would think I was a sighted kid who wore glasses. If you watched me reading, you would suddenly realize that I was very near-sighted. Until my early teens, around age 14, I did not use or need a white cane. At school, my nickname was "Lepo." I was lousy at sports. If I tried playing baseball, the pitcher came up within 4 feet of me and softly lobbed a slow ball over the plate. At school, this became known as the "Lepo pitch." I never felt that it was meant as a flattering term but just let the barb slide off of me. I was used to having to stand out in a crowd, literally if not just figuratively. When the teacher wrote on the blackboard, the major educational technology in a 1960s classroom, I had permission to stand right behind them so I could read what was on the board. At a school assembly, with the television screen showing a program for our class to watch (likely no bigger than a 20-inch screen, I suspect), I either sat in the front row or stood up right beside the television.

In school, I always did very well academically, except in my Grade 1 reading group. I was assigned to the group of slower readers. I suspect I was learning to read more slowly due to my eyesight. However, David, the Grade 1 student, was left to think that maybe I just was not very intelligent. In my school playground, my peers frowned upon academic accomplishments. Only athletic prowess was glorified. We had no education on inclusion for people with disabilities, nor am I aware of any efforts at the school to ensure that I had a welcoming environment to participate on a footing of equality. It was sink or swim. I suppose that necessity led me to learn how to swim. That sure helped when it came time in 1980 to try to figuratively swim up Niagara Falls.

By the time I appeared before the Special Joint Committee of the Senate and the House of Commons on 12 December 1980, I had been totally blind for a little over 2 years. When I was a child, I had no idea that my eyesight would start to slowly drop in my teens and that I would end up totally blind in the summer of 1978. Quite unexpectedly, my eyesight in my good eye started gradually dropping in January or February 1971. I was 13 and in Grade 9, my last year at St. Andrews Junior High School. At first, I noticed that it was getting harder to read print. I somehow muddled through. I started seeing small white flashes or sparkles in my field of vision. I told others that it was like having snow (interference) in a television program that came over the air waves, via a television antenna.

Even back then, I was a huge *Star Trek* fan, and I watched the show religiously when it was on the air for its first run. Drawing on a *Star Trek* image I knew well, I then and now equated what I saw to the sparkling or flashing evil alien in the *Star Trek* episode "Day of the Dove" (season 3, episode 11, of the original *Star Trek* series that first aired on 1 November 1968), just 3 years before my vision started to drop. I have since learned that the *Star Trek* visual effect was multicolour. I had seen it as light coloured since I was then watching a black and white television. As such, my mental image of the *Star Trek* alien was white, as was the flashing I started to see during the winter of 1971.

I had to try to see around or through this visual interference. My ophthalmologist thought there were prenatal strands attached to the cataracting lens in my left or good eye that were tugging on my retina as my lens was growing during my adolescent years. I gather these strands were in effect pulling off the retina. Over the next 6 years, my remaining eyesight got worse and worse. I developed cataracts. I recall one evening during high school that my dad was driving me somewhere, and I looked out the car window at passing streetlights. I could see the light splitting into two lights, diffusing around my cataracted lens, so much so that I felt I could almost see the shape of the lens itself. "Curious," I thought to myself.

I had to gradually learn skills like the use of a white cane to navigate independently. I took training to learn to read Braille. I also started using recorded audio books, then made available on large reel-to-reel tapes. From the time my vision started dropping in early 1971 until I reached the point where my useful vision was gone in the summer of 1978, we had no idea if it would keep on dropping until my vision was all gone or if it would level off at some point. We took things one day at a time. My eyes were too fragile to attempt surgery. As my eyesight kept getting worse, my ophthalmologist suggested an alternative experimental treatment. He offered to inject an enzyme into my good eye that might dissolve the prenatal strands in that eye that he thought were pulling my retina off. In a normal eye, those strands dissolve or disappear before birth. Who said I did anything the way everyone else does?

I think I was born hard-wired to think far outside the box when solving unusual problems. I asked my ophthalmologist whether maybe it would be wise to first try that enzyme injection in my bad right eye, to see if it had the desired effect. That right eye was already totally blind, so I had nothing to lose if something went wrong as a result of that injection. My doctor pondered my medical suggestion and then agreed with it! Wow! Should I have gone into medicine instead of law? That was a non-starter. I could not stand the sight of blood, and I get nauseous whenever someone describes medical details to me about anything. Imagine me decades later, trying not to gag when reading autopsy reports for homicide cases. My bad eye got the injection. It was a disaster. The injection triggered a massive and very painful response that lasted for months. It required a series of unpleasant follow-up treatments to neutralize it. Therefore, we decided not to try that injection in my good eye. It is a very good thing we tried it in my bad right eye first!

By the fall of 1976, as I began law school at the age of 19, my vision was so low that it was not very useful. By that time, I used a white cane when travelling outside my home. I tried with very limited success to use my remaining dwindling eyesight to detect landmarks to guide me when walking around. That became harder and harder over time. This was because my vision was so limited and because it varied from day to day. I never knew if and when I could count on it. There was an extraordinary synergy and symmetry between my mother and me (with whom I was very close, to whom I am forever indebted, and whom I miss every day since she died in 2013). It typified how we successfully worked together on so many challenging issues throughout the years of her life.

Her love for me drove her to not want me to feel impeded by a mother's natural worry about the possibility of further vision loss. Out of my love for her, I did not want her to worry that my vision loss was getting the better of me and holding me back. This led the two of us to together approach my vision loss with an unremitting "can do" attitude. It was something that needed to be successfully conquered, without doubts or second thoughts. She and I just sauntered ahead with doctors' appointments and whatever else awaited us, tackling each issue as it came up as a challenge to be strategized and bested. My mother is forever a shining role model to all parents. Parents of a child with a disability play a decisive role in their child's success. They can either hold them back or help them move forward. As a parent now myself, I have an inkling of how hard it was for her to keep her worry about me in check as well as she did over my formative teen years, while I slowly transitioned from low vision to total blindness.

One day in the first month of law school in the fall of 1976, my good eye did not seem right, even for me. I went to my parents' bedroom to talk to my mother about it. I took her reading lamp and aimed it right into my face. This totally freaked out my mother. The lamp I had directed point blank into my face from inches away was blazingly bright. I saw bright red. I said: "Mom, I'm seeing red, literally!" A rushed trip to my ophthalmologist revealed that my eyeball had internally hemorrhaged and was filled with blood. Gradually, blood vessels had been popping. This made it harder for me to see. My eye doctor explained to me that the only real option to end all these eye problems was to have both eyes surgically removed and replaced with artificial eyes. I was wrenchingly queasy at the thought but game in principle. I felt that there was nothing really to lose and something to gain from that surgery. Yet I was anything but eager to sign on the dotted line to subject myself to this surgery, no matter how clearly I knew that I should do it. I was a busy law student. I did not want to stop everything and spend days in the hospital and in recovery.

My parents were extremely reluctant about my having this surgery. To them, it seemed so final and irreversible. My mother especially worried about permanently severing my optic nerve. That could prevent me from ever being able to see again, should some amazing futuristic new technology or treatment come along that could restore my eyesight. The downward slide of my vision loss came to a climax in July 1978. I was 21, between second and third years at law school, and working as a counsellor at a Jewish educational summer camp in Ontario called Camp Ramah. I did not have much residual eyesight to speak of. One day, I was sitting in the camp library, schmoozing with someone. I flipped open a file folder to extract a piece of paper to discuss. The folder somehow flipped up towards my face. Its corner or edge gently jabbed my left eye, the eye with a bit of residual vision. It hurt a bit at the moment but seemed like nothing to worry about.

Later that night I awoke in my cabin with searing eye pain. That file folder had triggered another huge hemorrhage in my eye. I spent two stressful days medicated in the camp infirmary. The camp then shipped me off to a Toronto hospital, 2 or 3 hours away. I told the camp director not to notify my parents until I arrived in Toronto and the hospital gave me a diagnosis. I did not want to worry them, at least until I knew what was going on. Two months earlier, my father had had a heart attack, his second that year. I did not want to add to his stress level. This eye accident was the catalyst that got me to agree to have my eyes surgically removed. I was terrified about the surgery but delighted to get it over with. My parents were very reluctant.

I had incorrectly thought that, after the surgery, I would be left with two grotesque holes in the middle of my eye sockets. I also believed that artificial eyes were round balls, like a pair of marbles that I would have to somehow stuff into those gaping holes. That sounded nauseating to me. It was not until after the surgery that I found out that this was all wrong. An artificial eye is like a thick contact lens that I could easily slip under my eyelid. A ton of unnecessary stress would have been eliminated had the medical staff given me the most rudimentary advance briefing on the surgery and its consequences. But heck, I am just the patient, right?

Once I decided that I wanted the surgery, I had to convince my parents to agree. I drew heavily on my reservoir of nascent lawyering skills to convince them to accept my decision. I knew I wanted to go ahead with the surgery whether or not they agreed. However, I wanted their support for my decision and was eager to avoid familial stress. My parents ultimately agreed with my decision but not happily. That surgery in early August 1978 utterly liberated me. Afterwards, I told friends that it was the only medical treatment on my eyes that had actually improved my life! I came out of the surgery looking like I had convincingly lost one heck of a bar fight. My face above my nose was very swollen. I was bandaged in a way I described as making me look like the masked Robin the Boy Wonder (from the Adam West 1960s television series that I still visually remember very well). After a few painful post-surgical days, the swelling around my eyes gradually went down. I no longer had the deep, penetrating intermittent eye pain that had plagued me for several years.

Weeks later, the time came to be fitted for my artificial eyes. I got to choose my eye colour! An outrageously funny discussion ensued over the choice of eye colour. I was going to be a lawyer, so would blue pinstripe be the best choice? How about chartreuse? Could I get different pairs of prosthetic eyes coloured to match different outfits? My new artificial eyes looked like regular eyes, far better than my discoloured, disfigured natural eyes. I never again had to fear a bump to the head or a minor poke in the eyes that could send me to the hospital in agony. Sometime after this surgery, I walked right into a tree branch. It jabbed one of my new artificial eyes. It did not bother me in the least. Who else would happily celebrate a tree branch jabbing them in the eye? I just laughed it off, recalling the visuals of bullets harmlessly bouncing right off the chest of Superman in the hokey live action 1950s television series starring George Reeves.

I have often been asked what I now "see." Is it darkness, as popular lore and many television shows suggest? Do I live in a world of black? Is it like the experience of sighted people when they try turning off the lights at home at night in a sincere but misguided effort to see what the world is like for blind people? I experience absolutely none of that. Blindness is NOT darkness. It is the absence of any visual input. Look at it this way: I would be just as totally blind if I was immersed in a world of pure white or red or any other colour. Black is not what I experience. All those movies, television shows and books that equate blindness with darkness are, to be blunt, nonsense.

When school kids ask if I see black, I ask them to try to look at me through their belly button. Do you see blackness when you look at me through your belly button, I ask? Puzzled, they laugh. They tell me they don't see anything at all through their belly button. Well, that is the same for me, when I try to look using my eyes. Or is it? Actually, not all the time!

Sometimes my brain tries on its own to automatically generate something of a visual image of the world in front of me. That mental image lacks the rich detail that sighted folks see. It tends to be skewed towards the left side of the world in front of me. This is because back when I could see, I could only see through my left eye. Shortly after we met in 2002, my beloved wife Jill told me that I had to adjust how I aim my face when I want to look at someone. Until then, it turns out that, unknowingly, I used to routinely look at a person a bit off centre. This is because when I could still see, I had to turn my head slightly to get a person into the centre of my visual field. After I was no longer able to see, I retained this automatic practice until Jill straightened me out (literally). She has done that in a great many other ways as well.

Here is another odd layer to what my brain produces as a mental image whenever it generates anything at all. In my last years of useful vision, my visual field was overlaid with snow or visual static, like that evil *Star Trek* alien that I mentioned earlier. That visual special effect stuck with my brain and still persists in my mind's eye today if I try to conjure up a mental image of the world in front of me. For those who wonder how deeply *Star Trek* could possibly be embedded in my brain, mull over that one! I am keenly aware of two major advantages that I enjoy compared to some other blind people. First, my vision dropped very slowly over 7 years. In contrast, some others have total vision one day, driving a car and doing all the other things that a totally sighted person might do. The next day, they are suddenly totally blind due to an accident, injury, or medical condition. What a shocker that must be.

I had years to gradually adjust to vision loss. By the time my last bit of eyesight vanished, I was fully armed with all the adaptive skills I needed to live independently without eyesight. I did not need a crash course on how to use a white cane or do other tasks of daily living for which sighted people use their eyes. The only functional loss I noticed after my eyes were surgically removed in August 1978 — a change that felt a bit unnerving at first — came at some family function a few weeks after my surgery. We all posed for a photograph. I had heard long before this that, for some people who only have light perception, the loss of this residual ability was challenging. That had made no sense to me previously. When the photograph was snapped that day using a camera with a flash bulb (ancient technology compared to today's smartphones), I instinctively braced myself for the jarring effect of a flash. Shortly before my eye surgery in 1978, I could still see a camera flash, even when I could no longer see much else. What? I saw no flash that day! It was not a big deal, viewed objectively. Yet it stunned me for a moment. I guess I really cannot see anything now, I cleverly reflected to myself.

The second advantage for me was that, before I lost my last remaining vision, I had had the first 13 years of my life to visually learn about the world using the limited eyesight I then had. I learned to read print and to understand what the world looks like. No one had to teach me what the traffic pattern is at a four-way intersection. I had seen that traffic pattern since I was a child. Those who are born with no eyesight have to be actively taught this and a host of other visual and spatial concepts. Those concepts can be and are effectively taught to those who are born blind. For me, these were things I did not have to learn once I became completely blind. Importantly, in August 1978, I already knew what the Starship Enterprise looked like, at least the one bearing the serial no. NCC-1701. To learn about later versions of the Enterprise over the years after I lost my residual vision, I had to buy a plastic model of each — models that surround me in my home office as I write these words.

Here is an especially weird feature of my experience with total blindness. Seven or eight years before I lost my last residual vision, a blind adult came to my high school to talk to my class about blindness. I listened with interest, not knowing that, years later, I would end up totally blind myself. A student asked him if he remembered colours. He had previously been sighted. I vividly recall him explaining that he remembered the primary colours but none of the others. How ridiculous, I thought. How can you remember some colours but not others? Well, decades later, I discovered that he was right. 44 years after losing my remaining eyesight, I can remember the primary colours but none of the others. Let's not even start with teal or taupe, which I never saw or knew about when I could see. Popularizing new colour names after I lost my sight is just plain nasty!

In the end, I have had a foot in two very different camps. When I had good but limited eyesight, I viewed totally blind people as "others." I remember that, when I was a pre-teen, some totally blind youth treated me at some event as an outsider because I had useful vision. I am now living on the other side of that visual divide. My journey from partial vision to eventual total blindness was very gradual. There was no one single moment when I declared to myself that I would thence forward use the word "blind" to describe myself. For several years before my eyes were surgically removed, many people looking at me thought I was blind because I used a white cane. Many incorrectly think that anyone using a white cane must be totally blind. In fact, many people with partial vision use a white cane as an orientation and mobility aid. The white cane is a symbol of some degree of vision loss, which may or may not amount to total blindness.

When I started using the white cane early on in high school, my diminishing eyesight helped me find my way around. I needed the cane for two reasons. First, it helped me detect steps down. I was less and less able to see them. Second, it alerted others that, if I bumped into them, it was by accident and not on purpose. Yet members of the public so often misunderstand what a white cane really signifies. Some students who did not know me criticized me in the halls at school for using a white cane: "Hey! You shouldn't be using a white cane! It's obvious that you can see some things! You're not really blind!" This pervasive misunderstanding is made all the worse by the widespread use of the problematic and misleading term "legally blind." It implies that a person with that label cannot see at all and that this is truly a legal definition. In fact, there is no single, all-purpose legal definition of blindness. Blindness is defined differently in different laws for different purposes.

Over the years, some blindness agencies have unfortunately used the term "legally blind" to describe people who are either totally blind or who have a specified amount of partial vision. Yet the public correctly understands that "blind" means that a person cannot see anything. It confuses many when a person who obviously can see some things is described as "legally blind." I have learned that there is a huge difference between going blind, on the one hand, and being blind, on the other. If a sighted person suddenly loses their vision, they experience a deeply traumatic catastrophic loss ("going blind"). At that moment, there is so much that they can no longer do. They had always depended on their eyesight for almost everything. Now, it is gone!

Yet living with blindness ("being blind") is a very different experience. After a person experiences vision loss, whether shockingly sudden or, as in my case, gradually, they can learn many effectively alternative ways to do things to replace the role that their eyesight used to fulfill in areas like reading, getting around safely, and doing activities of daily living, such as dressing, cooking, and cleaning. Being blind — namely, living with blindness — is like learning to live using a different language. If you only speak English and you were suddenly deposited in a place where only Greek was spoken, you would be lost and incapable of using spoken or written language to communicate. It would all be Greek to you. But once you learn to speak Greek, you could fully function and thrive. Adjustment to blindness is very similar. Trying to experience what it is like to be blind by plunging oneself into total darkness is nothing like what I experience as a blind person.

As mentioned earlier, some sighted people unfortunately seek to find out what it is like to be blind by turning out the lights at home and trying to manage. This would be analogous to parachuting a monolingual English speaker into a Greek-speaking community and trying to converse with others there. When a sighted person does that "lights out" experiment at home, they are unknowingly contributing to long-term, harmful attitudinal barriers from which we blind people regularly suffer. Long afterwards, they remember the wrenching feeling of panic, fear, and disorientation that shook them when they turned off the lights and tried to safely get around. Too often, they incorrectly think that this is what living with blindness is like for me. I have had people over the years reveal the following thoughts: "David, it is just unbelievable what you blind people can do. I tried it once at home. I turned off the lights. It was terrifying. I could not last 5 minutes. You must really be amazing!" It is quite hard to disabuse people of that attitude. It can be very deep-rooted, fueled by strong emotions. It is even harder when a person saying this genuinely feels that they are paying you a huge compliment.

## B. The Meandering Path That Led Me to Disability Rights Advocacy

### *1. Not Pre-Destined*

As a child or early teen, I never had any idea that I would take up the cause of equality for people with disabilities. My mother thought that I wanted to be a lawyer since shortly after I first landed on the delivery room table in 1957. However, disability rights advocacy was not part of my neonatal plans, and, in fact, I had never heard of it up to my early teens. If there was anyone then publicly doing disability rights advocacy in Canada, none had come to my attention. There was no role model influencing me in that direction.

In my pre-teens and early teens, when I still had the full amount of near eyesight with which I was born, I had little if any idea about disabilities generally. I was once sitting on a bus when an older companion who was with me told me that there was a blind person sitting across from me. Unknowingly, I started staring at them. "David, stop staring at that blind person," my companion quite properly instructed me. Can you imagine me, now a blind disability rights advocate, having years ago reflexively stared at a blind person just because they are blind?

A few years later, when I was a teen and using a white cane, it drove my mother bonkers when she saw strangers staring at me. She devised a clever counter-measure. "David, stare at 9 o'clock," she would devilishly prompt me. I would turn to my left, white cane in hand, and unleash a killer stare. The stranger, who had been staring at me, instantly would break off their stare and turn away, quite embarrassed, my mother proudly informed me. Did this become something of a game that my mother and I enjoyed? Did my friends enjoy it too, when walking with me in public?

Over time, several transformative moments in my early years dramatically shaped my understanding of equality for people with disabilities and ignited within me a powerful compulsion to advocate for this cause. Separated in time, the incidents were not connected. Looking back, I see how they worked together.

## *2. The Swimming Pool Incident*

A transformative moment likely happened when I was less than 10 years old. I was swimming in a pool with my eyes closed. I swam face first into the pool's side wall. I stood up, nose throbbing. I had a look of terror on my face. I held my hand out in front of me, palm up. "Don't worry David!" said someone who saw my evident panic. I was looking down at my palm, which looked like it was full of blood. "It's just a few drops of blood that fell out of your nose, David. You're okay! When a little bit of blood hits all that water in your hand, it looks like a lot of blood!"

Why was this so transformative for me? I would not know the answer for more than a decade. I learned its significance during my disability advocacy activities in my adult years, such as the campaign for the disability amendment to the *Charter*. The moral of that swimming pool story is this: during our volunteer disability advocacy efforts, we will, at most, be able to marshal the efforts of a limited number of people with disabilities and disability organizations in support of our cause. We will, at best, amount to only a few drops of blood. We will never be able to organize 2.9 million Ontarians with disabilities, much less over 6 million Canadians with disabilities. However, our goal as community advocates is to get the government to think that our efforts add up to a major torrent or geyser rather than a few drops!

## *3. The Bar Mitzvah Incident*

On 9 May 1970, I reached a Jewish teen's traditional milestone, a bar mitzvah. At age 13, I was called up to the front of a Sabbath religious service at my family's synagogue in Toronto, Holy Blossom Temple, to fulfill the solemn ritual of reading aloud in Hebrew from the Torah. The Torah is the Hebrew text of the first five books of the Hebrew Bible, beautifully hand-scribed in an ornate scroll. The Torah has been rabbinically divided into weekly portions. Successive passages are assigned for each week of the year in the lunar Jewish calendar. I stood up, looked down at the Torah scroll, and visually read the portion assigned to me from that week's reading. I had studied it for months. I had never before stood upright, looked down, and read aloud any text. I ordinarily had to lean forward within a few inches of text to read it.

How did we pull that one off? Once again, it was due to my mother's endless drive and ingenuity. She had cleverly arranged for the text of my Torah portion to be photographed from a book. She had it massively enlarged so that each letter was well over an inch tall. The enlarged text was printed into a poster-sized document. Our synagogue then rolled it into the largest Torah they had, so that it would fit. When the Torah was ritually taken out from the ark that Saturday morning and unrolled on the pulpit, at the right spot was this large print version of the Hebrew text that I was to read in front of the congregation. Back then, of course, we had none of the current technology for enlarging text like this. I do not remember how my mother figured out how to do this.

For me, it was important to read my Torah portion aloud, standing up straight. Yet that was not the morning's seismic feature with long-term consequences for me. It was instead one of the verses in the passage from the book of Leviticus, Chapter 19, that I was assigned to read aloud in Hebrew. The decisive sentence that has echoed over the following decades for me and that I have quoted many times since then in speeches on disability rights issues, which I read aloud in Hebrew that morning, means this in English: "Do not curse a deaf person or place an obstacle in front of a blind person."

To me, that verse is the biblical birthplace of the duty to accommodate people with disabilities and the duty not to create barriers against people with disabilities. Those duties lie at the core of the guarantee of equality to people with disabilities in section 15 of the *Charter* and in human rights legislation that bans discrimination against people with disabilities in the workplace and in access to goods, services, and facilities. The ancient Biblical Hebrew word for "obstacle" in that verse is also the modern Hebrew word for "barrier." When I have tried to use my limited Hebrew to speak in Israel about disability issues, it is that Biblical Hebrew word that I often use.

On 9 May 1970, I had no inkling that disability rights would become a core cause for me or that the principle enshrined in that Biblical verse would, consciously or unconsciously, pervade so much of what I do. I also had no clue back then that my vision was going to start dropping less than a year later or that it would eventually lead to total blindness.

## *4. The Summer Camp Incident*

A third incident took place 3 months later in early August 1970 in a relatively unknown town, Oconomowoc, Wisconsin. At age 13, I had arrived for the first time at a Jewish educational summer camp there, now known by the name Olin Sang Ruby Union Institute Camp or, more lovingly, as OSRUI. On my first night at camp, as my fellow bunkmates were settling in for bed, I did what I did most nights to ready myself for sleep. I pulled out a novel to read. I held the paperback book about an inch away from my nose, as I lay on my bunk bed, starting to read. I braced myself for the inevitable comments that I fully expected from my cabin mates, all of whom just met me for the first time a few hours earlier that day: "Why are you holding the book so close to your nose?" "Why don't you get stronger glasses?" "Why do you read like that?" "What's the matter with your eyes?" I typically got comments like those whenever I started reading in front of other people who had just met me for the first time. Unlike strangers, my classmates at school were used to how I read. For me at age 13, such remarks from strangers were a normality, a fact of life. I did not hope for or expect anything different. I did not experience such remarks as a searing wound but as something I had to routinely endure as a fact of life, whether I liked it or not.

On that warm summer evening, not one of my cabin mates asked me any of those questions. No one made a single comment about the unusual way that I read. This was a first for me. It felt bizarre, jarring, and even shocking. What was the matter with these kids, I puzzled to myself? I did not then know, and did not find out for some time, that under the leadership of the camp director Jerry Kaye, the camp staff had proactively taken discrete steps earlier that day to educate my bunkmates about my disability in order to ensure that I had a welcoming environment to fully participate at camp. This was in 1970! Earlier that day, one of my counsellors had taken me away from my cabin for a few minutes, purportedly to orient me to the camp's layout. That had seemed odd to me at the time because, the day before, my parents and I had been given a similar tour by someone else. My young mind, not yet schooled in analyzing circumstantial evidence, did not piece the clues together.

My guided camp tour was a pretext to get me out of the cabin so that my other counsellors could talk to my bunkmates about my low vision and explain how to treat me as a full and equal member of our cabin group. What a simple step to take, with huge positive results. From the moment I picked up that book in my cabin that night, I was treated by my fellow campers and counsellors as just another kid in the group. It was the first time I had this experience with total strangers. Who would have thought that a social group could be created in which I, an adolescent with vision loss, could be simply welcomed as one of the guys? My bond with that camp continues to this day. Decades later, that same camp director had me return to teach new generations of campers about inclusion of people with disabilities, regaling them with this story at the very place where it had originally taken place.

Let me put that camp experience in context. A few years earlier, in the mid-1960s, my mother ran into immovable roadblocks when trying to find a day camp in Toronto that would let me attend as a camper. With my significant low vision, I had no real accommodation needs back then, except a need to avoid a major blow to my head that could trigger a detached retina. Of course, any camp must protect any camper from blows to the head. Only one wonderful day camp, Toronto's Camp Robin Hood, said yes. Several others said no. I have returned to Camp Robin Hood many times to do staff training on achieving inclusion for campers with disabilities, a goal on which that camp, like OSRUI, has a stupendous record. That first night at OSRUI taught me that it is possible and easy to create a truly inclusive social environment for someone like me. Many years later, the enormity of this life lesson was to take on much broader significance.

## *5. The Battle to Remain in My Local School*

A fourth defining moment took place a year later in a battle with my local school board that my mother tirelessly fought after my eyesight started to drop. In the winter and spring of 1971, my family had to tackle the question of where I would go to school in September 1971 when I would enter Grade 10 at age 14. Up until then, I always went to my local public school with my friends. For me, that was only natural. However, as the winter and spring unfolded in 1971, I lost the ability to read print. I had to have a way to read and write if I was to proceed with my education.

In the latter half of Grade 9, when I had just started losing the ability to read using my eyesight, a cohort of my junior high school teachers swung into action. Under the wonderful leadership of my French teacher, Rifka Phillips, a friend until her death years later, several teachers at St. Andrews Junior High in Toronto rallied to record books on tape for me. The CNIB gave me some recorded books. One CNIB staff member started teaching me Braille, 1 day a week. Another instructed me on white cane skills. This was all going on as I continued my school studies. Oddly, someone at the CNIB had started to teach me white cane skills years earlier when I still had all my initial vision and when we had no idea it was going to later drop. I have no idea what ridiculous chain of reasoning led them to think it was a good idea to teach me white cane skills needed by totally blind people when I was then still happily riding a bicycle. Ridiculous, perhaps, but ultimately very fortunate for me! I still use those same white cane skills to this day. Being pretrained on them when I had no foreseeable need made my later adjustment to gradual vision loss and eventual total blindness that much easier.

In the summer of 1971, a battle with our school board was brewing over where I would go to school that fall. Blindness "experts" at the North York Board of Education were pressuring my family to agree that I would leave my local school and family home to go to the W. Ross McDonald School for the Blind in Brantford, Ontario, some 2 hours away by car. Back then, the overwhelming practice in Ontario was to segregate blind students at this school throughout their school years up to the end of Grade 12. My mother and I toured the school for the blind. Our immediate, overwhelming reaction to it was the same. It was not for me. I did not want to leave my home, my family, and my friends. I did not want my learning environment to be populated exclusively with blind students. School staff left us with the impression, rightly or wrongly, that I would be in small classes that would probably progress at the pace of the slowest learner. I was just finishing Grade 9 with a number of awards for high academic achievement. I was not interested in a learning environment that risked slowing me down.

"Leave no stone unturned" was my mother's approach to everything. She and I also explored Boston's internationally renowned Perkins School for the Blind whose most famous alumna is Helen Keller. I did not want to go to school there either. I have no idea whether they could or would have admitted me. How did I end up staying in my community's local public school system for the rest of my education, despite strong opposition from my school board's blindness professionals? Over the summer of 1971, I returned to the wonderful OSRUI camp. I needed to quickly make progress in learning Braille. Jerry Kaye, the same camp director who had created such a welcoming environment for me at camp the summer before, stepped up to the plate again. During my second amazing summer at OSRUI, he arranged for me to get Braille lessons twice a week in nearby Milwaukee.

After camp ended that summer, my local school board's vision itinerant teachers assessed my Braille skills. While doing so, they (the people who had pressured my family to send me to the school for the blind in Brantford) told me it was important for me to know Braille. I snapped back that it was important for me to successfully complete my studies in school. They retorted that it was important for me to learn Braille. I saw Braille as a means to an end. They seemed to see it instead as the ultimate end, pure and simple. I do not denigrate Braille or undervalue the great importance that it can serve. They did not then tell me what is certainly widely known now and should have been widely known then. One's Braille reading skills are never as good for those like me, who lose their eyesight in their teens after earlier learning to visually read print, as it is for those who are born blind and learn Braille as their first medium of literacy.

My mother had to confront the North York Board of Education's vision itinerant program. I am forever indebted to her for this and for so much more. She pressed them to support me in the public school system in my community. I was never told that the North York Board of Education would reject my attendance at my local school. The only question at issue was whether the school board's vision itinerant program would agree to provide support services to me if I continued to attend my local school. The board's vision itinerant teacher program heavily pressured my mother to agree to send me to the school for the blind. Most mothers would be cowed by such pressure. Yet she stood up to them, stared them down, and fought back. She was asked what she would do if the vision itinerant program refused to support me. Defiant, my mother shot back that if they would not support me, she would learn Braille and support me herself. It was in the face of this that the vision itinerant program backed down and agreed to support me. One of their teachers was later to tell me that this program only grudgingly provided me with "token service" in high school. Whether or not that is so, I succeeded in getting through high school with high grades and some Braille skills but without being fluent in Braille.

I many times thanked my mother for battling to keep me from having to go to the W. Ross McDonald School for the Blind. This was amplified in recent years when it was publicly revealed that a class action had been successfully brought against that school for mistreatment and abuse of some of its students, including during the years when I would have studied there.[1] My Braille skills have never been good enough for reading entire books. I use Braille to label objects, jot down phone numbers, or write up terse notes for a speech or plan for examining a witness or presenting an oral argument in court. I was keenly aware of my lack of Braille proficiency on the night before I was to address Parliament in 1980 about the need for the disability amendment. Years after that, new technology such as talking computers and smartphones have provided me with ample means to succeed. I wish I could read Braille better than I can. However, I did not fail in my education or my work life due to my limited Braille skills, as those so-called experts intimated back in 1971.

That is, however, not the end of this transformative incident. Sometime between 1974 and 1976, after I started my studies at York University, the CNIB invited me to speak to a group of parents of blind or low vision children about my experience in school. I came to the CNIB's Toronto offices one evening to tell my story, pulling no punches. I told those parents how the vision itinerant experts had suggested that I would fail if I did not go to the W. Ross McDonald School for the Blind and how they turned up the heat on my mother. I explained that my mother had stood up to them, that I did not go to school in Brantford, and that I did not end up failing. I shared the lesson I learned from my mother: Stand up for your rights. Do not be intimidated by seeming experts if their reasoning does not hold up

1 See Michelle McQuigge, "Class Action over Alleged Abuse at Ontario School for the Blind Ends in $8-Million Settlement," *Toronto Star* (8 April 2017), online: <www.thestar.com/news/gta/2017/04/08/class-action-over-alleged-abuse-at-ontario-school-for-the-blind-ends-in-8-million-settlement.html>.

under scrutiny. I told them that their children need them to do the same. The audience was quite quiet in response.

Shortly after I got home, the phone rang. I could hear a devilish grin in the voice of the CNIB staff member at the other end of the call. He had been at my talk. He asked if I knew who was in the room when I gave my talk? I answered that there were parents of blind and low-vision children and some CNIB staff. That's not all, he told me. Sitting in the back of the room was a large contingent from the North York Board of Education's vision itinerant program. I had completely and justifiably skewered those folks, not knowing they were there. No wonder the room was so silent when I invited parents to ask me questions. It should have been obvious to all in attendance that I had no idea those school board employees were there.

The events in 1971 regarding my schooling comprised my first lesson in the importance of speaking truth to power. I learned from my mother that you can stand up to large inflexible bureaucracies. Sometimes you can even win. However, you cannot win unless you try. Since those formative events in 1971, the right to a barrier-free equal education for students with disabilities has been a defining passion in my life. It was top of mind when I spoke about the disability amendment to Parliament's Joint Committee on 12 December 1980 and when I later reflected back on what we won when the disability amendment was passed.

Decades later, it played a central part in my advocacy from 1994 to 2005 for the *Accessibility for Ontarians with Disabilities Act* [*AODA*].[2] It has driven my advocacy since 2009 to get an Education Accessibility Standard enacted under the *AODA* to tear down the many barriers that still impede students with disabilities in school. It lay behind dozens and dozens of hours of meetings and negotiations while I served from 2018 to 2022 on the Ontario government-appointed Kindergarten–Grade 12 Education Standards Development Committee. It is at the core of my advocacy efforts since 2015 as a member of the Special Education Advisory Committee of Canada's largest school board, the Toronto District School Board, and as that committee's chair in 2016 and 2017. It is top of mind when I undertake advocacy on behalf of students with vision loss as a member of the board of directors of the Ontario Parents of Visually Impaired Children.

2 *Accessibility for Ontarians with Disabilities Act*, SO 2005, c 11 [*AODA*].

## 6. *The Unexpected Transition from Being Teased to Being Pitied Because of My Vision Loss*

The fifth source that dramatically changed me was not a specific isolated incident but, rather, an accumulation of innumerable isolated events. By the time I was 15, my first-hand experience with strangers in public had taught me a jarring lesson about human nature and public attitudes towards people with disabilities. During my first 13 years, I carried no symbol of vision loss such as a white cane. I did not need one to get around. During those years, I had become accustomed to occasionally being treated as weird and at times being teased by strangers (and especially by kids who did not know me), all because of my eyesight. Whether or not I felt at some conscious or unconscious level that it was unfair, I just sucked it up.

I do remember an unpleasant feeling in the pit of my stomach at times when this would happen. I likely never talked about it much if ever with anyone. I can only ruminate now how much better off I would have been had I spoken up back then and had I gained professional or other insights to help me better understand and react to it. There were memorable incidents. Among the worst, a junior high school English teacher got my class to laugh out loud at my expense one day while he was recommending a book to our class to read. "This book doesn't have the kind of small print that would make you have to hold up the book close to your nose to read, the way David Lepofsky does," he joked to my class, as I silently sat there among my peers. Their laughter felt quite painful to me. Of course, I didn't talk about it with anyone. As always, I just forged ahead.

Please do not get the impression that I was walking around in a state of misery. I was generally a happy guy. However, I did not then have the confidence in myself that I would gain years later through the successful pursuit of my law career and my volunteer disability advocacy. Those who knew me in my early teens as being caustic at times perhaps had more insight into me than did I. I was not subjected to the horrific and blistering public mockery, or anything close to it, that the adolescent Quebec teen singer Jeremy Gabriel was subjected to decades later by Mike Ward, a very public comedian in Quebec. Ward decided that vilifying Jeremy for his disability was a clever thing to do over and over in his public comedy performances. Jeremy brought a disability discrimination claim against Ward. The Quebec Human Rights Tribunal decided the case in favour of Jeremy. In 2021, a majority of the Supreme Court of Canada overturned the Quebec

Human Rights Tribunal's ruling in *Ward v Quebec (Commission des droits de la personne et des droits de la jeunesse).*[3] Ward, the comedian, won.

I was struck with the staggering disconnect between the Supreme Court's majority opinion and the reality of bullying and teasing facing too many kids and teens with disabilities in the school yard. The majority's conclusion that ridicule and comedy-based bullying can rarely lead to discriminatory treatment is categorically out of touch with our reality.[4] This recently drove me to write a law journal article, spelling out how the Supreme Court of Canada's majority went off the rails. Check out "A Professional Comedian's Fundamental Right to Publicly Bully a Child Because of His Disability? Scrutinizing *Ward v Quebec Human Rights Commission* through a Disability Lens."[5]

When I was 13 and 14, I was staggered to find that things suddenly changed dramatically when I started to use a white cane in public as a mobility aid, due to my increasing vision loss. Strangers around me expressed a dramatically different attitude towards me. No longer was I teased or skeptically questioned about why I held a book so close to my face when reading. Instead, I was subjected to melodramatic pity. "How sad! Look at that poor blind boy" someone would say aloud about me, sitting right across from me in a subway car. "How long have you been blind?" I was regularly asked by strangers, with a voice saturated with patronizing, over-the-top pity for my seeming tragic plight.

What on earth is it with these people, I reflected over and over in my early to mid-teens. I was the same me that I was weeks ago when I was ribbed and teased for my vision loss. Add a white cane to the picture, and now I am the target of nauseating, unsolicited, and unwanted pity. This emanated from strangers who were members of the self-same public. I felt a grating sense of detachment. I knew I was very different from the me that strangers perceived, both versions of me, the one without the white cane as well as the one who uses that orientation and mobility tool. In my teens, I tried to make sense of this stunning shift in how strangers so often reacted

---

3 *Ward v Quebec (Commission des droits de la personne et des droits de la jeunesse)*, 2021 SCC 43, 463 DLR (4th) 567.

4 *Ibid* at para 88.

5 David Lepofsky, "A Professional Comedian's Fundamental Right to Publicly Bully a Child Because of His Disability? Scrutinizing *Ward v Quebec Human Rights Commission* through a Disability Lens" (2023) 108:2 SCLR 169.

to seeing me in public. All I knew was that it was strange, inexplicable, and, in a true sense, wrong. However, I did not then think it was my responsibility to do anything to try to fix it. That would come in the sixth ground-shifting incident along this zig-zagging path.

## 7. *The Subway Incident*

A sixth and remarkably life-changing incident took place on a subway car in Toronto in the fall of 1974. I was enroute to a class during my undergraduate studies at York University. I was carrying a briefcase on which a prominent York University sticker was affixed. I was chatting with a stranger seated next to me about my aim to go to law school. Another stranger walked over to me in that moving subway car. He handed me a dollar bill. Yes, we had dollar bills back then! He told me to buy myself a coffee. I was absolutely devastated. That person was actually handing me charity! This person looked at me holding a white cane. All he saw was a pitiful charity case.

Hurt, angered, and insulted do not even begin to describe my instantaneous shock and rage. Yet there was more to this event that made it so transformative for me. Before that day, I rarely if ever spoke publicly about my disability. I did not seek out or agree to speak to audiences to discuss the topic of living with a disability. Before that day, as far as I can now recall, I had addressed it publicly, at most, perhaps twice when speaking at a meeting or gathering. I did not then think of myself as being part of a broader disability community. I do not think I ever described myself as having a disability. I just thought of myself as having lousy eyesight.

Before that day, it was core to my understanding of the world that all I needed to do was to act like an equal. That would lead the public, I believed, to see me as an equal and, thereafter, to treat me like an equal. That would outweigh that slobbering pity business I had encountered in public since I started using a white cane. One dollar handed to me on the Toronto subway in the fall of 1974 obliterated my entire belief system in one fell swoop. There I sat, with a briefcase displaying a university's name, talking to a passenger (not the guy who gave me the dollar) about my plans to become a lawyer. What more could I do to show the public that I was a competent, functioning, and independent individual, not a blind beggar needing charity? I did not sport the university sticker on my briefcase nor talk about my plans for law school for that purpose. I was just being me. My world was shattered. At this turning point, I realized that if I wanted people to treat me as an equal, I had to do something more, something different.

When I was handed that dollar on the subway that day in 1974, I was completely speechless, a rarity for me! It would be another two decades or more before I would have a more articulate response. One day in the mid-1990s, while on the Toronto subway along with a buddy of mine who also happens to be blind, another stranger tried to put money in my hand. Finally, well into my law practice, I rapidly shot back with an impromptu acerbic response: "Do you make more money than a lawyer makes?" I pointedly asked him. "What?" he said to me. "Do you make more money than a lawyer makes?" I again asked. "You're a lawyer?" he asked me, with a note of surprise if not astonishment in his voice. "Yeah, I'm a lawyer, and you want to give me money, because you make more money than lawyers make. You think that lawyers just don't have enough money, is that right?" He walked away. He did not give me any money. I can only imagine the look on his face.

I have encountered many strange attitudes towards my blindness on the Toronto subway from time to time. However, I too can get it quite wrong when interacting with the public on the subway. Over the years, and in many different settings, total strangers have, out of the blue, asked me how I went blind. I have often answered in a matter-of-fact way, considering such inquiries just a routine part of my life.

However, one day over two decades ago, I totally and inexcusably blew it. Some stranger walked over to me while I was waiting on a subway platform and asked how I went blind. I had slept very poorly the night before. Irritated, I thought I would unleash a clever verbal snark: "Do you always ask strangers about their personal medical history?" I snapped. "What?" He asked. "Do you always walk right up to total strangers on the subway and ask them about their personal private medical history?" I retorted, thinking I had a rather good point to my jab. "I'm really sorry," he said, with an apologetic tone. "It's just that I'm losing my eyesight and I don't know what to do about it."

I felt worse than horrible. I have always felt a strong duty to be available to people who are dealing with the early stages of vision loss. I apologized profusely, bordering on grovelling. I offered to give him any information he needed to plug into helpful resources. I have no idea whether I gave him any information that helped him. However, I walked away from that incident disgusted with myself. I rededicated myself there and then to go back to my long-standing practice of always willingly and thoroughly answering any and all public questions about my blindness, no matter what, when, or where and no matter how fatigued I may be.

## C. A Disability Advocate's Journey Begins

After my unplanned experience in 1974 as an unwilling charity recipient on Toronto's subway, I began a journey akin to the odyssey that the disability community was then travelling. I was initially convinced, as were so many other people with disabilities, that our biggest problem was the attitude that the public held towards people with disabilities. From this, I, like many others, believed that all we needed to do was effective public education: if we change their attitudes, then we will change their behaviour. We argued that public attitudes towards our disabilities was our biggest problem. This sounded utterly revolutionary to me. So many people without disabilities figure my blindness is my big problem that holds me back. Nope, your attitudes are what hold me back! I did not invent that argument, but I unleashed it with passion and determination, time and again.

Over the next months, I gave quite a number of speeches to school kids and other audiences about the capacity of people with vision loss like me to be full and equal participants in society, living independently and learning how to do what everybody else does, just using other means. Some people read using their eyes. Others of us read using our fingertips or listen to audiobooks. Some people navigate using their eyes. Others navigate using a white cane or a guide dog. I really wanted to spread the word. In 1975 and 1976, I worked on student summer projects aimed at expanding public education on blindness. In the summer of 1976, I wrote a handbook for public speakers on how to give public talks about blindness issues. I ran a training session on this for the CNIB.

Over the next couple of years, I came to the realization that educating the public and raising awareness was not enough. I could give lots of speeches. So did many other people with disabilities and disability organizations. Audiences could get a good laugh at our witty jokes, feel moved by our message, and be very flattering in response. However, the wall of barriers against people with disabilities just persisted. How many members of any audience were in a position to leave such a talk, go right to their office, and issue authoritative directions that would change how a private company or government office treated people with disabilities? Not many! This fundamental change in my outlook led me far beyond giving "awareness-raising" speeches.

## D. How Little I Knew about Constitutional Disability Rights in the Summer of 1980

In the fall of 1974, I was admitted into York University's undergraduate Faculty of Arts program, without finishing high school. Back then, high school included a Grade 13. York admitted a few students after Grade 12 if their grades were good enough. I was one of them. In the fall of 1976, I got myself admitted to Osgoode Hall Law School after finishing 2 years in York's Faculty of Arts. I did not complete a Bachelor of Arts. Osgoode admitted some students with only 2 years of undergraduate university if their grades were high. My dad, always the loving jokester, teased me that I was a high school drop-out who just doesn't seem to finish anything! In the spring of 1981, at the official ceremony where I was admitted to the Ontario Bar as a lawyer, he audibly and jokingly sighed with relief: "Son, finally you graduated from something!"

Entering law school in the fall of 1976, I increasingly felt that, if our situation was going to improve, we needed the force of the law to get us there. At that time, the Ontario *Human Rights Code* did not forbid discrimination based on disability in any activity.[6] Canada's Constitution had no charter of rights that might make it unconstitutional for a government body to discriminate because of disability. Canada did not yet even have a national Canadian human rights act. For many years now, when I am introduced to give a speech in a law class or elsewhere, I am often described as a "constitutional law expert." Before I went to law school, that was about the last thing I ever thought I might be called. At some point when I was studying in York University's Faculty of Arts, my life-long plan to apply to law school was cast in serious doubt. I learned that in law school you must take a course in constitutional law. It sounded horrifically, insufferably boring. This made me seriously wonder whether I really did want to go to law school. I somehow managed to set aside my revulsion at the thought of studying constitutional law in order to proceed with my law school application.

My only thought about constitutions before that was at age 14 in Grade 9 when I was president of the junior youth group at my synagogue. For some reason that I cannot reconstruct, I decided that our youth group needed a constitution. Why I thought that is beyond me. Was I a teenage

6 *Human Rights Code*, RSO 1990, c H-19.

nascent closet constitutional nerd? I wrote a constitution and got our youth group to pass it.

In August 1976, I nervously walked into law school for my first day, fully intending to become a corporate tax lawyer and tax accountant. Arguing cases of any sort in court? Advocating on disability rights? Not a chance. Not me! None of that ever even crossed my mind. By 3 weeks into law school, I had given up on my corporate tax ambitions. I decided instead to aim for a civil litigation practice. I wanted to be up on my hind legs in court, arguing cases, any cases. In the second term of first year at law school, I took that mandatory constitutional law course that I had dreaded. It was not as bad as I had feared, but it was incredibly dull. We had no charter of rights to study nor anything truly resembling strong constitutional rights.

The course focused on the sleepy topic of division of powers between Canada's federal Parliament and the provincial legislatures. If a chicken is to be marketed, which level of government can establish a chicken marketing board to regulate it — a federal chicken marketing board or a provincial chicken marketing board? Is it an interprovincial chicken or an intra-provincial chicken? I know, the suspense is killing you, my reader. The cases we read rivalled watching paint dry. Imagine an impatient blind law student having to watch paint dry. We read a few cases on the question of whether the Constitution included an implied bill of rights. Would cautious Canadian judges read strong constitutional rights into the Constitution if Canada had adopted no explicit charter or bill of constitutional rights?[7] Don't hold your breath.

In my first year at law school, we had to form teams of two and take part in a moot court oral argument. We were given a fact situation and had to write a legal brief, called a factum, and then deliver an oral argument in front of mock judges. My partner and I were assigned to argue the case of *McNeil v Attorney General of Nova Scotia*.[8] At issue was the constitutionality of Nova Scotia's movie censorship board. The case had two issues, a federalism issue (can the province adopt legislation in this area, or can only the federal government do it?) and a fundamental rights question (does the Canadian Constitution protect the freedom of expression from infringements by provincial movie censor boards?). Astonishingly, I had

---

7 Walter Surma Tarnopolsky, *The Canadian Bill of Rights*, 2nd rev ed (Toronto: McClelland & Stewart, 1975) at 295–316.

8 *Nova Scotia Board of Censors v McNeil*, [1976] 2 SCR 265, [1975] SCJ No 77 (QL).

no interest in the case's freedom of expression issue. My mooting partner happily took that on. I preferred to argue the dry federalism issue.

Twists and turns seem to be the hallmark of my life and my law career. Freedom of expression later became a specialty of mine. It was a course subject of my 1981–1982 graduate studies at the Harvard law school. My master's thesis was on a freedom of expression topic. It was later expanded and published as a book.[9] I have written law journal articles on the freedom of expression, some of which have been cited by courts. I have argued freedom of expression cases at all levels of Canada's courts, including the Supreme Court of Canada. I have taught a course on freedom of expression and press at the University of Toronto's Faculty of Law for over 30 years and co-authored a casebook on that topic.[10]

In my first-year constitutional law course, we discussed absolutely nothing about equality rights. In 3 years at the Osgoode Hall Law School, I read no court cases nor ever had a class discussion on equality rights. Before starting law school, I once tried reading the Ontario *Human Rights Code*. I could not make any sense of it and gave up. My first-year constitutional law grade was far from stellar. In the very field by which I would later be described as an expert, I earned an underwhelming C.

Before 1980, I only once briefly pondered whether Canada should create a constitutional right to equality for people with disabilities. During the summer of 1977, the CNIB hired me to run a government-funded student summer project called the "Blindness Law Reform Project" [BLRP, which we pronounced "blurp"]. On my recommendation, the CNIB got a grant from the federal government that allowed it to hire me and a team of other law students to write a report that identified legislation that needed reform to advance the rights of people who are blind or have low vision. We explored things like the legal definition of blindness (proving that the oft-used term "legally blind" is a total misnomer, as I mentioned earlier in this chapter), protection from discrimination, rights to equal participation in education,

---

9 M David Lepofsky, "Open Justice: The Constitutional Right to Attend and Speak About Criminal Proceedings" (1985) 15:2 Manitoba LJ 243.

10 David Lepofsky, *Freedom of Expression and the Press,* 7th ed, vol 1 (Toronto: Faculty of Law, University of Toronto, 2017). The book includes materials drawn from David M Lepofsky, Jamie Cameron & Christopher Bredt, *Freedom of Expression and the Press in Canada: Cases and Materials*, 2nd ed (Toronto: Faculty of Law, University of Toronto, 1990–1991).

barriers, the design of buildings, and the like. I interviewed, hired, and managed the team of law students.

Over that summer, as I was brainstorming over the title to give our forthcoming report, I detected an overarching theme pervading all the issues we were addressing — namely, equality. I entitled our report *Vision and Equality*.[11] This foreshadowed the *Charter* venture that was to consume my attention 3 years later. A member of our BLRP team, a law student named Bruno Cavion, who later became Justice Cavion, wrote the chapter of our *Vision and Equality* report that addressed the need for human rights legislation to ban discrimination because of disability. As I reviewed his draft chapter that summer for inclusion in our final report, I embarked on a moment of brainstorming. Why, I asked, do we not include among our report's recommendations a proposal that Canada's Constitution be amended to ban discrimination because of disability? None of us foresaw that summer that the federal government would 3 years later propose a charter of rights that includes an equality rights provision.

Bruno dismissively rejected my recommendation out of hand. To him, it seemed unrealistic, if not fanciful. The discussion ended, with no further research or reflection. We never put that recommendation in our report. Ironic or what? We submitted our final report to the CNIB at the end of August 1977. I worried that the CNIB might not make it public. Even if the CNIB were not to use it, I wanted others in the blindness community to be able to read it and use the research collected in it. Help came through a person who later played an important role during my efforts in 1980 on the disability amendment, Dayton Foreman.

A volunteer member of the CNIB's national counsel, Foreman was a brilliant, deeply reflective, and ponderous retired psychiatrist who had lost his eyesight. He reached out to me that summer because he worried that the CNIB's senior management might impede our research or try to block our report from being made public. The CNIB's senior management was very secretive. That summer, Foreman assigned himself the role of my guardian angel who had my back. That relationship carried on after those events. One year later, he was incredibly supportive of me as I lay in hospital, wrestling with the decision whether to have my eyes surgically removed. Spoiler alert! Two years after that, this same man was there for me just when I needed him, when I got that phone call from Parliament inviting

[11] Canadian National Institute for the Blind, *Vision and Equality*, vol 1 (1997–1998).

the CNIB to present to the Joint Committee. After all this, I affectionately called him "my shrink!"

It was largely during my work on BLRP that I transitioned from believing that we could solve the barriers facing people with disabilities by raising awareness and educating the public to believing, ever since then, that we need law reform.

## E. Knowing How Disability Rights Legislation Gets Developed and Enacted? Not a Chance!

While in law school, I gave not a moment's thought to the idea of advocating for the rights of people with disabilities as a career objective. As I mentioned earlier, back then you would not hear the term "disability rights" in our law school's hallowed echoing halls. There were no courses in disability rights. Other law courses discussed nothing remotely approximating disability rights. By the summer of 1980, I also knew virtually nothing about the legislative process. How is a bill debated in the legislature, considered by a legislative committee, potentially amended along the way, and ultimately enacted and proclaimed in force? Law school taught us nothing about this. We studied how to interpret legislation and to apply common law legal principles. We took enacted legislation as a given. Decades later, as part of my disability advocacy for the *Accessibility for Ontarians with Disabilities Act*, I wrote and made public an introductory guide to the legislative process to explain all of this to our grassroots supporters.[12]

I also learned nothing in law school about the organizational structure of government and how proposed new legislation works its way through the government before it is brought forward to the legislature or Parliament. I later learned a great deal about this through my volunteer disability advocacy work and through my 33 years working as Crown counsel at the Ontario government. All of that knowledge is vital if you want to convince the government to bring forward legislation or to amend a bill that the government has brought forward. Who do you need to persuade? Who has the final say within government? How do they make decisions? What hot

---

[12] Ontarians with Disabilities Act Committee, "*ODA Committee Provides Introductory Guide on the Process That an ODA Bill Goes through at the Ontario Legislature*" (September 2004), online: <www.odacommittee.net/news159.html>; *AODA*, *supra* note 2.

buttons do you need to push to convince them? I have subsequently learned this through the school of hard knocks. In 1980, I knew zilch about this as I leapt into advocating for the disability amendment.

## F. Getting onto the CNIB's Ontario Divisional Board of Management

My platform for advocating for the disability amendment in 1980 had its genesis in steps that I had taken 2 or 3 years earlier. I never contemplated that those steps might lead me to a soapbox to advocate for constitutional reform and hand me a megaphone. Sometime after the summer of 1977, I somehow managed to get myself appointed to the CNIB's Ontario-division Board of Management. A national corporation, the CNIB is governed by its National Council. However, it delegates some authority to provincial Boards of Directors, with an unclear limited mandate to oversee provincial operations. I wanted to get on the CNIB's Ontario-division Board of Management in order to become a voice for reform within the CNIB so it would far better serve clients with vision loss. My primary objective was desperately needed internal CNIB reform, not external CNIB advocacy to the rest of the world.

I was certainly not the sort of person that the CNIB then sought to sit on one of its governing boards. Few members of the Board of Directors at the Ontario level had any knowledge of, or expertise in, vision loss or rehabilitation services. Only a minority of the board members were themselves people with vision loss. None were reformers or advocates of any sort. Other board members were all much older than me. The few other Ontario board members with vision loss were quite passive. They were very nice, genuine, and supportive of my objectives. However, they were very reluctant to ever speak up, challenge authority, question outdated practices, vocally support my efforts there, or try to make the organization more accountable to its consumers. I learned quickly that, among them, it was going to be up to me, flying solo, to actively advocate for reform at the CNIB.

The majority of sighted Ontario board members were overwhelmingly retired businessmen. Very few were women. They joined the board out of some sense of charity. They showed no drive to provide meaningful oversight. They unquestioningly rubber-stamped management reports. They did not warmly welcome my efforts to probe management and press for reforms. So how on earth did the board even let me join? It was thanks to its then chair, the late Harry Hyde. A lovely and thoughtful man, he was a former corporate senior manager. We met one day at the CNIB's cafeteria. He somehow became interested in getting me on board. I don't remember whether he or I first broached the idea. Hyde was something of a forward-thinking reformer, though not on the scale of my ambitions. However, it was my good fortune that he saw something in me that he liked. He must have thereafter done whatever was needed to get me on the Ontario board.

Once I got on the board, you did not need eyesight to know that I was seen as a young, out-of-place upstart. One of my proudest earliest moments came when I got an asterisk removed from the CNIB letterhead. It was printed next to the name of board members who were blind. That the letterhead listed board members was silly self-promotion. Moreover, that list showed the world just how few blind people were on the CNIB's Ontario board. It smacked of tokenism. I returned home from that board meeting, proudly proclaiming that I had been liberated from the CNIB letterhead asterisk! Take whatever victories you can get, big or small!

You might think that blind people, dissatisfied with the CNIB's services at that time, would be happy that a reformer like me had gotten on the Ontario board. Yet some were mighty unhappy with me. A newish advocacy group for people with vision loss called the Blind Ontario Organization with Self-help Tactics [BOOST] had understandably been very critical of the CNIB for being paternalistic and unaccountable to its consumers. Some of their members saw me not as a kindred spirit but, rather, as lending legitimacy to a dinosauric CNIB that should instead have been shut down, not reformed. Despite this, I forged ahead, driven by a pragmatic view that I wanted to do what I could to make progress.

One day in 1979, I presented to the CNIB's Ontario board a proposal I had written and which the CNIB staff had opposed. It would give the CNIB's clients a right of access to their client files, an embryonic form of freedom of information. Protesting in front of the CNIB's headquarters, BOOST exerted pressure from the outside while I presented my reform proposals on the inside. Our efforts were not coordinated. I was fuming with frustration after months of making little progress at the CNIB's Ontario board. I needed allies. I decided to try to stealthily slip some new like-minded members onto that board. The CNIB was not a membership organization. Any blind or visually impaired person could not simply join as a member of the CNIB and thereby have a vote on who sits on its governing boards. The board in effect appointed itself. It approved new board members as it wished.

The CNIB's Ontario board was not aware of my strategy of infiltrating it with new like-minded members. I got a handful of them appointed. However, we were still a powerless minority on the board. I needed to do something more. I decided to try to create a little island within the board structure where we might concentrate on making some progress. My next step was to get the board to allow me to form a board committee called the Public Education and Advocacy Committee (PEA Committee). Its members were all my new stealth board members. Most, if not all, of them were blind people. I was this new committee's chair. I got the board to approve our mandate. I wrote it in deliberately bland terms so that it would not trigger any red alerts among those who did not share my agenda. Sometimes, bland is beautiful, I was slowly learning. Here is our exciting mandate:

> The Committee shall be responsible for proposing and overseeing policy in the Ontario Division, with management and with appropriate staff members, in the areas of public education regarding the equality and capabilities of blind and visually handicapped Ontarians and advocacy by the Ontario Division to promote the advancement of the status of blind and visually handicapped Ontarians.[13]

Our PEA Committee was the tiny refuge of progressiveness amidst a sea of stultifying board stagnation and rubber-stamping. It was my hope that we could generate progress, flying below the radar. When our PEA Committee reported to the board on anything, we encountered, at best, bemused apathy. At least, the full board did not get in our way. This process was gradually teaching me the art of navigating issues through an organization even if you cannot persuade everyone on the way up the corporate ladder.

My capacity to have some impact on the CNIB's Ontario board got a real break in the late 1970s when there was a major turnover in the CNIB's senior management. Somehow, and I think due to manoeuvres on the national council for which my ally, Dayton Foreman, was a key player, the CNIB's national managing director was eased out. This was a very good thing. He was replaced by a younger man with low vision, Robert Mercer, who had a reform mandate. Mercer in turn eased out several senior managers, including Ontario's then executive director, who were ill-suited to organizational reform.

---

13 Resolution Establishing Public Education Committee (n.d.), "Proposed Terms of Reference."

I quickly developed a good relationship with the new Ontario executive director, Euclid Herie. It was seen as shocking that he was brought into the CNIB's senior management from the outside, then an unimaginable invasion of that cloistered insular organization. Throughout 1979 and 1980, he and I had innumerable phone calls, strategizing on how to stick-handle gradual reforms through the Ontario board. This taught me even more about front-line advocacy than I ever learned about in law school.

## G. The Last Preparatory Step: Getting Active in the Ontario Coalition for Human Rights for the Handicapped

Early 1980 witnessed the final stage in my formative education in the art of disability community organizing and advocacy. I had graduated from Osgoode the previous June and was toiling away at all hours as an articling student at a private law firm. I was learning all about law practice that had nothing to do with disability rights or disability issues. In 1962, the Ontario legislature was the first provincial or federal law-making body in Canada to enact a human rights code. It was meant to create a comprehensive ban on discrimination and an effective enforcement process to resolve disputes. The *Human Rights Code* spelled out certain economic activities in which discrimination is prohibited, such as employment, housing, services, and facilities. It banned discrimination in those activities based on named grounds such as race, religion, and creed. It created a new provincial arm's-length public agency to enforce that law, the Ontario Human Rights Commission.

Before that, Ontario had a few isolated statutes on the books that banned certain kinds of discrimination. They were enforced only by prosecution in court. They were weak, limited, and ineffectual. In 1980, a campaign was already underway to get the Ontario government to amend the Ontario *Human Rights Code* to ban discrimination in employment, accommodation, goods, and services and facilities based on disability. I had nothing to do with that campaign's birth or early weeks. Over the years after 1962, the Ontario legislature had gradually expanded the list of grounds on which discrimination was banned. However, disability was not one of those expanded grounds. In 1977, a committee of the Ontario Human Rights Commission released a report, entitled *Life Together*.[14] Among other things, it recommended that the Ontario *Human Rights Code* should be amended

[14] Ontario Human Rights Commission, *Life Together* (July 1977).

to prohibit discrimination based on physical disability. That recommendation did not include mental disability.

By the mid-1970s, the Ontario legislature had taken baby steps to address discrimination because of disability. In 1976, the Ontario legislature passed the *Blind Persons' Rights Act.*[15] It prohibited discrimination against a blind person accompanied by a guide dog in services and facilities that were customarily available to the public. This prohibition was enforced through the ineffectual avenue of prosecution in court, not through a complaint to the Ontario Human Rights Commission. Imagine an overloaded criminal prosecutor with a bulging docket of charges like sexual assault, armed robbery, attempted murder, and failure to let a blind person with a guide dog into a bar. You can guess where the prosecutor and courts concentrated their serious efforts.

From 1976 to 1979, the *Life Together* recommendations appeared to be going nowhere. The Ontario labour minister then responsible for this area, Bette Stephenson, did not appear particularly interested in this topic. In 1979, a new and much more progressive labour minister, Robert Elgie, entered the scene. A lawyer and neurosurgeon who later entered politics, he was a tremendously forward-thinking member of Premier Bill Davis's Progressive Conservative Ontario government. In 1979, Elgie took a first stab at this issue. His initial efforts faltered. However, they ultimately led to very positive reform. In his first attempt, he did not bring forward a bill to amend the Ontario *Human Rights Code* to prohibit disability discrimination. Instead, he introduced a separate bill into the legislature for First Reading, entitled the *Handicapped Persons' Rights Act.*[16] It prohibited disability discrimination in activities such as employment, accommodation, and goods and services. The bill assigned the Ontario Human Rights Commission with responsibility to enforce this new ban.

Ontario had no widely recognized cross-disability movement in place before this to press the Ontario government to amend the Ontario *Human Rights Code* to prohibit disability discrimination. The introduction of this bill led a number of disability organizations and groups to come together in the fall of 1979 to plan a response. I was not there and knew nothing

[15] *Blind Persons' Rights Act*, SO 1976, c 14.

[16] See the introduction of Bill 188, the proposed *Handicapped Persons' Rights Act*, in the Ontario legislature. Legislative Assembly of Ontario, *Hansard Transcripts*, 31st Parl, 3rd Sess (22 November 1979) (which began at 3:30 p.m.).

about it at the time. Elgie's bill spawned the creation of this new coalition, not vice versa. That pattern recurred 15 years later. In 1994, a private member's bill in the Ontario legislature triggered the birth of the grassroots movement to fight for the enactment of the *AODA*. I recount that saga in a law journal article I wrote almost two decades ago.[17]

In late 1979, that new as-yet-unnamed coalition's primary objection to Elgie's bill was not that its guarantees were weak, though they were exceedingly so. The bill banned only knowing discrimination.[18] It made intent to discriminate a mandatory element of any claim. That would have left unaddressed most of the systemic discrimination that people with disabilities face. Rather, anger spilled forth, first and foremost, about the fact that this bill did not include people with disabilities as a protected group in the Ontario *Human Rights Code*. It was an insult, they thought, that rights for people with disabilities were to instead be enshrined in separate legislation. It was blasted as "separate but equal." Ironically, 15 years later, disability advocates who I would lead for a decade united for the specific goal of winning separate disability accessibility legislation, culminating in the enactment in 2005 of the *AODA*.

In late 1979, leaders of this ad hoc coalition met with the Ontario government of the day, including Davis himself. How I wish I had been involved and had been part of that historic moment. They got the government to withdraw Elgie's bill and to agree to bring forward a bill that would add disability protection to the Ontario *Human Rights Code*. Shortly after that breakthrough, I got involved in this coalition, which eventually called itself the Ontario Coalition for Human Rights for the Handicapped. I am sure no one remembers this coalition's very dated name. We no longer use the term "handicapped." We also avoid referring to people with disabilities as "the disabled," without using "people" or "persons." For years, it has been central to the disability rights movement that we wish to be known as people first. A major organization of people with intellectual disabilities is, for that reason, called People First.

This new effort was a coalition of disability organizations, not a grassroots coalition of individuals with disabilities. My gateway in was

---

[17] M David Lepofsky, "The Long, Arduous Road to a Barrier-Free Ontario for People with Disabilities: The History of the *Ontarians with Disabilities Act* — The First Chapter" (2004) 15:2 NJCL 125.

[18] See *Handicapped Persons' Rights Act*, *supra* note 16.

my persuading the CNIB to get involved in the coalition, with me as their representative. This coalition had real internal tensions. I was unlucky enough to be caught in the crossfire. There was no dispute over any policy issues, such as what we wanted to add to the Ontario *Human Rights Code*. Rather, it was a disability politics/ideology-driven turf contest. The coalition included two kinds of organizations. The first were charitable agencies that provide services to people with disabilities, such as the CNIB, the March of Dimes, and the Canadian Hearing Society. The second were organizations of individuals with disabilities, commonly referred to as consumer organizations. Some consumer organizations were very critical of, and hostile to, some of the service agencies, seeing them as unaccountable and paternalistic. I was a consumer, a person with vision loss. However, I represented a service-providing agency on this coalition, the CNIB. The hostility that BOOST, a vocal consumer group of people with vision loss, had for the CNIB was loud, angry, and visceral.

Despite this dynamic, I got myself included on this coalition's steering committee. This is the first time I took on any kind of leadership role in the disability community. I learned many important lessons through this activity. It served as a foundation for my subsequent activities over the next decades, including my work in pursuit of the disability amendment to the *Charter*. At one point, I ran for a slot as a co-chair of this coalition. However, I was defeated. Someone opposed me because I was not a "true consumer" who was there to represent a consumer organization. As a member of the steering committee, I took an active part in developing our positions and co-presenting at meetings with senior Ontario government officials, including Elgie. Early on, I concluded that we needed to be as specific as possible about the wording we wanted in the Ontario *Human Rights Code*. I believed that we should draft specific amendments. I reasoned that we should not leave it to public servants to come up with the legislative wording, lest we be snookered by the details. I ended up doing a chunk of the drafting of our proposals, having never taken a course in legislative drafting or statutory interpretation. Make it up as we go along, I figured, not for the last time in my disability advocacy career.

In meetings with the labour minister and his team, I learned hour by hour how to build credibility, how to try to find out what issues were troubling the government, and how to search for our natural allies. Elgie was my tutor, though I doubt he knew that at the time. I appreciated his encouragement later in my career. His later letter of reference helped open doors to get my first job with the Ontario government in December 1982 after these events were behind us. The lessons I learned at those meetings have helped me at innumerable meetings with senior government officials over the ensuing decades. Thanks Bob!

Meanwhile, back at the CNIB, its new Public Education and Advocacy Committee held its first meeting on 14 September 1980. According to the minutes for that meeting, which I thankfully kept and recently excavated from my garage, we agreed that I, as its chair, would "continue to serve as CNIB Ontario's representative to the Ontario Coalition on Human Rights for the Handicapped and would continue as the spokesperson generally on Ontario Human Rights matters."[19] The stage was now fully set for October 1980 when Prime Minister Pierre Trudeau tabled his proposed constitutional reform package, including its proposed charter of rights that was glaringly missing equality for people with disabilities.

---

19 Ontario Division Board of Management Committee, *Minutes of the Meeting of the Ontario Division Board of Management Committee on Public Education and Advocacy* (14 September 1980).

# IV. THE 1980 DISABILITY ADVOCACY CONTEXT: STONE KNIVES AND BEARSKINS

## A. The Tools I Wished We Had

A person coming of age in the 21st century must find it puzzling to fathom how anyone could possibly muddle along as a disability rights advocate in the prehistoric days of 1980 when we had none of the ubiquitous tools that pervade 21st century social justice advocacy. In *Star Trek* terms, how did we find out what important data were recorded in that 23rd century, hand-held tricorder device, when all we could use were stone knives and bearskins (*Star Trek*, Original Series, season 1, episode 28, "The City on the Edge of Forever")? We could not instantly share our views with the world. There was no Internet, email, or World Wide Web as a low-cost, high-yield means to quickly reach a wide audience. There were no hashtags that now enable us to discover and quickly connect with like-minded people anywhere. There was no YouTube to distribute our video message to the world or to stream a meeting or event to the public for free. Forget about anything like virtual meeting platforms to bring people together from far and wide, such as Zoom, Microsoft Teams, or Google Meet. If you wanted to meet with others to build a consensus, plan action, or compare strategies, you had to physically assemble in the same room at the same time! Heck, in 1980, we did not yet have personal desktop computers at home, much less portable laptops. If you wanted to prepare a written document, it had to be manually typed on a typewriter.

About 20 minutes into my first-year criminal law exam in December 1976, the first law exam I ever took, I had no idea that, although I was hurriedly typing away to get my answers down on paper, my beloved IBM Electric typewriter's ribbon had broken. The first pages of my brilliant answers all came out as invisible indentations on blank paper. When I discovered this to my horror, I had to rapidly fix the ribbon and re-type the answers. By the way, I got an "A" on that exam, my only A in first-year law school! Too bad the typewriter ribbon did not break more often.

In 1980, I could not imagine the idea of time-saving software like word-processing programs. Voice dictation software was something I would associate with the 23rd century (*Star Trek*, Original Series, season 2, episode

26, "Assignment Earth"). If you wanted to send a personalized letter to each member of a parliamentary committee or to all members of parliament, it had to be manually typed individually for each recipient. Once it was typed, you dared not even think about changing a word of it if you were struck by a last-minute moment of inspiration. You would risk enraging the typists who toiled to accurately type each copy of the letter. If you needed potential supporters to receive printed information, a brief, or newsletter, you had to send them a hard copy by snail mail — there were no fax machines — which meant days of delay.

Okay, so we actually did have landline telephones for talking to each other. That was quite a step forward from the first half of the 1800s. However, in 1980, mobile phones were more than a decade away for the average consumer. Smart phones, and, later, tablets, came sometime after that. This average consumer also had to physically wait by their landline phone if they wanted to be sure not to miss an important call. Consumer voice mail and personal answering machines lay in the future. Only some businesses may already have acquired pricey new physical telephone answering machines.

Four decades ago, the only real way to get our message through to the broad public was via the conventional media, television, radio, or newspapers. If you wanted to see what stories made the news, you had to be watching television or listening to the radio at the precise time of the broadcast. Few people had video recorders. What if you managed to get a good story on radio or television news? There was no way to share it with others who missed the broadcast in the same way we easily do now via the web, email, and social media. If a disability organization wanted to send the media a news release on an issue like the need for the disability amendment, it had to be sent out via snail mail. It might not arrive in newsrooms for a couple of days. Surely, disability organizations had newsletters that we could use to alert their broader community about an issue, no? When they did, they might only be produced a few times per year. There was usually quite a lag time between when they went into production and when they reached their audience. This is hardly a way to rapidly share breaking news.

It was unimaginable in 1980 to shoot a video to support a disability advocacy effort that was coming up on short notice. You would need expensive video recording and editing equipment. Only the media and professional photographers normally had that gear. Even if you managed to record and edit a video, there was no free way to instantly reach a mass audience. Copies of that film or video would have to be produced in sufficient numbers at significant cost and then mailed to recipients. Private homes and many offices did not have equipment to screen that film or video. Had you told me back then that we would eventually be able to shoot a video using a small, light-weight ubiquitous smartphone, edit it on a laptop personal computer, and then post it on YouTube for the world to see — all at incredible speed and at no cost — I would have told you that you were dreaming in technicolour (a vintage 1960s term you can google if you wish)!

If you want to organize people with disabilities to advocate on a disability issue, you need to be sure your organizing efforts are barrier-free. That was a huge challenge back then and could be impossible to achieve. Many of the tools we now take for granted had yet to be invented. Now, people who cannot read printed content due to vision loss, dyslexia, or other disabilities have a host of options. Computers and smartphones read text aloud to us using screen-reading software, some of which is expensive and some of which is free. Digital text in an email, a Microsoft Word document, or a website is instantly readable without needing anyone to read it to me as long as it is formatted to be accessible. I now plow through zillions of emails and piles of documents every week, without any human being reading a word of them aloud to me.

What if someone now hands me a hard copy printed page? I can take a picture of it with my iPhone, have the smartphone perform optical character recognition on it, and then read the text on that page aloud to me. It is instantaneous. Contrast the world of 1980! I needed a human being to read that printed material aloud to me either in person or over the phone. Another option was for a volunteer recording service like the CNIB to line up volunteers to record it on tape. The CNIB supported the reading needs of people with vision loss all over Canada, including reading for work, school, or recreation. However, such efforts would gobble up a lot of time to get the document to the CNIB, for the CNIB staff to put it in their backlogged lineup of materials to record, and then for it to be produced as audio cassettes and distributed by snail mail. Fortunately, those tapes went by mail postage free. However, that service for the most part recorded books, not individual letters or other documents.

During my Harvard studies in 1982, 1 year after the disability amendment was passed, I played around with the revolutionary new Kurzweil Reading Machine. The great-great-grandparent of the technology we now use, it was the first desktop device that could scan a page of print and then read it aloud. It was slow and clunky. It also cost a mere $50,000 USD, which would be $157,000 CAD in 2023. Today, the comparable iPhone app is not only free, but it is much faster, more accurate, and, of course, totally portable.

What is available for people who read Braille? There is an exceedingly large supply of books already available in Braille. However, Braille readers now enjoy a feast of options for instantly converting printed material into Braille. You do not need the help of anyone who knows how to transcribe Braille. You can buy a Braille printer that you connect to a computer in order to crank out hard-copy Braille. You can also buy a very small, light, and portable refreshable Braille display. Pair it with your computer or smartphone, and it instantly produces Braille via a refreshable line of raised pins, one line at a time. Those Braille displays are not cheap, but lower-priced models have appeared in recent years.

If you wanted to read a document in Braille in 1980, the CNIB had to line up a Braille transcriber who had trained for months to learn the Braille code. It is not just letter-by-letter typing. Braille is usually produced using over 200 contractions, which the transcriber must learn. The backlog for Braille transcription, like the one for recording audio content, was enormous. Technology emerged around 1980 called "computer Braille." A sighted transcriber could type content on a print keyboard. The computer translated the text into Braille. It would then be machine printed in Braille. The transcriber need not learn the Braille code to input the text. I do not remember when that first became available in Toronto. This technology was very expensive. A large organization like the CNIB might acquire it. An individual would not be able to afford it.

What about accommodating deaf people at a meeting? Now, you can arrange for instant captioning of spoken word or sign language interpretation for a meeting, a virtual meeting, or a private conversation, for a fee. The transcriber or interpreter need not come to you. They can remotely provide their services from anywhere on earth. Although less accurate, there are automatic online captioning options, which, I gather, are better than no captioning at all. In contrast, back in 1980, a sign language interpreter would have to be hired to attend a meeting in person. There have always been major shortages of this service.

## B. The 1980 Socio-Political Milieu: Disability Rights Were Unheard of in the Mainstream

If that was the 1980 technological landscape, what was the socio-political landscape for taking a run at advocating for the disability amendment? As of 1980, only one province included protection from disability discrimination, both physical and mental, in their human rights statutes: Quebec.[1] Five provinces included protection against discrimination based on physical, but not mental, disability: New Brunswick, Saskatchewan, Prince Edward Island, Nova Scotia, and Alberta.[2] Four provinces included no protection from discrimination based on either physical or mental disabilities: British Columbia, Newfoundland, Ontario, and Manitoba.[3]

Some people assume that, for every sector of society, there is a well-oiled, well-researched advocacy team or lobby group on standby, primed and ready to leap into action on any issue, even on short notice. For people with disabilities, that was certainly not the case in 1980. At that time, few in the mainstream of Canadian society had even heard of "disability rights." The rights, needs, and interests of people with disabilities were relegated to charities and to government agencies to "take care" of our needs. To most, we were viewed as the recipients of aid and help, not as rights holders entitled to equality, full participation, and full inclusion in society. Disability organizations and groups did not have a long track record of success in joint political advocacy. I would later learn how important such a track record can be, beyond generating enthusiasm within the disability community. It

---

1 The Quebec *Charter of Human Rights and Freedoms* prohibited both physical and mental disability discrimination in 1979. *Charter of Human Rights and Freedoms*, CQLR, c C-12.

2 See *Act to Amend the Human Rights Act*, SPEI 1980, Cap 26; Prince Edward Island Human Rights Commission, *Celebrating Our Journey of Human Rights* (2016) at 14; *Act to Amend the Human Rights Act*, SNB 1976, c 31; *An Act to Amend Chapter 11 of the Acts of 1969, the Human Rights Act*, SNS 1980, c 57; *Individual's Rights Protection Act*, RSA 1980, c I-2; *Saskatchewan Human Rights Code*, SS 1979, c-24.1.

3 *BC Human Rights Act*, SBC 1984, c 22. See also the *Official Report of Debates of the Legislative Assembly*, Hansard, 2nd Sess, 33rd Parl (12 April 1984) at 4373. See the amendment to the *Human Rights Code*, 1988, c 62, reprinted in *Statutes of the Province of Newfoundland* 1988, 4th Sess, 15th General Assembly; *Human Rights Code*, RSNL 1990, c H-14; *Human Rights Code*, RSO 1980, c 340; *Human Rights Code*, CCSM 1987, c H-175.

can infuse a movement with credibility. That can be crucial when trying to get the attention of busy, easily distracted politicians and journalists.

Among individuals with disabilities, there was little experience with or organizational infrastructure for collective disability rights advocacy. The expression "disability rights" was typically not on our lips. Where disability organizations existed, they were, for the most part, charities that provided services to people identified with a specific disability, such as the CNIB. Especially at the national level, these charitable disability service providers had no expertise in, and knew precious little about, disability rights, grassroots community organizing and advocacy, or training people with disabilities to advocate for themselves. With some exceptions, most of them had little or no history of taking hard-hitting positions on major disability issues.

Those service providers operated in a charity milieu. People with disabilities were viewed as their "clients," the passive recipients of their charitable services. When those charitable agencies approached the government, it was typically to seek funding to finance their services. "Government relations" was merely a facet of their fund-raising operations. A fear of "biting the hand that feeds you" too often made them reluctant to "rock the boat." Give me points for two overused cliches in one sentence that drive home the point! I have always felt that a number of the rehabilitation services that those charities provided to people with disabilities should have been delivered by the government itself as public services. But why should the government bother when non-profit charities took care of these needs? Whatever may have been my view about this issue, that was the world in which I found myself in 1980 when approaching the need to advocate for the disability amendment.

Society's dominant perception of people with disabilities as the objects of charity was then and remains today a major cause of discrimination facing people with disabilities. It also served as a serious barrier to our effectively advocating for the disability amendment. For many disability organizations — private charities that had to fundraise for their ongoing existence — voicing a strong disability rights message to a government was foreign to their thinking. Few of those charities had even a single staff member responsible for advocacy in the modern sense of that term. To many people with disabilities in Canada in 1980, and especially to those who were older, the charity paradigm was the world with which they were familiar. To speak out and fight for their disability rights would not have seemed a natural thing to do. I do not suggest for a minute that none would want to speak out, had they felt that they could. Yet undertaking vigorous disability rights advocacy was an exceptional step for many, if not most, at that time. If you had approached one of those disability charities with a disability advocacy issue, you would typically have found them overloaded, providing the rehabilitation services for which they were mandated. Any new advocacy initiatives ranked low on their priority list.

Complicating this even more, when it came to the question whether to advocate for the disability amendment in 1980, some disability service-providing charities were torn over extraneous concerns unrelated to the disability amendment itself. A major public controversy surrounding the Trudeau government's proposed patriation of Canada's Constitution focused on whether the federal government required all provinces to agree to this constitutional reform. I had heard that at least one major national disability organization was internally divided on whether to support the call for a disability amendment to the *Canadian Charter of Rights and Freedoms* because of divisions within that national charity over the federal-provincial turf squabble.[4] I do not know how pervasive this concern was among national disability organizations in Canada in 1980. I thankfully heard not a whiff of it within the CNIB, for whom I advocated on the *Charter*'s disability amendment, but I had to worry about the possibility that it was lurking out there somewhere in the background.

In 1980, the logistics of rapidly organizing disability organizations across Canada to devise a joint position would have seemed overwhelming. It would require educating them on the constitutional issue, getting them to agree to a common agenda, convincing them of the need to make this a priority, and finding someone in their staff who could competently put this into action. In 1980, Canada was in a very different place than was the United States. The United States had gone through wrenching years of the civil rights movement, the anti-Vietnam War movement, and the women's rights movement (called women's liberation). In the early 1970s, incredible American disability rights advocates, reinforced by the flood of US soldiers returning from Vietnam with new disabilities, drew on those civil rights strategies to win federal disability rights legislation. The campaign of those

4 *Canadian Charter of Rights and Freedoms*, Part 1 of the *Constitution Act, 1982*, being Schedule B to the *Canada Act 1982* (UK), 1982, c 11.

spiritual forerunners to Canada's disability rights movement is magnificently described in the Netflix documentary *Crip Camp*.[5]

To fully understand the 1980 milieu in Canada for advocacy on disability issues, it is important to ponder how willing the print and broadcast media were to cover our issues. While it is always difficult to get the media to cover disability issues, it was orders of magnitude harder four decades ago. This was infuriating since, as I mentioned earlier, radio, television, and newspapers were the only effective way to reach and win over the public and turn up the heat on politicians. Experience on the front lines showed me in the early 1980s that news outlets did not think of disability issues, like the fight for the disability amendment, as a political story. Reporters typically knew very little, if anything, about disability issues. It seemed that reporters and editors had in mind only a few prefab paradigms of a disability story. If you did not fit into one of those prefab stories, you felt like you were trying to swim up Niagara Falls!

What were those four prefab, virtually cliché news stories? First, there was the tragic story of a person suffering due to their disability, which falls into the category of "Isn't it awful?" Second, there were the inspiring stories of a person succeeding at something "despite their disability": "Isn't it amazing what those inspiring people can do?" Third, let's not forget the heart-warming stories of the Anne Sullivan miracle workers, the heroic people without disabilities who defied the odds and selflessly helped a person alleviate the misery of living with their disability. Fourth, and only on occasion, there were the "David versus Goliath" stories. Some person with a disability or their family member valiantly and heroically vanquishes an unfair barrier or cold government bureaucracy to win something obvious and basic: "Why should those poor people with disabilities have to go through such an ordeal?"

Stories about advocating for new laws to protect our rights did not seem to fit into any of those templates. Even now, getting such stories into the media is still no picnic. Fortunately, we now have the option of using social media to reach the public even if the conventional media does not pick up on our news releases. In fact, I am now finding that blitzing an issue on social media can be the best way to get the sluggish conventional media to take interest in it. At the core of most of those four prefab news

---

5 See the film *Crip Camp*, directed by Ames Lebrecht and Nicole Newnham (2020), online: *YouTube* <www.youtube.com/watch?v=OFS8SpwioZ4>.

stories was an implicit, inaccurate, unfair, and harmful assumption that people with disabilities could not do much at all. Any achievement by people with disabilities was, by definition, amazing, inspiring, and heart-warming. People with disabilities were cast either as helpless, pitiable, and pathetic or as superhuman superstars capable of overcoming any obstacle despite the impossibility of living independently with a disability. This all undervalues and under-estimates what people with disabilities can do if they are just given the chance. It embodies the all-too-common disability experience of the soft bigotry of low expectations.

Throughout the fall and winter of 1980, the debate over the patriation of Canada's Constitution was an ongoing hot news story. It was all over the media, often at or near the top of the news. However, much of that coverage did not focus on anything to do with the specific contents of the *Charter*. Reporters appeared obsessed with the political battle between the federal government and many of the provinces over whether the federal government could unilaterally ask the UK Parliament to amend Canada's Constitution or whether the proposal required the support of some or all of the provinces. Early in the process, only Ontario and New Brunswick supported the federal government. Quebec and the western provinces were especially vehement that all, or at least most, of the provinces must approve the reforms. This issue landed in the Supreme Court of Canada in the famous 1981 patriation reference.[6]

So many media reports depicted this as a battle of personalities. Prime Minister Pierre Trudeau (portrayed at times as trying to win his place in history) versus certain of the more colourful provincial premiers or as a personal grudge match between Trudeau and his nemesis, Quebec separatist and premier Rene Levesque. In that media environment, it was brutally hard to get any reporters to even focus on an issue that related to the wording of section 15 of the *Charter*. I once called a CTV news reporter to try to get coverage of our call for an amendment to section 15 to include equality for people with disabilities. The reporter heard the word "amend," confused it with the debate over the Constitution's amending formula, and asked me what kind of amending formula we wanted. I was stunned at a television news reporter's obvious lack of fluency with the basics of the biggest story in the news. I was not talking about a constitutional amending formula! I realized that I had a lot to learn about the need to explain a story like this

6 *Re: Resolution to Amend the Constitution*, [1981] 1 SCR 753, [1981] SCJ No 58.

to reporters in a simple, step-by-step way, while never assuming the reporter knows anything about it.

## C. A 1980 Legal Profession Unequipped for Effective Disability Rights Advocacy

In 1980, our legal profession was ill-equipped to effectively handle disability rights issues. Ontario's first disability rights legal aid clinic, the ARCH Disability Law Centre, had just opened its doors in 1980. There were few, if any, lawyers practising in Ontario who would self-identify as practising in the area of disability rights. Few disability rights were enshrined in our law at that time for them to try to enforce.

Law schools then taught little or nothing about disability rights. Years would pass before even a few law schools started to offer an optional disability rights course for the small percentage of students who chose to enroll in it. It was a huge breakthrough in the mid-1980s when the mandatory Ontario bar admission course started to devote a half-day of its lengthy 6-month program to the entire topic of representing clients with disabilities. That was an effort to make up for the lack of this training in law schools. I was centrally involved in the design and delivery of that program. It was symbolic of the world in which we then lived that I had to fight the Law Society time and again to avert that tiny offering from being cancelled. Sadly, its contents were optional and not mandatory during some of those years, when it was offered at all, even though it was well received by law students. I understand that such disability content has long since vanished from Ontario's bar admissions program.

After four decades since the *Charter* was adopted replete with a guarantee of equality for people with disabilities, Canadian law schools still do not effectively ensure that law students are trained to meet the legal needs of clients with disabilities. In 1983, then Family Court Judge (later Supreme Court of Canada Justice) Rosalie Abella authored a landmark report finding that Ontario's legal profession was not meeting the legal needs of people with disabilities.[7] Abella's report concluded that law schools needed to reform their curriculum in order to effectively train lawyers to meet the legal needs of people with disabilities. I hazard a guess that most law deans

7 Rosalie Silberman Abella, *Access to Legal Services by the Disabled: Report of a Study* (Toronto: Ministry of the Attorney General, 1983).

then and now did not even know about Abella's report and its blunt findings. A decade after Abella's report, I was invited to deliver a talk on this topic at a meeting of all of Canada's law deans. I turned my presentation into a published law journal article, entitled "Disabled Persons and Canadian Law Schools: The Right to the Equal Benefit of the Law School."[8]

As I write this retrospective, I am immersed more than ever in the challenge of expanding law school curriculum on disability issues. Over the first 7½ years since I retired at the end of 2015 as counsel with the Ministry of the Attorney General for Ontario, I worked on a part-time basis at the Osgoode Hall Law School on expanding the disability curriculum that is taught to law students. I have held the title of visiting professor of disability rights and legal education at Osgoode. I gave guest lectures in a diverse spectrum of law school courses, primarily on disability issues and disability rights. Starting in September 2023, I have taken on a similar role at the University of Western Ontario's Faculty of Law. I repeatedly find that law students welcome the chance to learn about this topic. So many law professors are delighted to have it included in their courses. Yet there are still so many barriers to overcome the entrenched failure to systematically cover this topic, even in an era where law school curriculum is being revamped to better address equity issues of various sorts.

In 2021, I delivered a report to the Osgoode Hall Law School, which was brimming with a comprehensive set of recommendations for curriculum reform.[9] Those recommendations are now included in a law journal article whose title says it all: "People with Disabilities Need Lawyers Too! A Ready-to-Use Plan for Law Schools to Educate Law Students to Effectively Serve the Legal Needs of Clients with Disabilities as Well as Clients without Disabilities"[10] When it comes to legal education on this topic, things are somewhat better now than they were in 1980. However, Canada's legal

8 David Lepofsky, "Disabled Persons and Canadian Law Schools: The Right to the Equal Benefit of the Law School" (1991) 36:2 McGill LJ 636.

9 David Lepofsky, *Educating Law Students to Serve the Legal Needs of Clients with Disabilities: A Practical Plan for Making Progress*, Report to Osgoode Hall Law School (January 2022).

10 David Lepofsky "People with Disabilities Need Lawyers Too! A Ready-to-Use Plan for Law Schools to Educate Law Students to Effectively Serve the Legal Needs of Clients with Disabilities as Well as Clients without Disabilities" (2022) 38 Windsor YB Access Justice 148.

education system and its legal profession are still far behind where they should be.

## D. What Was It Like Doing It Again over 35 Years Later?

In 2015, while a federal election was underway, some disability advocates (of which I was one) were pressing the federal parties to pledge that, if elected, they would enact a national disability accessibility law. Canada had no such legislation. The federal Tories had promised one on their own initiative in 2006 but took no meaningful action to keep that promise over their ensuing decade in power. In 2015, I planted an idea with the March of Dimes, one of Canada's big disability service providers, that they might convene a summit of disability organization chief executive officers [CEOs] about doing some concerted action on this issue. They quickly agreed. It was pulled together within a very short time. The 2-hour summit produced a unanimous statement, released to the media shortly afterwards, calling for a national disabilities law.

In 1980, nothing like that CEO gathering was likely conceivable. Had such a gathering been called back then to discuss a joint national effort on the disability amendment, I doubt many CEOs would have even showed up. It was not that they were against disability rights. Disability rights was either not on their agenda or was buried at its bottom. By the time we would have assembled them in one room, it could well have been too late for much concerted action.

Over the ensuing campaign for the *Accessible Canada Act* from 2015 to 2019, I thought back many times on the advantages we then enjoyed by tackling a national disability rights advocacy blitz with all the tools we did not have back in 1980.[11] The Internet and social media, and especially Twitter, played a vital role in our 2015–2019 campaign. News releases were instantly sent out across Canada at the push of a button. Any news coverage, of which there was far too little, was quickly posted on our website and shared via email and social media to thousands of people. Our progress could be and was instantly tracked around the world.

We rapidly pulled together brainstorming meetings with other disability advocates online or by phone, at little or no cost. Accommodations such as captioning for such meetings were remotely delivered over the web. We could

11 *Accessible Canada Act*, SC 2019, c 10.

follow all parliamentary proceedings on Bill C-81, the proposed *Accessible Canada Act*, from anywhere, by computer or smartphone, in real time. We swiftly posted online my presentations on behalf of the *Accessibility for Ontarians with Disabilities Act*'s Alliance to a Standing Committee of the House of Commons on 25 October 2018 and to a Standing Committee of the Senate on 11 April 2019.[12] Others around the world could watch those videos whenever they wished. Hansard, the official transcript of parliamentary proceedings, was often readily available online for us to monitor.

Compare the 1980–1981 public hearings and debates at the Special Joint Committee of the Senate and the House of Commons on the Constitution of Canada. As I mentioned earlier, they were the first proceedings of any parliamentary committee to be televised in Canada. If you did not see their proceedings live or catch them being replayed (reruns of proceedings in Parliament were then very unusual), you were out of luck. Together with the ARCH Disability Law Centre and the Council of Canadians with Disabilities, a key strategy in our campaign for amendments to strengthen Bill C-81 when it was before Parliament was to create an open letter to Parliament. In it, we set out key priorities for amending the bill and then got as many disability organizations as possible to sign on. Working together and using email, the web, and social media, we pulled this off twice, with incredible speed, once in the fall of 2018 when the bill was before the House of Commons and in the 2019 spring, when it was before the House for a second time after the Senate passed several amendments that we wanted the House of Commons to ratify. In 1980, this would have taken months and many more hours of volunteer or staff work.

12 *Accessibility for Ontarians with Disabilities Act*, SO 2005, c 11. See "Presentation by the Accessibility for Ontarians with Disabilities Alliance Chair David Lepofsky to the House of Commons Standing Committee on Human Resources, Skills and Social Development and the Status of Persons with Disabilities on Bill C-81, the Proposed Accessible Canada Act" (25 October 2018), online: *Youtube* <www.youtube.com/watch?v=T_nkPeSUPHg>; Senate, Social Affairs Committee, "David Lepofsky Addresses Concerns on Bill C-81 to Senate Committee" (11 April 2019), online: *Youtube* <www.youtube.com/watch?v=FERCAljHbrw>.

# V. WHY I GOT INVOLVED IN THE DISABILITY AMENDMENT CAMPAIGN

## A. A Careful Goal-Directed Plan?

Before I would dive head-first into a major effort like a campaign to get an amendment to Canada's Constitution, you would expect me to carefully deliberate over whether to take on this challenge at all, to studiously estimate the time it would demand of me and the time I had available to devote to it, and to meticulously formulate specific goals that I want to achieve. Not this time! My decision to campaign for the disability amendment was slap-dash, with no such pondering or contemplation. I cannot remember where I was or when it was that I decided to dive into this. So why did I jump on this issue? Of course, I was driven by an impulse to win the disability amendment itself. It was just plain ridiculous that people with disabilities were left out of section 15 of the *Canadian Charter of Rights and Freedoms*.[1] But there was more that I eventually had in mind.

## B. An Uphill Battle, to Say the Least

I knew from the start that it was extremely unlikely that we would succeed, for several reasons. With hindsight, it was even more uphill than I then thought. Prime Minister Pierre Trudeau was laser focused on rushing his Constitution patriation package through Parliament at warp speed.[2] He seemed iron-willed and inflexible. There was so little time to mount a serious campaign for the disability amendment — something I had never done before. Very little time was initially allotted to the Joint Committee for public hearings. That committee was the only major high-profile public platform that I knew of where the case for the disability amendment could be pressed. Many groups competed for the Joint Committee's precious time slots to raise a host of different issues. My chance of getting one of those time slots felt like approximately zero.

---

1 *Canadian Charter of Rights and Freedoms*, Part 1 of the *Constitution Act, 1982*, being Schedule B to the *Canada Act 1982* (UK), 1982, c 11.

2 Robert Sheppard & Michael Valpy, *The National Deal: The Fight for a Canadian Constitution* (Toronto: Fleet Books, 1982) at 16–64.

I heard of no politician and no political party championing this issue themselves in the early fall of 1980. Voters with disabilities were not seen as a constituency for politicians to court. Politicians were not fretting about alienating or winning over the disability vote! Getting media coverage of the need for the disability amendment also looked like an uphill battle. As I said earlier, the media and public discussion and debate over the Constitution's patriation was overwhelmingly preoccupied with the politics of whether Trudeau's federal government could unilaterally patriate the Constitution without the agreement of most, if not all, of the provinces. There was no broad public dialogue across Canada and in the media on any of the *Charter*'s finer details, such as on what rights needed to be added to it.

It was and remains to me bizarre that there could have been so little public and media attention on the actual rights to be included in the *Charter* when the *Charter* was the very centrepiece of the patriation package. I earlier discussed that the constitutional rights to be enshrined in the *Charter* were going to touch everyone's lives in one way or another. Strange as it seems, what the *Charter* said and whether it should say it better were seemingly viewed as irrelevant or inconsequential. Canada's disability community was in no position in October 1980 to organize a swift, loud, sophisticated nation-wide campaign. There was no groundswell about this issue among people with disabilities themselves. I can remember hearing of no earlier issue that led people with disabilities to turn out in any numbers in front of the Parliament buildings in Ottawa or the Ontario legislature in Toronto.

I anticipate that very few people with disabilities even knew that the *Charter* was written in a way that left them out of its equality rights guarantee. If they thought about it at all, it would likely have seemed disconnected from their daily lives. I would later relearn over decades of volunteer disability advocacy that people with disabilities and their organizations are often overwhelmed with coping with the immediate burdens of getting through the next day or week. Abstract goals like a legislative amendment to win a constitutional right to disability equality would not rank high in their immediate priorities. Under such daily pressure just to keep one's head above water, people with disabilities and disability organizations generally would not have the time or inclination to research what a constitutional right to equality for people with disabilities would mean for them.

## C. A Collateral Goal Was My Main Goal

If winning the disability amendment looked impossible and was absolutely not my primary objective, why did I bother at all with this? Believe it or not, I was at least equally thinking that it could help our campaign in Toronto, in which I was immersed, to get the Ontario legislature to amend the Ontario *Human Rights Code* to prohibit discrimination against people with disabilities.[3] What did a disability campaign aiming at the Ontario government and a provincial statute (the Ontario *Human Rights Code*) have to do with whether Parliament in Ottawa should amend a different proposed law (the *Charter*) to protect against disability discrimination? Was I a very confused law student who could not get my levels of government straight and who conflated two very different laws and different levels of government? No, but my chain of tactical reasoning on this question in 1980 was, on reflection, more than a tad contorted, as I will explain.

Just to remind you of what I briefly discussed in Chapter III, the Ontario *Human Rights Code* is a provincial statute. It made it illegal for anyone to discriminate because of sex, religion, race, or certain other grounds. It banned discrimination in access to things like employment and the enjoyment of goods, services, and facilities.[4] It created a public law enforcement agency, the Ontario Human Rights Commission, to investigate, mediate, and, where appropriate, publicly litigate against those who discriminate.[5] The Ontario *Human Rights Code* had been on the books in Ontario since 1962. However, even as late as 1980, it still did not forbid discrimination because of mental or physical disability.

The *Charter* was meant to impose restrictions on activity by governments, legislatures, and the public sector. The *Charter* was not meant to impose restrictions on private businesses or non-profit private organizations. In contrast, a provincial anti-discrimination law like the Ontario *Human Rights Code* bans unlawful discrimination in both the public and private sectors. As I also explained back in Chapter III, a group of Ontario disability community organizations had been toiling away since late 1979 to get protection for people with disabilities included in the Ontario *Human Rights Code*. In the spring of 1980, I had joined the leadership team

---

3 *Human Rights Code*, RSO 1990, c H-19.

4 *Ibid*, ss 1, 5(1).

5 *Ibid*, ss 27–31.7.

of that group, the Ontario Coalition for Human Rights for the Handicapped. I was pickled in drafting some of the detailed amendments to the code that we wanted. This was an instant crash course in disability rights advocacy, with one heck of a high-stakes practicum!

In 1980, we went to the media in order to reach the public. Our aim was to mount pressure on Ontario's Conservative government under Premier Bill Davis. We wanted to turn up the heat on the Ontario government. However, we did not want to target or, in any way, undermine its lead minister, Robert Elgie, with negative media coverage. Premier Bill Davis and Labour Minister Elgie had seemed receptive to our message, but their government was moving far too slowly. That was something I would encounter time and again over the next four decades when dealing with politicians. We feared that the Ontario government might keep delaying. When it finally got moving, it might again bring forward weakly worded legislation. The governing Conservatives had some members who wanted nothing to do with expanding human rights for people with disabilities. We did not want to inadvertently empower that faction within their caucus by making it look like this was a no-win issue that would trigger bad press for the government, no matter what proposed legislation it brought forward. The nay-sayers in the Conservative Party could use that to press the Tory caucus to shelve the whole disability human rights reform issue.

How do we square that circle? How do we turn up the heat without undermining Elgie? We decided to keep our message to the media positive and encouraging towards the Ontario government. At the same time, I thought I would take it on myself to unleash a good hard-hitting verbal swipe at the federal government. Remember that this Ontario coalition was formed before Prime Minister Trudeau brought forward the proposed *Charter* in October 1980. It did not expand its efforts beyond the provincial sphere to advocate for the disability amendment to the proposed *Charter*. It was solely devoted to advocacy at the provincial level in order to achieve amendments to the Ontario *Human Rights Code*. It was not a choice of getting one or the other — amendments to the Ontario *Human Rights Code* or an amendment to the proposed *Charter*. We needed both. However, our Ontario coalition's members stayed focused on the provincial objective alone. It had taken a great deal of collective effort (of which I was a part) just to keep them working together on that goal.

So how did I draw a strategic connection between the campaign in Toronto to win amendments to the Ontario *Human Rights Code*, on the one hand, and a fight in Ottawa to get disability equality added to the proposed *Charter*, on the other? Try to follow my tactical thinking, if you can! I naively saw the fight in Ottawa for the disability amendment as a way of showing the Ontario government that we were capable of unleashing real media muscle. We could blast the Trudeau government in the media. This would show the Ontario government in Toronto that we could do the same to them if it did not deliver strong amendments to the Ontario *Human Rights Code*. That could make the Ontario government take our concerns more seriously. It could empower Elgie if he tried to convince his more reluctant caucus colleagues.

I have no idea if this dubious, contorted strategy ever helped with our campaign regarding the Ontario *Human Rights Code*. I seriously doubt it made any difference. I do not think I ever discussed my tactical thinking within our coalition or with anyone in the Ontario legislature or government. No one within the Ontario government of the day has ever intimated to me that they were influenced by our federal media blitz in deciding how far to go on reforms to the Ontario *Human Rights Code*. The odds were slim that the senior officials at Queen's Park were even following the scant media coverage we secured that was targeted at the Trudeau government in Ottawa. I know from years of experience since then that, had senior provincial political officials seen us unleashing a barrage at the Trudeau government, they would have been delighted. We were diverting our firepower to Ottawa and away from Queen's Park. Politicians love when a community advocacy group is distracted by another target. I had a lot to learn in 1980.

One positive thing that I can now say about my attempt at strategic thinking was that it was good to try to engage in strategic thinking. You need to try, even if feebly, before you can ever hope to become good at it. Moreover, this dubious tactical thinking helped lead me to engage in the fight for the disability amendment to the *Charter*. I am certainly happy, with hindsight, that I did end up leaping into that issue, whether or not my reasons for doing it made any sense at all!

## D. Lessons Lepofsky Learned

The collective effort to get the *Charter* amended to include a disability equality guarantee ended up succeeding, despite my severe well-founded skepticism about its potential for success. That lesson has carried forward with me over decades of disability advocacy since then. The obvious unlikelihood of success has typically not deterred me. My willingness to take part in, and later to lead, the decade-long campaign that led in 2005 to the enactment of the *Accessibility for Ontarians with Disabilities Act* [*AODA*] was never slowed or deterred by the overwhelming impediments that made our likelihood of success seem equally slim.[6] In retrospect, I attribute my willingness to disregard the seemingly insurmountable odds of winning the *AODA* from 1994 to 2005 in large part to my experience in 1980–1981 with the seemingly unwinnable campaign for the disability amendment that we collectively won.

The question I have difficulty answering to this day is why I really did engage in the campaign for the disability amendment at all. Beyond my bogus tactical thinking that I just described, why did I take on this fight when it was so obviously and completely hopeless? Why did I not instead invest that time into more efforts in our campaign to get disability into the Ontario *Human Rights Code*? Why was I not deterred from taking action on the disability amendment by the minimal interest in it expressed by others with whom I was engaged within the small disability advocacy community? I suppose the answer is the same as it is for all my disability advocacy efforts over the past four decades. I just feel driven to do it. The issues are important to me and have become a deeply embedded passion. I feel blessed that I have the opportunity and the time to dive into these issues. I have had a career path that gave me a level of comfort and security as well as a skill set on which I could draw.

In 1980, it seemed that every time I turned on the television to watch the nightly news, there was non-stop coverage of the patriation battle. Yet there was no discussion of the need for the disability amendment. Our policy arguments in support of the disability amendment were overwhelming, as I explore later in this retrospective. There was no visible opposition to it. I had no idea if anyone else was fighting for the disability amendment. I thankfully had access to a platform via the CNIB to try to get attention on the issue. Because I was in the bar admissions course in the fall of 1980, I had ample time on my hands.

I felt quite isolated doing advocacy on this issue back then. It is very exciting and invigorating to dive into community advocacy when I am working closely with a team of other like-minded people. We can go out for a beer, celebrate successes, grumble about failures, yack on the phone late into the night, and encourage each other along the way. When it feels

---

6 *Accessibility for Ontarians with Disabilities Act*, SO 2005, c 11.

like you are doing it alone, you have to sustain yourself by being driven to take on the issue. I certainly had and have no delusions of my own importance. I now know that others were actively campaigning for the disability amendment. In 1980, we had no Internet or social media to help us discover each other and compare notes. In each instance from the 1980 fight for the disability amendment and other battles that have arisen since then, I have felt that I would have difficulty living with myself if I sat idly by and did not take on the issue. Perhaps it is just who I am. That is why I do it. That is also why I do not stop doing it.

# VI. GOING IT ALONE: BECOMING THE CNIB'S OFFICIAL CONSTITUTIONAL SPOKESPERSON, WHATEVER THAT IS!

## A. Finding a Soapbox

How do you get started on a campaign to try to win the disability amendment? I didn't have a clue. I needed an organizational platform from which to speak. David Lepofsky, a 23-year-old blind law student, acting alone, was not going to get any attention from the media, the public, or any politicians. I had been in the media a handful of times in my late teens, talking about disability issues purely from a blindness perspective. Otherwise, I was a complete unknown beyond the close circle of my family, friends, classmates, and my immediate colleagues within the Ontario Coalition on Human Rights for the Handicapped.

There was no pre-existing coalition that had formed to win the disability amendment, as far as I had heard. To build one from scratch was out of the question. I doubt I even thought about it as an option. There was no time, given the Trudeau government's rushed timetable for Parliament passing its constitutional patriation package. I had never before taken part in starting a coalition of any sort. I asked some of my compatriots in the Ontario Coalition for Human Rights for the Handicapped if they would like to jump on a disability amendment bandwagon. It sparked exactly zero excitement. There was no real interest in broadening our advocacy efforts beyond the provincial Ontario *Human Rights Code* to include the federal *Canadian Charter of Rights and Freedoms.*[1] My fellow coalition members were too busy with other things. Getting organizations to help with our provincial coalition campaigning for inclusion of disability in the Ontario *Human Rights Code* was enough of a project.

My solution was to turn to the one disability organization with whom I had already established a relationship in order to see if I could undertake a blitz on their behalf to win the disability amendment. I planned to offer

---

1 *Human Rights Code*, RSO 1990, c H-19; *Canadian Charter of Rights and Freedoms*, Part 1 of the *Constitution Act, 1982*, being Schedule B to the *Canada Act 1982* (UK), 1982, c 11.

to volunteer to be the CNIB spokesperson (back then we said "spokesman") on constitutional issues, a title I invented. It sounded mighty authoritative. I did not actually know what it meant, but I hoped someone might be impressed by it. Founded shortly after the First World War, the CNIB was Canada's largest non-profit charitable organization providing rehabilitation services to people who were blind or had low vision. I had been a CNIB client since I was a child.

When deciding to seek out the CNIB as my soapbox from which to speak on the disability amendment, I knew that this risked some controversy among some people with vision loss who were outside the CNIB tent. A good number of CNIB clients, and especially younger ones, understandably had pent-up frustration and even anger at the CNIB as a paternalistic, poorly run service provider. Many CNIB clients shared with each other a litany of jaw-dropping stories of problems they had experienced when trying to get services from that agency. The CNIB had dominated the sphere of providing vision loss rehabilitation services for decades.

In Chapter IV, I explained that, in the mid-1970s, a group of especially frustrated individuals with vision loss in Ontario formed an organization to raise serious criticisms of the CNIB, the Blind Ontario Organization with Self-help Tactics [BOOST]. Quite a number of their criticisms of the CNIB were well founded. The CNIB had reacted to their criticisms very poorly, treating them as marginal, radical riffraff. I was concerned that members of BOOST might not take kindly to my using the CNIB as my soapbox for advocating for the disability amendment. I turn out to have been correct. It must sound bizarre that this should even have been a worry, given what was at stake in the fight for the disability amendment. Yet disability community politics over the years can be confusing and confounding. Infuriating as it can get at some moments, I have considered it my job to learn how to stick-handle around such things. It is surprising how rarely it has ended up getting in the way.

The CNIB had resources and had a very good reputation in Canadian society. For me, the choice to try to get the CNIB to let me speak for them on the disability amendment issue was easy but not risk free. As soapboxes go, it was the best one, not to mention the only one open to me.

## B. Getting the CNIB to Appoint Me as its "Official Constitutional Spokesperson"

Once I decided on the CNIB route, it was by no means an easy task to get the CNIB on board. It was not a certainty that the CNIB would want to take any action on this or would want to assign this effort to me. The CNIB was then a very traditional, reserved, private non-profit charity that was reluctant to "rock the boat." The CNIB had no one on staff who knew anything about this subject or about how to campaign for legislative reform. In the 3 years since the CNIB had received the report and recommendations of our 1977 Blindness Law Reform Project, I doubt they had done much to take action on our recommendations, beyond taking part in the Ontario Coalition for Human Rights for the Handicapped and sending our report to Prime Minister Joe Clark the previous year, on my suggestion. Earlier in 1980, I had asked the CNIB to get involved in the Ontario Coalition for Human Rights for the Handicapped. The CNIB had not come to me, expressing any desire to join that coalition.

I had a few things working in my favour. I was already on the CNIB's Ontario board, chaired its brand new Public Education and Advocacy Committee [PEA Committee], which I had founded, and spoke for the CNIB as its representative on the Ontario Coalition for Human Rights for the Handicapped. I had created and directed the CNIB's 1977 Blindness Law Reform Project. And, oh yeah, I was a blind guy with a law degree! Also working in my favour was the fact that, a short time earlier, the CNIB's National Council had brought in a new senior management team to replace the stodgy incumbents who were a legacy of a bygone era. They were truly a breath of fresh air. I had a good working relationship with the CNIB's new national managing director, and the new Ontario division executive director who was brought in as part of this wave of reform. This new management team was expected to undertake major reform at the agency.

My first challenge was to come up with a way to formally raise this issue in order to get the CNIB to take a position on the disability amendment and to appoint me as its spokesperson. As noted in Chapter III, before the *Charter* became a public issue, I had not been able to achieve much progress at the CNIB during my efforts as a member of its Ontario Board of Directors. In fact, looking back now, my only big accomplishment serving for several years on that board was using it as my platform to get the CNIB engaged in the disability amendment campaign — one that was worth the many earlier long, tedious, and boring board meetings through which I had impatiently suffered. Most of the Ontario board members viewed me skeptically as an unorthodox troublemaker, out of touch with the CNIB's traditional gray-flannel, conservative deportment. They knew little, if anything, about human rights, constitutional rights, or law reform. I needed a way to somehow get those folks to give me a mandate that I thought they neither knew nor cared about and one for which they had no predisposition to trust me to handle.

Knowing just a tiny bit about corporate law and about the CNIB's organizational structure, I anticipated that it would be the CNIB's National Council that would have to give me the mandate. I was a member of the CNIB's subsidiary Ontario board, not a member of its National Council. My solution was to craft a seemingly convoluted resolution and to first present it to the CNIB's PEA Committee. My resolution for the PEA Committee urged the CNIB's Ontario board chair to recommend that the CNIB's National Council advocate for the disability amendment. I expected no difficulty getting the PEA Committee's members to pass this resolution. I had recruited most of them for the Ontario board and all of them for the PEA Committee. They were all my allies and supportive of this agenda.

I called an emergency meeting of the PEA Committee for 30 October 1980 and chaired the meeting. The PEA Committee quickly and easily passed this motion, which I had composed:

> Whereas the proposed new Canadian Constitution, which is before the Senate and the House of Commons, includes a Charter of Rights which in Section 15 provides: "everyone has the right to equality before the law and to equal protection of the law without discrimination because of race, national or ethnic origin, colour, religion, age or sex."
>
> and whereas this provision does not make reference to the handicapped as a group entitled to equality before the law and to equal protection of the law;
>
> and whereas the proposed wording of the equality clause will likely not involve the proper protection of egalitarian liberties in Canada;
>
> and whereas The Canadian National Institute for the Blind has a policy and goal, the advancement of the legal rights of visually handicapped Canadians;
>
> be it therefore resolved: that the Public Education and Advocacy Committee recommend to the Chairman of the Ontario Division Board of Management, or a person so designated by him, and propose the following motion on behalf of the said Committee at the November 1980 meeting of National Council, namely:

> "Be it resolved that National Council supports the inclusion of handicapped persons in Section 15 of the proposed *Charter of Rights* to be included in the Canadian Constitution; and be it further resolved that CNIB National Management be directed and empowered to take all necessary steps to bring CNIB's position on this issue before the public and before the Government of Canada as soon as possible; and that Management be directed and empowered to advocate for the use in a constitutional equality clause of words which will give it broad and effective scope and meaning."[2]

I did not care why the CNIB's Ontario board might pass this motion or, after it, why the CNIB's National Council might adopt it. I only cared that they actually passed it. I have learned time and again over the decades since then that it can be very effective to present a request or recommendation that is written in terms that a person feels they cannot refuse, whether or not it is something to which they want to agree. Maybe that is a contorted spin on Marlon Brando's legendary "offer you can't refuse" in the movie *The Godfather*.

Our motion would first come up at the meeting of the CNIB's Ontario board on 12 November 1980. I wanted the Ontario board to say yes to our position and thereby send it to the National Council for its approval. I was not able to make the Ontario board's meeting because of my studies for the Ontario bar admission exams. Instead, I wrote the volunteer who chaired the Ontario board and who also sat on the CNIB's National Council, Jack Pequegnat. In my letter to him on 10 November 1980, I quoted the motion that the PEA Committee had passed. I urged him to support us and to advocate at the National Council for the CNIB to adopt our motion and agree to advocate for the disability amendment.[3] In my letter, I pressed the *Charter* issue's urgency. I feared that it otherwise could get lost in the shuffle at the CNIB. I also tried to impress the issue's importance on him in order to win his support:

> It is the Committee's view that this matter should be raised at National Council in its November meeting, because the Federal Government's current plans for patriation include the passage by the Senate and the House of Commons of its

---

2 Canadian National Institute for the Blind (CNIB), *Minutes of the Meeting of the Public Education and Advocacy Committee of the Ontario Board of Management* (30 October 1980) at 2.

3 Letter from M David Lepofsky, Chairman, Public Education and Advocacy Committee, to JA Pequegnat, Chairman, Ontario Division Board of Management, Re: Human Rights and the Proposed Canadian Constitution (10 November 1980).

> now-famous resolution by early December. If CNIB is to take action on this issue, the National Managing Director must be mandated to do so as soon as possible or else the opportunity to grant handicapped persons the same right to equality as all other Canadians will be irrevocably lost.
>
> I realize that there is much controversy in Canada over whether the Government of Canada should unilaterally patriate the Constitution, and whether such patriation should include the entrenchment of a charter of rights. CNIB should, I feel, not express any opinion to the public on whether the Government's plan in this direction is good or bad. However, our Committee is of the view that CNIB can and should take the position publicly that if the Government of Canada is to entrench a charter of rights in a new Canadian Constitution, then any right to equality which is provided for Canadians should not be denied to handicapped Canadians.[4]

I had no idea whether Pequegnat would support our recommendation or if he even agreed with the prime minister's plan to patriate the Constitution. I had no reason to expect him to be favourably disposed to our position. I had no working relationship with Pequegnat. When he chaired meetings of the CNIB's Ontario board, he was, to say the least, not receptive to issues and perspectives that I raised. He did not appear to know much about blindness. Yet he was the one who I had to convince at this stage. To me, this was not encouraging.

With hindsight, I should have moved mountains to enable myself to go to the 12 November 1980 Ontario board meeting to speak to this issue myself. I had arranged for a colleague on the PEA Committee to do so, but it was certainly not a sure thing that the Ontario board would listen to her and adopt our motion. I should also have taken a deep breath and tried to set up a face-to-face meeting with Pequegnat. In my letter to him, I should have made the case in more detail on why the CNIB must advocate for the disability amendment. Fortunately, my not taking those steps did not turn out to matter. The CNIB's new reform-minded national managing director, Robert Mercer, was agreeable to the CNIB's taking on this issue and to my serving as its constitutional spokesperson. I recall a pleasant meeting in his office to discuss this idea. No doubt, his support played a key role, if not the decisive role, in the CNIB's ultimate approval of my motion.

Our motion was eventually taken to the CNIB's National Council during the week of 17 November 1980. I was not invited to that meeting nor given a chance to explain our motion to that council. I was later told

---

4 *Ibid.*

that it was passed. I have no idea if there was any discussion or debate over it. I thereby became the official constitutional spokesman of the CNIB. Heck, maybe that sounds impressive to somebody. I was honoured that the CNIB's chief executive officer trusted me enough to appoint me to this volunteer role. He was new to the job and did not really know me at all. Disability law reform advocacy was not his turf. His plate was more than full, trying to belatedly lug the CNIB into the second half of the 20th century.

## C. Hitting the Ground Running: Trying to Get Media Attention

As I think back to that time, I instantly conjure up that amazing final scene in the 1972 movie *The Candidate*, starring Robert Redford. His character spends the whole movie trying to get his party's nomination for senator. At the end of the movie, he wins the nomination. Stunned and clueless about what to do now that he has won the nomination, the candidate ends the movie by looking at us, the audience, with a stunned visage, and asks aloud: "What do we do now?" I am no Robert Redford, but I was just as clueless. I knew that it would be up to me to do all the work on this campaign. There was no one at the CNIB with any expertise on advocacy who could assist. Naively, I decided to kick off our campaign by trying to get media coverage. The media was our only possible way to win public support for our cause, especially on short notice.

Even before we got the blessing of the CNIB's National Council to advocate for the disability amendment, I wanted to quickly generate some kind of mandate for me to speak out on this issue. Back on 30 October 1980, when the Public Education and Advocacy Committee held its emergency meeting on the need for the disability amendment, we did not yet have a mandate from the CNIB. This is because our motion calling for the CNIB to take action had not yet been considered by its Ontario board or its National Council. My solution was to get the Public Education and Advocacy Committee to give me a mandate to speak out on this issue on its behalf. At that 30 October 1980 meeting, the CNIB Public Education and Advocacy Committee passed this motion that I drafted:

> Whereas inclusion of handicapped in the proposed *Canadian Charter of Rights* is a matter of urgent and pressing necessity, needing immediate action,

and whereas CNIB National Management has taken the position before the special Parliamentary Committee on the Disabled and Handicapped in favour of inclusion of handicapped in the *Charter*;

and whereas CNIB National Management has also taken the same position at a recent meeting concerning the International Year of Disabled Persons, and joined with that meeting in making a public statement to that effect;

be it therefore resolved:

that the Public Education and Advocacy Committee immediately bring to the attention of the public in Ontario its concerns over the current constitutional proposals and that the Committee Chairman be authorized to express the views of the Committee.[5]

The "whereas" clauses in that motion were designed to put as much pressure on the CNIB as I could to let me forge ahead. I wanted to avert any risk that someone could complain about my speaking about the disability amendment before the CNIB's National Council got time to discuss this issue.

So what sizzling news story did I have to offer the media after our 30 October 1980 meeting? How about something like "Committee of CNIB's Ontario Board Launches Campaign to Get Proposed Charter of Rights Amended to Protect Disability Rights" or something like that. You can just imagine news assignment editors leaping over each other to jam their microphones in my direction! The news release that the CNIB issued, likely on 31 October 1980, was an edited version of a text that I brainstormed onto paper:

"The exclusion of handicapped people from the right to equality under the proposed Constitutional *Charter of Rights* has made the *Charter* meaningless to hundreds of thousands of handicapped Canadians," states David Lepofsky, Chairman of the Ontario Public Education and Advocacy Committee of The Canadian National Institute for the Blind. The proposed Bill establishes the right to equality before the law and to equal protection of the law without discrimination because of race, national or ethnic origin, color, religion, age or sex. However, its wording excludes equal protection to handicapped people.

"The repudiation of handicapped persons' human rights is made all the more shocking because the *Charter* is proposed to be enacted in 1981, during the International Year of Disabled Persons," says Mr. Lepofsky. "Indeed, Canada seconded the motion in the United Nations to declare 1981 the International Year of Disabled Persons."

---

5 CNIB, *supra* note 2 at 1.

> Mr. Lepofsky adds that if the government intends to entrench the civil liberties of all Canadians in the Constitution, then it is essential that handicapped Canadians be guaranteed their civil liberties as well. He pointed out that the Committee is also concerned with the use of the term "equality before the law" in the *Charter*. Canadian courts have interpreted these words as not protecting citizens from obvious discriminatory legislation.
>
> While the CNIB Committee on Public Education and Advocacy is most directly involved with the legal rights of visually impaired Canadians, it is concerned for all handicapped persons whose rights will be excluded in the proposed *Charter*.[6]

My efforts to get media attention starting the day after that emergency PEA Committee meeting and over the following 2 months were abysmally unsuccessful, with just a few critically important exceptions that I discuss later. This was my first of many instances over the ensuing four decades where I learned through bitter experience how difficult it is to get media to cover our issues, especially when reporters and editors think our issues are marginal and do not understand them. I had not yet learned a lesson I was to come to understand years later — namely, that the news media does not cover issues; it covers events. To get media attention on the need for the disability amendment, it was not good enough for our news release to argue the issue. We needed to choreograph some event tied to that issue.

I had no training in how to compose a news release nor any list of media contacts. Working from the CNIB's Toronto offices, I vividly recall phoning around to media outlets to announce our news story to any assignment editors I could reach: "CNIB's Ontario board of directors Public Education and Advocacy Committee demands that the proposed Charter of Rights be amended so that people with disabilities are not left out." I recall yawns at the other end of the phone.

In one of these calls, I put on my most official-sounding voice and told a reporter that I was calling from the CNIB and that we demanded an amendment to the *Charter* to protect people with disabilities. The CTV reporter immediately asked me what there is in the story that is "visual?" Stunned, I stared at the phone. I tried to calmly explain with a bit of exasperation in my voice that I was calling from the Canadian National Institute for the Blind!!! (emphasis on the word "blind") Needless to say,

---

6 CNIB, Ontario Public Relations Department, Press Release (on or about 31 October 1980) at 30.

CTV did not get it or cover the story. It would be years before I learned how to dash off a punchy news release to make it attractive to reporters. Television stations need concrete examples and attention-grabbing images. If there is nothing visual in the story, then it is not news, so they think. Since then, I have learned how to create a story with a visual background, to make it appeal to television reporters. Blind or not, I have got to think visually or "sighty," as I sometimes call it!

We got no media coverage from that initial blitz. Later that fall, I made very limited efforts to get some other disability organizations to support the CNIB's blitz to win the disability amendment. The only positive response I got was a letter from a federation of groups of people with different physical disabilities under the rubric of the Ontario March of Dimes. I tabled that letter with the Joint Committee, but more about that later. One-and-a-half decades later, I learned about the importance of going through the time-consuming effort of building a coalition one member at a time, often through an exhausting process of individually meeting senior managers of major disability organizations to patiently explain the issue on which we were campaigning.

Unknown to me at the time, efforts were underway elsewhere within the disability community to press for the disability amendment. Two major national disability organizations were hard at work, the CAMR (since renamed the Canadian Association for Community Living and, more recently, renamed again as Inclusion Canada) and the COPOH (since renamed the Council of Canadians with Disabilities). Our goals and messages were the same. Our efforts were isolated from each other rather than being coordinated. Scrambling to get the CNIB's blitz underway, I did not know about the efforts of those organizations and had no practical way to find out about them. Chapter X describes some of their key contributions to the disability amendment cause.

## D. What a Difference Four Decades and Rapidly Evolving Technology Makes! How I Would Get Started Today

Things would have been incredibly different had I been embarking on the blitz for the disability amendment four decades later. First, I have the good fortune that I am now Chair of the Accessibility for Ontarians with Disabilities Act Alliance [AODA Alliance]. I already have a well-established platform to advocate on a wide spectrum of issues concerning accessibility and inclusion. I would not have to write some three-tiered motion to take up the CNIB'S corporate ranks. We have a robust email list of people who get our email updates. Our tweets on Twitter reach over 12,000 people. We reach thousands more with updates on Facebook and LinkedIn. Our YouTube videos have together gotten over 100,000 views. We have a track record and helpful media contacts who regularly reach out to us for comment on disability issues.

Operating from our AODA Alliance platform, or even if acting as an individual, it would be considerably easier for me to reach out to like-minded people and community organizations to rapidly assemble an ad hoc coalition. A broadcast email and solicitations over social media could invite interested folks to come together on a Zoom meeting to be scheduled within a couple of days if the issue was very time sensitive. We could ask one of our partner organizations to fund needed disability accommodations, such as real time captioning and sign language interpretation. These can be delivered over the Zoom platform from anywhere in the world. At an inaugural Zoom meeting, a new coalition can be founded and an ad hoc leadership team can be identified. An email list can quickly be launched so that all can keep up with our efforts. A new website and Facebook page are easy to set up. Other than the captioning and sign language interpreters, none of these steps costs any money. They can bring people together from across the country, if necessary.

Drawing on years of experience, we could quickly slap together a news release and basic statement of principles and share them around the leadership team to make sure people are happy with them before firing them off to the media and to members of parliament via email and social media. Once again, the cost is zero, apart from the volunteer hours of doing the writing and emailing/tweeting. Yet another time-tested strategy is the wonderfully helpful "open letter" to Parliament, even if we do not have time to construct a formal coalition to wage a campaign on an issue. It is much easier and quicker to pull together like-minded allies and work together informally without any of the burdens of a formal organizational structure. A core of us can craft an open letter to Parliament, which explains the issue and outlines the action we seek. It should be detailed enough to explain the issue to someone who knows nothing about it. It should be short and clear enough to be quickly read and absorbed. To give it more oomph, it can and should include hyperlinks to supporting background information and corroborating documentation. In 1980, the word "hyperlink" did not yet exist!

Once the open letter is drafted, it can be shared among disability organizations and groups to amass an impressive list of organizational co-signatories. Once a few organizations have signed on, other organizations are more motivated to join in. All of this can be done within a week or two. It only requires a small core of dedicated volunteers or paid staff members of disability organizations. Once there is momentum, it can pick up speed amazingly quickly if the circumstances are right. That the disability community won the disability amendment to the *Charter* with none of those tools at our disposal is, to me, rather mind-boggling!

## E. Submitting a Brief to Parliament on the Need for the Disability Amendment

The next urgent task I faced in the fall of 1980 was drafting a CNIB brief to Parliament, arguing why we needed the disability amendment. Along with that brief, we needed to request a chance to present at the Joint Committee's public hearings, mindful of the fact that we had virtually no chance of getting a time slot to present there. I had never drafted a brief for legislative hearings. I had never even read such a brief. I did not really know what a brief was, who would read it, or what it was supposed to include. It turns out that a brief is just a written document that says what we want and why we want it. There is no magic to how it is written or formatted, though I did not know that in 1980.

As discussed earlier, I knew absolutely nothing back then about the procedure that a bill goes through in Parliament in order to become a law. I now know that, ordinarily, when a bill goes through Parliament, it first proceeds through the House of Commons. The House of Commons must vote to pass it three times. These three successive debates and votes are called first, second, and third "readings." Once a bill is passed at second reading, it is often sent to a Standing Committee of the House of Commons to study the bill in detail before it goes back to the House for third reading and debate. As part of its study of the bill, the Standing Committee may hold public hearings. Members of the public can request a chance to speak to the committee at public hearings and tell them what they think of the bill. The Standing Committee decides which organizations or individuals get to speak at the hearings. There is no guarantee that a Standing Committee will agree to let our organization or individual make a presentation. It can take a lobbying blitz to agree to let us present, which I sadly did not know in 1980.

After the House of Commons Standing Committee's public hearings are finished, the Standing Committee reviews and votes on the bill one section at a time. This is called "clause-by-clause" review. During this part of its work, members of the Standing Committee can propose amendments. The committee votes on the proposed amendments one at a time. If a majority of the members of the Standing Committee vote in favour of an amendment, that amendment becomes part of the bill. The bill goes back to the House of Commons, including any amendments that the Standing Committee made, for a final vote at third reading. Once the House of Commons passes a bill, it is sent to the Senate. The Senate goes through the same steps as had the House of Commons. This can include a second set of public hearings before a Senate Standing Committee. If the Senate passes the law "as is," in the same terms as the House of Commons, it is considered to have been passed by Parliament. If the Senate makes any changes to it, it must go back to the House of Commons for a vote on the Senate's changes. It becomes a law only when both the House of Commons and the Senate pass the bill in identical terms. Finally, the bill then goes to the governor general for the automatic formality of royal assent, at which point it is signed into law.

This all can take a long time. The Trudeau government was in a hurry. To speed things up, Parliament created a Special Joint Committee of the Senate and the House of Commons on the Constitution of Canada (Joint Committee). It included members of parliament and senators. It had two co-chairs, one member of parliament, and one senator. It was assigned responsibility to deal with the constitutional reform package. To avoid a duplication of separate hearings in the House of Commons and later in the Senate, the Joint Committee held one set of public hearings. I had no one to turn to at the CNIB for advice on how to navigate this process or write a brief. Over the years since then, I have written dozens and dozens of briefs to legislatures and other public bodies. I have given talks to students and community groups on how to write a brief and how to make a presentation to a parliamentary committee. Yet I wrote the first and most important brief I have ever written with no knowledge, no experience, no guidance, and no clue.

Floundering, I called the House of Commons for help. Someone in the office of the Joint Committee's clerk told me that he had a huge pile of briefs in front of him. Some of them were very long. He told me that if I want the politicians to read the brief, keep it short! I faithfully followed that advice when writing the CNIB's 1980 brief on the disability amendment. I have wantonly violated that advice far too many times when writing briefs since then. I have been teased over and over by fellow disability rights advocates that only I could write a document that is over 100 pages long and still call it a "brief." My three-page brief was so short that I include it here. I lost my own copy of it many years ago. In preparation for this retrospective, I managed to get a copy from the Archives of the Library of Canada. The brief, I am proud to say, has all the key ingredients. I cringe while rereading it because it uses the out-of-date term "handicap" that was in vogue back then. The entire 600-word brief, dated 1 December 1980 is as follows:

INTRODUCTION

The CNIB, Canada's largest organization providing rehabilitation services to visually handicapped persons in Canada, has, as a goal, the legal, social and economic equality and equality of opportunity for visually handicapped persons. Its concerns, as set forth below, are applicable not only to the interests of blind and partially sighted Canadians, but to all mentally and physically handicapped Canadians, who number in the millions. This brief addresses only those handicapped-related issues arising in the proposed *Charter of Rights*.

THE PROBLEM

One of the worst problems confronting handicapped persons is discrimination imposed by able-bodied Canadians. The attitudes of well-intentioned but misinformed persons are often the greatest barrier to the full integration of handicapped persons into Canadian life.

Patronizing and discriminatory attitudes towards the handicapped has resulted not only in employment and housing discrimination, but also in legislative discrimination against the disabled. Jury statutes deny blind persons the right to serve as jurors, whether or not their blindness would affect their ability to serve. Marriage laws preclude some mentally handicapped persons from the right to marry. Immigration laws provide harsher standards for handicapped immigrants than for able-bodied ones. Handicapped people are sometimes denied minimum wage protection.

Laws which discriminate against handicapped persons are likely attributable to anachronistic and inaccurate public attitudes towards the handicapped. Accordingly, there is a pressing need for handicapped persons to have their right to equal treatment by the law safeguarded in the Constitution, entitling them to the same rights to equality enjoyed by the non-handicapped.

PROBLEMS WITH THE PROPOSED *CHARTER OF RIGHTS*

1. The Equality Clause

Section 15 of the proposed Non-Discrimination Clause provides "everyone has the right to equality before the law and to the equal protection of the law without discrimination because of race, national or ethnic origin, colour, religion, age or sex."

Since 'mental or physical handicap' is not listed as a protected class, this proposal ensures the handicapped persons shall remain disentitled to equality before the law. Legislative discrimination against the disabled will continue unchecked.

Recommendations:

a) That "mental or physical handicap" be included in the non-discrimination section,

b) Alternatively, the list of protected classes in the Equality Clause should be non-exhaustive, so that handicap can be read into the clause by the courts.

Section 15 is too similar to Section 1(b) of the Statutory Canadian Bill of Rights, a provision the courts have repeatedly interpreted as failing to invalidate discriminatory legislation.

Recommendation:

c) In Section 15, the right to equality should be spelled out in strong language, unequivocally directing the courts that discriminatory legislation is to be rendered inoperative.

2. The Exemption Clause

Section 1 of the proposed *Charter of Rights* provides "The *Canadian Charter of Rights and Freedoms* guarantees the rights and freedoms set out in it, subject only to such reasonable limits as are generally accepted in a free and democratic society with the parliamentary system of Government."

An exemption clause should not apply to either the right to an interpreter, (Section 14) necessary for deaf and deaf-blind persons, or the right to protection from discrimination (Section 15), since these rights should be absolute.

Recommendations:

d) Certain rights enumerated in the *Charter*, including those in Sections 14 and 15, should not be restricted by an exemption clause such as Section 1,

e) Alternatively, the wording of the exemption clause should be made much more specific and narrow than is provided in Section 1. The present

> Section 1 would likely be interpreted by the courts as rendering constitutional virtually all legislation passed in Canada, whether it infringed the fundamental rights listed in the *Charter*.[7]

Today, I would write the brief myself, using a laptop computer. For at least 40 years, I have been able to write and edit myself, using a computer equipped with a screen-reading program. The computer reads back to me what I am typing. If I make a typographical error, I may well hear it as I am typing because the computer will mispronounce the word. The computer merely reads what it sees. I edit documents without needing assistance of a sighted person. A spell checker, grammar checker, and similar software help ensure that my documents are presentable. Even then, I still need a sighted person to look over documents that I now create using all of this fancy technology to make sure that they are formatted properly, look presentable, and are free of typing mistakes.

40 years ago, I had none of this futuristic *Star Trek* technology. Instead, I drafted the brief from scratch, using an electric typewriter. I could not proofread it at all. If I made a mistake while I was typing, and if I was aware of it, I could not correct it. When that happened, I would put an X in brackets, and then I would keep on typing. A sighted person would then go over what I had written and correct it, looking for errors and for my "X" code. I would then need a sighted person to retype the whole messy document. In 1980, I knew I needed editorial help. I had recently befriended a young journalist. I invited her out for dinner. I do not recall if she thought that this was a date. I explained why I wanted to get together when we got to the restaurant. On arriving, I sprung on her a volunteer work assignment. I said I needed help editing a brief on why we needed a change to Canada's proposed new Constitution. She looked at me like I had just landed from another planet. Yes, even I could tell! Thankfully, she agreed to help. A couple of hours later, after dinner and some editing at a restaurant table, our brief was finished and ready to be retyped and submitted to Parliament. For me, it did not feel weird to spend a dinner date editing a brief to Parliament on Canada's Constitution. Subsequently, I have foraged time and again for volunteer help on our causes from wherever I can find it.

---

7 CNIB, *Brief Submitted by the Canadian National Institute for the Blind to the Special Joint Committee of the Senate and of the House of Commons on the Constitution of Canada* (1 December 1980).

If I were writing this brief today, I would draw on years of experience and a healthy accumulated bank of knowledge about equality rights, constitutional adjudication, and disability barriers. I could get editing and proofreading help if I wanted it via email in no time. I have so many wonderful allies in the disability rights movement who selflessly volunteer their time at all hours of the day or night when they can (and despite pleading with me that they are overloaded and have no time) to review a draft brief. They offer great ideas and constructive criticisms. This includes legal professionals as well as many non-lawyers who have acquired an amazing reservoir of knowledge in this area. We have all been learning together on the fly.

Today, a brief such as this, once finalized, would be posted on the Internet within minutes of finishing touches being applied. Tweets and Facebook posts would publicize the brief to the world. A news release would instantly put this brief into the hands of hundreds of reporters. Not a single piece of paper would be consumed. In the case of the brief that I wrote for the CNIB on the disability amendment, I doubt that anyone read it or even saw it, other than some of those politicians on the Joint Committee and their staff.

# VII. GROUNDWORK I SHOULD HAVE DONE AT THE START

## A. Discovering Who Calls the Shots

Over the years, I have given tons of talks on the art of community organizing and advocacy. There are key principles I always share. In 1980, I knew none of them. I am astonished at how far we managed to get in 1980 despite this. If only we had learned some of this in law school and had the Internet to search for strategies or YouTube to watch TED Talks on community organizing action tips. No CNIB staff knew how to do any of this, as far as I could tell. One of the first steps I impress on audiences is to figure out who the real decision-maker is. Who really calls the shots? Who can make the decision you are trying to influence? I am not talking about finding out who is the person or body with legal authority to do what you want. That person or body is quite often not the real decision-maker.

Do you want to approach any government organization to press for some sort of social reform? If they identify you as someone to talk to at all, which is often not the case, they almost invariably direct you to someone who has absolutely no authority to make the change you want. The real decision-maker does not want to get anywhere near you. Instead, you get the pleasure of talking to a "spear-catcher," someone who is the public face but nothing more. The real decision-maker happily hides behind that shield. You get to converse with a warm, smiling, and welcoming person who thanks you so very much for your thoughtful input and wise feedback and who solemnly pledges to ensure that it gets right to the people who have the authority to decide the issue.

I implore disability advocates to penetrate further into the bureaucracy. Find out where the real power lies. That includes unearthing the formal decision-making hierarchy and then discovering whether it is someone on that hierarchy or someone else who holds the true reins of power in question. To the uninformed public, of which I was a card-carrying member in the fall of 1980, it looked and smelled like the decision-making authority over the disability amendment was the Special Joint Committee of the Senate and the House of Commons on the Constitution of Canada (Joint Committee). That was the body that held the public hearings. That was the body that would then undertake a clause-by-clause review of the *Charter* and that would debate and vote on amendments. Not so fast, Lepofsky, I would love to have whispered into my 23-year-old ear. Just because the Joint Committee was holding public hearings and casting votes over the wording of the *Charter*, it is wrong to think that that was where the ultimate decisions were to take place over the disability amendment.

I have since learned that a committee of the legislature or Parliament that undertakes public hearings and clause-by-clause debates over a bill rarely makes the actual decisions over what amendments to adopt. Especially in the case of a majority government, such as Pierre Trudeau then led, others in the government make these decisions in the backrooms, thoroughly insulated from public scrutiny and accountability. They then quietly issue instructions to the members of a legislative committee. Years later, I was again involved in advocacy on a bill before the Ontario legislature that had made its way to a standing committee for clause-by-clause debate. In the standing committee's meeting room at the Ontario legislature, while the formal proceedings were going on, I wandered over to the political staffer who was passing the written instructions to their governing party's members of the legislature, directing how they were to vote on some amendment. I quipped that I would be happy to write their notes for them if they would leave it to me to tell them how to vote on the upcoming amendments. This may have earned a brief chuckle. Maybe not.

Years later, when I appeared before the House of Commons Standing Committee on Human Resources, Skills and Social Development and the Status of Persons with Disabilities on 14 November 2022 to blast the problems with Bill C-22, the proposed new *Canada Disability Benefit Act*, paper notes were no longer passed to members of parliament. Instead, the party brass who were calling the shots evidently texted messages to the members of parliament on the standing committee as the hearings proceeded, while sitting mere metres away in the seats allocated to public observers. During our 1980 campaign for the disability amendment, there were senior officials in the Prime Minister's Office and/or the Justice Department who were calling the shots. Now, the shots would all be called by political staffers in the office of the justice minister or the prime minister. Yet, back then, it is possible that career public servants had more of a say. I never investigated this, then or later.

In 1980, I should have worked the phones to try to discover who was actually in charge of making decisions over the contents of the *Charter*.

I could have started with my own Liberal member of parliament as a possible source of intelligence. Calls to the Justice Department could have led me to the Crown lawyers working on this issue. You never know which of these inquiries will hit the motherlode. I did none of this. In government, there is an important division between the professional public service, on the one hand, and political staff who work in the office of a cabinet minister or of the prime minister, on the other. I did not fully understand this until a few years later. A ministry's public servants from the deputy minister on down the ranks are full-time permanent employees of the public service. They are non-partisan and politically neutral. They are not officially identified with, or loyal to, any political party. They do not lose their jobs when a new government is elected. The neutral public service serves each government that successively takes power.

In contrast, above the office of a deputy minister in a ministry or department is the very political and partisan office of the cabinet minister. The cabinet minister is, of course, a politician, usually a member of the legislature or of Parliament. They are most assuredly not politically neutral. The staff in their office are called "political staff." They are loyal to the party in power. They are not permanent employees. When the government changes, after an election or if the minister is shuffled out of that portfolio, political staffers lose their jobs unless the successor minister decides to keep them on or another minister's office hires them. Those who work in the Prime Minister's Office, like those who work in a minister's office, are also political staff, not permanent public servants.

I explain in Chapter XIII that, on the fateful day when I appeared before the Joint Committee to advocate for the disability amendment, one of Justice Minister Jean Chrétien's political staff, Eddie Goldenberg, came over to say hello to me in the meeting room as I was walking out. I had met him the year before when I worked as an articling law student at the Lang Michener law firm. He and I had done a small amount of work together on one case. I now see it as an invaluable goldmine to have had a connection with a senior staffer in the justice minister's office. I should have leapt at the chance to convince him of the merits of the disability amendment. "Hey Eddie, how about going out for a coffee?" I should have said then and there. However, I was oblivious to this at the time. I did not reach out to him for over a month. We will reach that later in this story.

Public servants and political staff who are ready to whisper in your ear can help provide desperately needed insider information on who is making the ultimate decisions, on what is being discussed, and on what we need to do to advance our cause. If you dig hard enough, you can connect with public servants and political staff who are very supportive of your concerns and who welcome an opportunity to quietly share helpful information. Some feel an important duty to the public to elucidate how mysterious government procedures work inside the impenetrable labyrinth of government. Some just happen to have a spouse, sibling, child, parent, or dear friend with a disability, making them eager to help our cause. Of course, I must take their tips with a grain of salt. Some try to work me, just as I am trying to work them. Ah, the joys of an elegant, graceful waltz.

## B. Get Opposition Parties on Side

It is extremely important to reach out to opposition parties as soon as possible in the legislative process. Who is the opposition critic with lead responsibility on our issue? Do they know and care about our issue? Are there any other members in the opposition caucus who might be sympathetic to our goals? Who has this file within the staff of the office of the opposition leader? Each opposition party usually has a research office, which may be separate from the leader's office. Who if anyone, within that team, has our file? Have they even heard of our issue? This requires me to unearth information on the hierarchical structure within the party's establishment.

An opposition party's leader has their own office and staff. Sometimes there may be no one in the leader's office or the research office who has been assigned our issue. That can happen if the issue has not gotten any public attention. Because the *Charter* was all over the media, I am virtually certain that there were officials in each opposition party leader's offices and research offices who were all over the constitutional reform file. Each political party is its own little universe. Overlaying any formal structure is the party's informal hierarchy. You could be told that a specific member of parliament is the opposition party's critic on an issue. Yet some other caucus member could for practical matters be the party's centre of gravity on that issue. The sands of power within a party can quietly shift from week to week. From the outside, this can all be impenetrable.

How do you piece together information on this organizational maze? I have found that there are always friendly folks if you look hard enough. Some are friendly because disability has touched their lives or the life of a loved one. Others are naturally attracted to the inherent justice of our cause. Still others feel bad that we keep getting the runaround. There are other people to approach to explore the power landscape, and this includes community advocates who have been trying to penetrate this fog. Experienced journalists can have keen insights to informally offer, if asked. How I wish I had known some of this back in 1980! As I think back on my advocacy efforts in 1980, I feel like a lawyer who has argued zillions of cases cringes as they reread the transcript of their very first trial.

In 1980, both the Conservatives and the New Democratic Party [NDP] were in the opposition in Parliament. I should have tried early on to get both of these parties to go on the record as officially supporting our call for the disability amendment. Had they publicly done so early in the fall of 1980, this would have ramped up pressure on the Trudeau government. If the government had known early on that the opposition would unite to bring a motion in the Joint Committee to adopt the disability amendment, this would have put the heat on the government to decide how they were going to vote on that motion. Would they want to be on the record voting against equality for people with disabilities during the International Year of Disabled Persons? This would have been a great opportunity to use the strategy I have used many times since then, orchestrating a motion that a government may not want to vote for but which it could not be seen as voting against.

Winning early opposition support for the disability amendment would have made it easier to get the media to pay attention to our issue. The media love to cover political disagreements and conflicts. Had we gotten an opposition party to issue an early news release that they supported a disability amendment, we could have encouraged reporters to press the government on how they planned to vote on the disability amendment. If one opposition party said they would support the disability amendment, we could also use this to pressure the other opposition party to do the same. A great way that opposition parties can help is by confronting the government on our issue during Question Period in Parliament. It would have been amazing had we approached an opposition party to ask the justice minister something like this: "The government claims that the *Charter* is to be enacted to guarantee equality for everyone. Yet the government has left out people with disabilities. Will the government amend the *Charter* so that people with disabilities, like all other Canadians, will enjoy the constitutional right to equality?"

Chapter XV recounts the one instance I could find where a question was asked of the Trudeau government about the disability amendment during the patriation debate. I had nothing to do with that and only learned about it while preparing this retrospective. Ironically, that question came from a Liberal member of parliament rather than from either of the opposition parties. It is never easy to get an opposition party to ask a question on our issues in Question Period. It typically takes a protracted and concerted advocacy effort. Each party gets to pose only a few questions during Question Period. Those parties have many priorities and issues vying for attention during Question Period. Opposition parties scour the newspapers each day to decide what juicy, sizzling issues they should raise the next day during Question Period. An opposition caucus's members compete for airtime during Question Period to shine public attention on their pet issues.

I now have years of experience lobbying opposition parties to get them to ask a question in Question Period. It makes their job easier for me to draft the question for them. It also makes it more likely that they will ask the specific question that you want asked. It is frustrating to win a party's agreement to pose a question to the government on your issue during Question Period, only to have the opposition politician flub the question. I have seen that happen. Once an opposition party raises a question in Question Period, it can generate media coverage. Reporters watch Question Period to track which issues are getting top billing that day. As one example, I managed to get an opposition question unleashed in the Ontario legislature in 2013 on an accessibility issue in which I was deeply involved.[1] It triggered great media coverage and, even better, a supportive editorial in the *Toronto Star* on 31 October 2013.

In the fall of 2013, the Accessibility for Ontarians with Disabilities Act Alliance [AODA Alliance], which I chaired, was trying to get the Ontario government to make public information on what little, if anything, it was doing to enforce the *Accessibility for Ontarians with Disabilities Act* [*AODA*].[2] For months, we got no answers from the Ontario government. Frustrated, I filed a freedom of information request. The government responded by saying that I would have to pay over $2000 to get an answer. I asked the government to waive this fee because the AODA Alliance is a

1 Legislative Assembly of Ontario, *Hansard Transcripts*, 40th Parl, 2nd Sess (29 October 2013) at 3996–3997.

2 *Accessibility for Ontarians with Disabilities Act*, SO 2005, c 11.

non-profit unfunded organization with no money. The government would not budge.

Opposition NDP member of the provincial parliament Cheri Di Novo confronted the government about this in Question Period on 30 October 2013.[3] Her question triggered a *Toronto Star* editorial the next day that slammed the government about this fee. In face of this blistering bad press, the Ontario government backed down and waived the fee. It disclosed to us a pile of damning documents that we had requested. These documents showed that the government was doing nothing to enforce the *AODA*, especially *vis-à-vis* private sector organizations that the government knew to be in violation of that law. We forked those documents over to the *Toronto Star*. That generated more *Toronto Star* editorial support for us.[4] All of this was spawned by one question in Question Period.

In 1980, I missed out on all these potential avenues for political persuasion by not approaching the opposition parties to get their support. Time and again, I have observed an invisible tacit dance between the media and the political parties. The media scrutinizes the political parties to see what issues the politicians are emphasizing. This influences the media's choice over which stories to cover, which to ignore, and which to bury on a newspaper's back pages. As part of this dance, political parties sniff out the media to see what issues they are profiling and prioritizing. If an issue is on the front pages, opposition parties are more likely to ask about it in Question Period. The government of the day will be more likely to want to have a good marketable position to respond to issues that the media puts on the front page.

The challenge of a community organizer and advocate is to try to cut in on this dance, to propel our issue higher up on the hit parade of both the media and the parties. It is not easy to do. If you are oblivious about it, as I was in 1980, you do not even try.

---

3 Legislative Assembly of Ontario, *Hansard Transcripts*, 40th Parl, 2nd Sess (29 October 2013) at 3996–3997.

4 "Ontario Must Enforce Equality Rules for Disabled: Editorial," *Toronto Star* (18 November 2013), online: <www.thestar.com/opinion/editorials/2013/11/18/ontario_must_enforce_equality_rules_for_disabled_editorial.html>.

## C. Find Other Natural Allies

In 1980, it would have been wise for me to try to find other potentially influential organizations in society that could have supported our cause. As I discuss in Chapter IX, it was fortunate that I turned out to have a connection with the Canadian Jewish Congress, which helped our efforts. I should have reached out to other influential opinion-making organizations for support. The very process of doing so would have let me test out and sharpen the arguments to be made in support of the disability amendment. It could have helped us discover if anyone was opposed to us and, if so, why.

# VIII. TRYING TO FIGURE OUT WHY THE FEDERAL GOVERNMENT LEFT DISABILITY OUT OF THE *CHARTER*'S EQUALITY RIGHTS PROVISION

## A. How Little I Knew Back Then

When campaigning for the disability amendment, an obvious first question jumps out: why on earth had the federal government left disability out of section 15 of the *Canadian Charter of Rights and Freedoms*' equality rights provision?[1] It was on my mind, and no doubt on the minds of others advocating for the disability amendment. As far as I knew, the federal government gave no explanation of this glaring omission when it first introduced the constitutional patriation package into Parliament in October 1980. Sadly, in the fall of 1980, I did not even take the obvious step, then technologically possible, to excavate the federal government's reasoning — namely, writing the prime minister. I nevertheless got a glimmer of at least some of the government's reasons from bits of information that reached us indirectly. This was enhanced by our own guestimates.

Some time that fall, I finagled my only opportunity to publicly speak face to face with a federal cabinet minister. Cabinet ministers were trying to sell the Trudeau initiative around the country. The synagogue where I belonged, Toronto's Holy Blossom Temple, hosted a Sunday morning breakfast event where federal External Affairs Minister Mark MacGuigan was to make the Trudeau government's pitch. I leapt at the chance to attend this event and to ask a question during the question-and-answer period. As the past president of Holy Blossom Temple's junior youth group from 1971 to 1972 and of its senior youth group from 1973 to 1974, I was a familiar face there. This event was held one floor below the sanctuary where, a decade earlier, I had publicly recited in Hebrew those life-defining words from the Torah during my bar mitzvah: "Do not curse a deaf person or put a barrier in front of a blind person." I did not then draw the connection in my own mind with my bar mitzvah portion as I asked the minister why the

---

1 *Canadian Charter of Rights and Freedoms*, Part 1 of the *Constitution Act, 1982*, being Schedule B to the *Canada Act 1982* (UK), 1982, c 11.

government left disability out of the *Charter*'s equality guarantee and pressed him to support the disability amendment.

A former law dean, the minister no doubt quickly grasped our argument's compelling force. I heard in his voice a certain lack of enthusiasm as he struggled to defend the failure to include disability in section 15 of the *Charter*. He said that what people with disabilities needed was to be protected by human rights/anti-discrimination statutes, not by the *Charter*. That Sunday morning, I did not then realize that this exchange laid a helpful foundation for the argument I would make before the Special Joint Committee of the Senate and the House of Commons on the Constitution of Canada (Joint Committee), just a few short weeks later. Like an effective cross-examination of a key witness during a trial, grilling a cabinet minister can provide an opportunity to build an informal record to buttress the case to be made to politicians, journalists, and the public.

## B. If Only I Had Known What Justice Minister Jean Chrétien Told the Joint Committee

How I wish I had known that fall that, on 12 November 1980, Justice Minister Jean Chrétien would publicly spell out his government's reasons for leaving disability equality out of the *Charter*. When I appeared before the Joint Committee in December, I had pieced together or surmised only some bits and pieces of this rational. Alas, there was no online Hansard (official transcripts of Parliamentary proceedings) for me to instantly search from the convenience of a home computer, as I now do. During a public meeting of the Joint Committee on 12 November 1980, Justice Minister Chrétien was pointedly asked about the omission of people with disabilities from section 15 of the *Charter*.[2] His answer was a rare revelation that would have helped me formulate strategy in response. His rambling answer sounds to me like he was working from an answer that his officials had prepared. Public servants routinely equip a minister with a fulsome briefing note with carefully scripted answers that they might read or paraphrase in response to anticipated questions. Answering a Liberal member of parliament's question on another topic, Chrétien had this exchange:

---

2 Canada, Parliament, *Minutes of Proceedings and Evidence of the Special Joint Committee of the Senate and of the House of Commons on the Constitution of Canada*, 32nd Parl, 1st Sess, No 3 (12 November 1980) at 85.

**Chrétien:** Thank you, Mr. Mackasey. Of course, I said I do not want to turn back the clock, as you described. The rights should be there and we hope that the same rights will eventually be extended to all Canadians.

To go back to the first point you made, of course this amending formula will be used. Mr. Robinson put it in a negative way, the possibility of some rights being taken away from the *Charter*. I explained to him how complex the mechanism is, and it will not be easy. Now, with the Provincial *Charter of Rights*, it can be done like that.

Now, in the future there will be consultation between the provinces and the national government. There will be the whole process, there will be a year delay after the deadlock and the referendum, but eventually amendments to the Bill of Rights can be made.

Another thing, too, is that it might be with the evolution of rights, some rights eventually can be entrenched in the Constitution that are not now there, and that could be objected to by some provinces, but by that time we could let the people of Canada decide. This *Charter of Rights* is not perfect, it is a minimum. There are a lot of rights that will evolve in the society, will mature in the society and will be capable of precise definition so as to be in a Charter of Rights, but in the meantime, the evolution of these rights will be measured and bring about into Parliament through the *Bill of Rights*, through the Human Rights Bill that will come outside of the *Bill of Rights*, because the Human Rights Commission will still be there, will analyze the problems, the evolution of society, the mechanism to protect the rights of some minorities today, that their rights are not quite defined, such as the physically handicapped, and so on. So these things have to mature, to find their place in a Charter of Rights, but in the meantime, the Human Rights Commission will be called upon to follow up the evolution and the drafting and the regulations and so on, that it will be easier in the future. However, you are right, I do not want to turn back the clock, and I said in my own personal view that, the more provinces will accept it, the better…[3]

Later the disability amendment topic came up again, raised by another member of the Joint Committee:

**Robert Bockstael:** Mr. Chairman, I have one very short last question dealing with non-discrimination. As it is stated that "everyone has the right to equality before the law and to the equal protection of the law without discrimination because of race, national or ethnic origin, colour, religion, age, or sex," does the minister see any difficulty in adding the handicapped, either physical or mental, to that list?

---

3 *Ibid* at 60.

> **Chrétien:** There are, of course, some drafting problems which would arise. That is why I stated earlier that the Human Rights Commission will continue to exist as well as the Human Rights Act. Very often, rights which are being asserted at this time are very difficult to define in legal terms. There are many degrees of disability involved; some are physically handicapped, others are mentally handicapped. Fortunately, society is becoming increasingly more aware of the protection of those rights. However, it is very difficult to draft a precise legal wording which could be easily incorporated into the constitution and into the human rights charter.
>
> We are examining that problem at the moment. It is not for want of sympathy or personal desire that I say that I do not know whether it is possible today. If it is not, the amending formula will allow us, in future, to add to it rights which are not clearly defineable today.[4]

Had I known of that statement, I would have made refuting it the centrepiece of my efforts. Alas, I was to piece together only bits of its contents before I would get my brief shining moment to make our case at Parliament.

## C. A Unique Insight I Got 1 Year Later

In the fall of 1981, a year after these events and months after the Joint Committee eventually passed the disability amendment, I got an incredible, if not unique, insight into the real reasons that had driven the federal government to resist the idea of including equality for people with disabilities in the *Charter*. That fall, I had the life-changing opportunity to study for a master of law at the Harvard Law School in Cambridge, Massachusetts. While there, I met a thoughtful, intelligent, and insightful man who was enjoying a year as a scholar in residence at the Harvard Law School, Barry Strayer. He had certainly earned that opportunity, having just served as one of the top lawyers at the federal Justice Department, working on the *Charter* project. He would later go on to an admirable career as a judge in Canada.

He took me to lunch one day at Harvard in the fall of 1981. I could not resist the chance to ask the question! Why did we face such opposition to the disability amendment? As he spoke, I was all ears. I had then and have now no reason to doubt his answer's sincerity or accuracy. He was a principled, accomplished, highly competent public official and a former law professor. He certainly did not come across to me as a posturing political partisan for the Trudeau Liberals. He told me that, shortly before

4 *Ibid* at 85.

the introduction of the constitutional patriation package, there had been quite a struggle within the government just to get some limited disability protection included in the Canadian *Human Rights Act*.[5] As such, he explained that it seemed that getting disability into the *Charter* could not get much traction within the government or at least within the public service.

It took me many years to fully appreciate the enormity of what he told me over four decades ago and to integrate it into my strategic advocacy thinking. I have spent years since then waging various disability campaigns, without being fully aware of how much invisible, strong opposition we face from within a public service. Sometimes elected politicians are more willing to agree with our requests, only to be substantially held back or even undermined by recalcitrant public servants. Four forces can converge to cause this. First, pejorative stereotypes among the public about disability can be as pervasive in the public service as they are elsewhere in society. Second, even though the public service is supposed to be politically neutral, when it comes to issues like equality for disability, the public service can collectively resist this, fearing it as a new burden on them. Over the years, I have heard people surmise that the business community is the major opponent to laws and policies that seek to ensure equality for people with disabilities. Contradicting that view, I have found over and over that the public service tends to be far more resistant and that the business community is far more accepting. Any number of business leaders have said to me: "Just tell us what we need to do, so we can do it!"

The third factor is a disturbing hive mind mentality that I have seen too often in the public service as well as in some other large organizations. I have met many, many public servants who, individually, are incredibly supportive of disability inclusion, equality, and accessibility. I would hazard a guess that a majority of them are supportive of our goals if a decision were up to them as individuals. Yet when they combine together within a public service organization, department, or ministry, a harmful groupthink takes over. They far too often act like the collective "hive mind" of that organization, department, or ministry, reflexively thinking that they must resist and oppose. They tend to subordinate their own judgment to that perceived hive mind, which leads the hive mind to become a dominant force that sets the collective direction. It is far too often a direction opposing our aims.

---

5 *Human Rights Act*, SC 1976–1977, c 33.

As one illustration of this, I led the AODA Alliance's campaign for over 7 years, starting in 2009, to get the Ontario government to agree to develop an Education Accessibility Standard under the *AODA*.[6] That regulation would be designed to tear down the many disability barriers that impede students with disabilities from fully participating in, and benefiting from, Ontario's education system. I eventually learned that the greatest opposition to this proposal — one I hoped would have been widely seen as beneficial for our education system — was Ontario's Ministry of Education. Most of the officials at that ministry with whom I spoke individually seemed supportive of our proposal. Yet, behind closed doors, the hive mind took over, which led the ministry to oppose our proposal. Under the *AODA*, the Ontario public service is the single largest obligated organization with the greatest number of duties. As such, it is in an enormous conflict of interest when it comes to law enforcement under that legislation. In effect, that legislation mandates that the Ontario Public Service enforce that law against itself. Unsurprisingly, it does a demonstrably poor and lax job of it.

Fourth, it is common for some, though certainly not all, policy advisors and legal advisors within government to serve as a negative drag on any number of new initiatives. They can make an industry out of conjuring up all the problems, real or imagined, that a new policy innovation may create. They can caution ministers to go slow, to be cautious, to not stick their necks out. It has no doubt led any number of politicians, on taking power, to become very frustrated, eager for public servants to stop telling them what they cannot do and wishing they would instead start figuring out what they can do!

## D. An Additional Perspective about Which I Learned Years After the Fact

During my research for this memoir four decades after these events, I read a fascinating account about the reasons that drove the federal government to leave disability equality out of the *Charter*. These were recorded in the published recollections about the fight for the disability amendment by veteran disability advocate and lawyer Yvonne Peters in a book chapter entitled, "From Charity to Equality: Canadians with Disabilities Take

---

6 *Accessibility for Ontarians with Disabilities Act*, SO 2005, c 11. These efforts are documented at <www.aodaalliance.org/education>.

Their Rightful Place in Canada's Constitution."[7] I have known Yvonne for decades and consider her a friend but did not know of her in 1980, nor did I know of her efforts to get the disability amendment passed in conjunction with the COPOH, which is now called the Council of Canadians with Disabilities. Our paths were destined to cross time and again during our careers. We are both lawyers, both blind, and both devoted to human rights, disability organizing, and advocacy.

Peters described COPOH's early efforts at pressing for the disability amendment and the answer they got from the government:

> In a telegram addressed to Jean Chrétien, Minister of Justice, dated September 18, 1980, COPOH denounced this restrictive wording. On October 20, 1980, Jacques A. Demers, Special Advisor, responded on behalf of Jean Chrétien, and explained that careful consideration had been given to the grounds that should be included in a non-discrimination clause. The letter states:
>
>> Since an entrenched Charter is by its very nature a generalized document which does not lend itself to detailed qualifications and limitations, it was ultimately decided to limit the grounds of nondiscrimination to those few which have long been recognized and which do not require substantial qualification. Unfortunately, such is not yet the case with respect to those who suffer physical handicaps and consequently provision has not been made in the *Charter* for this ground.[8]

Peters wrote this about Jim Derksen, a key player in COPOH's efforts to get the disability amendment passed: "During his stay in Ottawa, Jim Derksen attempted to unravel the misconceptions about disability that were being cited as barriers to amending the Charter. He contacted the federal Department of Justice and after several phone calls he was put in touch with a Justice lawyer who agreed to an evening meeting to discuss the government's position."[9] Out of that meeting, two main concerns emerged: fear of unmanageable costs and concern about how to define disability in the *Charter*. The government appeared to be worried that inclusion of disability in the *Charter* would somehow expose it to large lawsuits that would bankrupt the government coffers.

---

7 Yvonne Peters "From Charity to Equality: Canadians with Disabilities Take Their Rightful Place in Canada's Constitution" in Deborah Stienstra & Aileen Wight-Felske, with Colleen Watters, eds, *Making Equality: History of Advocacy and Persons with Disabilities in Canada* (Concord, ON: Captus Press 2003) 119.

8 *Ibid* at 124–125.

9 *Ibid* at 130.

## E. The Issue of LGBTQ2S+ Rights and the Disability Amendment

I had a well-founded worry while campaigning for the disability amendment that an unstated reason for the government's resistance to including disability in section 15 was a concern about the one other major equality-seeking group that also sought inclusion in that provision. That was the efforts on behalf of the LGBTQ2S+ community to get section 15 of the *Charter* amended to make it unconstitutional to discriminate based on sexual orientation. I can point to no speech or public statement by any federal public official or any of the few conversations I had then or later with any public officials that provides evidence of this concern. I have never asked them about this issue.

Why did I suspect this? Back then, it seemed unimaginable that the federal government would agree to amend the *Charter* during the patriation debate to ban discrimination because of sexual orientation, no matter how unjust that discrimination is. In 1980, the idea of legally protecting equality rights from discrimination based on sexual orientation was, regrettably, far from publicly accepted. At that time, only one province's anti-discrimination law banned discrimination based on sexual orientation in economic activity such as employment. Quebec had taken this step only in 1977.[10] Four decades later, Canada has commendably come a long way when it comes to extending legal protections against discrimination because of sexual orientation.

Events in 1980 at the provincial level in Ontario reinforced my suspicion. I explained earlier that in 1980 the Ontario legislature was considering a major overhaul of the Ontario *Human Rights Code*, including adding a ban on discrimination because of disability.[11] Four years earlier, in its landmark *Life Together* report,[12] the Ontario Human Rights Commission recommended adding physical disability as well as sexual orientation to the Ontario *Human Rights Code*'s ban on discrimination. Ontario's Progressive Conservative government under Premier Bill Davis was willing to add disability to the *Human Rights Code*. It was categorically unwilling to

---

10 See *Charter of Human Rights and Freedoms*, RSQ, c C-12, s 10. For the 1977 amendment of section 10 to include sexual orientation, see <www.legisquebec.gouv.qc.ca/en/version/cs/C-12?code=se:10&history=20170607>.

11 *Human Rights Code*, RSO 1990, c H-19.

12 Ontario Human Rights Commission, *Life Together* (July 1977).

add sexual orientation. In 1980, Ontario's Conservative government introduced a bill to comprehensively revamp the Ontario *Human Rights Code*. That bill included disability protection but did not include sexual orientation protection.[13]

Ontario's opposition NDP supported adding sexual orientation to the Ontario *Human Rights Code*. The opposition Ontario Liberal Party appeared to me to be conflicted on this issue. It had certainly not gone on the record as supporting a ban on discrimination based on sexual orientation, as far as I had seen. A delegation of the Ontario Coalition on Human Rights for the Handicapped got a rare meeting with the Ontario Liberal caucus. We were asked what our position was on the sexual orientation issue. It was my sense that they were sussing us out as part of their struggle to figure out where they stood. Our coalition expressed no position on that issue because our mandate was felt to be limited to the disability issues for which we were advocating. Nevertheless, I regret we did not collectively and publicly recognize the commonality between the need for disability protection and for LGBTQ2S+ protection.

Information was then circulating that there may have been some backroom discussions among the three Ontario political parties about the possibility of slipping the human rights reform bill through the legislature extremely quickly, without holding any public hearings. Ontario then had a minority government. This legislative manoeuvre might have been on the table as a way for the parties to duck public attention on the sexual orientation issue. I cannot document that suspicion or rumour nor the underlying reason for such a legislative move. We made it clear that our coalition opposed any such procedural shortcuts. We wanted to get the Ontario bill before a standing committee of the Ontario legislature in order to press for amendments to improve it. It is good we did that because over the next year we succeeded in getting amendments to strengthen it.

This all showed me that, in Ontario, there was all-party political support for a provincial law that would ban discrimination because of disability but political division and fear among some politicians about touching the sexual orientation issue. It was not rocket science for me to have pondered that the same politics would come into play as the Trudeau government grappled with the *Charter*. In Chapter XIV, I discuss in more detail how

13 Legislative Assembly of Ontario, *Hansard Transcripts*, 31st Parl, 4th Sess (25 November 1980) (first reading of Bill 209 began at 3:30 p.m.).

on 12 January 1981, Justice Minister Chrétien proposed revising section 15 to open up the list of grounds of discrimination that it would prohibit. Chrétien's proposal on that day would not add any new grounds of discrimination to section 15 by name. His revised wording would let courts add new grounds to section 15 by judicial interpretation.

At that time, I saw Chrétien as rather obviously ducking both the sexual orientation and disability issues. He was offering to give courts the power to add new grounds to section 15, without taking a position on which grounds the courts should add. Later that month, we eventually succeeded in getting disability explicitly added to the *Charter*. The LGBTQ2S+ community did not succeed in getting sexual orientation explicitly listed. It would take another 14 years for the Supreme Court of Canada to add sexual orientation to section 15 through judicial interpretation in 1995.[14] The effect of the Supreme Court of Canada's rulings in this area was to in effect insert "sexual orientation" to section 15, as if it were written into its list of prohibited grounds of discrimination.

What an irony it is that in 1980 and 1981, there was broader political support for including people with disabilities but not sexual orientation in section 15. It was frankly emblematic of how quickly things changed on the political front that, in 1986, the Ontario legislature revised the Ontario *Human Rights Code* to ban discrimination based on sexual orientation with little if any fanfare. That which had appeared politically impossible 6 years earlier became manifestly possible without even triggering major media and public attention. Sometime over four decades ago, I recall chatting on a bus with one of my Osgoode Hall Law School classmates who was advocating for legal protections against discrimination because of sexual orientation. We contrasted what he experienced in response to his advocacy efforts and what we were receiving as reactions to our disability efforts. Since then, I have had similar conversations with other LGBTQ2S+ advocates about the stunning irony that, in 1980, they could not get Parliament to add sexual orientation to the *Charter*. Yet, two decades later, the LGBTQ2S+ community won considerably more social change through the *Charter* than have people with disabilities. For example, same-sex marriage was

---

14 *Egan v Canada*, [1995] 2 SCR 513, [1995] SCJ No 43 (QL).

legalized.[15] Social benefits traditionally available to heterosexual couples were extended to same-sex couples.[16]

## F. The Federal Government's Reasons for Not Including Disability in the *Charter*'s Equality Section Were Transparently Bogus

In *The National Deal: The Fight for a Canadian Constitution*, journalist Robert Sheppard and Michael Valpy describe how, through the summer of 1980, the Trudeau government was hard at work, vigorously trying to negotiate an agreement with the provinces to patriate the Constitution, replete with a new charter of rights.[17] Most provinces were dead set against it. These journalists recounted how the federal government was at that point reluctant to be too aggressive on what to include in the *Charter* because of the provincial resistance to it. At the time, this looked like the usual tiresome bickering between two levels of government. Yet we members of the public were not just spectators. Our rights were on the negotiating block. The hold-out provincial premiers and governments were acting like any foot-dragging entity that simply does not want to be regulated or to change their practices.

Let's assume that the federal government was reluctant to go further than it did in section 15 of the *Charter* in the summer of 1980 during its negotiations with the premiers. By October 1980, those negotiations had failed. The federal government had decided to go it alone. It would have made abundant sense for the federal government to have then come up with a more robust section 15 to make it as appealing as possible to the public. Yet they did not do so. There was, in its initial wording of section 15, tabled in Parliament in October 1980, at the very least, a model of calculated governmental timidity. I now understand far more clearly than in 1980 that when a government gives bogus reasons for its position on an issue, it is typically because those are not the true reasons.

In this case, the federal government's stated reasons during the patriation debate for opposing the disability amendment were transparently meritless. First, disability cannot be defined. The government never worried about

---

15 *Ibid.*

16 *Modernization of Benefits and Obligations Act*, SC 2000, c 12.

17 Robert Sheppard & Michael Valpy, *The National Deal: The Fight for a Canadian Constitution* (Toronto: Fleet Books, 1982) 38–64, 65–77.

defining all the other vague terms of the *Charter* before proposing to entrench them in the Constitution. If you want to see vague constitutional terms, take a gander at "freedom of expression" (section 2(b)) or "the principles of fundamental justice" (section 7). How about taking "unreasonable search" (section 8) for a spin? Moreover, interpreting mushy constitutional and legislative language is exactly what courts do. Law books are jam-packed with cases illustrating this. Entire texts and law school courses are available on the topic of how to interpret legislation.

Second, people with disabilities do not need constitutional equality because their rights are otherwise sufficiently protected in the law. The litany of discriminatory laws and practices in Canada in 1980 prove this to be demonstrable nonsense. A good illustration of that is the fact that, at the same time as we were fighting for the disability amendment to the *Charter*, we were embroiled in a simultaneous multi-year fight to get the Ontario *Human Rights Code* amended to ban discrimination because of disability. Equality for people with disabilities had not yet matured sufficiently to be included in the Constitution? How on earth does a form of discrimination "mature" enough? Is the problem that, in 1980, we did not yet collectively feel guilty enough about it? The essence of the guarantee of equality in the Constitution is protecting those who have been constitutionally left out. Being left out is not something that matures.

Third, people with disabilities can fight later for equality through a constitutional amendment? Why burden people with disabilities, a highly vulnerable and disadvantaged population in Canada, with having to suffer their way through an uncertain, lengthy, and arduous amending formula that was not likely to ever produce any constitutional amendments because so much provincial support must be secured? No new constitutional right has been added to the *Charter* over the four decades since 1982 using that amending formula. I will eat my white cane if I am proven wrong and some new right is inserted into the *Charter* in my lifetime!

## G. What I Would Do If I Were Fighting This Campaign Today

If I were waging this campaign now, I would treat as a top priority unmasking why the federal government opposed the disability amendment. We had multiple ways to flush out answers. I did not do any of this back in 1980, even using the antique technology at hand. First, I would immediately write the prime minister and justice minister. I would pointedly ask why disability was left out. Our letter would explain why disability equality should be enshrined in the *Charter*. I would ask the government to agree to support the disability amendment or explain why not. I would copy this letter to the opposition leaders to pique their interest.

Having written so many letters of this kind over the years, I now understand that letters like this should simultaneously speak to several audiences, ones that come to the letter from very different perspectives. Of course, it should be written to speak to the prime minister or cabinet minister to whom it is addressed. However, they rarely read such letters, though, at times, they may. The letter should therefore aim to push the buttons to which so high placed a person might react. It should be written in a way that puts them on notice of our concerns. If we want to later go public to complain that we have not gotten an answer, this letter should make all the major points to support our position. That would make a failure to respond to us even harder to justify.

A second important audience includes senior government officials. It should arm them with the key information that you want them to have to potentially get the government to act on an issue. A third audience for this letter should be other members of parliament in the government caucus. I want to persuade them that the government as a whole should want to support us. Those members of parliament can press the government leadership on our behalf behind closed doors, even if they must vigorously defend the government in public. A fourth audience for this letter includes the opposition parties. They should get from the letter that we are raising a great issue worthy of opposition pressure. A fifth important audience for this letter is the media. It should explain the issue, our request, and the reasons supporting it in convincing terms for a busy reporter who knows nothing about the issue. It should lead the reporter wanting to cover this issue, who is feeling frustrated, and who is left wondering why we have not gotten an answer to our reasonable request that is so obviously backed by compelling reasons. The letter can include questions directed at the letter's named recipient, which can inspire a reporter to ask the same questions. The letter's final audience, surprising as this may sound, includes people with disabilities and disability organizations. It helps keep them up to date. It motivates them to want to support our efforts. For those who want to take action, it gives them words to use and arguments to make.

Were I doing this today, within moments, this letter would be posted on our website for all to see. I would tweet it all over the place to our thousands of Twitter followers. A link to this letter could also reach thousands very quickly by posting it on LinkedIn and Facebook. Second, I would try to entice the media to probe the government for answers. I have done this many times over the years since then on many different issues. Sometimes reporters can get answers from public officials, when all we have gotten from a government is icy cold radio silence. Reporters could confront the prime minister or minister of justice at news conferences, public events, or just in passing. They regularly send written inquiries to a prime minister's or minister's office when on the trail of a news story.

As I explained earlier, in 1980, the media was not the least bit schooled in disability rights issues. If we were covered at all, it was likely in soft feel-good inspiring stories, not in their hard-hitting political coverage. At a news conference back then, we could not expect that reporters would come up with this issue on their own if we did not spoon-feed it to them. For decades, as a core part of disability rights advocacy, we have had to educate reporters one at a time, convincing them to pop the question. In recent years, things have very gradually improved in that regard.

Third, I would seek out other creative ways to publicize the fact that we have asked the government for an answer but have gotten none. Social media is great for this. Earlier, I explained that sometimes the media picks up on stories from our social media blitzes, even though they did not give it a moment's thought when we first broke the story in a news release. I don't care one bit why they pick up our story as long as they do run with it. If we get no answer from the government, I would run a daily count on social media. Picture a daily tweet saying: "It's been 37 days since we wrote @PierreTrudeau asking why he left people with disabilities out of his great new *Charter of Rights*. Equality for some = equality for none! Millions of Canadians with disabilities deserve an answer! Pass the #DisabilityAmendment!" In this tweet, I would include a link to the web page where we posted our unanswered letter to the prime minister. To turn up the heat and try to squeeze out an answer, why not tweet this separately to each member of parliament?

# IX. AN IMPORTANT STOP ALONG THE WAY: THE HOUSE OF COMMONS SPECIAL PARLIAMENTARY COMMITTEE ON THE DISABLED AND HANDICAPPED

## A. What Was the Special Parliamentary Committee on the Disabled and Handicapped?

The first round in the battle for the disability amendment was a most important one. At the time, it appeared marginally relevant, if not useless. Looking back, it was anything but that. It provided a staging ground that brought disability organizations together with a common cause and, ultimately, a centre of gravity for politicians who became convinced that Canada's Constitution should include a constitutional right to equality for people with disabilities. For us, it was a huge stroke of luck that the United Nations [UN] had declared 1981 to be the International Year of Disabled Persons [IYDP]. Even better, IYDP's theme was declared to be all about equality and full participation for persons with disabilities. Stir into the mix Canada's having been a co-sponsor of the UN resolution that declared 1981 as IYDP, and you have the recipe for a great argument in support of the disability amendment. How could Canada adopt the *Canadian Charter of Rights and Freedoms* during the IYDP but leave people with disabilities out of its *Charter*'s vaunted equality provision?[1]

Beyond arming disability advocates with this blistering, unanswerable argument, IYDP helped our cause in an additional way. Because the IYDP was coming in 1981, the federal government felt it had to do something public and visible in advance to look like it cared, even if this was likely pure symbolic tokenism. In 1980, Parliament established an all-party committee to inquire into the needs of Canadians with disabilities. The Special Parliamentary Committee on the Disabled and Handicapped (Smith Committee), chaired by Liberal member of parliament David Smith, held public hearings in the fall of 1980 to gather input on what the federal

---

1 *Canadian Charter of Rights and Freedoms*, Part 1 of the *Constitution Act, 1982*, being Schedule B to the *Canada Act 1982* (UK), 1982, c 11.

government could do to improve the status of persons with disabilities in Canada.

Canada's Parliament took steps to establish a special parliamentary committee on the disabled and handicapped well before Prime Minister Pierre Trudeau launched his October 1980 constitutional patriation initiative. One year earlier, plans for such a House of Commons committee were well underway. In the fall of 1979, the federal Progressive Conservative Party was briefly in power. On 1 October 1979, at my urging, the CNIB national managing director Ross Purse wrote Prime Minister Joe Clark to send Canada's prime minister the Blindness Law Reform Project's *Vision and Equality* report that I and my team of fellow law students had prepared 2 years earlier, described in Chapter III.[2] His letter to Prime Minister Clark included:

> For your interest and information, and that of The Hon. Walter Dinsdale, as Chairman of the above-mentioned special Parliamentary Committee, I am forwarding under separate cover the report on a study conducted by a group of law students in 1977, under the leadership of a blind law student, Mr. M. David Lepofsky, entitled "Vision and Equality, Blindness Law Reform Project".[3]

That letter might seem less than consequential. However, it had been quite an advocacy journey for me to reach that point. In 1977, I had to appeal to the CNIB's National Council chair, over Purse's head, to get the CNIB to be willing to let anyone outside the CNIB see the *Vision and Equality* report. Here we were, 2 years later in October 1979. I was able to convince Purse to promote this report to the prime minister of Canada. That would have been unimaginable to me in 1977. In December 1979, the Joe Clark minority government fell after an opposition non-confidence motion, and this triggered a national election. In January 1980, Pierre Trudeau's Liberals were re-elected, which set the stage for Trudeau's constitutional patriation initiative later that year.

On 23 May 1980, the House of Commons approved the establishment of the new Smith Committee. Its mandate included:

> to evaluate the scope and effectiveness of existing government programs for the disabled and handicapped, as well as the degree to which they interlock with voluntary programs and services, with the objective of suggesting measures

2 Canadian National Institute for the Blind, *Vision and Equality*, vol 1 (1997–1998).

3 Letter from RC Purse, Managing Director, Canadian National Institute for the Blind, to C Joseph Clark, Prime Minister of Canada (31 October 1979) at 1.

to improve the quality of services provided to such persons, provided that the examination shall include the following subjects:

- fundamental and civil rights
- employment opportunities
- vocational training
- business incentives
- income supplement programs
- health services and medical rehabilitation
- quality of life of institutionalized persons
- community support services
- access to public buildings and services
- coordination within and between jurisdictions
- transportation
- housing.[4]

I must have quickly learned about the establishment of the Smith Committee. I have no idea how. On 6 June 1980, I wrote the CNIB's new national managing director, Robert Mercer. I alerted him that the Trudeau government was to continue with the previous government's plans to set up a parliamentary committee on the disabled and handicapped. This was 2 months before we established the CNIB board's Public Education and Advocacy Committee and 3 months before Prime Minister Trudeau unveiled his constitutional patriation package. I told him how I had recommended that his predecessor's CNIB managing director send our Blindness Law Reform Project's *Vision and Equality* report to the previous parliamentary committee. I cautioned that the chances were good that our report never made it to its intended recipients.[5]

I encouraged the CNIB to get involved with the work of this new Smith Committee. I volunteered my help and advice. I alerted Mercer of the volunteer work I had been doing for the CNIB to support efforts to get

---

4 Special Committee on the Disabled and the Handicapped, 32nd Parl, 1st Sess, Vol 1, No 1 (23 May 1980) at 3.

5 Letter from David Lepofsky to Robert Mercer, Managing Director, Canadian National Institute for the Blind (6 June 1980).

disability protection added to the Ontario *Human Rights Code*. Looking back at my letter to Mercer, I unknowingly was laying a firm foundation for later taking on the role as the CNIB's spokesperson regarding the patriation of Canada's Constitution a few months later. On learning about the Smith Committee, I skeptically surmised that the Trudeau government convened those public hearings without having any intention of doing anything significant or new to advance equality for people with disabilities. It is not unusual for a government to stage a public relations exercise, such as holding public hearings on an issue, merely to make it look as if the government cares and is attentively listening. There may be no prior government agenda to do anything in response to those hearings. In this way, public hearings can be designed to divert attention from government inaction, while happily kicking the policy can down the road.

That committee's chair was a junior member of parliament. When a parliamentary committee is meant to deal with a major government priority issue, a higher profile member of parliament is assigned to chair the hearings. Yet to our potential advantage, a junior member of parliament can be hungry to move up the party's ladder. Doing a good job at hearings like this can help achieve that. If we can show that hungry member of parliament a way to succeed in their mission, we may convert low-profile public hearings into a win-win situation for us and the committee chair. If that member of parliament is convinced that our cause is a good one and worth fighting for, they can become a pivotal asset in our campaign, slogging away on our behalf behind the scenes. Once again, I knew none of this in 1980.

Though not originally intended as such, the Smith Committee turned out to give the disability community a fantastic platform to press for equal rights for people with disabilities. From it, I learned an important lesson that I have encountered over and over: grab every platform you can find to press your case. Even if it looks like a public hearing is mere tokenism, use it as a soapbox. You have nothing to lose and tons to gain.

## B. Tagging onto the Canadian Jewish Congress Delegation to the Smith Committee

In the late summer of 1980, I got a call from Osgoode Hall law professor Fred Zemans. I knew Zemans from law school, as I had graduated just 1 year earlier. He headed a social action committee at the Canadian Jewish Congress [CJC]. He told me about the Smith Committee, explained that the CJC planned to make a presentation at its public hearings, and invited me to be part of the delegation. I don't think the CJC had much, if any, idea of what it wanted to say to the Smith Committee. I told Zemans that the CJC should advocate for amendments to federal legislation to comprehensively protect people with disabilities from disability discrimination. Prime Minister Trudeau had not yet announced his constitutional reform initiative so I was not yet engaged in advocating for the disability amendment.

The CJC filed a comprehensive brief with the Smith Committee. I had been involved in the development of the 20 pages of the brief that detailed amendments to various federal laws that we sought, including changes to the *Canadian Bill of Rights*, the Canadian *Human Rights Act*, and the federal *Income Tax Act*.[6] Some of these would not jump out at anyone as especially innovative. For example, the Canadian *Human Rights Act* had only addressed discrimination because of physical disability. The CJC urged that it be expanded to ban discrimination because of mental disability as well.

Yet one passage in the brief now stands out. It unknowingly foreshadowed the battle for the disability amendment to the *Charter* that none of us then knew about or could have predicted. The CJC's brief recommended that the statutory *Canadian Bill of Rights* should be amended to prohibit federal legislation from discrimination because of disability. As I explained in Chapter II, the *Canadian Bill of Rights*, which had then been in force for two decades, was a federal statute that set out a series of basic rights and freedoms that federal laws could not violate, unless a federal law stated that it operated notwithstanding the *Canadian Bill of Rights*. I do not recall to what extent I was directly involved in creating this passage. The brief stated:

> The Canadian Bill of Rights is a symbolic statement of the goals and philosophical outlook of the people and government of Canada; it may also serve to prevent the government itself from passing discriminatory legislation against those groups protected by its provisions. Should it be entrenched in a new Canadian Constitution, its significance will be even more greatly enhanced; it will form part of a document which proclaims to the world our aspirations and fundamental concerns, against which our actual progress, or lack of it, will be assessed.

---

6 *Canadian Bill of Rights*, SC 1960, c 44; *Human Rights Act*, SC 1976–1977, c 33; *Income Tax Act*, RSC 1985, c 1.

Section 1 of the *Canadian Bill of Rights* reads as follows:

> 1. It is hereby recognized and declared that in Canada there have existed and shall continue to exist without discrimination by reason of race, national origin, colour, religion or sex, the following human rights and fundamental freedoms, namely,
>
> a. the right of the individual to life, liberty, security of the person and enjoyment of property, and the right not to be deprived thereof except by due process of law;
>
> b. the right of the individual to equality before the law and the protection of the law;

Surely, the handicapped also have the right "to life, liberty, security of the person and enjoyment of property," which in the broadest sense can be construed to mean a high quality of life, employment, and security of dignity, and, surely, the handicapped are also entitled to the protection of the law. There should be no doubt that the federal government may no more discriminate against the handicapped in its own legislation nor deny them "human rights and fundamental freedoms" than it can discriminate and deny rights "by reason of race, national origin, colour, religion or sex":

> Recommendation One
>
> Therefore, we recommend that Section 1 of the Canadian Bill of Rights be amended to include the physically and mentally handicapped as a protected class.[7]

It now seems quite odd that the CJC's brief recommended amending the *Canadian Bill of Rights*. As Chapter II describes, Canada's courts had by then interpreted that law so narrowly that it was functionally useless. Why dredge it up? An amendment to it would achieve nothing for us. Yet that recommendation had the potential to help us in a way that we could not have predicted. Once the Trudeau government's constitutional patriation package was made public on 2 October 1980, and once the battle began for the disability amendment, the very same arguments that we mounted in the CJC's brief in favour of a disability amendment to the *Canadian Bill of Rights* would equally show why a disability amendment to Trudeau's proposed *Charter* was needed.

---

7 Canadian Jewish Congress, *Legal Perspective*, Brief to the House of Commons Special Committee on the Disabled and the Handicapped (17 September 1980) at 41–43.

On 17 September 1980, our CJC delegation went to Ottawa to present to the Smith Committee. Were this today, I would have a video recording of the hearing to post on YouTube and tweet to the world. Back then, only a handful of people in the room would ever hear and see what we had to say. I was the last of six speakers in the CJC's delegation that had to divvy up our short slice of speaking time. Before I got my chance to speak, the other CJC speakers addressed other issues. After they finally finished, I had to jam the entire case for the need for federal legislation to be reformed to protect equality for people with disabilities in the remaining 5 minutes or less. I tried to calmly make the best use of what little time they left for me, despite my frustration almost boiling over. Over the years since then, I have had to learn how to manage that frustration when I am given far too little time to present an important issue, while keeping a running ever-shortening mental list of the most important points to squeeze into the few speaking moments I have left.

This was my debut appearance before any parliamentary committee, federal or provincial. It gave me an opportunity to get experience on my feet and to test out our broader message in favour of equality and human rights for people with disabilities. I have learned over the ensuing years that my arguments get tighter and sharper each time I get to try them out in action, whether in the media or when addressing a parliamentary committee. Especially important, this appearance in Ottawa gave me a chance to meet Liberal member of parliament David Smith and try to establish an impression on him. That alone made the trip worth it.

That would have been enough. However, there turned out to be another benefit to my appearing at the Smith Committee's hearings. It was there that I first met a young reporter who was covering our presentation for the *Canadian Jewish News*. She was the same person who I would invite to dinner later that fall to help me edit the CNIB's brief to the Special Joint Committee of the Senate and the House of Commons on the Constitution of Canada (Joint Committee).

## C. The Smith Committee Publicly Calls for the Disability Amendment

Some of the Smith Committee's hearings took place before Prime Minister Trudeau tabled his constitutional patriation package in Parliament. Groups like our Canadian Jewish Congress delegation, which made their presentations before 2 October 1980, had no chance to advocate in person to the Smith Committee in support of the disability amendment to the *Charter*. However, we all had a great chance to educate and motivate the members of that committee on the need to pass new legislation to protect people with disabilities from disability discrimination. It was a short and obvious step from there for the Smith Committee's members to see the need for the disability amendment to the *Charter* once Trudeau made public his constitutional reform package.

Responding to the strong feedback that it received from many quarters at its hearings, the Smith Committee decided to take action. On 30 October 1980, the same day that our CNIB Public Education and Advocacy Committee held its emergency meeting to kick off our campaign for the disability amendment, the Smith Committee took the unusual step of publicly releasing an interim report. That report expressed exceptional unity among Parliament's fractious three major parties. The Smith Committee cleverly stick-handled its way around the headline-grabbing controversial division among the federal parties about the appropriateness of Trudeau's constitutional reform package. The interim report expressed its recommendation in conditional terms. It ducked the question whether Canada should get a *Charter*. The Smith Committee declared that, if the *Charter* was to be enacted, then it should be amended to include equality for people with disabilities.

Recently, I found a 31 October 1980 article from the *Toronto Sun* collecting dust in my garage. The article, with the headline "Grant Rights to Disabled, MPs Say," stated:

> The Commons committee on the disabled said yesterday full and equal rights should be granted to the handicapped in a Bill of Rights contained in the constitution.
>
> Committee chairman David Smith told a news conference that the committee felt that human rights and increased parliamentary services to the disabled required immediate attention by the federal government.
>
> "Should it be the will of Parliament to entrench rights in a patriated constitution, the committee believes that full and equal protection should be provided for persons with physical or mental handicaps," Smith said.
>
> Smith, Liberal MP for Don Valley East, said the all-party committee was unanimous in its decision to confer equal status on the handicapped.
>
> Under the current Human Rights Act, a law passed by Parliament in 1977, disabled Canadians are protected under the law, but the committee recommended

> the government take those rights a step further and entrench "Equal opportunity" for them in Canada's fundamental law.
>
> The act says every individual should have an equal opportunity to make for themselves a life that he or she is able, or wishes to have, without being hindered from doing so from discriminatory employment practices based on physical handicap.
>
> "This is what we are taking issue with," Smith said. "We think the time has come to broaden it so that it [the act] does not Just apply to cases relating to employment."
>
> He added that the committee wanted to highlight that people with mental handicaps, including people with learning disabilities, mental retardation or mental illness, be added to list of grounds for protection under the Human Rights Act.
>
> "What we're saying there is that we should also include in the Human Rights Act specific reference to people with various mental handicaps," Smith said.[8]

In her published account of the COPOH's advocacy efforts in support of the disability amendment, Yvonne Peters explained how COPOH got the Smith Committee (which she called the "Obstacles Committee") to hire COPOH staffer Jim Derksen to work for the Smith Committee:

> During his work with the Obstacles Committee, Mr. Derksen had many opportunities to speak with Committee members about the government's refusal to include people with disabilities in the proposed *Charter*. Thanks to the hard work and persistence of Mr. Derksen, Committee members soon sympathized with the struggles of people with disabilities and began earnestly lobbying their respective caucuses for their support.[9]

In one decisive sentence, the Smith Committee catapulted itself from unnoticed troubling tokenism to a prominent force in the campaign for the disability amendment. Its interim report was the first major endorsement of the disability amendment from within the political process. It handed us a punchy new argument — namely, that an all-party parliamentary committee supports the right of people with disabilities to have equality rights enshrined in the proposed new *Charter*.

---

8 "Grant Rights to Disabled, MPs Say," *Toronto Sun* (31 October 1980).

9 Yvonne Peters "From Charity to Equality: Canadians with Disabilities Take Their Rightful Place in Canada's Constitution" in Deborah Stienstra & Aileen Wight-Felske, with Colleen Watters, eds, *Making Equality: History of Advocacy and Persons with Disabilities in Canada* (Concord, ON: Captus Press 2003) 119 at 128 [footnotes omitted].

Unknown to us at the time, a major benefit for our cause from all of this was that it also produced a critically important advocate for our cause within the Liberal caucus, Member of Parliament David Smith. I later learned that Smith took it upon himself to press members of his own caucus over and over to get them to support the disability amendment. Had he not done this, I do not know whether we would have won the disability amendment. Four decades later, on his death after a long career in politics as a member of parliament and later as a senator, I honoured David Smith's contribution to the disability amendment with a guest column in the *Toronto Star*, entitled "Sen. David Smith an Unsung Hero of Disabled Canadians."[10] See Appendix 2 for the full article.

Since those events, I would learn time and again how public hearings, while frustrating and seemingly pointless at the time, gradually give members of the legislature or of Parliament an education on an issue, whether they want it or not. As they sit through those hearings, trying to sympathetically smile as if they are carefully hanging on every word, they can consciously or unconsciously internalize our concerns, while hearing witness after witness vividly illustrate them in gritty real-life terms. It was tremendously helpful for us that some members of the Smith Committee also served on the Joint Committee that was to hold hearings on the contents of the patriation package, including the proposed *Charter*. When the disability amendment was discussed, they spoke about the feedback they heard from the disability community during the Smith Committee's hearings, drawing on the crash course in disability rights that those earlier hearings delivered.

For example, on 21 November 1980, during the Joint Committee's hearings on the patriation package, one member of the Smith Committee (who was also a member of the Joint Committee) stated that the Smith Committee had heard from over 400 witnesses. They all called for the disability amendment: "Mr. Young: … I am also a member of the Special Committee on the Disabled and the Handicapped, and over the summer months, we had over 400 witnesses who made presentations to that Committee and without exception, everyone argued that disability and

---

10 See David Lepofsky, "Sen. David Smith an Unsung Hero of Disabled Canadians," *Toronto Star* (2 March 2020), online: <www.thestar.com/opinion/contributors/2020/03/02/sen-david-smith-an-unsung-hero-of-disabled-canadians.html>.

handicap should be included in any new charter of rights and freedoms."[11] I would relive this experience two decades later, in 2005, when the Ontario government held public hearings on the proposed Bill 118, the *AODA*.[12] One of the Standing Committee's backbench liberal members who took part in the legislative hearings was newly elected Member of Provincial Parliament Kathleen Wynne. In 2005, she could make no decisions on her own over how to vote during that Standing Committee's proceedings. Party officials handed her marching orders, which she faithfully followed. Eight short years later, she became Ontario's premier. When I met in person with her in that role to press for needed action to more effectively implement the *AODA*, I knew I was dealing with a premier who had received the unique education on our issues that came from listening at days of public hearings on Bill 118 in 2005. It no doubt helped, for example, when we eventually convinced her in the fall of 2016 to agree to develop and enact an Education Accessibility Standard under the *AODA* in order to tear down the accessibility barriers that impede hundreds of thousands of students with disabilities in Ontario's education system.

There are still more lessons that I learned from this experience, though as is often the case for me, I only got the total picture much later. A lay observer would think that a movement in support of a cause starts from the grassroots, picks up steam, and then culminates with pressure on the government for change. Eventually, the government takes action in response to this pressure that originated at the grassroots. Yet there are times when there is initially no such grassroots movement for the reform in issue. Counter-intuitively, it is sometimes government action that ignites grassroots efforts in support of a cause, instead of the reverse. As I noted in Chapter I, in the summer of 1980, there was no grassroots disability movement calling for disability equality to be enshrined in Canada's Constitution. It was the introduction into Parliament of Trudeau's patriation package, combined with the Smith Committee's public hearings, that became the lightning rod that brought out voices from the disability community. Had it not been for the appointment of the Smith Committee, no such generation of consensus in support of the disability community would likely have been forthcoming,

---

11 Canada, Parliament, *Minutes of Proceedings and Evidence of the Special Joint Committee of the Senate and of the House of Commons on the Constitution of Canada*, 32nd Parl, 1st Sess, No 10 (21 November 1980) at 14.

12 *Accessibility for Ontarians with Disabilities Act*, SO 2005, c 11.

for all the reasons, spelled out in Chapter VI, that led me to decide to "go it alone" on the disability amendment issue.

My participation in the CJC's deputation to the Smith Committee is illustrative. Had there been no Smith Committee, the CJC would not have focused its efforts on federal policy on disability issues. At that time, the organized Canadian Jewish community had a very long way to go to recognize and address disability issues as they related to participation by people with disabilities in Jewish communal activities and services. However, because the Smith Committee was appointed and had convened public hearings, the CJC decided to make a deputation to it. It was in turn because of this action that the CJC's Social Action Committee chair Fred Zemans reached out to me. And the rest, as they say, is history.

The Smith committee spawned a larger disability community consensus. I was to witness something very similar again 14 years later. In 1994, there was no major Ontario disability community movement to press for a provincial disabilities act. As I have recounted elsewhere, only a few of us were pushing for it.[13] Others in the disability community did not turn their minds to it, did not agree with it, did not consider it a priority, or did not even know about it as an issue. Despite this absence of a grassroots disability community groundswell in 1994, backbench Ontario Government New Democratic Party Member of Provincial Parliament Gary Malkowski decided that year to introduce his own private member's bill, named the *Ontarians with Disabilities Act*. His bill triggered legislative public hearings. Those public hearings in turn brought a pivotal group of disability advocates together in one room at the Ontario legislature on 29 November 1994. It was there that the organized movement was spontaneously born that fought for a decade to win the enactment of the *AODA* in 2005. 20 or so disability advocates grew into Ontario's largest cross-disability advocacy movement in memory. I had the privilege of being there right at the start and of eventually co-chairing and then chairing the Ontarians with Disabilities Act Committee that led that effort. There, as in the case of the Smith Committee, it was legislative committee hearings that triggered the creation of a major disability community advocacy effort, not the other way around.

---

13 M David Lepofsky, "The Long, Arduous Road to a Barrier-Free Ontario for People with Disabilities: The History of the *Ontarians with Disabilities Act* — the First Chapter" (2004) 15:2 NJCL 125 at 155–157.

# X. TWO OTHER DISABILITY ORGANIZATIONS' IMPORTANT DEPUTATIONS TO THE JOINT COMMITTEE IN SUPPORT OF THE DISABILITY AMENDMENT

## A. Meet Two Other Key Organizational Advocates for the Disability Amendment

Before I was to appear before the Special Joint Committee of the Senate and the House of Commons on the Constitution of Canada (Joint Committee) on 12 December 1980, two major disability organizations had made presentations to that committee calling for the disability amendment. On 21 November 1980, the Joint Committee heard from the Canadian Association for the Mentally Retarded [CAMR]. That group was supported at its presentation by People First, a long-standing organization of people with intellectual disabilities whose name signals the fact that they want to be known as people first. Four days later, on 25 November 1980, COPOH got their turn at the plate.

In the fall of 1980, I did not know about the CAMR's or COPOH's presentations, their efforts in support of the disability amendment, or that they were coordinating their efforts. So many of our arguments in support of the disability amendment were similar and mutually reinforcing, though I arrived at mine independently of theirs. Coordinating our efforts would have made my life much easier and, no doubt, would have improved my advocacy efforts. I presented to the Joint Committee days after they made their presentations. This is a prized opportunity that I have always sought out, whether arguing a case in court or speaking to a parliamentary committee. When you speak last, you can build on, summarize, and supplement the arguments that were made earlier and try to land a concluding knock-out punch. I have analogized this to batting clean-up in baseball. I want others to load the bases, tire the pitcher, and get the crowd pumped up before I get my time at bat.

A read of the CAMR's, COPOH's, and, later, the CNIB's presentations to the Joint Committee immediately reveals how much our disability terminology has changed since then. All the three disability organizations that appeared before the Joint Committee invoked the outdated phrases "handicapped people," "the handicapped," or "handicapping condition." The term "handicapped" has since been discarded as pejorative. It has been associated, correctly or otherwise, with begging for charity, cap in hand. Years later, COPOH changed its name to the Council of Canadians with Disabilities, eliminating its use of the term "handicapped." I am mortified that throughout my presentation to the Joint Committee, I used the term "handicapped." I asked that the term handicapped be added to section 15.

The term "mentally retarded" was also used. The CAMR's very organizational name used the term "mentally retarded." That expression is now widely rejected as a term of humiliation, ridicule, and belittlement. Since then, the CAMR changed its name to the Canadian Association for Community Living and, again, most recently to Inclusion Canada. Its provincial and municipal counterparts also changed their names to remove "mentally retarded." The terms "developmental disability or intellectual disability" are now preferred. These important terminology changes are not empty wordsmithing. They aim to get away from harmful stereotypes and to have our words accord with our dignity.

## B. Advocacy Efforts by the CAMR

The core of CAMR's 21 November 1980 presentation to the Joint Committee was delivered by lawyer and strong disability rights advocate David Vickers. He later served as British Columbia's deputy attorney general and, after that, as a justice on the Supreme Court of British Columbia. A member of CAMR's delegation who did not have a speaking role was Toronto lawyer Orville Endicott. He selflessly dedicated his long legal career to advocating for the rights of people with intellectual disabilities. For me, he was a wise mentor and a strong ally in our disability advocacy efforts. So often, he humbly kept himself in the background while slogging tenaciously to advance our cause.

Addressing the Joint Committee, Vickers emphasized that the CAMR's core objective was to promote the integration of people with disabilities in society. He emphasized that they were not seeking special rights. It is amazing that he needed to make that point.[1] I also had to do so in my

1 Canada, Parliament, *Minutes of Proceedings and Evidence of the Special Joint Committee of the Senate and of the House of Commons on the Constitution of Canada*, 32nd Parl, 1st Sess, No 10 (21 November 1980) at 7–8 [*Minutes of Proceedings, 21 November 1980*].

efforts to advocate for the disability amendment. We were reacting to our genuine fear that our claim for equality for people with disabilities might irrationally be rejected as a demand for special rights:

> We ask you to pause for a moment, if you will, to consider the needs of an average Canadian citizen. Think of your own needs and how they have been met throughout your life. Canadians who are handicapped are no different in that regard than you or I. To achieve the limits of their potential they require, first of all, the ability to live, and in particular adequate health care.
>
> Second, they require an appropriate education in the least restrictive alternative.
>
> Third, they need appropriate vocational training and thereafter appropriate vocational opportunities.
>
> Fourth, they need appropriate residential accommodation, again in the least restrictive alternative.
>
> Fifth, they need appropriate recreational and social opportunities. Antidiscrimination clauses in charters and human rights codes contains statements of conduct that is prohibitive. In addition to such statements of prohibitive conduct, our association favours a statement of positive rights. We say that those values to which we all subscribe as Canadians can be and ought to be stated as basic conditions of social, economic and cultural rights in Canada.[2]

The CAMR urged the adoption of language in the *Canadian Charter of Rights and Freedoms* that would guarantee positive rights.[3] Beyond that, it focused on the need for the disability amendment:

> The year 1981 will be International Year of the Disabled. It would be an appalling commentary on our Canadian values if we failed to entrench in that year, in our new constitution. protection for all Canadians who live with a handicap whether real or perceived. The usual objection raised to inclusion of handicapped as a prohibited ground of discrimination is that such a measure might obstruct programs designed to remedy the effects of the long history of negative discrimination. We believe that the usual exceptions to affirmative action programs can relieve this concern. And you have dealt with that in the subsection to Section 15.
>
> There is a second objection from those who say that in order to benefit from antidiscrimination clauses a person would first have to identify himself or herself as handicapped. This objection can be overcome if the terminology used is

2 *Ibid* at 9.

3 *Ibid* at 9, 10, 11; *Canadian Charter of Rights and Freedoms*, Part 1 of the *Constitution Act, 1982*, being Schedule B to the *Canada Act 1982* (UK), 1982, c 11.

> defined broadly, such as we find in a definition of "handicapped person" which can be found in the U.S. Rehabilitation Act of 1973. There "handicapped person" is defined as any person who has (a) a physical or mental impairment which substantially limits one or more of such person's major life activities; (b) has a record of such impairment; or (c) is regarded as having such an impairment.
>
> It is noteworthy that particularly under subsection (c) of this definition the focus is clearly on the act of discrimination rather than on whether the person discriminated against can be fitted into the protected category. That is the essential purpose of the statutory definition.[4]

Vickers gave examples of people with intellectual disabilities who were detained for years and decades by the criminal justice system as unfit to stand trial, even though they were only charged with minor offences such as purse snatching. They were detained under the outdated and arbitrary Lieutenant Governor's warrant system.[5] A decade later, the Supreme Court of Canada would strike down that outdated *Criminal Code* regime, though without invoking the disability amendment in support of its ruling.[6] He talked about the fact that a disability amendment to the *Charter* could help signal to trade unions, among others, that barriers to jobs for people with disabilities should be torn down:

> Now, like employers and like public and private organizations, they are a long way away from actually accommodating the needs of our handicapped friends. That is why to entrench the value is simply to signal, if you will, to the trade union movement that all people, including handicapped people, have that as a basic Canadian right and that is why it is important. It is a beacon, if you will, and it affords our people the opportunity for vocational experiences which they heretofore have not had an opportunity to grasp.[7]

Vickers spoke extensively about the need to promote deinstitutionalization and community living opportunities. In response to a committee member's question, he explained that where there have been efforts to de-institutionalize people with intellectual disabilities, and establish group homes, some have

---

4 *Minutes of Proceedings, 21 November 1980*, *supra* note 1 at 10–11.

5 *Ibid* at 14–16.

6 *R v Swain*, [1991] 1 SCR 933, [1991] SCJ No 32 (QL); *Criminal Code*, RSC 1985, c C-46; M David Lepofsky, "A Report Card on the Charter's Guarantee of Equality to Persons with Disabilities after 10 Years: What Progress? What Prospects?" (1997) 7:3 NJCL 263 at 273, 294, 302–302, 373–374.

7 *Minutes of Proceedings, 21 November 1980*, *supra* note 1 at 17.

objected at the municipal level to these group homes.[8] He did not specifically discuss how the disability amendment could be used to oppose this. However, he tied the rectification of this to the benefits that would extend to having children learn about disabilities in school:

> Well, there is not doubt it is happening across the country and there is no doubt it is happening for a number of reasons.
>
> The first reason it is happening, it comes back to the question of attitudes again and where do we begin to change attitudes, and my plea again is that we begin with our youngsters in school accepting the disabilities that our fellow Canadians have.[9]

One brief moment during the CAMR's presentation is both jarring and emblematic of how employment for people with disabilities was so often viewed back then by some governments and others. It was then common to hear people speak of a limited number of "jobs that people with disabilities can do," implicitly presuming that we could not do most other jobs. The CAMR was asked if it had known of any unions that opposed letting people with disabilities join them. In response, the CAMR's president stated in part:

> There are cases — and I will ask Mr. Vickers to provide details — where employers ... [i]n Quebec, the Bureau for the Handicapped is trying to increase the number of jobs available to the handicapped and the mentally retarded.
>
> There have been several cases involving handicapped persons where an attempt has been made to have jobs considered as being suitable for the handicapped, but union rules, particularly with regards to seniority, have prevented this from being done.
>
> There was, for example, darkroom work for the blind. We wanted photography companies to give blind people priority for darkroom work and the request was turned down by the unions. This is the type of thing that is related to the union membership issue.[10]

In 1980, long before we had digital cameras and smartphones, if you wanted to take a photograph, you had to snap that picture using a film camera and then send the film to be developed in a "dark room." It appears that someone had thought that working in a dark room would be a great job category that blind people could do. It would even be good to give them

---

8 *Ibid* at 19–20.

9 *Ibid* at 19.

10 *Ibid* at 16–17.

preferential access to those jobs. A long time would pass before we reached the stage of having leading decision-makers understand that we can do far more than a few pre-defined jobs and that the burden is on an employer to show that our disability precludes us from doing a particular job, even with accommodation up to the point of undue hardship.

## C. Advocacy Efforts by COPOH

### *1. Who Was COPOH?*

COPOH described itself as a coalition of nine provincial organizations of people with disabilities: the British Columbia Coalition of the Disabled, the Alberta Committee of Action Groups of the Disabled, the Saskatchewan Voice of the Handicapped, the Manitoba League of the Physically Handicapped, the United Handicapped Groups of Ontario, Carrefour Adoptation Québec, the Nova Scotia League for Equal Opportunities, the Prince Edward Island Council of the Disabled, and the HUB.[11] These member groups were grassroots organizations of people with disabilities themselves. They were not charities that provided services to people with disabilities like the CNIB or the March of Dimes. In the world of 1980 technology, assembling and sustaining such a coalition was impressive.

### *2. COPOH's Initial Advocacy Efforts in Support of the Disability Amendment*

From what I have been able to unearth with limited sources at my disposal, it appears that COPOH was the most active of any disability organization advocating for the disability amendment. Yvonne Peters, a disability rights advocate and a member of the COPOH delegation presenting at the Joint Committee, describes COPOH's efforts in support of the disability amendment in her book chapter entitled "From Charity to Equality."[12] As

---

11 Correspondence from the Coalition of Provincial Organizations of the Handicapped (COPOH) to the co-chairman of the Joint Committee (7 November 1980) at 1; COPOH, *Brief to the Special Joint Parliamentary Committee on the Constitution* (November 1980) at 1.

12 Yvonne Peters, "From Charity to Equality: Canadians with Disabilities Take Their Rightful Place in Canada's Constitution" in Deborah Stienstra & Aileen Wight-Felske, with Colleen Watters, eds, *Making Equality: History of Advocacy and Persons with Disabilities in Canada* (Concord, ON: Captus Press 2003) 119.

addressed in Chapter IX, a key member of COPOH's leadership team, Jim Derksen, had also staffed the Special Parliamentary Committee on the Disabled and Handicapped (Smith Committee), which gave him a unique opportunity to have a well-placed voice at a critical time. In her book chapter, Peters wrote that, before the *Charter* debate began, the Smith Committee had met with COPOH's leadership as part of its work. Peters described COPOH's front-line lobbying efforts as follows (calling the Smith Committee the "Obstacles Committee"): "The work of the Obstacles Committee coincided with an intensive telegram and letter writing campaign spearheaded by COPOH and its provincial affiliates. The COPOH garnered support from a wide range of parliamentarians as well as from other community and equality-seeking groups."[13] COPOH wrote an open letter on 28 October 1980 to members of parliament and senators, pressing for the disability amendment and arguing:

> To fail to prohibit discrimination on the grounds of disability in any constitutionally entrenched Charter of Rights and Freedoms which (prohibits) discrimination on the grounds of race, national or ethnic origin, colour, religion, sex or age is tantamount to rejecting the fundamental humanity of disabled Canadians.
>
> If the *Charter of Rights and Freedoms* is entrenched as it is presently written, people who bring complaints of discrimination on the grounds of sex, age, race, religion and other grounds listed in 15(1) (the non-discrimination clause) to human rights commissions at the federal or provincial levels, will also be able to appeal to higher courts on constitutional grounds if they are not satisfied that they have been protected from discrimination by the Commission. Complaints of discrimination on the grounds of disability, however, will not have a similar constitutional back up and therefore obviously will not be given the same priority by human rights commissions when allocating limited staff resources.
>
> In fact, it will become quite clear that discrimination against a person because he or she is disabled, while prohibited, is not as prohibited as discrimination against a person because of sex, age, race, religion and the other grounds listed in the constitution.[14]

Years later, I and other disability advocates would use the strategy of an open letter to government on issue after issue. We now try to get as many

---

13 *Ibid* at 128.

14 COPOH, *An Open Letter to the Commons and the Senate* (28 October 1980). The national chairman was Allan Simpson.

organizations as possible to sign on to such an open letter and spread it far and wide on the web and social media to massively amplify our message.

According to Peters, she took part in a demonstration on Parliament Hill on 3 November 1980 in support of the disability amendment. COPOH could stage this event on short notice because its national board was meeting in Ottawa. Peters wrote:

> I believe that the demonstration on Parliament Hill was the first time that people with a variety of disabilities from across the country gathered together to publicly express their frustration and dissatisfaction with government. People with disabilities were just beginning to experience the promise of rights, and we were resolved not to let the architects of the *Charter* diminish or undermine this potential by ignoring our claim to legally recognized equality.[15]

The demonstration on Parliament Hill, referred to earlier, intensified COPOH's commitment to the *Charter* project. Following the demonstration, Ron Kanary, COPOH's vice chair, and I were asked to extend our stay in Ottawa to engage in the direct lobbying of key politicians. Most of the politicians we met with were genuinely interested and receptive to our issue and were obviously trying to make sense of how a *Charter* would function in the Canadian context.[16] Peters reflects on what COPOH experienced in response to their efforts:

> Like many institutions in society, the COPOH lobby revealed that politicians and bureaucrats alike displayed diverse opinions about disability. They ranged from a simple lack of understanding to ignorance and a deeply felt bias towards disability.
>
> In the late '70s and early '80s, many people did not understand the social consequences associated with having a disability. Nor were they familiar with the idea of according equality rights recognition to people with disabilities.[17]

As its next step, in November 1980, COPOH submitted a brief to Parliament. It drew on and responded to the information it garnered from discussions with politicians, according to Peters.[18] COPOH wanted to ensure that it would get a time slot to speak to the Joint Committee. Its spirits were buoyed when it got an invitation to do so.[19] On 25 November 1980, COPOH's

---

15 Peters, *supra* note 12 at 121.

16 *Ibid* at 128–129.

17 *Ibid* at 129–130.

18 *Ibid.*

19 *Ibid* at 127–129.

delegation to the Joint Committee hearings included Monique Couillard, Yvonne Peters, Ron Kanary, and Jim Derksen.[20]

### *3. COPOH's Three Core Arguments in Support of the Disability Amendment*

COPOH's written brief and its 25 November 1980 oral presentation to the Joint Committee combined to mount a solid, detailed case in support of the disability amendment. This is especially striking since COPOH had so little time to prepare, and Canada had such a limited understanding of disability equality rights in 1980. COPOH's argument covered ground that was not addressed at all, or in the same way, either by me on behalf of the CNIB or by the CAMR. COPOH's oral presentation to the Joint Committee on 25 November was almost a verbatim recitation of its written brief. The appendix to COPOH's brief (which was not read aloud at the 25 November 1980 Joint Committee meeting) and COPOH's answers to Joint Committee members' questions during their oral presentation combined to unleash a barrage of additional salvos supporting the disability amendment.

COPOH told the Joint Committee that the disability amendment was supported by the Smith Committee, the Canadian Human Rights Commission, the Canadian Jewish Congress, the Royal Canadian Legion, and the Canadian Labour Congress.[21] COPOH thereby showed that it was far more on top of the key events unfolding at the Joint Committee than I was. COPOH's core contention was that we need the disability amendment because people with disabilities face discrimination in Canada. The Joint Committee was told:

> The growing awareness and concern about this in society is based on a true understanding that disabled people are a minority who have suffered discrimination which has limited their participation in society and who therefore require protection of the law. This social understanding calls on you to include disability or handicap as a prohibited ground of discrimination in Section 15(1) of the proposed *Canadian Charter of Rights and Freedoms*.[22]

---

20 Canada, Parliament, *Minutes of Proceedings and Evidence of the Special Joint Committee of the Senate and of the House of Commons on the Constitution of Canada*, 32nd Parl, 1st Sess, No 12 (25 November 1980) [*Minutes of Proceedings, 25 November 1980*].

21 *Ibid* at 26–27.

22 *Ibid* at 27.

To do justice to it, I quote in full the three advantages of the disability amendment that COPOH presented to the Joint Committee. I then describe how COPOH responded to real or anticipated arguments against the disability amendment:

> Firstly, constitutional protection of the rights of disabled people would give high symbolic profile to the social concern to recognize and protect these rights. It would set the tone for an improved future. When we are denied service in a restaurant simply because of our blindness, or employment because of deafness, or housing because of a spastic movement disability, we are often injured twice — once by the act of discrimination itself and again by the shocking realization that the state offers us no protection from such discrimination. This situation still pertains in three provinces of Canada; in the other seven provincial jurisdictions, the provinces have taken, to various degrees, a leadership role in providing human rights protection. It will be a profound joy in such circumstances to substitute for the helpless feeling of being relegated to the refuse as if with no value or right to expect better than the prejudice or discrimination offered to us in the past, the reassuring knowledge that we are protected from such prejudice and discrimination by the Canadian constitution.
>
> The *Canadian Charter of Rights and Freedoms* will articulate the most basic and cherished values of our society and place them in the basic legislation of the land. This alone will set a new tone which of itself will do much to redress the injuries of exclusion and prejudice that have been our inheritance.
>
> Secondly, the inclusion of disability as a prohibited cause of discrimination as it applies to the substance of the law will do much to change existing laws at municipal, provincial and federal levels which do discriminate against disabled people. A good example of such a needed change is the legislation which denies disabled people the protection of minimum wage legislation in various provinces and in the federal labour code.
>
> No longer will we remain the only category of adult Canadians whose labour and productivity can be bought for twenty-five cents a day and less. Lest this example should be misunderstood, the constitutional change we recommend to you will not mean that all centres offering daytime activity for disabled people will be required to pay minimum wages, but it will mean a distinction will have to be made between daycare activity centres where people do not work and which are therefore exempt from minimum wage standards and settings where people work, which will be subject to such standard protections from exploitation.
>
> The amendments we are recommending to you would also help preclude any future legislation at municipal, provincial or federal levels which would discriminate against disabled people. Forty years ago, Nazi Germany enacted legislation which called for compulsory sterilization of certain disabled people

in the name of racial eugenics. Other disabled people were murdered although the word used was euthanasia. Even today in this country, compulsory sterilization is sometimes talked about for certain disabled people, and the Ontario Association for the Mentally Retarded is required to have a public policy against any form of passive infant euthanasia.

The Canadian Jewish Congress, in its presentation to you a week ago today, speaking for the inclusion of handicap in Section 15(1) referred to a brief they submitted to the Special Parliamentary Committee on the Disabled and Handicapped wherein they made the same recommendation. They said in that brief that the ramifications of our failure to firmly establish equal legal rights for our handicapped and of our near automatic exclusion of them from the mainstream resulted in events in the not-too-distant past which still cast shadows over us dark enough to send cold shivers running through our souls.

For those of us who still remember, or who have taken the trouble to learn about it, it was in Hitler Germany that the retarded, the gypsies, the physically and emotionally handicapped so easily became early fodder for the destruction machine.

It is interesting how little is said about this dimension of the holocaust. This neglect to recall or analyze this particular dimension of the holocaust gives us a frightening insight as to the state of our present moral crisis in respect to what we describe as the disposables of our society.

We value the dignity of the individual and his right to life and security of the person and have already articulated these values in our draft constitution Section 7. However, in light of history and the ongoing association with disability of concepts such as racial eugenics and passive euthanasia, disabled Canadians deserve the same reassurance of the amendment we recommend to ensure the right ... to the equal protection from the law without discrimination because of ... disability or handicap, so that forty years from now such atrocities could not so easily be perpetrated in Canada. Disabled Canadians need to know they are secure from such dangers and that their fellow Canadians hold values which embrace the right to life and security of the person for everyone. including disabled people. The amendment we recommend would articulate and help preserve these most important values which are held by the Canadian people today.

The third general advantage that the inclusion of disability or handicap as a prohibited ground of discrimination would produce, as applied to the administration of the law, is to reinforce human rights protection as an ordinary legislation level. We have struggled for and achieved this in seven of the ten provinces and have it at the drafting stage in the remaining three. This ordinary legislation level protection, through setting up Human Rights Commissions as courts of first recourse in matters of discrimination, represents

> the major means by which non-discrimination rights are implemented for the individual who experiences discrimination.
>
> We agree with Chief Canadian Human Rights Commissioner Gordon Fairweather that the *Charter of Rights and Freedoms* should apply to both the substance and the administration of the law.
>
> We believe that Section 15(1) of the proposed *Charter* will then make it possible for the decisions of human rights commissions to be appealed to higher courts on constitutional grounds. This will do much to improve the quality of protection on grounds which are listed in Section 15(1). The listing of disability or handicap in Section 15(1) then will be important to disabled Canadians as it will improve the protection already available at ordinary legislation levels.
>
> The omission of disability as a listed category in Section 15(1) would probably significantly damage the quality of protection already achieved at the ordinary legislative level for disabled Canadians. It seems obvious to us that once the *Charter of Rights and Freedoms* is in place, together with Section 15(1), human rights commissions, when allocating their necessarily limited staff and legal resources will give higher priority to complaints of discrimination on grounds which are listed in the constitution because of their potential for appeal to higher courts on constitutional grounds.
>
> Hence, if disability is not among the listing in Section 15(1), complaints of discrimination on grounds of disability will be dealt with using whatever resources the commissions have left over after dealing with complaints on grounds which are listed in Section 15(1). Inadvertently, the *Canadian Charter of Rights and Freedoms* will create a first and second class of rights to protection from discrimination.[23]

What happens if I now scrutinize these three arguments under a legal microscope, using my understanding of equality rights that I have garnered over the decades since 1980? It turns out that two of COPOH's arguments are at least in part legally incorrect. Under the disability amendment, people with disabilities cannot bring a constitutional claim when a private business discriminates against them because of their disability, at least if no public program is in issue.[24] That could knock out COPOH's first argument. Human rights commissions were and are not likely to allocate more enforcement

---

23 *Ibid* at 27–30.

24 *Eldridge v British Columbia (Attorney General)*, [1997] 3 SCR 624 at paras 40–44, [1997] SCJ No 86 (QL).

resources to disability cases if the *Charter* was amended to include disability equality. That puts an end to at least part of COPOH's third argument.

So what, you properly ask? I immediately toss that legal microscope aside. Such an evaluation of COPOH's argument is, to me, mildly interesting but ultimately immaterial. Those holes in COPOH's arguments took nothing away from COPOH's powerful and influential presentation in support of the disability amendment. I am confident that few 1980 legal scholars and no members of the Joint Committee would have detected, understood, or given a hoot about those weaknesses in the COPOH case. As the late and much-loved television *Jeopardy* game show host Alex Trebek often said: "No harm, no foul."

## 4. *Answering the Concern That the Disability Amendment Would Cost Too Much*

The appendix to COPOH's brief gave a comprehensive answer to any fear that the disability amendment should be rejected because it would cost too much:

> The fearful spectre of a court interpreting non-discrimination because of disability in the Constitution to mean that suddenly all buildings, airplanes, train coaches, ferries, bus systems, and so on in Canada are in violation of the Constitution because they are not accessible to persons in wheelchairs has been suggested. We are familiar with this phantom. We find these fears even humorous at times, such as, for example, during the time of the last government when the minister of justice, in trying to explain the continuing delay in improving the Canadian *Human Rights Act* to our benefit, as had been promised in a letter to us by the former prime minister, suggested that the *Human Rights Act* amendment would mean all telephone books would have to be published in Braille. Of course, part of the humour lies in the fact that such a Braille telephone book would be almost completely unusable and would fill a large room.
>
> In this example, of course, the concept of "program access" (to which I will return later) is already at work giving disabled Canadians free access to telephone company operator assistance information services, which is an easy, inexpensive, and usable alternative. This spectre begins to evaporate with close critical examination. First, we must give judges and lawyers credit for being human and part of our social fabric. This spectre of impossible

> overnight change seems to imply that the courts exist in a vacuum outside of our human social experience.[25]

COPOH argued that the reasonable limits clause in section 1 of the *Charter* would protect against the "spectre of future bankruptcy because of a court order for universal and complete wheelchair accessibility."[26] Of interest, the COPOH brief's appendix argued that section 1 would also protect against other similar excessive claims, such as a claim that a ban on sex discrimination requires that fathers should be entitled to paid maternity leave, not just mothers.[27] Of course, we now know that, far from an absurdity, paid paternity leave is now a reality, in no small part because of a recognition of gender equality.

COPOH argued that courts could rely on the Joint Committee's proceedings as an aid to interpret the *Charter*. To calm any fears of excessive costs, the appendix to COPOH's brief stated: "For our part, we are intentionally articulating the position that including 'disability' in 15.1 of the Charter of Rights and Freedoms will not result in the imposition of catastrophic or unreasonable costs by the courts on society."[28] I fully understand COPOH's tactical thinking in the heat of that moment. Yet no one is bound for all time by what COPOH then stated. The Supreme Court of Canada ruled in an early decision (one that involved no disability issues) that statements by public officials during the Joint Committee proceedings, while admissible, get little weight as a guide to interpreting the *Charter*.[29]

If the statements of the government's legal advisors get little weight on what the *Charter* was meant to achieve, the statements to the Joint Committee in the appendix to a brief by a community group might not get any more weight. Although irrelevant here, I happened to be co-counsel to the attorney general for Ontario on that Supreme Court case. In that case, Ontario, among other governments, tried to get the Supreme Court of Canada to place significant weight on what senior public servants told the

---

25 COPOH, *Brief to the Special Joint Parliamentary Committee on the Constitution* (November 1980) at i, Appendix: On Cost/Definition and Other Objections to the Inclusion of Disability or Handicap in 15(1) of the Proposed Canadian Charter of Rights and Freedoms [COPOH Appendix].

26 *Ibid.*

27 *Ibid.*

28 *Ibid* at ii.

29 *Re BC Motor Vehicle Act*, [1985] 2 SCR 486 at paras 35–53, [1985] SCJ No 73 (QL).

Joint Committee. The Supreme Court of Canada ended up interpreting a *Charter* provision in a manner that directly contradicted what those public servants had told the Joint Committee.[30] But I digress. As a further response to the fear of an enormous cost, COPOH's appendix argued:

> The nucleus of the disruptive costs argument is the fear that existing equipment and facilities would have to be immediately retrofitted for wheelchair accessibility. This must be so as wheelchair accessibility is generally accepted to add only 0.5% to total project cost if incorporated into the design or planning stage in the development of new equipment and facilities. Since all equipment and facilities must be, sooner or later, replaced with new, the obvious direction to take is to ensure non-discriminating accessible design in all new equipment and facilities and then to carefully limit the application of non-discrimination legislation to what is reasonable in the area of retrofitting what already exists. The Human Rights Acts with their accompanying administrative criteria and interpretive regulations which we have described, take just this direction, mandating the very inexpensive non-discriminating accessible design for new buildings and so on; and limiting the application of their protection vis-à-vis existing facilities with safe-guarding clauses and phrases such as "exempt from compliance because of undue hardship" and "reasonable accommodation."[31]

How things have changed! In arguing against objections to the disability amendment on the grounds that it would cost too much, COPOH advanced an argument in 1980 that today would be met with strong objections from many in the disability community. COPOH's appendix contended that access to services may be sufficient if provided through alternative means rather than through the mainstream. For example, it asserted that para-transit services may be a sufficient means of access rather than through conventional public transit. COPOH also contended that, over time, services are expected to evolve to include effectively serving people with disabilities.[32] With the benefit of more than 40 years of experience since then, I can state with confidence that such a "separate-but-equal" view, which is usually anything but equal in many cases, is now, at best, only accepted as a temporary transition to full equality. For example, decades later, para-transit services remain separate, but far from equal, for public transit passengers with disabilities.

30 *Ibid.*

31 COPOH Appendix, *supra* note 26 at vi.

32 *Ibid* at vi–vii.

Here is how COPOH addressed this in its brief's appendix:

> Disabled people by the very nature of their disabilities often require a different kind of access to a given program or service than is required by the public at large. Protection from discrimination because of disability in the provision of goods, services, facilities and accommodation has to do with access to the provision of these. It does not specify what form this access should take. The suggestion of a Braille telephone book may well be an obvious form of access for those who are unfamiliar with the needs of disabled people and the means of meeting these needs, but it is in fact, as has been shown earlier, not a useful or valuable means of access to telephone book information for the disabled person. The far less expensive and more useful access to this information can be had from the operator.
>
> This kind of easy and inexpensive, common-sense access to a difficult drinking fountain in the South Block of the Parliament Hill complex was intended by Canadian Human Rights Commissioner Gordon Fairweather when he recommended the provision of a 500 box of paper cups nearby.
>
> Similarly, elevators, ramps and new rolling stock may be the obvious means of access for wheelchair users to the Toronto Transit System to a person ignorant of the real needs of disabled people and the means of meeting these needs. In fact, access to the public transit service for disabled people is often far better achieved by the provision of a parallel door-to-door special public transportation service, and this form of program access is already provided in Toronto. A government office offering service to the public in some instances may have to be on the fifth floor of a building without an elevator. Program access can be achieved for disabled citizens by a system wherein the disabled person telephones prior to arriving at the building and is met on the ground floor by the government official who will then supply the information or other service his office makes available to the public. Of course, over time, as more and more disabled people participate in society and make demands of services, services will evolve to provide easier and simpler forms of access to the public at large including disabled people, who are part of the public. The importance of the amendment we recommend to you is that with its passage, disabled people would have the constitutional right not to be discriminated against in employment and the provision of goods, services, accommodation and facilities. The means of access to this employment and so on will of course have to be a reasonable and cost effective one.[33]

In an attempt to calm concerns about the cost issue, COPOH contended in its appendix that some changes were already budgeted for, such as retrofitting

---

33 *Ibid.*

the federal government's facilities.[34] An especially cruel irony was COPOH's optimism that Via Rail was addressing the need to ensure that new passenger train cars were accessible:

> It is also interesting to note that VIA Rail in its orders for new passenger rail cars has already specified that they be designed in such a manner as to be accessible to wheelchair users.
>
> It is also interesting to note that VIA Rail which originally had pled undue financial hardship, when forced by the Canadian Transport Commission last spring to provide reasonable access to wheelchair users at all its major stations across Canada, found that the total cost of renovating these stations and providing lifts was well under 3% of the subsidy they receive in one year from the Canadian taxpayer and that this cost would be pro-rated over many years use and would benefit 5% of the Canadian public for many years to come. This was hardly an unreasonable cost, considering the public benefit that accrued.[35]

Why is this a cruel irony? 37 years later, COPOH, renamed the Council of Canadians with Disabilities, would take VIA Rail to the Supreme Court of Canada over this very issue. In *Council of Canadians with Disabilities v VIA Rail Canada*, the Supreme Court held that VIA Rail had violated federal disability anti-discrimination requirements by purchasing less accessible passenger train cars to replace older more accessible ones.[36] I was ecstatic when the Supreme Court cited with approval a law journal article that I had authored that explains why it violates human rights requirements to create new accessibility barriers.[37]

COPOH's appendix drew on an argument that many disability advocates would use over the years. It argued that guaranteeing equality to people with disabilities would enable them to transition to being taxpayers, contributing to our economy, and away from receiving social assistance from our economy. In an attempt to show that it is unfair to hold cost concerns

---

34 *Ibid* at vii.

35 *Ibid.*

36 *Council of Canadians with Disabilities v VIA Rail Canada Inc*, 2007 SCC 15, [2007] 1 SCR 650.

37 *Ibid* at paras 178, 181; M David. Lepofsky, "Federal Court of Appeal De-Rails Equality Rights for Persons with Disabilities — *Via Rail v Canadian Transportation Agency* and the Important Duty Not to Create New Barriers to Accessibility" (2005–2006) 18 NJCL 169; M David Lepofsky, "The Duty to Accommodate: A Purposive Approach" (1993) 1 Canadian Labour LJ 1.

against people with disabilities, COPOH also contended that the cost of guaranteeing sex equality would be much higher than the cost of disability equality.[38] Synthesizing these written responses in its oral presentation to the Joint Committee, Derksen summed up why cost is not a good reason for not including equality for people with disabilities:

> This seems to be based on the idea that simply to place disability or handicap in Section 15(1) without any limiting clauses might result in the courts imposing disruptive change on our society: for example, that all buildings without elevators be equipped with elevators.
>
> Now, we see that religion, sex and age are also included in that section without any limiting clauses. We see that Section 1 or Section 15(3) as proposed by the Human Rights Commission, would allow the courts to interpret the reasonableness or the justifiable necessity of limiting that protection from discrimination for age, sex and religion.
>
> Sections 1 and 15(3) would make possible an interpretation, in regard to protection from discrimination on the basis of age, by the courts that would uphold 18 as the minimum age for, say, the purchase of liquor, firearms, voting in federal elections. There seems to be a misunderstanding that there is no comparable limiting clauses in existing statutes and no comparable precedents in existing case law to limit reasonably, where justifiably necessary, that right to protection from discrimination.
>
> In our appendix, we point out the fact that seven provincial human rights commissions and the Acts that they administer include limiting kinds of clauses which take into account undue hardship for the vendor of a service; which take into account the need for the employer to require bona fide occupational requirements; which take into account and allow a mechanism whereby the commission or tribunal can determine reasonable qualifications to the right.
>
> Now, all of these things are in place. The courts will not have to. We will not desire that in a vacuum in interpreting the constitutional protection for disabled people from discrimination.
>
> We believe that those mediating mechanisms which are already in place will enable an orderly process of change to a point where disabled people would not be discriminated against in the provision of goods, services and in their endeavour to achieve employment and so on.
>
> We believe, in fact, and this has been shown by the strong economies of Northern Europe, that enabling disabled people to participate in society would be an extremely cost-effective course of action for this country to take.

---

[38] COPOH Appendix, *supra* note 26 at vii–viii.

> We know that in Sweden technical aids are made available to disabled people who require them for employment and for independent living within the community. The same is true in West Germany.
>
> We believe the cost argument which underlies much of the resistance or objections to the inclusion of disability in the constitution is not a real one.[39]

## 5. *Answering the Argument That It Is Too Hard to Define Disability*

COPOH's brief and oral presentation also fully answered any concern that it was hard to define the term "disability" or "handicap." Its brief's appendix set out the definitions of disability in the Canadian *Human Rights Act* and provincial anti-discrimination legislation in Quebec. It set out the definition of physical disability in anti-discrimination statutes in New Brunswick, Manitoba, Prince Edward Island, Nova Scotia, and Saskatchewan. It quoted the definition of "physical characteristic" in Alberta's anti-discrimination legislation.[40] COPOH argued that similarities in these definitions show a consensus on how to define disability. Moreover, it argued that experience with those human rights protections shows that including disability in the *Charter*'s equality rights provision provides for its sensible implementation and not a "cataclysmic" result.[41]

COPOH addressed the objection to these definitions in its oral presentation. Kanary stated:

> Mr. Chrétien indicated in your committee meeting of Wednesday, November 12, in response to a question from Mr. Bockstael that the difficulty in adding "handicap" to the list of prohibited grounds was one of drafting a precise legal definition for incorporation into the *Charter*.
>
> In our view, the *Charter of Rights and Freedoms* is not an appropriate place for definitions. Neither is it necessary to define disability or handicap or degree of these in the proposed *Charter*. We note that it has not been necessary to define "religion" in the *Charter*, despite the plain fact that we will continue to discriminate against religions which practice human sacrifice.[42]

---

39 *Minutes of Proceedings, 25 November 1980, supra* note 20 at 38–39.

40 COPOH Appendix, *supra* note 26 at ii–v.

41 *Ibid* at v–vi.

42 *Minutes of Proceedings, 25 November 1980, supra* note 20 at 27–30.

Derksen argued:

> [I]n our brief we call on those who object to the inclusion of handicapped in the constitution to come up with demonstrably clear and justifiable sound objections, not merely the kind of vague implications or references to drafting and definitional problems. The definitions exist; they are very similar from one jurisdiction to another, which tells us that they have been tested and that they work.
>
> We believe that Chief Commissioner, Gordon Fairweather, has a good deal of experience in administering protection from discrimination for disabled people. We think that his opinion should carry a lot of weight here.[43]

## 6. *Answering a Grab Bag of Other Arguments against the Disability Amendment*

It has been my experience time and again that, when an organization wants to positively address a disability issue, they usually find a way. On the other hand, if they do not want to, they devote time and energy to conjuring up the most bizarre mix of arguments to justify their desire to do nothing. COPOH felt that it had to respond to a mix of other arguments against the disability amendment. This illustrates the kind of push-back they either encountered or feared. COPOH answered a suggestion by the justice minister that adding disability to the *Charter* should be put off to sometime after Canada's Constitution has been patriated. Speaking for COPOH, Kanary told the Joint Committee:

> We wish to note that, indeed, the inclusion of the entire *Charter* could wait until such a time-but in fact as Mr. Chrétien indicated on page 77 of *Proceedings* for the Committee meeting of November 13, there are some reasons why entrenching a *Charter of Rights and Freedoms* for all Canadians should be done now. We believe these reasons also apply for the inclusion of handicap in Section 15(1) now, and not after patriation.[44]

COPOH's appendix responded to a concern that protection for equality for people with disabilities under the *Charter* might be less than the protections otherwise available in law. COPOH said that, if this is a real risk, the same risk also exists for all others whom section 15 would protect from discrimination on other grounds such as race or sex.[45] It was oxymoronic

43 *Ibid* at 38–39.

44 *Ibid* at 30–31.

45 COPOH Appendix, *supra* note 26 at viii.

for anyone to fear that courts would be so liberal in implementing equality for people with disabilities as to bankrupt Canada (a worry that COPOH earlier refuted), on the one hand, while fearing that courts would be too restrictive in implementing disability equality, on the other hand. COPOH responded to a concern that one's race or sex is innate while some disabilities are self-inflicted, such as a disability arising from an attempted suicide.[46] In my decades of disability advocacy, I had thought that I had heard every argument under the sun against disability equality. Before reading COPOH's brief, I had never heard this especially outlandish one.

COPOH correctly responded that all people with disabilities should be protected by the *Charter*'s equality rights provision, including people with self-inflicted disabilities.[47] COPOH's appendix also accurately noted that most suicides result from severe depression, itself a disability, emphasizing: "A person who is unjustly discriminated against because of any degree of disability is still unjustly discriminated against and deserves protection from this."[48] COPOH's appendix rejected any suggestion that lesser or minor forms of disability should not be protected. Its appendix noted that discrimination because of one's colour should be prohibited even if a person's skin is a lighter shade of black.[49] COPOH emphasized that protecting people with disabilities from discrimination does not extend any privilege to them.[50] As I noted earlier, this was a theme that I was later to find I had to emphasize in my own advocacy in support of the disability amendment.

## 7. *COPOH's Additional and Sundry Arguments in Support of the Disability Amendment*

COPOH emphasized the international dimension of the case in favour of the disability amendment. Kanary told the Joint Committee:

> Mr. Fairweather and others have spoken to your Committee about the advantages of fitting the *Canadian Charter of Rights and Freedoms* to the international context including the international covenants Canada is party to.
>
> We call your attention to the fact that Canada was one of fifty co-movers at the United Nations at the Universal Declaration of the Rights of Disabled

46 *Ibid.*

47 *Ibid.*

48 *Ibid* at ix.

49 *Ibid* at viii.

50 *Ibid* at ix.

> People in 1976. Canada was also one of two co-movers of the resolution in the United Nations which established 1981 as the International Year of Disabled Persons with the themes of full participation and equality. Including handicap in Section 15(1) of the proposed *Charter* would be a good demonstration that our domestic actions are in line with the policies we are promoting in the world.[51]

COPOH drew attention to the fact that disability affects people from all walks of life. It eventually extends to people who now have no disability at all. Kanary told the Joint Committee: "As you can see by our delegation, disabled Canadians are also men and women, Mennonite, French. Irish, and so on; indeed disabled Canadians are all colours, races, religions and ethnic origins. For this reason, our concerns about the proposed *Charter* naturally go far beyond the inclusion of 'handicap' in Section 15(1)."[52] He added:

> Some disabled people in Canada apply the label TAB to Canadians without disabilities. TAB is an acronym for temporarily able-bodied and is used to remind society that disability is a condition which can occur to anyone at any time, at any level of society. Transport Canada's demographic study indicates that 34 percent of all persons who reach the age of 80 are disabled in relation to mobility. It may be useful to think of the amendment we propose as a kind of insurance or assurance. It is in fact an assurance that the society we live in will continue to progress toward a society which is supportive and open to the continued participation of people who are or become disabled. It is an assurance that in the event of disability, one will not be relegated to inferior education, low income and the poverty of experience and lifestyle symbolized by the institutional residence and attached historically to the condition of disability.[53]

The fact that students with disabilities face so many barriers in the education system became part of the case for the disability amendment that COPOH presented. One member of parliament on the Joint Committee who also served on the Smith Committee invited COPOH to speak to barriers that students with disabilities can face in the education system, noting:

> **Mr. Young:** … I used to think in this country that the rights to education were a principle, and yet we have experienced over the summer months, and in listening to people, we have discovered that there are thousands of kids across this country who are disabled or handicapped in one form or another who are denied access to education, so we are not only talking about access to

51 *Minutes of Proceedings, 25 November 1980*, *supra* note 20 at 30–31.

52 *Ibid.*

53 *Ibid* at 31.

> education, we are talking about accommodation, transportation and other goods and services that, as I say, we take for granted.[54]

Peters replied:

> I think that what you have said is very true, that disabled people need to have equal access to education. Unfortunately, that is not always the case. There are not only architectural barriers that can get in the way, there are needs for facilities such as sign language interpreters for deaf people and access to Braille material and so on for blind people. If we go back to the constitution, what we look to from the constitution is a document that will set a tone for disabled persons in this country so that we can build legislation, or at least use it as a foundation to build legislation so that we can start improving things like educational opportunities and we can start providing equal access in necessary facilities and so on.[55]

COPOH directly addressed the possibility of an irrational fear about what equality for people with disabilities might mean. COPOH expressed a clear vision of what the disability amendment was hoping to achieve:

> [W]e look to the Constitution for a final recognition that disabled Canadians are in fact Canadians as well and that the Constitution, hopefully, will set a mood so that we can become included in the planning and decision making process over the coming years; so that we could allow for adequate housing, and support services for individuals who require such services, and the many other services, accommodations and facilities which we are presently being denied. We are looking for the Constitution to set a tone so that changes may come about, not overnight but over a period of years, that we can become fully integrated and active and contributing as a force of people in society.[56]

Speaking for COPOH, Derksen added:

> I want to follow that up by saying that presently disabled people and their problems are often viewed through a very biased cloud of emotional responses. This has resulted in a situation which has become clear to the Special Committee on the Handicapped and Disabled wherein the people are institutionalized at 20, 30 or 40,000 dollars a year, where they could be integrated in the community if they had, say, five thousand dollars worth of support services.
>
> Now, it is economically sound to de-institutionalize most disabled people who are presently in institutions.

[54] *Ibid* at 35–36.

[55] *Ibid* at 36.

[56] *Ibid* at 36–37.

> There has also been a kind of emotional reaction to our call for human rights based upon fear that human rights for disabled Canadians will somehow have a disruptive effect on our society.
>
> We have shown in the appendix to our brief that that fear is really not based upon any sound reasoning, and that it is an unnecessary fear generated out of the kind of bias and emotion that people feel within themselves when confronted by disabled people.
>
> What we need is a clear-minded, objective approach to our problems; and that approach, I would suggest, starts with an articulation that disabled people are Canadians and should have the right to protection from discrimination as a matter of Canadian heritage or, if you like, of constitutional right.[57]

## 8. COPOH's Troubling Internal Debate over Whether to Seek Equality for People with All Disabilities or Only Those with Physical Disabilities

In 1980, COPOH had an internal debate over whether it should ask Parliament to include all people with disabilities in section 15 or only people with physical disabilities. Peters described this in her book chapter: "The COPOH also built alliances with other disability rights groups. Of particular importance was the alliance established with the then Canadian Association of the Mentally Retarded, now known as the Canadian Association for Community Living." The discussion between the two organizations centred on whether to push for the inclusion of both physical and mental disability in the *Charter* or to restrict the campaign to physical disability. Some people were concerned that combining mental disability with physical disability would weaken the chance for success for persons with physical disabilities. However, other people recognized that disability, no matter what the origin, was largely a product of social attitudes and systemic barriers. As a result, after much discussion, it was decided that both organizations would advocate as a united front for both physical and mental disability.[58]

It is of course very good that COPOH's written brief to the Joint Committee and its oral presentation to the Joint Committee on 25 November 1980 called for disability or handicap to be added to section 15. This was not limited to persons with physical disabilities. It is troubling that COPOH had any internal debate over this in 1980. Today, the Council of Canadians

57 *Ibid* at 37.

58 Peters, *supra* note 12 at 128–129.

with Disabilities, the current incarnation of COPOH, would never even consider this subject as requiring any internal deliberation or debate, according to my experience with them over the years. In cross-disability advocacy efforts in which I have been involved over the decades, a core priority has been to ensure that no disability gets left behind. We advocate together. We advocate for each other. We are stronger when we speak in support of each other's needs. When a blind person talks about the need for sign language, or a deaf person talks about the need for ramps instead of stairs, or a person using a wheelchair talks about the need for Braille, the message is clear that our cause is a unified, shared one.

There are, of course, times when an identifiable disability group will understandably and justifiably advocate for a specific measure they need. However, on something as momentous and as once in a lifetime as the enactment of a constitutional charter of rights, the notion of seeking equality for people with some disabilities but not others is utterly wrong. Moreover, as a practical matter, disabilities do not come in a watertight siloed package. There are many people who have a combination of mental and physical disabilities. Their disability-related needs, like an omelet, are not easily unscrambled.

It is a credit to COPOH that it decided to do the right thing on this score. It is puzzling that, well after COPOH went on the record, calling for all disabilities to be included in section 15, it sent a telegram to the Joint Committee that called for "physical handicap" to be added to section 15. The telegram from COPOH's national chairperson, Allan Simpson, on 9 January 1981 stated:

> COPOH, the Canadian Coalition of Provincial Organization of the Handicapped, represented Canadians with all kinds of physical disabilities across Canada, respectfully urges you to recommend an amendment to the proposed *Charter of Rights and Freedoms* so as to include physical handicap as a prohibited reason for discrimination under Section 15 sub section 1 of the proposed Act.
>
> It is our position that "clearly demonstrable and justifiably sound objections" to this amendment have not yet been brought forward by either government or any witness before the special Joint Parliamentary Committee on the Constitution on which you serve. The honorable Jean Chrétien's concern as to the unavailability of a workable definition suggested to you on November 12 1980 was, we believe, amply refuted by our presentation of November 25 1980 which listed nine example definitions already found in Canadian human rights legislation in various jurisdictions.

> It is now a widely held conviction that protection from discrimination is the single most important issue facing Canadians with disabilities today. We, therefore, anticipate further consideration of this matter in the Committee's discussions with the honorable Jean Chrétien this week and in its final deliberations on the proposed *Charter* prior to February 6th. We ask for your support.[59]

This telegram was dated a month and a half after COPOH spoke at the Joint Committee and a mere 3 days before Justice Minister Jean Chrétien was to give his all-important speech to the Joint Committee, outlining which amendments to the *Charter* the Trudeau government would approve (a speech that I discuss at length in Chapter XIV. I have no idea why COPOH's national chairperson would deviate in this telegram from COPOH's earlier position. Moreover, this telegram refers to the appendix included in COPOH's brief, which itself sets out definitions of disability that, in some cases, included both physical and mental disabilities. This may have been sloppy drafting in that 9 January 1981 telegram.

In the end, this odd telegram did not change the outcome. The Joint Committee eventually adopted the disability amendment, including both mental and physical disability.

## D. Postscript: A Dramatic Public Statement to the Joint Committee by David Smith, Chair of the Smith Committee

On 25 November 1980, an extraordinary event took place at the end of COPOH's presentation to the Joint Committee. Member of Parliament David Smith made this statement to the Joint Committee:

> The members of the Committee will be aware that I am the Chairman of the Special Committee for the Disabled and the Handicapped; and one point I would like to make is that we have had an opportunity of hearing over 600 witnesses right across Canada in 8 different cities and it is quite clear to us that COPO which is represented here today by four very articulate people, is in fact the voice of disabled people in this country. They are very legitimate spokespersons for the disabled community and their headquarters is in Winnipeg. They are well organized and have been most helpful to the work of the Committee.
>
> I thought it might be useful to give just a brief background as to the position of the Committee on the constitution. The first report was really primarily released

[59] Telegram sent from Allan Simpson, National Chairperson of COPOH, to Senator Hays (9 January 1981).

> prior to our final report which will be coming out at the end of the year in order to make our position known on it. This is found in the third paragraph of the first page. It is one sentence, and there was considerable discussion about it, but that presents the unanimous position of the all-party committee. I believe it has already been read by Dr. Lang but it is only one sentence: "Should it be the will of Parliament to entrench human rights in a patriated constitution, your Committee believes that full and equal protection should be provided for persons with physical or mental handicaps."
>
> I think it is important to point out that it would be unreasonable to conclude that if specific reference is not included that somehow the constitution will not cover disabled Canadians.
>
> It is quite clear to me that it will cover everyone, but I think that our Committee was of the viewpoint that we wanted the clearest possible indication that disabled Canadians are in fact covered and all their rights are protected.
>
> Now, I appreciate that there is some concern over the question of definition and what is reasonable. There has of course been legislative precedent in Canada in the Human Rights Act. I am not aware of any difficulties that have been encountered in the interpretation the courts have given to the reference in the Human Rights Act concerning disabled Canadians.
>
> I know that there is also the concern about, well, once specific reference is given to one minority group, does this open the Floodgates to all minority groups? I think it could be argued that the rationale that prompted the reference to disabled Canadians in the Human Rights Act would also exist in the case of the constitution.
>
> Those are really the points that I wish to make. Mr. Chairman, I appreciate your definition problems but this is the position of the Committee and I wanted to reinforce the conclusions of the Committee.[60]

How I wish I had known about Smith's statement when I was preparing for my presentation to the Joint Committee some 2 weeks later. He blew out of the water most of the government's arguments against the disability amendment. Only one line in his statement could give rise to concern: "I think it is important to point out that it would be unreasonable to conclude that if specific reference is not included that somehow the constitution will not cover disabled Canadians."[61] That was perhaps aimed at calming some of his Liberal caucus members. It nevertheless did not undermine the core thrust of his compelling statement.

---

60 *Ibid* at 42–43.

61 *Ibid* at 43.

## E. Who Else in the Broader Community Endorsed the Disability Amendment?

In any public advocacy effort, it helps to have allies. It would have been helpful for me to know whether anyone else speaking before the Joint Committee had endorsed our call for the disability amendment. This was not easy to do. If only someone would have been nice enough to invent the Internet a couple of decades earlier! A few Google searches would have solved my problem. The only way an organization like the CNIB, far removed from Ottawa's Capitol Hill, could do this was to watch the entire televised Joint Committee proceedings whenever they were on the air. Its schedule varied week to week. I, for one, had to study for my bar admissions exams as much as hours of those hearings would have been a thrilling suspense-filled distraction! It would be a few years before I would buy a video cassette recorder, then an emerging kind of consumer electronic, so I could record programs. Without one, you had to watch the hearings live if you knew when they would air or catch a rerun if you had any way to find them! We had no other way to archive video for later viewing if you did not work for a television network.

Contrast that almost four decades later with my much easier and more fulsome preparation to appear in October 2018 before a House of Commons standing committee to make submissions on Bill C-81, the proposed *Accessible Canada Act.*[62] That standing committee's official Hansard transcript was posted online within hours or days after each meeting. These can easily be read online, searched, or downloaded. The video of the standing committee was streamed live and quickly archived online, making it accessible for instant viewing from anywhere with a few clicks. When a cabinet minister spoke to such hearings, I could analyze it and post a detailed analysis of it online within a day. Social media and email blitzing spreads the word to thousands in no time and at no cost.

In dramatic contrast to 1980 when I was doing most, if not all, of my advocacy on the disability amendment on my own steam, I had the benefit in 2018 of an amazing team of volunteer law students from Osgoode Hall Law School helping me prepare for my standing committee appearance. They summarized each standing committee meeting for me, keeping me right up to date. As well, when time permitted, I could and did read any of

---

62 *Accessible Canada Act*, SC 2019, c 10.

the hearing transcripts myself, without needing a sighted reader to read them aloud to me. The hearing transcripts were posted online in an accessible format. I could download and read them at home, in a hotel, or in transit, either using my laptop computer or trusty iPhone. My laptop is loaded with a sophisticated screen-reading program. Every iPhone comes with a free dashboard screen-reading program called Voiceover.

Four decades earlier, the formal transcripts of each meeting of the Joint Committee were produced in hard copy documents that I could not read myself unassisted. Moreover, the turnaround time for their hard copy production was no doubt longer than the production of the online Hansard today. In 1980, I would need to get my hands on a hard copy of a volume of Hansard. That alone was a major challenge. I would then need to line up a sighted volunteer to read them aloud to me. That was another daunting challenge, given the demands on the time of sighted volunteer CNIB readers and the backlog of requests for books to be recorded on tape. Commercially produced audio books were years in the future. Even if I had a team of volunteer readers on stand by in 1980, I would have to get the Hansard transcripts to them and, thereafter, get the recorded audio tapes from the readers to me. Who would have thought that you eventually would be able to quickly download an MP3 recording from the Internet?

Despite all of these impediments, I knew in 1980 that the Joint Committee had heard presentations that supported the disability amendment. I referred to this in my deputation to the Joint Committee on 12 December 1980. You'll get there in Chapter XIII. The disability amendment was supported in one form or another by the Canadian Human Rights Commission,[63] the Canadian Jewish Congress (referring to their earlier submission to the Smith Committee, of which I had been part, as discussed in Chapter IX),[64] the Mennonite Central Committee,[65] the Canadian Council

---

63 Canada, Parliament, *Minutes of Proceedings and Evidence of the Special Joint Committee of the Senate and of the House of Commons on the Constitution of Canada*, 32nd Parl, 1st Sess, No 5 (14 November 1980) at 8.

64 Canada, Parliament, *Minutes of Proceedings and Evidence of the Special Joint Committee of the Senate and of the House of Commons on the Constitution of Canada*, 32nd Parl, 1st Sess, No 7 (18 November 1980) at 93.

65 *Minutes of Proceedings, 25 November 1980*, *supra* note 20 at 45.

on Social Development,[66] New Brunswick Premier Richard Hatfield,[67] the Canadian Council on Children and Youth,[68] the Coalition for the Protection of Human Life,[69] the Canadian Citizenship Federation,[70] the United Church of Canada,[71] the National Black Coalition of Canada,[72] the British Columbia Civil Liberties Association,[73] and the New Brunswick Human Rights Commission.[74] In its presentation to the Joint Committee on 25 November 1980, COPOH said that the Canadian Labour Congress and the Royal Canadian Legion also supported the disability amendment.[75]

A number of presenters at the Joint Committee spoke explicitly in terms of covering physical or mental disability. Unfortunately, some only talked about physical disability. I was not aware of this at the time. Reading those transcripts now, I do not get the sense that those who mention only physical disability in each case consciously wanted to exclude mental disability. They offered no reasons or arguments why physical disability should be added while mental disability should continue to be left out, with the exception of the Saskatchewan Human Rights Commission, whose aberrant position is put under my own kind of microscope in Chapter XI.

---

66 Canada, Parliament, *Minutes of Proceedings and Evidence of the Special Joint Committee of the Senate and of the House of Commons on the Constitution of Canada*, 32nd Parl, 1st Sess, No 19 (4 December 1980) at 29.

67 *Ibid* at 49.

68 *Minutes of Proceedings, 8 December 1980*, *supra* note 5 at 31.

69 Canada, Parliament, *Minutes of Proceedings and Evidence of the Special Joint Committee of the Senate and of the House of Commons on the Constitution of Canada*, 32nd Parl, 1st Sess, No 22 (9 December 1980) at 26–27 [*Minutes of Proceedings, 9 December 1980*].

70 Canada, Parliament, *Minutes of Proceedings and Evidence of the Special Joint Committee of the Senate and of the House of Commons on the Constitution of Canada*, 32nd Parl, 1st Sess, No 29 (18 December 1980) at 53.

71 *Ibid* at 81.

72 *Minutes of Proceedings, 9 December 1980*, *supra* note 70 at 10.

73 *Ibid* at 110–11.

74 Canada, Parliament, *Minutes of Proceedings and Evidence of the Special Joint Committee of the Senate and of the House of Commons on the Constitution of Canada*, 32nd Parl, 1st Sess, No 11 (24 November 1980) at 35–36, 42.

75 *Minutes of Proceedings, 25 November 1980*, *supra* note 20 at 27. I have not found any documentation on this with regards to the last two groups.

The Canadian *Human Rights Act* was enacted in 1977, just 3 years earlier.[76] It included a ban on discrimination because of physical disability but not mental disability.[77] That law prohibited discrimination because of physical disability only in the area of employment and not in any of the other important economic activities that this new federal human rights legislation covered.[78] As a federal law, it regulated discrimination only in federally regulated organizations like the Government of Canada itself, banks, airlines, and telecommunication companies.[79] It was up to provincial human rights laws to address discrimination in the vast majority of other organizations in Canada, which the provinces could regulate. It would be some time after the constitutional patriation battle before the Canadian *Human Rights Act* would be amended to cover both physical and mental disability and to extend protection from disability discrimination to all economic activity that the Act addressed.[80] Justice Minister Chrétien told the Joint Committee hearings that the federal government was then considering proposals to this effect. Before the *Charter* was enacted, and certainly before the disability amendment was adopted, the federal government had not committed to make those amendments to broaden the Canadian *Human Rights Act*.

76 *Human Rights Act*, SC 1976–1977, c 33.

77 *Ibid*, ss 2(a), 3.

78 *Ibid*, ss 2(a), 3.

79 *Ibid*, s 2.

80 *Canadian Human Rights Act*, RSC 1985, c H-6, ss 2, 3(1).

# XI. TROUBLING ARGUMENTS FROM THE MOST UNLIKELY SOURCES

## A. Background to a Little-Known Troubling Part of this Saga

While this saga was unfolding, others presented three arguments to the Special Joint Committee of the Senate and the House of Commons on the Constitution of Canada (Joint Committee), which, if accepted, would have created serious problems for those of us campaigning for the disability amendment. Whether or not they meant or wanted to create these obstacles, their arguments did just that. Thankfully, those arguments all flopped. Brace yourself for a quick, deep, and hopefully painless plunge into constitutional law. When Parliament was struggling to figure out how to word the equality provision of the *Canadian Charter of Rights and Freedoms*, several meaty, important, and potentially overlapping issues arose.[1] Two of them became especially important to our fight for the disability amendment.

First, what grounds of discrimination should section 15 prohibit? In other words, who will be protected from discrimination? Second, if someone proves that the government engaged in discrimination prohibited by the *Charter*, what kinds of justifications, if any, should a government be able to present to a court to successfully defend its conduct? Since the *Charter* was enacted, legal scholars have happily pickled themselves in these issues in law journal after law journal, conference after conference, dissertation after dissertation, and, at times, in barroom squabble after tavern tussle. However, before the constitutional patriation imbroglio, Canada's legal and public policy experts had precious little experience with these constitutional issues. We never cracked a book on them in law school before 1980.

In contrast, by 1980, the United States had decades of experience and rich scholarship on these constitutional questions, which sprang from the massive case law under the equal protection clause of the US Constitution's

1 *Canadian Charter of Rights and Freedoms*, Part 1 of the *Constitution Act, 1982*, being Schedule B to the *Canada Act 1982* (UK), 1982, c 11 [*Charter*].

14th Amendment.[2] In the fall of 1980, Canada's patriation political marathon hit the headlines so fast that there was no chance to marshal a legal academic self-education blitz on these issues. As I explained in Chapter III, Canada's legal professoriate and legal profession were not brimming with expertise in constitutional equality rights or disability rights advocacy. As well, our law schools did not ensure that law students received effective training on serving clients with disabilities or on disability-related legal issues.

## B. The First Harmful Proposal to the Joint Committee: Amend Section 15 to Eliminate Any Reference to Specific Prohibited Grounds of Discrimination

### *1. Who Advocated for This Position and Why*

Several well-meaning but ill-informed organizations harmfully urged the Joint Committee to rewrite section 15 in order to strip out of it any and all specific prohibited grounds of discrimination. They wanted this provision to simply say that it guarantees the right to equality. It should not name any of the grounds of discrimination that it prohibits, they contended. Those pressing for this change to section 15 appeared to feel that equality should be a right that everyone enjoys. It was wrong to just list some discrimination grounds, to the exclusion of others, they thought. For them, the quick fix was for section 15 to list no grounds at all. They certainly were not driven by any opposition to equality rights for people with disabilities.

For reasons I will expand upon shortly, this would have been horrible for us. It would have let politicians duck our call for the disability amendment. They could just state that they would love to add disability to the list but there was no longer a list of prohibited grounds of discrimination in section 15 to which disability could be added. Who pressed for this? Ironic as it now seems, this argument that was so harmful from a disability perspective came from some leading equality-seeking organizations. The most influential of these was the Canadian Human Rights Commission, represented by its widely respected first chief commissioner, Gordon

---

2 See Laurence H Tribe, *American Constitutional Law*, 2nd ed (Mineola, NY: Foundation Press, 1988) at 1436–1672, 930–964, 1297–1320 [Tribe, *American Constitutional Law*, 2nd ed] (for more information on the 14th Amendment).

Fairweather.[3] Endorsing them were, among others, the Canadian Jewish Congress[4] and the Canadian Federation of Civil Liberties and Human Rights Associations.[5] Fortunately for us, a number of the organizations pressing this view also proposed a fall-back second option: if section 15 were to include a list of forbidden grounds of discrimination, they contended that this list should be expanded to include people with disabilities.[6]

I got a major jolt while writing this retrospective to discover that the New Brunswick Division of the Canadian Association for the Mentally Retarded was one of the community organizations that took this harmful position. As I detailed in Chapter X, the CAMR was one of the three disability organizations that appeared before the Joint Committee with the core aim of winning the disability amendment. The CAMR's brief to the Joint Committee made a strong argument in favour of adding disability to section 15.[7] Its brief made a modest and inconsequential side reference to the possibility of merely proclaiming a right to equality, without listing any prohibited grounds of discrimination.[8] However, in a letter to the Joint Committee on 24 November 1980, the New Brunswick division of the CAMR went further, stating that its first preference was for section 15 to simply ban discrimination, without listing any forbidden grounds of discrimination.[9] That problematic letter thankfully went on to say that if section 15 were to list specific grounds of discrimination to be prohibited,

3 Canada, Parliament, *Minutes of Proceedings and Evidence of the Special Joint Committee of the Senate and of the House of Commons on the Constitution of Canada*, 32nd Parl, 1st Sess, No 5 (14 November 1980) at 8–9 [*Minutes of Proceedings, 14 November 1980*].

4 Canada, Parliament, *Minutes of Proceedings and Evidence of the Special Joint Committee of the Senate and of the House of Commons on the Constitution of Canada*, 32nd Parl, 1st Sess, No 7 (18 November 1980) at 93 [*Minutes of Proceedings, 18 November 1980*].

5 Canada, Parliament, *Minutes of Proceedings and Evidence of the Special Joint Committee of the Senate and of the House of Commons on the Constitution of Canada*, 32nd Parl, 1st Sess, No 21 (8 December 1980) at 8 [*Minutes of Proceedings, 8 December 1980*].

6 *Minutes of Proceedings, 18 November 1980*, *supra* note 4 at 93; *Minutes of Proceedings, 8 December 1980*, *supra* note 5 at 8; *Minutes of Proceedings, 14 November 1980*, *supra* note 3 at 8–9.

7 Canadian Association for the Mentally Retarded (CAMR), *Brief to the Special Committee of the House of Commons and Senate on the Resolution on Patriation of the Constitution of Canada* (10 November 1980).

8 *Ibid* at 3.

9 Letter from CAMR, New Brunswick Division, to the Joint Clerks of the Special Joint Committee on the Constitution of Canada (24 November 1980) at 3.

then disability should be included in that list.[10] That letter from the New Brunswick division of the CAMR to the Joint Committee included the following:

> In keeping with this direction, we would in many ways prefer that discrimination simply be barred by the Canadian Constitution, without any list of grounds. We believe that there should be no discrimination. Period.
>
> But if there must be a list of persons against whom there must be no discrimination, we ask that persons who are mentally retarded be included in that list.[11]

## 2. *Why It Would Hurt Disability Equality to Delete from Section 15 the Enumerated Grounds of Prohibited Discrimination*

When the government's legal team set out in the summer or early fall of 1980 to compose section 15's wording, it had to decide which grounds of discrimination to prohibit as unconstitutional. When they first put pen to paper, they had these three choices. First, section 15 could list all the grounds of discrimination that it would prohibit. It would include an exhaustive list. If a ground of discrimination, like disability, was not named in that list, then we would be left out, freezing in the constitutional cold. Second, section 15 could list absolutely no grounds of discrimination whatsoever. It would just state that everyone has the right to equality. This would dump onto the courts the entire mess of deciding on a case-by-case basis what grounds of discrimination the *Charter* would forbid and on which grounds it would be perfectly fine for governments to discriminate. Third, section 15 could list several grounds of discrimination that are prohibited, just like in the first option. However, it could be worded to also let courts recognize additional grounds of discrimination on a case-by-case basis. By this option, those who are listed as "in" can rest assured that they are protected by section 15. Those who are not in that lucky list will not know if section 15 protects them until Canada's courts finally and authoritatively rule on the question.

In October 1980, the federal government's initial draft of section 15 went for the first option. It listed seven grounds of prohibited discrimination:

---

10 CAMR, *supra* note 7 at 4.

11 *Ibid* at 3.

race, national or ethnic origin, colour, religion, age, and sex.[12] Disability was not in that list. Section 15's original wording would not let courts add any additional grounds of discrimination to that list. We were freezing out in that constitutional cold. Along came us pesky disability rights advocates in the fall of 1980, complaining that it was wrong to leave us out of section 15. What were Parliament's options once we raised that argument and once members of the Joint Committee asked questions of witnesses, concerned about the fact that disability was left out? First, Parliament could just say "no" to us, leaving section 15 as it was initially worded. We would be guaranteed that people with disabilities would have no constitutional right to equality. Second, Parliament could add disability as an eighth ground of discrimination that section 15 would prohibit but keep that list as a closed and exhaustive one. People with disabilities would win, but others who had been left out of that list, such as the LGBTQ2S+ community, would remain shivering out in the cold. Third, Parliament could remove any list of grounds of discrimination from section 15. We would be free to go to court and try to argue that the constitutional ban on discrimination included discrimination based on disability. Fourth, Parliament could refuse to explicitly add disability to the list of seven grounds of discrimination named in section 15. However, Parliament could have expanded the wording of section 15 to let courts later add additional grounds, like disability, on a case-by-case basis. First spoiler alert: the federal government tried this as its first response in early January 1981, but we were not happy and lobbied onward, as Chapter XIV reveals! Sorry to undermine the suspense. Fifth and finally, Parliament could have kept the initial list of prohibited grounds of discrimination, added disability to that list and also modified section 15's wording so that courts could later add more grounds of discrimination on a case-by-case basis. This would ensure that disability was included. It would also let courts later extend the reach of section 15 to other unenumerated equality-seeking groups. Second spoiler alert: this was where our *Charter* eventually ended up at the end of this saga.

How did these options look to us? Here is my analysis now. Before I made my presentation to the Joint Committee in December 1980, I turned my mind to only some of this. I made some arguments at the Joint Committee on this issue but discuss it here in much greater depth than I had thought of back then. The worst of all possible worlds was the one

---

12 *Ibid.*

where section 15 started in October 1980. People with disabilities had only one solid guarantee, which was that we had lost out of any bid for constitutional equality. We would be left having to fight for an amendment to the Constitution to add disability to section 15 at some future time. Our chances of that were pretty much nil. Just getting disability added to the Ontario *Human Rights Code*, an ordinary statute, was a massive multi-year ordeal that had not yet succeeded when we were immersed in the battle for the disability amendment to the *Charter*.[13]

The best of all possible worlds for us was the one for which we pressed: write disability explicitly into section 15! Only that would guarantee that we had the full protection of that provision. For us, it was less preferable for Parliament to refuse to add disability explicitly to section 15 while taking the less effective step of expanding the provision to empower courts to later add additional grounds of discrimination. With that option, we would not be guaranteed from the start that we would eventually be included, but at least we were not categorically and irreversibly excluded from the start. If the provision listed the original seven grounds of discrimination, we would at least be able to later try to argue in court that disability should be judicially added because it is analogous to those enumerated grounds as one that anti-discrimination legislation was increasingly addressing.

The option of having section 15 list no grounds of discrimination at all was better than being permanently excluded but was also the second worst of all of these options from a disability perspective. Yes, we were not guaranteed that we would be excluded. Yes, courts would have the power to later add disability. However, section 15 would include no guideposts that could help point judges to disability as a ground of discrimination that should be constitutionally forbidden. Making this worse, if Parliament deliberately chose to wipe out of section 15 the original seven grounds of discrimination, clever government lawyers would later argue in court that the very fact of this deletion while the *Charter* was being debated in Parliament signified a legislative intent that they should not serve as interpretative guideposts. We had no prior assurance that every judge, hearing that argument, would reject it.

From a disability perspective, there were two humungous problems with leaving it to the courts to add disability to section 15's list of protected grounds of discrimination. These arose if Parliament ripped all named

[13] *Human Rights Code*, RSO 1990, c H-19.

grounds out of section 15 or if it left in the original seven grounds that did not include disability while giving courts the power to add grounds like disability to that list. I was aware of only the first of these dangers in 1980. I became painfully aware of the second one in the earliest years of my law practice (both described below). First, it would burden the disability community with lawyering up and going to court for a ruling that section 15 makes it unconstitutional for government bodies to discriminate because of disability. It was not just a matter of getting any judge to rule in our favour. We needed a decisive overwhelming win in the Supreme Court of Canada. That could take years. It would cost thousands and thousands of dollars. We had no assurance that our issue would ever get to the Supreme Court of Canada. If a case made it all the way to the Supreme Court, there would be no guarantee that it would produce a categorical, unambiguous win for us. We would need a case with the most compelling facts. Bad facts can produce very bad legal rulings.

What if the first case bringing this issue to the Supreme Court of Canada had poor facts for our cause? What if the lawyer arguing that case was not up to the task? In my years of law practice, I appeared on over 30 cases in the Supreme Court. I witnessed many good lawyers in action there. I also suffered through some lawyers who were less than stellar. It can have a real impact on the case's outcome. We cannot show up at the Supreme Court and ask it to dump that case and wait until a case comes forward with better facts or a more persuasive lawyer. If the *Charter*'s wording did not make it 100 percent clear that it banned disability discrimination, it was quite predictable that government lawyers would argue in court that section 15 did not guarantee disability equality. Especially in the *Charter*'s earliest years, governments across Canada repeatedly argued in court for the most exceedingly narrow interpretation of the *Charter*.

On the expensive multi-year climb up the court ladder to the Supreme Court of Canada, there would be the danger that lower courts could rule against section 15 covering disability discrimination. If one lower court found in our favour, that would not be good enough. Other courts could take the opposite view. It was quite possible to get conflicting decisions from lower courts — one saying disability is included and another ruling that it is not. That could set back the cause of disability equality for years. It took years after 1982 for Canada's courts to get a serious handle on the *Charter*. When the *Charter* came into operation, many judges, and especially those in lower courts, were very cautious and conservative when it came to interpreting its new battery of constitutional rights. I lived through this as one of the Crown lawyers arguing constitutional cases for Ontario in the lower courts in those years.

Canada's pre-*Charter* judicial treatment of equality rights was nothing to write home about. As I discussed in Chapters II and IX, two decades before 1980, Parliament passed the *Canadian Bill of Rights*.[14] It was an ordinary statute, not part of Canada's Constitution. It guaranteed that a federal law could not violate the rights that are set out in the *Canadian Bill of Rights* unless that legislation states that it overrides the *Canadian Bill of Rights*.[15] (This was an early incarnation of the infamous "notwithstanding clause" that later found its way into the *Charter*). Section 1(b) of the *Canadian Bill of Rights* guaranteed the right to equality before the law and the protection of the law.[16] Before the 1980 constitutional patriation marathon began, the Supreme Court of Canada had decided in widely condemned decisions that section 1(b) of the *Canadian Bill of Rights* was not an egalitarian provision at all.[17] It was interpreted in an extraordinarily narrow, impoverished way so that it guaranteed little, if anything.[18] In 1980, equality-seeking groups worried that there was a real risk that courts could take the same impoverished approach to the right to equality in section 15 of the *Charter* unless Parliament vigorously swung a constitutional sledge hammer when wording that provision.

We had no reason to be confident in 1980 that Canada's judiciary would quickly and consistently rule that section 15 banned discrimination because of disability unless the *Charter* said so in loud, clear, and unambiguous terms. In 1982, our judiciary was not geared up to implement the *Charter*, much less a sparkling new equality rights provision. As I pointed out earlier, when the *Charter* became part of Canada's Constitution, very few, if any, judges on the bench had ever studied constitutional rights and freedoms. It would not be until the late 1980s that the first crop of new lawyers graduated

---

14 *Canadian Bill of Rights*, SC 1960, c 44.

15 *Ibid*, s 2.

16 *Ibid*, s 1(b).

17 Walter Surma Tarnopolsky, *The Canadian Bill of Rights*, 2nd rev ed (Toronto: McClelland & Stewart, 1975) at 295–316.

18 See e.g. *Bliss v Canada (Attorney General)*, [1977] 2 ACWS 190, 77 DLR (3d) 609; *Bliss v Canada (Attorney General)*, [1979] 1 SCR 183, 92 DLR (3d) 417; *Attorney General of Canada v Lavell*, [1974] SCR 1349, 38 DLR (3d) 481; Tarnopolsky, *supra* note 17 at 295–316.

from Canadian law schools with even a basic introduction to the *Charter*. More years had to pass before law schools had a robust body of authoritative *Charter* case law to teach in first-year constitutional law courses. It was not until at least the mid-1990s, if not later, that Canada was appointing judges to the bench who had even studied the *Charter* in law school. Add another 5 to 10 years before our courts would be populated with any judges who, as law students, had earlier been immersed in *Charter* case law in law school and who as lawyers later litigated *Charter* cases in their law practices.

Even if a case on point got to the Supreme Court of Canada in the *Charter*'s earliest years, with excellent facts and superb lawyers to present it, we had no assurance that the Court would get it right, much less that it would get it right the first time around. Even with section 15 amended to include equality for people with disabilities, I have argued in more than one law publication that the Supreme Court has failed to even identify a core disability equality issue in some notable cases where it was screamingly obvious.[19] This is so even though there have been other compelling cases where the Supreme Court has expressed a very good understanding of disability equality principles.[20]

As for the second serious danger, I was monumentally oblivious to it in 1980. This was the risk that our courts could take a completely untethered approach to section 15. Judges might invoke it to address any claims of different treatment that are not tied to the enumerated grounds or any human rights grounds that are analogous to them. US courts have done that for decades under the equal protection clause in the US Constitution's 14th Amendment. Individuals or companies in the United States who want to challenge the constitutionality of legislation or regulations that they do not like can complain that the law they attack impermissibly treats them differently or worse than some other business or some other sector of the

---

19 See David Lepofsky, "*Carter v Canada (Attorney General)*: The Constitutional Attack on Canada's Ban on Assisted Dying: Missing an Obvious Chance to Rule on the Charter's Disability Equality Guarantee" (2016) 76:5 SCLR 94 at 95–97 [Lepofsky, "*Carter v Canada*"]; M David Lepofsky, "A Report Card on the Charter's Guarantee of Equality to Persons with Disabilities after 10 Years: What Progress? What Prospects?" (1997) 7:3 NJCL 263 at 294–298, 302, 317, 339–340, 373–374.

20 *Eldridge v British Columbia (Attorney General)*, [1997] 3 SCR 624 at paras 53–67, [1997] SCJ No 86 (QL) [*Eldridge*]; *Council of Canadians with Disabilities v VIA Rail Canada Inc*, 2007 SCC 15, [2007] 1 SCR 650 at paras 119–124, 127–137.

economy.[21] The so-called "discrimination" they contest may have nothing to do with human rights grounds like race, sex, religion, or disability.[22]

This was no fanciful fear in Canada. A number of Canada's trial and appeal courts did just that from the time section 15 went into effect in 1985 until 1989. They used the fact that the final version of section 15 gave them the power to add additional grounds of discrimination to that provision beyond those enumerated in it. The clear majority, if not overwhelming preponderance of, section 15 cases that came to court during those 4 years had nothing to do with any of the enumerated grounds of discrimination listed in section 15 or any human rights grounds analogous to the enumerated grounds.[23] During section 15's first 4 years in operation, for example, the Ontario Court of Appeal ruled that section 15 was violated wherever a law did not treat people similarly if those people were judicially found to be similarly situated.[24] If you were in court listening to the submissions in one of those cases and the questions from the bench, or if you read the court's decision, you would have scratched your head, wondering what on earth the argument had to do with equality, discrimination, and human rights. I sure did scratch my head over this, and I was there, arguing some of those cases!

Overwhelmingly, in four short years, our section 15 case law degenerated into a totally misguided non-egalitarian approach to equality rights.[25] One case seriously entertained that a provincial law violated section 15 of the *Charter* because it treated the manufacturers of aluminum pop cans differently from the manufacturers of steel pop cans — *Re Aluminum Co. of Canada, Ltd. and the Queen in Right of Ontario*.[26] I actually had the privilege of getting all gussied up to go to court in order to argue that the

---

21 Laurence H Tribe, *American Constitutional Law*, 3rd ed (Mineola, NY: Foundation Press, 2000) at 1059–1068, 1107–1113 [Tribe, *American Constitutional Law*, 3rd ed]; Tribe, *American Constitutional Law*, 2nd ed, *supra* note 2 at 1437–1439, 1454–1462.

22 Tribe, *American Constitutional Law*, 3rd ed, *supra* note 21 at 1059–1068, 1107–1113; Tribe, *American Constitutional Law*, 2nd ed, *supra* note 2 at 1437–1439, 1454–1462.

23 David Lepofsky & Hart Schwartz, "Constitutional Law: Charter of Rights and Freedoms — Section 15 — an Erroneous Approach to the Charter's Equality Guarantee: R. v Ertel" (1988) 67 Can Bar Rev 115 at 121–122.

24 See e.g. *R v Ertel*, [1987] OJ No 516, 20 OAC 257 at paras 68–69 (QL).

25 Lepofsky & Schwartz, *supra* note 23 at 121, 125–128.

26 *Re Aluminum Co of Canada, Ltd and the Queen in Right of Ontario; Dofasco Inc, Intervenor*, (1986) 29 DLR (4th) 583, 55 OR (2d) 522.

*Charter* protects people, not pop cans, while trying not to explode in court in derisive laughter at the absurdity of it all. Fortunately, my argument succeeded. The *Charter* does protect people but not pop cans. Phew!

In the first legal publication of mine that the Supreme Court of Canada ever cited with approval, co-authored with my colleague and friend, constitutional lawyer Hart Schwartz, we argued against that "similarly situated/similarly treated" definition of section 15's equality guarantee.[27] We sighed with relief in 1989 when the Supreme Court of Canada attempted to put an end to this chaos in the equality rights case law. In its first decision interpreting section 15 — *Law Society of British Columbia v Andrews* — the Supreme Court thankfully held that section 15 bans discrimination based only on the grounds listed in it and in any additional ground analogous to those enumerated grounds.[28] Among the many great opportunities that I had during my career as an Ontario Crown, I got to appear as co-counsel for Ontario, which intervened in the *Andrews* case. Also exciting for me was the fact that the Supreme Court of Canada, in *Andrews*, cited with approval the article that Schwartz and I had written, which lambasted the Ontario Court of Appeal for having taken its problematic "similarly situated, similarly treated" approach to section 15.[29] Schwartz and I were humbled to see that, among the authorities cited in that case, were Justice Rosalie Abella, Aristotle, and us![30]

In 1980, my strategic view on whether disability should be explicitly listed in section 15 was simple, but I hope not simplistic. If you want the law to guarantee something, say it! Say it clearly! I had already come to believe this when I worked on drafting detailed proposals earlier in 1980 for the Ontario Coalition on Human Rights for the Handicapped on how the Ontario *Human Rights Code* should be amended to ban disability discrimination in activities like employment, housing, and services. Over my decades of disability advocacy since then, I have been strengthened in this view. This lies at the core of my efforts on behalf of the Ontarians with Disabilities Act Committee from 1994 to 2005 to get the *Accessibility*

---

27 Lepofsky & Schwartz, *supra* note 23.

28 *Andrews v Law Society (British Columbia)*, [1989] 1 SCR 143, [1989] SCJ No 6 at 4 [*Andrews*].

29 *Ibid* at 10, McIntyre J.

30 *Ibid* at 10, 18, McIntyre J.

*for Ontarians with Disabilities Act* enacted.[31] It is central to my activities since then to get strong and effective accessibility standards created under that statute.[32]

I have increasingly come to realize that most people who read and use laws are not lawyers, blessed with the joys of a robust legal education. They have not learned the tricks of the trade of interpreting legislation. They do not go to lawyers every time they read a law to find out what it means. For those people, if not for overworked judges as well, we need laws to include plain, clear, unambiguous wording. If you want them to understand that discrimination because of disability is forbidden, tell them in straightforward unambiguous terms that discrimination because of disability is forbidden! This is not some major new insight on my part. A movement in the 1800s in the United States, inspired by Jeremy Bentham, promoted the idea that the masses of court decisions that together comprise the maze of the common law should be codified.[33] I first heard of the US codification movement during an incredible course on American legal history that I took at Harvard in 1981–1982 during my master of law studies. Had I been born a century or more earlier, I could well have become an activist in the codification movement instead of the 21st century disability rights movement. I think I got the better deal!

## C. The Second Harmful Proposal to the Joint Committee: Amend Section 15 to Create a Hierarchy Among Equality-Seeking Groups

### *1. A Hierarchical Approach to Equality Rights?*

The second argument presented to the Joint Committee that threatened to create impediments for our campaign for disability equality came from two influential women's rights organizations. They asked the Joint Committee to rewrite section 15 so that certain discrimination grounds, like sex and

---

31 *Accessibility for Ontarians with Disabilities Act*, SO 2005, c 11. For the history of this campaign up to 2003, see M David Lepofsky, "The Long, Arduous Road to a Barrier-Free Ontario for People with Disabilities: The History of the *Ontarians with Disabilities Act* — the First Chapter" (2004) 15:2 NJCL 125 at 159–333.

32 These activities are documented at <www.aodaalliance.org>.

33 Andrew P Morriss, "Codification and Right Answers" (1999) 74:2 Chicago-Kent L Rev 74 at 355, 360, 379.

racial discrimination, would be harder for governments to justify than discrimination on any other grounds. What they sought would entrench a hierarchical approach to equality. Under it, some disadvantaged groups, like women, would be treated as more equal than others, such as people with disabilities. To me, this is an especially disturbing part of section 15's history. I suspect that very few know about it.

This all arises from a basic constitutional question to which I adverted earlier in this chapter: how strong a justification should a court require a government to present in order to defend a claim that a law or other government action has discriminated contrary to section 15? This constitutional issue has plagued US courts, legal scholars, and social justice advocates for decades. The result in the US case law is far from satisfactory. There was a real risk in 1980 that it could harmfully influence how Canada's courts approached section 15 of the *Charter*. In US constitutional law cases in 1980, it had been much harder for a government to justify racial discrimination than discrimination on other grounds.[34] In the language of American constitutional cases, US courts applied different "levels of scrutiny," depending on the ground of discrimination at issue.[35] US courts subjected racial discrimination to "strict scrutiny," the most exacting and probing judicial oversight available.[36] At the other end of the spectrum, a wide range of other grounds for unequal treatment were subject to only minimal scrutiny by courts. In those cases, government action needed to be only minimally rational. That lower level of judicial scrutiny applied, for example, to unequal treatment of different businesses by virtue of the specific business in which they operated.[37] In the middle was "intermediate scrutiny," which applied to some grounds of unequal treatment, such as sex.[38]

The US approach established a hierarchy of equal rights protection under the equal protection clause of the 14th Amendment to the US Constitution. A looming question facing Canada in the fall of 1980 was whether Canada's courts would or should go down that same road when interpreting the new section 15 of the *Charter*, and, if they did, who would get preferential status in that new constitutional hierarchy of equality rights

---

34 See Tribe, *American Constitutional Law*, 2nd ed, *supra* note 2 at 1451–1454.

35 *Ibid* at 1439–1474.

36 *Ibid* at 1451–1454.

37 *Ibid* at 1439–1450.

38 *Curtis Craig et al, Appellants v David Boren, etc, et al*, 429 US 190, 97 S Ct 451 (1976).

claimants? Put simply, should Canada adopt the US "levels of scrutiny" approach when interpreting section 15 of the *Charter*? If so, should this be written into the text of section 15?

The original text of section 15 that was introduced into Parliament in October 1980 did not dictate anything about this issue. Had that wording been enacted as is, Canadian courts might have decided to take an approach similar to their US judicial counterparts. On the other hand, our judges might have taken a different approach. They might have demanded that governments present the same level of justification no matter which ground of discrimination was alleged. This was a subset of a much bigger issue that was before the Joint Committee — namely, how courts would assess any justification of an infringement of any *Charter* rights that a government presented in defence of its impugned law or other government action. The very first section of the *Charter*, section 1, allowed for a "reasonable limits" defence to be mounted for a violation of any rights listed in the *Charter*, including those guaranteed by section 15. Extending far beyond equality rights issues alone, there was a substantial debate at the Joint Committee over how section 1 of the *Charter* should be worded.

The initial draft of section 1 was extremely broad. It provided: "The *Canadian Charter of Rights and Freedoms* guarantees the rights and freedoms set out in it subject only to such reasonable limits as are generally accepted in a free and democratic society with a parliamentary system of government."[39] That initial version of section 1 would have made it very easy for a government to defend almost any *Charter* rights infringement. It was predictable that, under it, governments would argue in case after case that, if Parliament approved a measure, it must automatically be generally acceptable in a parliamentary system.

That version of section 1 was roundly criticized at the Joint Committee's public hearings, including by me. On 12 January 1981, Justice Minister Jean Chrétien agreed to substantially tighten up section 1 because of all the criticism of it during the public hearings.[40] It now provides: "1. The *Canadian*

---

39 Canada, Parliament, *The Canadian Constitution: 1980, Proposed Resolution Respecting the Constitution of Canada* (Ottawa: Government of Canada, 1980), s 1 [*Canadian Constitution: Proposed Resolution*].

40 Canada, Parliament, *Minutes of Proceedings and Evidence of the Special Joint Committee of the Senate and of the House of Commons on the Constitution of Canada*, 32nd Parl, 1st Sess, No 36 (12 January 1981) at 11.

*Charter of Rights and Freedoms* guarantees the rights and freedoms set out in it subject only to such reasonable limits prescribed by law as can be demonstrably justified in a free and democratic society."[41] Further complicating things, there remains to this day a debate whether any justification to a discrimination claim can be mounted under section 15, even before resorting to section 1. A book could be written on that topic alone. Happily, I will spare you that!

In 1980, two key women's organizations argued at the Joint Committee that section 15 should be rewritten in a hierarchical way. They would likely not have readily accepted as correct my use of the term "hierarchical." They were the National Advisory Council on the Status of Women[42] and the National Association of Women and the Law.[43] The presentation to the Joint Committee by a third organization, the National Action Committee on the Status of Women, could also be read as appearing to support this hierarchical approach.[44] However, the transcript of their hearing is far from clear on this. They did not explicitly call for a hierarchical approach to be added to section 15. A leading question from New Democratic Party Member of Parliament Pauline Jewett suggested that they support a two-tier approach to equality rights. The presenters from the National Action Committee did not specifically answer her when responding to her long multi-part question.[45]

The lead champions advocating for this hierarchical approach to equality were Mary Eberts, speaking for the National Advisory Council on the Status of Women, and Deborah Acheson and Pamela Medjuck, representing the National Association of Women and the Law.[46] Let me analyze their arguments from a disability perspective. In the next section, I set out key excerpts on point from their presentations to the Joint Committee. I invite you to size them up for yourself. The advocates for this position wanted to

---

41 *Charter*, *supra* note 1, s 1.

42 Canada, Parliament, *Minutes of Proceedings and Evidence of the Special Joint Committee of the Senate and of the House of Commons on the Constitution of Canada*, 32nd Parl, 1st Sess, No 9 (20 November 1980) [*Minutes of Proceedings, 20 November 1980*].

43 Canada, Parliament, *Minutes of Proceedings and Evidence of the Special Joint Committee of the Senate and of the House of Commons on the Constitution of Canada*, 32nd Parl, 1st Sess, No 22 (9 December 1980) [*Minutes of Proceedings, 9 December 1980*].

44 *Minutes of Proceedings, 20 November 1980*, *supra* note 42 at 68–70.

45 *Ibid* at 68–70.

46 *Ibid* at 127–28, 146–47, 150–51; *Minutes of Proceedings, 9 December 1980*, *supra* note 43 at 57–60, 64–65, 67–68.

ensure that gender, religious, racial, and national/ethnic origin equality got the maximum protection from governmental discrimination.[47] They wanted to avoid the risk of certain other grounds of discrimination, such as disability, somehow diluting their equality by lowering the bar across the board.[48] They evidently feared that, if courts applied the same level of judicial scrutiny to unequal treatment based on any grounds of discrimination, this would lead to a diluted protection for some groups such as women and racialized communities.[49] They asked for section 15 to be amended so that unequal treatment based on certain grounds like race and sex should never be permissible or so that it would be judicially tested in a far more critical and exacting way. In contrast, unequal treatment on other grounds such as age or disability should be justifiable if it is reasonable when assessed on a case-by-case basis.[50] To me, that would have created a hierarchy of different levels of equality rights protection for different equality-seeking groups.

I profoundly disagreed with their proposals. I had learned about some of them in the fall of 1980. I was stunned that any equality-seeking advocates could take a position that was so obviously hurtful to our cause. However, I was so focused on just getting the disability amendment passed that I did not devote time and energy to mount a concerted campaign against their harmful recommendations. Fortunately, Parliament did not accept their hierarchical recommendations. Why was I so upset? Equality is, at its core, all about eliminating hierarchies. Embedding a hierarchy in section 15 contradicted egalitarian principles. To repeat and re-emphasize, it treats some as more equal than others. Central to this proposed hierarchical approach to equality was the idea that courts should treat discrimination on the short list of preferentially protected grounds as "the most grave," as Eberts put it to the Joint Committee. Yet there should be no elites among disadvantaged equality-seeking groups. Moreover, it was implicit in their proposal that different equality-seeking groups live in mutually exclusive silos. Yet the world does not work that way.

---

47 See, respectively, *Minutes of Proceedings, 20 November 1980*, *supra* note 42 at 127–128; *Minutes of Proceedings, 9 December 1980*, *supra* note 43 at 57–60.

48 *Minutes of Proceedings, 9 December 1980*, *supra* note 43 at 58.

49 See, respectively *Minutes of Proceedings, 20 November 1980*, *supra* note 42 at 127–128, 147; *Minutes of Proceedings, 9 December 1980*, *supra* note 43 at 57–58, 65, 67–68.

50 *Minutes of Proceedings, 20 November 1980*, *supra* note 42 at 151; *Minutes of Proceedings, 9 December 1980*, *supra* note 43 at 58–59.

Since then, it has been far more widely and wisely accepted, especially within many equality-seeking circles, that we must be alive to the intersectional effects of different equality-seeking designations. Women with disabilities are doubly disadvantaged because they are women and because they have disabilities. The same goes for racialized persons with disabilities or Indigenous persons with disabilities. This is not an "either/or" situation. As you add equality-seeking identities, you multiply a person's disadvantages, one disability rights advocate once told me. I love their mathematical metaphor. An intersectional approach to equality takes all of this into account in a holistic approach to equality issues. In it, equality should deliver equality to everyone. A two-tiered approach to section 15 is anathema to this.

It is good that intersectionality has become axiomatic in the organized disability rights community in Canada. For example, during advocacy in 2018 and 2019 over the development of the *Accessible Canada Act* and from 2022 to 2023 over the creation of the *Canada Disability Benefit Act*, a good number of disability advocates from across Canada strongly pressed for each of those laws to be amended to include principles of intersectionality.[51] In 1980, to support their desire for preferred protection against discrimination based on sex, race, religion, or national or ethnic origin, the proponents of this hierarchical approach to section 15 argued in part that discrimination on those grounds is never reasonable. They contended that, in contrast, discrimination on other protected grounds can be reasonable in some situations and unreasonable in others. They also argued that the features of a person's sex, race, religion, or national or ethnic origin are immutable.

These propositions are either wrong *per se* or overstated. For example, neither one's sex nor one's religion is immutable. A person can choose to undertake gender reassignment surgery. A person can opt to convert to another religion. Moreover, disability is at least as immutable as a person's race or national/ethnic origin. The immutability of a condition is, in any event, hardly a compelling justification for a hierarchical approach to equality

---

51 See e.g. *Accessible Canada Act*, SC 2019, c 10, s 6(e). See also Accessibility for Ontarians with Disabilities Act Alliance, *Brief on Bill C-22, the Canada Disability Benefit Act* (24 April 2023), online: <www.aodaalliance.org/whats-new/please-email-senate-standing-committee-on-social-affairs-urge-them-to-amend-bill-c-22-in-accordance-with-the-aoda-alliance-brief-that-we-submitted-today/>.

rights. I elsewhere have criticized a Supreme Court of Canada judge for urging such a troubling approach to equality in 1997, during oral argument in the first case where the Court ruled on a disability discrimination claim based on section 15 of the *Charter*.

In *Eaton v Brant County Board of Education*, young Emily Eaton, a child with a disability, filed a *Charter* claim against her school board.[52] The school board had forced her, over her family's objection, to attend a segregated class for students with disabilities. She wanted to be educated in a regular classroom with all students, not just with students with disabilities. Her counsel relied on the US Supreme Court's landmark ruling in *Brown v Board of Education* that separate but equal education for black students in the United States was inherently discriminatory.[53] During oral argument in the *Eaton* case, Supreme Court of Canada Justice Charles Gonthier tried to downplay the impact of *Brown v Board of Education* because you are born with your race but not your disability. Emily Eaton's counsel properly responded to that incorrect and troubling judicial remark by politely reminding the Court that Emily was born with her disability.[54]

Hard as it may be to believe, advocates at the Joint Committee who pressed for a two-tiered approach to equality, where disability would be on the lower tier, urged that this would be helpful for people with disabilities. They argued that, otherwise, courts could strike down programs that give a benefit to people with disabilities as discriminating because of disability. Eberts argued: "We want the courts to have the flexibility to say, 'Look, this is a program designed for handicapped persons.' We do not want it to be struck down because of a categorical idea of what is just."[55] Acheson argued:

> One of the questions that is often addressed at this point is the question of the physically handicapped person. Why should not the compelling reason test apply there. There is a very good reason, because you want to be in a position to make some discrimination in respect to a physically handicapped person. You want to be able to pay additional benefits to that person; you want to be able to require three apartments in every housing complex to be accessible to

---

52 *Eaton v Brant County Board of Education*, [1997] 1 SCR 241 at paras 6–8, [1996] SCJ No 98 (QL).

53 *Brown v Board of Education of Topeka*, 347 US 483 (1954).

54 Lepofsky, "*Carter v Canada*," *supra* note 19 at 93–94.

55 *Minutes of Proceedings, 20 November 1980*, *supra* note 42 at 151.

> physically handicapped persons. So the court needs more flexibility to deal with those issues and we do not want to hamstring the court.[56]

Their argument was transparently wrong, even if viewed through the lens of the law as it was understood in 1980. First, the very programs about which they were worried would easily be saved from constitutional attack by section 15(2) of the *Charter*. It provides that it does not violate section 15(1) if such a program has as its purpose the amelioration of the conditions of disadvantaged people. As originally introduced into Parliament, section 15(2), like section 15(1) did not include disability. However, our call for the disability amendment would of necessity have led to disability being added to both sub-sections 15(1) and (2).

The original text of section 15(2) in October 1980, when the Joint Committee was holding these hearings, was: "(2) This section does not preclude any law, program or activity that has as its object the amelioration of conditions of disadvantaged persons or groups."[57] After the disability amendment was passed, the finalized text of section 15(2) reads: "(2) Subsection (1) does not preclude any law, program or activity that has as its object the amelioration of conditions of disadvantaged individuals or groups including those that are disadvantaged because of race, national or ethnic origin, colour, religion, sex, age or mental or physical disability."[58] Section 15(2) totally refutes their argument that the hierarchical approach to equality was needed to help people with disabilities. However, if needed, a second argument similarly disposes of it. If a person without a disability tried to make one of the arguments about which Eberts and Acheson proposed, attacking a program because it only extends benefits to people with disabilities, their attack would be summarily dismissed as bogus, without having to have any section 15(2) or section 1 justification advanced in the program's defence. To invoke legal protections against disability discrimination, you need to have a disability. A person with no disability cannot object to a government disability benefit on the grounds that it discriminates against them because they have no disability.

Earlier I noted that the National Action Committee on the Status of Women might be taken to have supported the idea of a hierarchical definition of equality rights in section 15, although the transcript of their hearing

---

56 *Minutes of Proceedings, 9 December 1980*, *supra* note 43 at 65.

57 *Canadian Constitution: Proposed Resolution*, *supra* note 39, s 15(2).

58 See the *Charter*, *supra* note 1, s 15(2).

does not clearly show that they did. When they appeared before the Joint Committee to speak to section 15's wording, they had not investigated in advance about a need to add disability to section 15. The National Action Committee on the Status of Women asked the Joint Committee to amend section 15 to add marital status, sexual orientation, and political belief.[59] They did not ask that disability be added to section 15. Conservative member of parliament Flora Macdonald asked if they would also recommend adding disability to section 15. Lynn McDonald, the president of the National Action Committee on the Status of Women, answered that they had not internally explored this issue but felt that women's organizations would broadly support it:

> **Flora Macdonald (Kingston and the Islands):** You made the suggestion of adding certain other categories to that, in that section. I think the ones you suggested are marital status, sexual orientation and political beliefs. Now, I would ask you if in that too you would consider, because I think that it should certainly be known that women support this kind of thing, that you include as well the mentally and physically handicapped.
>
> **Lynn McDonald:** We have never canvassed on this point, but I expect that that would find very broad support among women's organizations.[60]

It was troubling that any equality rights advocates were pressing for any harmful amendments to section 15 before the Joint Committee. That was made worse by the fact that some others echoed their recommendation.[61] This culminated in January 1981 when the New Democratic Party itself proposed wording for section 15 that would have entrenched a hierarchical approach to equality in the wording of section 15.[62]

I did not argue against this hierarchical approach to equality, or even mention it, when I appeared at the Joint Committee on 12 December 1980. Should I have? What would I decide to do about that if the issue came up

---

59 *Minutes of Proceedings, 20 November 1980*, *supra* note 42 at 59.

60 *Ibid* at 65.

61 See e.g. Canada, Parliament, *Minutes of Proceedings and Evidence of the Special Joint Committee of the Senate and of the House of Commons on the Constitution of Canada*, 32nd Parl, 1st Sess, No 20 (5 December 1980) at 19–20 [*Minutes of Proceedings, 5 December 1980*]; Canada, Parliament, *Minutes of Proceedings and Evidence of the Special Joint Committee of the Senate and of the House of Commons on the Constitution of Canada*, 32nd Parl, 1st Sess, No 42 (21 January 1981) at 8 [*Minutes of Proceedings, 21 January 1981*].

62 *Minutes of Proceedings, 21 January 1981*, *supra* note 61 at 8.

now, given my disability advocacy experience since then? I would be heavily tempted to call out this hierarchical approach to equality and offer a few punchy sentences showing why it should be rejected. Yet there are times when I choose to keep my presentation as simple as possible and focus on one solitary message without distractions when speaking to a parliamentary committee. That might lead me to leave out any remarks on the proposal to entrench a hierarchical approach to equality in my presentation to a parliamentary committee, even today. With the luxury of hindsight, I know that my silence on the issue when addressing the Joint Committee in 1980 did not work to our ultimate disadvantage. Such are the uncertainties and after-the-fact ruminations in the life of a volunteer disability rights advocate.

Were this today, and whether or not I would address this issue in my deputation to Parliament, I would most assuredly issue some sort of public statement somewhere about it. For example, I would write an update from the Accessibility for Ontarians with Disabilities Act Alliance identifying the proposal of a hierarchical approach to equality and spelling out our counter-arguments. This would be emailed to our supporters, posted on our website, and widely distributed through tweets, Facebook posts, and the like. I might well send a letter to all members of parliament and senators, urging that section 15 not be rewritten to provide for two-tiered equality rights. If I thought there was a realistic chance of getting them to change their position, I would first reach out to the advocates for such a hierarchical wording of section 15, time permitting. Even if there was no chance that they would change their minds or their position, it could be worthwhile to reach out to them and to hear and learn from what responses they would offer to our critique.

The issue of hierarchical approaches to equality that we faced in 1980 has not gone away. I have been concerned about it ever since my participation in the fight for the disability amendment in 1980. I have seen it reflected in some equality-seeking efforts since then, where one equality-seeking group understandably seeks to advance their status but in a way that has the collateral effect of potentially disadvantaging other equality-seeking groups. In the 1980s, some organizations commendably established employment equity programs but provided employment equity only for women or for women and racialized persons. Of course, employment equity for women and racialized persons is extremely important. It needs to be expanded. However, when an organization establishes employment equity only for these two equality-seeking groups, it risks the damaging impact of causing further disadvantage for people with disabilities, Indigenous persons, and the like. This happens when an organization has an employment-equity program that is explicitly limited to women and racialized persons. It also can happen when an employer establishes an employment equity program that, on paper, identifies its targets as women, racialized persons, Indigenous persons, and people with disabilities but that, in operation, prioritizes only women and racialized people.

I witnessed this harm up close when I was working in the Ontario public service in the first half of the 1990s. Its so-called "Accelerated Employment Equity" initiative ended up reducing employment opportunities for people with disabilities and Indigenous persons.[63] Back then, I called it accelerated employment inequity for those two equality-seeking groups. The most recent incarnation of a pervasive troubling hierarchical approach to equality that I have seen occurs in some current equity, diversity and inclusion [EDI] programs. There has been a commendable proliferation of EDI policies and programs in the public and private sectors in recent years. However, too often, these programs focus only on EDI for racialized persons and Indigenous persons. Again, I strongly support such efforts for racialized communities and Indigenous persons. However, these initiatives must also equally include other equality-seeking groups, such as people with disabilities. Otherwise, people with disabilities end up being disadvantaged once again. Making that worse, those organizations' leaders think they are demonstrating leadership and making great strides in EDI, even though they are harming equity for people with disabilities along the way. I have become increasingly vocal on this issue.

Unknown to many, a hierarchical approach to equality rights ultimately found its way into the *Charter* but not until months later. In the fall of 1981, the federal government cut a deal with nine of the ten provinces to win their support for the *Charter* but only if the infamous "notwithstanding clause" in the *Charter*'s section 33 was added.[64] It allowed Parliament and provincial legislatures to immunize from attack a piece of legislation for 5 years under certain *Charter* provisions, including section 15, if the

63 Ontario Public Service Advisory Group on Employment Equity for Persons with Disabilities, *Brief to the Ontario Standing Committee on the Administration of Justice of the Ontario Legislature Regarding Bill 168 — the Ontarians with Disabilities Act* (November 1994).

64 See Robert Sheppard & Michael Valpy, *The National Deal: The Fight for a Canadian Constitution* (Toronto: Fleet Books, 1982) at 144, 297–299, 346.

legislation included a clause stating that it operates notwithstanding the *Canadian Charter of Rights and Freedoms*. I have more to say about this clause in Chapter XVI.

Some advocates for women's rights sought an amendment to the *Charter* to counteract this decision. They ultimately won the addition of section 28 to the *Charter*, which provides: "Notwithstanding anything in this *Charter*, the rights and freedoms referred to in it are guaranteed equally to male and female persons."[65] They sought section 28 so that a section 33 notwithstanding clause could not be used to immunize a law from being challenged on the basis of sex discrimination. If section 28 is so read, Parliament or a provincial legislature can invoke a section 33 notwithstanding clause to immunize a law from challenge under section 15 of the *Charter* as discriminating because of grounds like race, religion, or disability. Only sex discrimination could not be shielded from attack by a notwithstanding clause. Section 28 has had very little practical impact.[66] However, it stands as a constitutionalization of the notion that some people are more equal than others. In Chapter XVI, I explain why this troubles me and try to provide some broader context for the position taken by advocates for section 28.

### 2. *What the Joint Committee Was Told in Support of Inserting a Hierarchical Approach to Equality into Section 15*

Don't take my word for it. I invite you to read what was presented to the Joint Committee that, in my view, argued for a hierarchical approach to equality rights. To begin, Eberts, speaking on behalf of the National Advisory Council on the Status of Woman, argued:

> We have, thanks to the chance to contribute at the outset to the nature of our charter, a chance to get it right the first time around. We can include language, meant as a clear signal to the courts that whatever they may think about other bases of distinction, certain bases of distinction should never be regarded as reasonable.
>
> … We propose that the Section read:

---

65 *Charter*, *supra* note 1, s 28.

66 See e.g. Beverley Baines, "Section 28 of the Canadian Charter of Rights and Freedoms: A Purposive Interpretation" (2005) 17:1 CJWL 45 at 52–53; Cee Strauss, "Section 28's Potential to Guarantee Substantive Gender Equality in *Hak c Procureur général du Québec*" (2021) 33:1 CJWL 84 at 88–89.

> (1) every person shall have equal rights in law, including the right to equality before the law and to the equal protection and benefit of the law.
>
> (2) Such equal rights may be abridged or denied only on the basis of a reasonable distinction. Sex, race, colour, national or ethnic origin or religion will never constitute a reasonable distinction except as provided in Subsection (3).
>
> Our proposal does two things: it accepts the idea that some distinctions may possibly be reasonable or practical. That is the idea behind Subsection 1 and the first sentence of Subsection 2. This is, if you like, our first tier of analysis. Under this section, for example, a law denying drivers licences to married women might well be struck down even though there is no guarantee of equality before the law on the basis of marital status.
>
> We also feel it necessary to tell the courts what basis of distinction just will not be reasonable and that is the second sentence in Subsection (2). …
>
> … We think that if we keep the list of "never reasonable categories" which are explicitly expressed rather short, the courts and the legislatures cannot help but get the idea that in these cases they should and can respond to a signal to regard them as most grave.[67]

When answering a question from Conservative Member of Parliament David Crombie, Eberts made it clear beyond any doubt that, based on the approach she was urging, there would be two tiers of equality rights protection. Sex discrimination would be one of the new grounds that got the stricter protection. Disability was one of the grounds that would get the less strict protection. She had this exchange:

> **Crombie:** It is a welcome change because I think many entrenched rights in the world do not include age for that very reason. However, it is with Section 15(2) that I come to my next question if I could.
>
> While one could understand and indeed applaud excluding age because of its impact on social programs, I also note that you did not include in your list of case-by-case protective areas, you use sex, race, colour, national or ethnic origin or religion and you did not include either sexual orientation or the handicapped, mental or physical, in your preferred list and I wondered why you did not.
>
> **Eberts:** I think that the rationale would be the same as that for age and it has been pointed out by, for example, the Lamontagne-McGuigan Committee that to include marital status in a list of distinctions that are always regarded as unreasonable would create practical problems with the administration of a number of social programs, for example. And our formulation remains the same: we have two tiers; where the ground is specifically mentioned in Subsection 2 of

[67] *Minutes of Proceedings, 20 November 1980, supra* note 42 at 127–129.

our proposal we intend that to be a signal to the courts that distinctions based on those grounds are categorically wrong, we should never have them.

**Crombie:** Which problems?

**Eberts:** Race, sex, colour and so on. Whereas distinctions based on other grounds can be judged by a court to be reasonable in certain circumstances and unreasonable in other circumstances, so that once again, as I mentioned in my initial presentation, a statute which denied a driver's licence to someone on the basis of marital status could well be challenged and found to be unreasonable, even though marital status is not explicitly mentioned. So that we hope that our formulation would be flexible enough to cover both sort of hard core types of distinction and also those that required more flexibility. Also, there is nothing in our formulation to prevent either the province or the federal government from passing detailed and articulate legislation to prevent specific kinds of discrimination on the basis of any category.

**Crombie:** So it is clear in my own head, Mr. Chairman, you have in your two orders of protected rights, as it were, age, sexual orientation and handicapped, mental and physical, are clearly in the second order which need to be dealt with in a case-by-case manner as opposed to categorical; is that what you are saying?

**Eberts:** Yes, that is right.[68]

Eberts argued that their approach accorded with the recommendations of the Canadian Human Rights Commission. In response, Crombie, who later in those proceedings would be the history-making politician to formally move that the disability amendment be added to section 15, gently responded to Eberts by flagging the call for the disability amendment, as follows: "I might say, Mr. Chairman, and indeed with kindness, that you may want to familiarize yourself with the brief of the Canadian Association of Mentally Retarded who take a somewhat different view."[69] Liberal Member of Parliament Coline Campbell further pressed Eberts on this issue, and she again made it clear that she was proposing two different tiers of constitutional protection, with disability being among those on the lower tier:

**Coline Campbell:** Let us go to Section 15. You have already said you like the list. You said at page 14 that you would go with those because:

We believe that these few additions reflect Canadians' views about what sort of discrimination is most grave.

---

[68] *Ibid* at 146–147.

[69] *Ibid* at 147.

You mention here today that you do not like age, and you would not include handicap, both marital status or sexual orientation.

I would like a little broader reasoning as to why you consider what you have included there — if you are going to go to a list, and I personally do not like a list because it has limitations within a legal context, unless you use words as the Civil Liberties people said. I personally would prefer to see a general statement of equal rights for all persons and no list and to revert to the Canadian Human Rights Act for expansion of the list and the reasonableness of future needs as they come up; but if you are going to start listing, then you might as well list as many as there are.

**Eberts:** I will try to be fairly brief. Our proposal has basically two tiers of protection within the context of a general guarantee. The first tier is that group which will never be regarded as a reasonable basis for distinction. I draw your attention to the remarks we have quoted from the speech of the Prime Minister which you will find on page 12, where he says:

There are, after all, only two permanent conditions attributable to human beings, one is sex, the other is race. All other distinctions from which discrimination may grow are temporary in nature or are subject to change.

That is not the complete rationale for our choice but it is to some extent the rationale for our choice. But I will continue. We propose that there be certain hard-core categories which, in our contemplation, could not give rise to reasonable distinction.

It is not reasonable to determine a right to vote, to drive, or whatever on the basis of your sex or race.

With regard to the other areas that are beginning to be introduced into human rights legislation and I would say Mr. Fairweather's legislation does not contain a protection against discrimination on the basis of sexual orientation anyway: with regard to those, it is our view that they lend themselves more readily to a consideration on the basis; is this particular distinction reasonable in the context in which it is proposed? Is it reasonable in the context of an income maintenance program to draw a distinction on the basis of age, or physical or mental handicap? So that you could consider, for example, a whole range of social legislation which would be invalidated by absolute categories and we do not want that to happen.

We want the courts to have the flexibility to say. "Look, this is a program designed for handicapped persons." We do not want it to be struck down because of a categorical idea of what is just. We want it to be upheld if it is reasonable. By the same token, we do not want the courts or the legislature to be given all sorts of leeway to apply stereotypes to the issue of what is reasonable in the area of sex and race discrimination and the other matters which we have made.

> So, our proposal, if you will, is an attempt to give some juridical structure to the really laudable sentiments and philosophy behind Mr. Fairweather's proposal. I do not think we differ from him in desire, but we do in the structure as to how we propose to achieve it.[70]

The National Association of Women and the Law advanced a similar position. Pamela Medjuck argued:

> Thus, the court will have a duty when interpreting Section 15 to determine which distinctions amount to discrimination and which are reasonable and should be allowed.
>
> The American courts have developed a "suspect classification" test in relation to discrimination on certain invidious grounds. For example, race can rarely form a proper basis for differential treatment in law. In such cases the onus is on government to prove a compelling state interest for the distinction in order for the law to be upheld. The court must not only evaluate the purpose of the legislation, but must also determine if the purpose could be achieved in another non-discriminatory way.
>
> However, a majority of the American court has not yet applied this "suspect classification," sometimes called "strict scrutiny," test to distinctions made on the basis of sex. It has, rather, adopted a middle test somewhere between "strict scrutiny" and "reasonable distinctions" to apply to sex inequality cases. ...
>
> Because immutable characteristics, such as sex and race, are unrelated to the ability or capacity of a person, we believe that a strict standard must apply to them. In the words of the paper presented by the Canadian Human Rights Commission, distinction should almost never be made on these grounds. We would like to point out, while we do support Mr. Gordon Fairweather's comments that these distinctions should never be made, we cannot agree with his recommendation which includes that age should be included with race and sex. We do not believe that. Otherwise, we are supporting his principles; not the wording of his recommendations. To ensure that our courts will take this approach, we believe it will be necessary to clearly state the standard in Section 15.
>
> We therefore recommend that Section 15 specifically provide that a compelling reason must be given for any distinction on the basis of sex, race, national or ethnic origin, or religion.
>
> Regarding other prohibited grounds, age, physical or mental handicap, marital status, political belief, sexual orientation and previous conviction, we would emphasise that not all "inherent" classifications are necessarily invidious, to use the American term. The example of age comes immediately to mind. While

70 *Ibid* at 150–151.

some legal distinctions on the basis of age are improper and therefore ought to be prohibited by Section 15, many distinctions based on age are perfectly appropriate because they fairly relate to different levels of capacity.

It is appropriate, for example, for children who have been convicted of committing criminal offences not to be given as severe a penalty as adults. Equally, we do not want to have the vote in Canada extended to children four years of age. These types of reasonable distinctions are acceptable in law.

This is not to say that unfair, unreasonable distinctions on the basis of age should be tolerated.

Certainly Section 15 should forbid discrimination on this ground. Our point is that the judiciary should apply a different, a more stringent, test to laws which distinguish on the basis of the invidious or the suspect categories, such as sex or race, than to laws distinguishing on other bases, age, handicap, et cetera.

To achieve this, Section 15 of the *Charter* must make it clear that a suspect classification test, that is, a strict scrutiny test, should apply to certain types of discrimination. To fail to do so will result in this standard for all differential treatment being reduced to the lowest common denominator, i.e. the reasonable classification test.

A number of grounds which should receive judicial scrutiny have been left out of the *Charter*. The more obvious ones are: marital status, physical or mental handicaps, political belief, sexual orientation and previous conviction. It is important to include marital status because often discrimination against women is disguised in this form. The language of Section 15 should permit the court to scrutinize legislation on these grounds. The present wording of Section 15(1), because it provides a finite list of prohibited grounds, will not permit the necessary expansion.

In addition, new ground may be recognized in the future which we cannot now anticipate. To achieve this, either no list should be included in Section 15(1), or words such as "on any ground including" should be added before the list to clarify that it is not all inclusive.

Our first preference would be to include no list at all to provide for the more expansive possible application of the section. However, we do recognize the concerns of groups such as the mentally handicapped who may prefer the protection of a list of grounds which includes them.

The difference in the terms "any distinction" and "any discrimination" is very significant to our point of view. The value-charged word "discrimination" should be avoided if at all possible. Problems have arisen in interpretation of the word "discrimination" in that courts generally feel that they must find that the complaining party has been subject to harsher treatment than others. In the Burnrhine case, 1974, the Supreme Court of Canada upheld the provision under the *Juvenile Delinquency Act* which imposed a much longer term of incarceration on a young person than an adult could have received for the same offence, on the ground that he was benefiting from a longer period of rehabilitation. The word "distinction" here would squarely focus the courts on the primary issue: differential treatment of persons in like circumstances.

I am just going to read now the recommended wording that we are putting to the Committee for Section 15: taking into account all of the points raised, we therefore recommend that Section 15(1) be redrafted in two subsections using the following approach:

Our first preference would be:

> Section 15(1) every person shall have equal rights in law including the right to equality before the law and to the equal protection and benefit of the law; and
>
> (2) a compelling reason must be shown for any distinction on the basis of sex, race, national or ethnic origin, colour or religion.

We prefer this because it is much cleaner. The only restriction mentioned in it is the compelling reason. It is an affirmative statement and not a negative denial on certain grounds.

However, another acceptable formulation would be:

> Section 15(1) every person shall have equal rights in law, including the right to equality before the law and to the equal protection and benefit of the law without unreasonable distinction on any ground including sex, race, national or ethnic origin, colour, religion, marital status, age, physical or mental handicap, sexual orientation, political belief and previous conviction; and
>
> (2) a compelling reason must be shown for any distinction on the basis of sex, race, national or ethnic origin, colour or religion.

Just to reiterate, we do prefer the drafting, I said it before, but my second suggestion is preferable to the present one, so if we have to be denied our first preference, we will take the second preference over Mr. Trudeau's offer.[71]

She listed the benefits of her organization's entire set of proposals for section 15, including:

> 4. A strict scrutiny test will apply to distinctions on the traditional grounds of race, sex, national or ethnic origin, colour or religion.
>
> 5. The court may apply a strict scrutiny test to the other grounds or reasonableness test as circumstances warrant.[72]

---

71 *Minutes of Proceedings, 9 December 1980*, *supra* note 43 at 57–59.

In answer to a senator's question, Acheson yet again clearly expressed her organization's intent: "All we are doing in Section 15(1) is setting a standard through those cases where discrimination can almost never be justified and we are leaving it open to the courts discretion to decide whether it will use a compelling reason test or a reasonableness test with respect to the other cases."[73] She went on to explain, in the following passage that I quoted earlier:

> One of the questions that is often addressed at this point is the question of the physically handicapped person. Why should not the compelling reason test apply there. There is a very good reason, because you want to be in a position to make some discrimination in respect to a physically handicapped person. You want to be able to pay additional benefits to that person; you want to be able to require three apartments in every housing complex to be accessible to physically handicapped persons. So the court needs more flexibility to deal with those issues and we do not want to hamstring the court. We want to show the court what our goal is, our ideal is a compelling reason test, but at the same time that you give the court a standard, you must give the court responsibility to act judiciously.[74]

## D. The Third Harmful Argument to the Joint Committee: Leave Out Mental Disability from Section 15 and Require All Section 15 Claims to First Be Vetted by Human Rights Commissions before Courts Can Rule on Them

### *1. A Bizarre Chain of Human Rights Reasoning*

Perhaps the weirdest harmful argument of all, and one of which I only became aware four decades after the fact, came from the Saskatchewan Human Rights Commission. Its lead spokesperson at the Joint Committee was its Chief Commissioner Ken Norman, an experienced professional in the human rights field. In his rather confusing answers to the Joint Committee's questions, it sounded like he was recommending against including mental disability in section 15. I had to reread his answers several times to try to figure out what he was saying. I remain unclear, confused, and, most of

---

72 *Ibid* at 60.

73 *Ibid* at 64.

74 *Ibid* at 65.

all, troubled by them. I set out the relevant passages in full in the next section of this retrospective. A Joint Committee member invited him to comment on, among other grounds, the lack of protection in section 15 for people with physical disabilities.[75] As a disability rights advocate, I would have hoped and expected that he would just give a resounding "yes" to this invitation and would have added mental disability as well. It had been just days before that the COPOH and the CAMR had called on the Joint Committee to add both physical and mental disability to section 15. My appearance at the Joint Committee was still 1 week away.

Thankfully, Norman agreed that grounds like physical disability could be added.[76] However, on the inclusion of mental disability, he appeared to contradict himself, supporting it at some points but possibly opposing it at others.[77] He was unclear on whether that was what he was saying and, if so, why he was saying it. He did not ever say why governmental discrimination because of mental disability would be *per se* acceptable. At points in his long answer, he sounded like he actually might support second-tier protection for people with mental disabilities as well as those with physical disabilities.[78] If his presentation remains confusing to me after multiple reads, it could well have led members of the Joint Committee to see the Saskatchewan Human Rights Commission as, at the very least, arguing for lesser protection for people with physical disabilities and perhaps no protection against discrimination based on mental disability.

I would have wanted him to tell the Joint Committee that disabilities do not necessarily come in neat, mutually exclusive, watertight compartments. A physical disability can also accompany a mental disability and vice versa. Excluding one from the *Charter* would *ipso facto* impair protection for the other. Making this worse, Norman heartily supported the National Advisory Committee on the Status of Women's proposal, critiqued earlier, that section 15 be amended to mandate two different levels or tiers of equality rights protection. He explicitly agreed with Ebert's proposed division in which some equality-seeking groups got stronger protection and others

---

75 *Minutes of Proceedings, 5 December 1980*, *supra* note 61 at 19–20.

76 *Ibid* at 19–20.

77 *Ibid* at 19–20, 24.

78 *Ibid* at 19–20.

got less. He appeared to list physical disability among those in the second tier of protection.[79]

It got worse still. Norman told the Joint Committee that he aimed "to raise serious questions of institutional competence with regard to the antidiscrimination provisions of the proposed Charter."[80] He sought to argue "that Section 15 creates serious difficulties with regard to the interface between the ordinary courts and statutory human rights agencies."[81] He had an understandable concern about how well the courts would deal with interpreting equality rights, given their unfortunate history in this area.[82] It took committee members several tries to find out whether he even agreed with or opposed entrenching a charter of rights in the Constitution.[83] Norman argued that statutory human rights commissions (like the one he headed) were created to do a better job of implementing equality rights.[84] That was the conventional legal wisdom since well before 1980. He advanced the incredibly harmful suggestion that a new section be added to the *Charter* to provide that a person could not go to court to try to enforce their section 15 equality rights until and unless they had used up all their other legal options.[85] He asked the Joint Committee to insert this into the *Charter*: "[N]o law or practice shall be construed as inconsistent with Section 15 unless any other remedy available and provided for by law has been sought."[86]

Had I known about this back in 1980, I would have wanted to tell the Joint Committee in loud and clear terms to resoundingly reject it. His proposal would have created a major, costly, and harmful new procedural roadblock to equality claimants. First you would have to file a complaint with a Human Rights Commission. Then enjoy spending years trying to get your case resolved satisfactorily. Only after that could you go to the courts to enforce your equality rights under the *Charter*. The human rights and constitutional adjudication processes were already replete with too many barriers to access to justice. Adding another new barrier? No thanks! That

---

79 *Ibid* at 17–18, 20.

80 *Ibid* at 5.

81 *Ibid.*

82 *Ibid* at 6–11.

83 *Ibid* at 14.

84 *Ibid* at 6–7.

85 *Ibid* at 11–12.

86 *Ibid* at 12.

amendment would have lengthened the lineups of complainants at Human Rights Commissions across Canada. Since then, and without this added *Charter*-based burden being imposed on them, those Human Rights Commission line-ups have only gotten scandalously longer due to chronic underfunding of those agencies and to the growing number and complexity of the cases they receive. Had Parliament accepted Norman's counter-productive recommendation, those delays in enforcing human rights would have gotten even worse, to the detriment of discrimination victims.

Another part of his presentation added a different indirect problem from a disability rights perspective. Norman had signalled to the Joint Committee a real concern with including protection in section 15 against discrimination because of age.[87] The original text of section 15 already included age as a prohibited ground of discrimination. We disability rights advocates now regularly emphasize that age is the most common cause of disability. Any reticence about effective constitutional protection against age-based discrimination was thereby harmful for people with disabilities.

## 2. What Was Said: The Saskatchewan Human Rights Commission's Key Troubling Remarks to the Joint Committee That Hurt the Case for a Strong Disability Amendment

There were two troubling responses from the Saskatchewan Human Rights Commission from a disability perspective. Here is the first:

> **Leslie Gordon Benjamin:** Now, again, the Saskatchewan Bill of Rights prohibits discrimination because of race, creed, religion, colour, sex, marital status, physical disability, nationality, ancestry or place of origin, and our resolution as it is worded does not mention creed, marital status or physical disability.
>
> Could you comment on the distinction between creed and religion, how the courts may view the absence of the word "creed," or absence of the words "marital status," or absence of the words "physical disability"?
>
> **Norman:** To begin with, sir, I think that "creed" is redundant. I may stand corrected by lawyers around the room more able than I, but in my experience it has been interpreted, on those few occasions when it has been considered, to be coterminous with freedom of conscience, religion. So if I can set that

[87] *Ibid* at 18, 22.

aside, I do not think its absence has any significance that one should be wringing one's hands over from the proposal.

Marital status, physical disability, and to those two could be added the categories which you have had advanced before you that exist in some jurisdictions that do not exist in Saskatchewan, and you have heard, of course, from organizations like the Mental Health Association seeking a further definition of disability beyond physical, to include forms of mental disability, retardation and so forth.

In my rather lengthy reply to Mr. Hnatyshyn's question, I tried to address that problem and I think, unless there is some other proposal that I am not aware of in my attempt to stay abreast of this Committee's proceedings, the most sensible and workable response has been provided in the brief of the Advisory Council on the Status of Women. I am very uneasy personally about setting down in the constitution today's list. We just held hearings in Saskatchewan on amendments to the code just last week. One group came forward, the Mental Health Association, in seeking to have that included in the code, and they gave a very interesting statistic. They said that in 1975, just five years ago, in the election they polled members of the legislative assembly and asked them: did they support the inclusion of physical disability in the code? The statistic they came up with was quite shocking; a very, very small number said yes. A very small number only five years ago.

Only two years ago the entire legislature unanimously supported the inclusion, so if that is any indication this field is moving and progressing quite rapidly, and I think it would be a shame to draft an antidiscrimination provision in such a way as to impede the opportunity of an organization like the Association for the Mentally Retarded to achieve legislative gains because now they are facing a constitution which seems to say: you are out.

**Senator John Connolly:** (inaudible).

**Norman:** Well, I am only saying they are making a very strong case in all jurisdictions to now be included in the legislation, and before you; I just cite them as a case in point.

**Joint Chairman (Senator Harry Hays):** Mr. Benjamin, go ahead.

**Benjamin:** Mr. Chairman, they want in, in terms of the Saskatchewan code?

**Norman:** Yes.

**Benjamin:** But you do not think it should be in the national constitution because it is for such a long period of time and in areas such as this there is a continuous progress and change?

**Norman:** In a nutshell, yes, sir, that is my position. I think it is better to have the two-tiered system and a broad invitation to the courts to consider questions of unreasonable distinction. I keep referring to Mary Eberts brief, but it did impress me. She gave an example on marital status, she said if you accept the

> language that was put forward by the advisory council, well then, it may well be that, I think she used the example of the drivers licence application which discriminated on the grounds of marital status, would be struck down in the courts, by the court saying that is not a reasonable distinction. So you have covered marital status without putting it in stone but not putting something else in stone such as economic status or such as mental disability or sexual orientation which only Quebec has had the courage to put forward into legislation to date.[88]

Here is the second troubling response:

> **Ron Albert Irwin:** Just one last question. You say that physically handicapped, mentally handicapped should be on, I think you called it a tier system. Many people have come before us and said unequivocally the physically handicapped should be in the *Charter*, but I think your experience is important. You are suggesting there are different types of rights that the physically handicapped have and we have to look at each one and what is reasonable. I put to you that maybe it is a good idea to put the right to employment of the physically and mentally handicapped in the federal charter and leave the right to services and so on to the human rights charters?
>
> **Norman:** Well, sir, I think that, as in my response to Mr. Benjamin on the question of the *Charter*, it is a constitutional document getting down to the detail of talking about a work place as distinguished from services or accommodation. I think that is a step in the wrong direction because even the work place alone, every human rights law in this country that deals with physical disability, and certainly those laws when they deal with mental disability, we have heard so from the Association of Mentally Retarded in their briefs to us as recently as last Friday, necessarily needs to have a reasonableness distinction standard because we have in this country all sorts of special employment provisions for people with multiple handicaps and disabilities, and they need to be addressed in a sensitive way by an agency or agencies, departments of labour included with human rights agencies, and I think to simply have a clear prescription is to invite the court to wonder what in the world to do with that, because it seems to be an invitation to upset a number of apple carts that have been put together by every government.
>
> **Irwin:** Thank you, Mr. Norman, your remarks have been informative.[89]

---

88 *Ibid* at 19–20.

89 *Ibid* at 24.

# XII. AN UNFORGETTABLE PHONE CALL

## A. Was There Any Hope That the CNIB Would Be Invited to the Joint Committee's Hearings?

After submitting the CNIB brief to the Special Joint Committee of the Senate and the House of Commons on the Constitution of Canada (Joint Committee), I had absolutely no expectation that we would be invited to make a presentation at its public hearings in Ottawa. Many groups had asked to make presentations. I earlier explained that the Joint Committee had very tight timelines because Prime Minister Pierre Trudeau was fast-tracking his constitutional patriation package through Parliament. Trudeau's speedy timetable maximized pressure on hold-out provincial premiers to cut a constitutional deal with him. It seemed that all hope for appearing at those hearings was lost. The Joint Committee's hearings were originally scheduled to wrap up by early December.[1] Our CNIB brief is dated 1 December 1980. No wonder we had not been invited to present at those hearings before it was originally slated to wrap up.

With the constitutional reform issue a headline grabber day after day, those who did not earlier ask to appear before the Joint Committee were no doubt coming forward to request a time slot. Moreover, being the first-ever televised meetings of any parliamentary committee, this was all getting more public attention. Back then, there was no parliamentary cable channel for watching proceedings of the House of Commons. For those of us who had cable television, a cable channel periodically televised public events. The Joint Committee was broadcast live through that channel, gavel to gavel. It was rerun during off-hours. Someone flipping channels to find something to watch could accidentally stumble on these proceedings. Public policy nerds like me tuned in on purpose to keep track of the proceedings.

This helped because, as I previously explained, mainstream media coverage of the patriation debates, though ample in quantity, included far too little discussion of which rights were included in or excluded from the

---

1 See Robert Sheppard & Michael Valpy, *The National Deal: The Fight for a Canadian Constitution* (Toronto: Fleet Books, 1982) at 343.

*Canadian Charter of Rights and Freedoms*.[2] The only possible exception was the controversial section 23 of the *Charter*, governing minority language education. This was a sensitive political topic because Quebec had elected a separatist provincial government. Quebec was restricting the opportunity to go to school in English for some children. Section 23 of the *Charter* could override that provincial policy.

A glimmer of hope for more groups to present at the Joint Committee hearings came after mounting public pressure and media criticism of the Joint Committee's tight timelines. I played no part in that pressure campaign, though I absolutely should have done so! On 2 December 1980 (the day after our brief's date), the Joint Committee was given authority to extend its hearings into the new year.[3] This extension was likely part of Prime Minister Trudeau's effort to try to win public support for his constitutional reform package over the heads of the objecting provincial premiers. Did this extension of the public hearings mean that we would get a chance to appear? I remember mulling that over on a walk home from the subway after a day in December at the boring bar admissions course. It was little more than daydreaming to fill the time. Did I not have anything better than public hearings on the Constitution to daydream about? This must have seemed exciting to me compared to the daily tedium of cramming for bar exams.

We heard nothing from Parliament over the week after the Joint Committee's hearings were extended. It seemed more and more unlikely that we were going to get invited to Ottawa. However, I still had a lingering tiny nagging thought in the back of my mind: "What if ...?"

## B. A Phone Call to Remember

The Joint Committee's Hansard transcript documents that, on 10 December 1980, there was still some wrestling going on over which organizations would next be invited to come to the public hearings.[4] The incredibly memorable phone call came unexpectedly that same day, sometime after 5:00 p.m. Parliament was inviting the CNIB to make a presentation at the

---

2 *Canadian Charter of Rights and Freedoms*, Part 1 of the *Constitution Act, 1982*, being Schedule B to the *Canada Act 1982* (UK), 1982, c 11 [*Charter*].

3 Sheppard & Valpy, *supra* note 1 at 343.

4 Canada, Parliament, *Minutes of Proceedings and Evidence of the Special Joint Committee of the Senate and of the House of Commons on the Constitution of Canada*, 32nd Parl, 1st Sess, No 23 (10 December 1980) at 32–37.

Joint Committee's hearings. Even before that call came, it had been quite a momentous week. During the afternoon of 10 December 1980, I was at Queen's Park, witnessing disability rights history unfold. Ontario Premier Bill Davis's Conservative government at long last completed second reading debates in the legislature on Bill 209, a comprehensive bill to amend the Ontario *Human Rights Code* to prohibit discrimination because of disability.[5] The biggest overhaul of that legislation since it was first enacted two decades earlier, this bill also made other substantial improvements to the Ontario *Human Rights Code*.

I anxiously watched the proceedings at Queen's Park along with other leaders of the Ontario Coalition for Human Rights for the Handicapped. We learned about the government's discussions with the opposition parties about possibly rushing this bill through the legislature without public hearings and, therefore, without any amendments. We decided to stand our ground and to insist on public hearings on this provincial bill so that we could get an opportunity to seek amendments. That day, I again skipped the lectures for the bar admissions course, which I and my classmates overwhelmingly found to be consistently unhelpful. We opted to simply study from the course's reading materials. It is no small irony that, 3 years later, I would begin a stint of over two decades of teaching in that same bar admissions course!

That afternoon, the Ontario legislature approved Bill 209 on second reading and sent it to a standing committee for public hearings.[6] That is where we would be able to seek amendments to the bill. I returned to my parents' home that day at dinner time. I planned to have dinner with my parents and then hit the tape-recorded books to study for my bar examinations. Our phone rang. It was incredibly good luck that I was home to take the call. We did not own an answering machine. Voice mail and cell phones were years in the future. Imagine if I had missed that call! I picked up the kitchen phone and casually said hello. A male voice at the other end of the call skeptically asked: "Is this the CNIB (Canadian National Institute for the Blind)"? I had no idea who was calling or why anyone would call our home number

---

5 Legislative Assembly of Ontario, *Hansard Transcripts*, 31st Parl, 4th Sess (9 December 1980), online: <www.ola.org/en/legislative-business/house-documents/parliament-31/session-4/1980-12-10/hansard>. Second reading of Bill 209 began at 5:00 p.m. *Human Rights Code*, RSO 1990, c H-19.

6 Legislative Assembly of Ontario, *supra* note 5. See the concluding remarks from 5:50 p.m. to 6:01 p.m.

to reach the CNIB. The CNIB's main phone number is very different from our family home phone number. Okay, so I am blind, but, still, what gives?

Shocked, my racing mind speculated whether this might be about the Joint Committee's hearings. Verbally stumbling, I asked who was calling. Sounding a tad dubious, the caller repeated his question rather than answering mine: "Is this the CNIB?" The caller said he was calling from Parliament on behalf of the Joint Committee of the Senate and the House of Commons on the Constitution of Canada to speak to the CNIB. I struggled to put on a professional businesslike voice. I told the caller that he had reached David Lepofsky, speaking on behalf of the CNIB. Still sounding skeptical, the caller said that the CNIB was invited to make a presentation to the Joint Committee on Friday, 12 December 1980, at 10:00 a.m. I was in stupefying shock. That was a mere 36 hours away. Pleading, I asked if we could make our presentation the next week. The caller gave me a categorical "no." I was told in effect that I had to take it or leave it. I said "yes" on the spot. I was thoroughly uncertain whether I had any authority to just accept this invitation without checking with anyone at the CNIB. I had not yet heard the expression that it is better to seek forgiveness than ask for permission. What a perfect illustration of that maxim!

One aspect of this otherwise disastrous timing was extremely fortunate. Throughout that fall and winter, I had one bar examination typically every 2 weeks, usually on Fridays. I had just survived a bar exam on the previous Friday, 5 December 1980. My next one would not be until Friday, 19 December. Thankfully, Friday, 12 December 1980, came smack in between those two exam Fridays. Had there been a bar exam on Friday, 12 December 1980, I would have had to refuse Parliament's invitation or to try to find a way to later take a make-up exam if there was such a thing.

## C. My First Reaction — Panic!

I now reflect on that phone call as the opportunity of a lifetime. I hit the disability rights advocacy jackpot after rolling the dice on an unbelievably long shot. However, on 10 December 1980, I experienced no joy, no excitement, and no awareness that such calls are very rare. After hanging up the phone at the end of that short call, I proceeded to panic! Terrified, I raced upstairs to my bedroom, lay on my bed, and stared at the ceiling. "What the hell do I do now?" I thought. Yes, blind people sometimes stare at ceilings! I had precious little time to get the CNIB's approval for this adventure, to make travel plans, to book a hotel, and to figure out who else from the CNIB would accompany me at Parliament. Oh, yes, I also had the exquisitely daunting task of doing all the needed research and of preparing an intelligent and intelligible presentation.

I had no idea what to do first. I am not sure I had ever booked an airplane flight before. I am certain that I had never reserved a hotel room. Back then you had to use a travel agent to book flights. It was already too late in the day to call one. In any event, I did not then have a travel agent or a credit card for booking a flight. It was inconceivable in 1980 that one might just sit down in front of an as-yet-uninvented personal computer and book flights and a hotel online in just a couple of minutes, day or night. I did not know what this would all cost. I had no pre-approved budget or signing authority to pay for any of it. I learned only well after the fact that Parliament would reimburse our travel expenses.

Terrified, the first thing I did was to phone Dayton Foreman, the volunteer vice president of the CNIB's National Council, at his home. In Chapter IV, I explained the important support I got from this blind retired psychiatrist, both when I faced surgery to have my eyes removed 2 years earlier and in battling resistance within the CNIB to some of my earlier advocacy efforts, 3 years earlier. I told Foreman about Parliament's invitation and pleaded for help. In his signature soft-spoken way, he was incredibly helpful and supportive. He instantly approved my decision to accept Parliament's invitation. It was him who ensured that the travel arrangements were made. The next afternoon, Foreman picked me up in a taxi to go to Toronto's airport. We flew together to Ottawa. It was my first experience travelling with a person who used a guide dog. Foreman also alerted the CNIB's managing director, Robert Mercer, who was at a meeting somewhere in Alberta. Because of a blizzard, it took Mercer 24 hours to fly to Ottawa to join Foreman and me as the CNIB's delegation at the Joint Committee.

## D. Rushed Legal Research on the Fly

The CNIB entirely relied on me to prepare and present our oral presentation to the Joint Committee. I do not recall whether Foreman, Mercer, or anyone else asked me to go over with them in advance what I planned to say to the Joint Committee. This blind pilot had to learn quickly to fly solo. After I got off the phone with Foreman, it was dinner time. My mother was serving steak, a perennial favourite of mine. My stomach was churning big time. I could barely bring myself to eat a thing. When I get very stressed, my appetite vanishes. I had a little over a day to prepare my presentation. The lack of any law school training on equality rights and on the legislative process came back to bite me with ferocious jaws.

What research could I do in the few hours available before I would be on stage and, unnervingly, on television cameras? All that was immediately available to me in a format I could read to help with my preparation for the Joint Committee were any pre-recorded audio books in the CNIB library and anything that I could get human beings to record for me to play back on audiocassette, all within 1 day or less. The CNIB's audio book library was extremely limited. As for law books, it only had books that I had earlier gotten them to record for my law school studies. None of those would help. Even if there had been something worth reading, they would not have been available to me after business hours,

Tackling this today, I could instantly access a wealth of legal sources online that my computer can read aloud to me. I could solicit help and advice over social media. Others could email helpful documents to me as attachments, including court cases, law journal articles, and even entire books. If they are in an accessible format like Microsoft Word, I can immediately read them or do searches within them without needing sighted assistance. In fact, today's embarrassment of electronic readable riches would present me with the problem of too much to read and insufficient time to read it all. In December 1980, such a problem would simply not compute in my mind!

After dinner, and again lying on my bed, staring at that uninformative ceiling, an idea suddenly hit me. It would help me big time if I could get my hands on examples of specific laws that discriminate against people with disabilities. I had no sighted assistant available to go to a law library with me at that hour to plow through thousands of pages of provincial and federal statutes and regulations in hopes of finding examples. Even if I had a volunteer willing to drive across Toronto that evening to invade my law school's library, it would not be possible to carry out the search that I desperately needed to do. There were no printed research tools for finding out which laws include terms like "disability." Emerging technology could come to my rescue, I thought, but it would be a long shot. Earlier that year, when working as an articling student at a private law firm (the required 1-year apprenticeship at a law office for law school graduates before they could take their bar exams and be admitted to the profession as a lawyer), I got an introduction to Quicklaw. It was then a very new and seemingly futuristic searchable computer database of court decisions, statutes, and regulations.

Currently operated by LexisNexis, you can now search these resources and other legal databases online from the comfort of home. To use Quicklaw in 1980, it was necessary to get your hands on a computer terminal at the Quicklaw office in downtown Toronto. Some large law firms apparently had terminals in their offices that were hard-wired to Quicklaw but that was quite new and exceptional.

How was I going to pull off a Quicklaw search in the evening of 10 December 1980? I did not work for a law firm at that time, much less one with a hard-wired Quicklaw terminal. I did not have a Quicklaw account. I had no time to race to the Quicklaw office in downtown Toronto at that hour, praying that an employee would still be there to do a search for me. What to do? I got Quicklaw's phone number from 411 and gave them a call. I was in luck. A kind and helpful Quicklaw employee answered. I feared she was heading out the door to go home. Grovelling abjectly, I told her my predicament and time crunch. On the CNIB's behalf, I needed to very quickly search all legislation in Canada to find any that talked about disability. I am sure I explained how I had earlier seen a demonstration of Quicklaw and was ever so impressed. I told her that the CNIB no doubt had no account with them and likely had not heard of Quicklaw. I told her that they could bill the CNIB later if they wished. I had no prior authorization for this and no idea what it would cost. She agreed to help me and never quoted me a fee. As far as I know, they never billed the CNIB.

I had to decide which search terms to use in databases of federal and provincial legislation and regulations. I had no experience doing any database searches. I had only once witnessed a short demonstration of Quicklaw, months earlier. What a time and case for on-the-job training. I asked her to search for terms such as disability, disabled, handicapped, deaf, or blind. She read aloud search results as they came up on her screen. How was I to keep track of the results? I scrambled to turn on a cassette recorder in my bedroom. It recorded me as I repeated aloud the search results that she read to me over the phone. It was painfully slow and cumbersome. Would we find any useful results? Who knew? Amidst the tension, some search results cracked me up. A *Highway Traffic Act* had provisions governing what to do if there is a "disabled vehicle" on the road. I did not feel that I was mandated to advocate for the pressing cause of the rights of disabled vehicles.

So many years later, I still vividly remember the dramatic background sound that I heard over the phone as she fed me the search results. Earlier that week, international rock star and beloved former Beatle John Lennon had been shot dead in front of his New York City home. I was one of the millions of devastated Beatles fans around the world who spiralled into deep shock and mourning that week. A huge memorial rally was underway across the street from the Quicklaw office in front of Toronto City Hall. Over the phone, I heard thousands singing "all we are saying is give peace a chance" as well as Lennon's song "Imagine," whose hopeful lyrics about fighting for social justice eerily befit our campaign for the disability amendment.

Apart from that Quicklaw research, I knew I needed a crash course in equality rights. Earlier that year, I had approached brand new Osgoode Hall Law School constitutional law professor Marc Gold. He had recently finished graduate studies at Harvard. I had contacted him for advice on what to do when undertaking my Master of Law at Harvard beginning in September 1981. Gold had written his master's thesis at Harvard on equality rights. As he was writing that paper, he could have had no idea how pivotal it would be in my preparation to argue at the Joint Committee for the disability amendment months later. Somehow, I managed to get my hands on a photocopy of his thesis. I rushed it to the CNIB's Toronto headquarters by taxi so that its volunteer readers could record it on tape. It was at least 100 pages long. A person reads about 25 pages aloud in an hour. I could not twiddle my thumbs for 4 hours before the entire thesis was recorded. Therefore, the CNIB sent each cassette tape to my home by taxi as a reader finished reading a part of the thesis so I could dive right into it. As each tape arrived at my home, I jammed it into my cassette player and inhaled whatever I could learn. The thesis took a broad theoretical look at the meaning of equality. It did not address the specific topic of disability equality. However, it was all I could get my hands on, so it was my veritable tree of knowledge.

As the hours ticked by on Thursday, 11 December 1981, I did not have the luxury of 4 hours to listen to these audio recordings. Once more, revolutionary new technology had come to the rescue. It enabled me to read Gold's thesis in half the time, freeing up two desperately needed hours for other preparatory work. Five years earlier, I got my hands on new technology that dramatically changed the lives of blind people. It was a specialized cassette player that could vary the playback speed. If I played a tape at faster than regular speed, the tape recorder adapted the reader's voice to sound normal despite talking more quickly. They did not sound like Alvin and the Chipmunks. This is now a standard feature on computers, smartphones, and tablets. For example, everyone can easily speed up a podcast or a commercially purchased audiobook. Now used by the broader public, that technology was originally invented to accommodate blind people.

Like many blind students, I had learned during my university studies to listen to audio recordings at double speed. I would typically absorb the information more effectively than I would if listening at normal speed. As an added bonus, it takes only 30 minutes to read 1 hour of audio. Over the years, many friends and colleagues have said to me: "It's amazing! I just don't know how you can possibly understand that!" I quip in response: "I just don't know how you sighted people can read that paper that is so flat! It's just utterly amazing what you sighted people are capable of!" Were these events occurring today, Gold could have emailed me his thesis, saving all the time and effort that it took to get his thesis to me in a form I could read. If he had it in hard copy, that would today create a short delay for me. We would quickly shoot the pages of his thesis through a document scanner. We would use widely available low-cost or free optical character recognition [OCR] software to speedily convert it to an electronic text that my computer could instantly read aloud to me. So often, the accommodations that are initiated to accommodate people with disabilities end up widely benefiting everyone. Like the technology for speeding up a tape, that OCR software is yet another measure that was originally invented to enable blind people to access printed text. It is now widely used by sighted people as well.

As I reflect back on these events, there is an amazing coincidence regarding Gold's helping me in my hour of maximum need. Almost four decades later, I plunged into disability advocacy at Canada's Senate. I previously mentioned how, in 2018, the House of Commons had passed Bill C-81, the proposed *Accessible Canada Act*, to tear down disability barriers that are within the federal government's regulatory reach. This was an outgrowth of the earlier campaign from 1994 to 2005 to get the Ontario legislature to enact the *Accessibility for Ontarians with Disabilities Act.*[7] Bill C-81, as passed by the House of Commons, was well intentioned but far too weak.[8] In 2019, the Accessibility for Ontarians with Disabilities Alliance and several other disability organizations campaigned to get the Senate to amend Bill C-81 to strengthen it. In the future, I plan to later write an account of the entire Bill C-81 saga.

---

7 *Accessible Canada Act*, SC 2019, c 10; *Ontarians with Disabilities Act*, SO 2005, c 11.

8 Canada, Parliament, *House of Commons Debates*, 42nd Parl, 1st Sess, Vol 148, No 359 (27 November 2018) at 24071.

I had no experience doing any advocacy at the Senate. I knew nothing about its formal procedures or the informal forces that drove senators' decisions on any issues. I had a massive need for a crash course. Where was I to turn? How about Senator Gold? After the events that first brought us together, we became friends in the early 1980s. We had been out of touch since then for no particular reason. As I was casting about in early 2019 for possible sources of wisdom, a colleague mentioned Senator Gold as a possibility. "He's a senator now?" I exclaimed. An email or two later, and we were back in touch. He delivered for me an indispensable crash course, one that I could not replicate elsewhere under unavoidable time pressure.

Unfortunately, 4 years later, when I and a cohort of other like-minded disability advocates tried to get the Senate to make amendments to another law, Bill C-22, the proposed *Canada Disability Benefit Act*, in the spring of 2023, that same senator became one of our most vigorous adversaries.[9] In the Senate, he served as one of the key representatives of the federal government of Prime Minister Justin Trudeau. He did all he could to strenuously oppose and scuttle the much-needed amendments we sought to that bill so that it would effectively achieve the government's stated goal of lifting people with disabilities out of poverty. Fortunately, we nevertheless got at least some helpful amendments passed. People with disabilities languishing in poverty needed as many amendments as we could secure.

Let's get back to 10 and 11 December 1980. I thought it might be clever to get the CNIB to transcribe our brief on the *Charter* into Braille and to record it on audio tape. I wanted to hand copies to each member of the Joint Committee. They had probably never seen Braille before and had never thought of the need for printed documents to be transcribed into alternative accessible formats for people with print disabilities. The CNIB had to get the brief transcribed in Braille and then copied. A reader needed to record it onto tape. That tape needed to be copied. We then needed to schlep all of this with us on the plane to Ottawa. I have no idea how the CNIB managed it all in under 24 hours.

9 *Canada Disability Benefit Act*, SC 2023, c 17.

## E. Assembling My Thoughts on the Night before My Day at Parliament

For reasons I did not know, Foreman and I booked into Ottawa's luxurious and historic Château Laurier hotel. I spent the evening alone in my hotel room, cramming and, most memorably, starving. I ordered room service. Doesn't that cost a fortune, I worried? Who is going to pay for all of this? I better pick something cheap, I thought. From one of Ottawa's nicest restaurants, I ordered a burger! That night, I got my earliest training in something that later became a regular part of my law practice over the next decades. Under ridiculous time pressure, I focused on systematically sifting through a blizzard of information, distilling the key points to make, structuring the presentation into a logical sequence, and trying to adorn it with zippy memorable turns of phrase. Even that early in my career, I had extemporaneously given many speeches. I knew that this one needed to be far more meticulously planned.

I now know so much more about tactical decisions to balance when designing a presentation to a legislative committee. How much of my allotted time should I use up delivering my speech? How many minutes should I leave for the Joint Committee to question me? What arguments will the members of the committee be thinking about? What is most likely to be troubling them? What hot button issues are they dealing with? Who within the government bureaucracy is likely giving pushback? How can I equip members of the committee to push back against the bureaucrats' pushback? What punchy lines might be most tantalizing for journalists? Most of these questions did not cross my mind that night.

## F. Preparing Speaking Notes: Not My Strong Suit!

I knew it was important to have detailed notes for my presentation. This presented a challenge that has recurred throughout my decades of law practice and community advocacy. How will I read notes if I indeed prepare any? I explained in Chapter IV that, in 1980 and all the way up to the present, my Braille reading skills have been very limited. As is typically the case with those of us who acquire literacy by visually reading print as a child and who later learn Braille in our teens or later, it would take me forever to read a book in Braille. Someone who learns to read Braille in their teens or afterwards, as a second mode of reading, cannot read Braille with the speed and proficiency or for the duration that is mastered by a person who learns Braille as a child as their first mode of literacy. Throughout my life, Braille has been a useful tool for jotting down a phone number or an address on an index card, having a few points written down as notes for a speech, labelling spice jars and cans of food products, CDs and DVDs, or reading a Braille label sewn into a shirt or pair of pants that says what colour the garment is.

I have never been able to use Braille to proficiently read aloud a quotation or other passage of text. This may surprise some people for someone like me who has had a long career as a courtroom lawyer, arguing complex appeals. In court, a lawyer is typically buried in paper, including transcripts, court decisions, legal research, and, of course, one's notes for their oral argument. Lawyers routinely read a judge some quotations aloud from cases or trial transcripts. I never do. Over the years, I have given hundreds of speeches, classes, lectures and seminars, oral arguments in court, legislative committee presentations, and other formal speeches. I never read a speech aloud from a prepared text because I cannot do so. I also happen to think that reading a speech aloud word for word is far less effective and compelling than speaking directly to an audience.

I almost never try to write a word-for-word script for a presentation. I certainly did not do so that night in Ottawa. I have found that composing a prepared text hurts rather than helps. I would quickly get distracted by trying to accurately memorize a prepared text. I instead prefer to develop and memorize a logical series of key points that I can deliver free of such distractions. My goal is to remember the points I want to make rather than the precise words for making them. When I am speaking to an audience, I am consciously thinking about what I want to say and how I want to say it. I hope that this makes me sound more natural and sincere. I aim to sound like I am talking to you, not speechifying at you. For anyone, this is a higher energy demand on the brain than merely reading a text aloud verbatim. I find that when people read a text aloud, they rarely sound like they are speaking naturally. For many speakers, it sounds more forced and less sincere. I marvel at newscasters who sound like they are not reading when I know that is what they are doing.

Throughout my career, I have succeeded with an evolving spectrum of strategies for notes. In December 1980, however, I had not yet had the chance to do that. Key technology had not yet been invented on which I have since heavily relied. Most notably, I did not then have a computer at all, much less a portable laptop with a screen-reading program to read speaking notes aloud to me through an earphone as I stand at a lecture. Braille was all I had in 1980, so Braille is what I used. That December night, I prepared Braille notes. For several years after that, I also spent hours on the night before a court appearance, transcribing my notes into Braille on a Perkins Brailler. It often turned out to be a monumental waste of precious last-minute preparation time!

I rarely get nervous when I am giving a speech. On the rare occasion when I do get jittery, like if I happen to be speaking to a parliamentary committee for the first time in my life about the very future of Canada's Constitution, my hands can get sweaty. Reading Braille with sweaty hands is like reading print through fogged-up eyeglasses. I do not recommend it! I do not know how much, if at all, I used my Braille notes when I was speaking to the Joint Committee. Over the years, when I have prepared Braille notes for a speech or courtroom oral argument, I rarely end up looking at them. They serve, at most, as a calming security blanket. When in law school, I set a standard for myself that I carried forward throughout my law practice. I have always wanted to know my topic so well that I would not need notes. My goal is to know it better than anyone else in the room. I also like to plan a logically structured presentation so that, once I begin, the rest of the presentation simply flows naturally. That, I believe, is what I did for the most part in the case of my appearance before the Joint Committee.

Adrenaline helps make up for my inability to fluently and quickly read Braille. That I am blessed with a good memory certainly makes this all easier. I wish I had been able to read Braille proficiently and fluently throughout my career. It would have been extremely helpful. I am in no way advocating against its use or against Braille education for students with vision loss. However, I have managed in my career without good Braille-reading skills.

# XIII. THE BIG DAY: ADDRESSING THE JOINT COMMITTEE

## A. Start Your Engines

I entered the Special Joint Committee of the Senate and the House of Commons on the Constitution of Canada (Joint Committee) meeting room on the morning of 12 December 1980, pumped, clad in a conservative-looking suit and tie, ready for action and more than a little nervous. A very weary CNIB managing director, Robert Mercer, met us there, exhausted after travelling for a full day to get to Ottawa. I apologized to him for putting him through that ordeal. Before the formal televised proceedings began, I got a brief chance to meet the committee's presiding co-chair for that day's proceeding, Senator Harry Hays. I may have been reading something into it, but his deportment seemed especially restrained. I was aware that, just a short time earlier, he had triggered embarrassingly bad press when he made a remark to representatives of the National Action Committee on the Status of Women, presenting at the Joint Committee, which reflected some of the very stereotypes about women against which they were campaigning:

> **Joint Chairman (Senator Hays):** We want to thank the National Action Committee on the Status of Women for being present today and for your brief. We appreciate you coming and as a matter of fact we are honoured. However, your time is up and I was just wondering why we do not have a section in here for babies and children. All you girls are going to be working and we are not going to have anybody to look after them.[1]

I quickly banished from my mind my vivid recollection of the senator's earlier and oft-re-aired embarrassing video clip. I needed to focus on my goal that morning.

Let me describe my presentation's key points and offer some reflections on them. The entire Hansard transcript of my presentation to the Joint Committee is set out in Appendix 1.

---

1 Canada, Parliament, *Minutes of Proceedings and Evidence of the Special Joint Committee of the Senate and of the House of Commons on the Constitution of Canada*, 32nd Parl, 1st Sess, No 9 (20 November 1980) at 75.

## B. Try to Quickly Grab the Joint Committee's Attention

I tried a double-barrelled opening to quickly grab the Joint Committee's attention. I wanted to show that there was strong support within the disability community for the call for the disability amendment. I feared that the committee's members might think that there was not a great deal of support for it. I presented a letter of endorsement from the Ontario Federation of the Physically Handicapped.[2] You will not find this coalition on Google. In 1980, it was a group of some 37 disability organizations that the Ontario March of Dimes had brought together. I had been working closely with the March of Dimes for months. The March of Dimes was a key player in the Ontario Coalition for Human Rights for the Handicapped as we campaigned to get the Ontario *Human Rights Code* amended to prohibit disability discrimination. It only took me one rushed phone call to get the March of Dimes to prepare this important endorsement letter.[3]

Next, to exemplify our commitment to equality, we passed copies of our brief in Braille and recorded on audio cassette to each member of the Joint Committee.[4] No doubt, these members of parliament and senators had only ever received briefs in print and had never given a moment's thought to the need to make printed information available to people with disabilities in accessible formats.

## C. My First Argument: Combatting Pervasive Problematic Attitudes Towards People with Disabilities

I pivoted to the core reasons why we needed constitutional protection against disability discrimination. My first salvo was one that I was quite comfortable launching. I had used it for a half dozen years in speeches and a few media interviews. I argued that we needed the disability amendment to combat the results of pervasive harmful public attitudes towards people with disabilities.[5] As touched upon in Chapter IV, for a half decade leading up to that day in speech after speech, I, like many other people with

---

2 Canada, Parliament, *Minutes of Proceedings and Evidence of the Special Joint Committee of the Senate and of the House of Commons on the Constitution of Canada*, 32nd Parl, 1st Sess, No 25 (12 December 1980) at 5 [*Minutes of Proceedings, 12 December 1980*].

3 *Human Rights Code*, RSO 1990, c H-19.

4 *Minutes of Proceedings, 12 December 1980*, *supra* note 2 at 5.

5 *Ibid* at 6–7.

disabilities, had tried to dispel the prevailing notion that the biggest problem we face is our disabilities. People look at a blind person, I thought, and too often all they see is the white cane. They so often assume that we are pitiful and utterly incapable of doing most things on our own. At that time, it was transformative and even fundamentally disruptive to tell an audience that our problem is not our disability but, instead, the attitude of others towards our disability.[6]

For that time, this was a revolutionary argument. The conventional wisdom within Canada was that our disability was our big problem. When a person with a disability achieved something, such as a blind person becoming a lawyer, we were viewed as amazing and inspirational. That was rooted in the basic belief that, with a disability, it is basically impossible to be independent. Anyone with a disability who accomplishes anything must be a superstar. Those who called us inspirational, amazing, or superhuman sincerely thought they were complimenting us. That description, however, was and remains hurtful and harmful, despite its being well intentioned.

In 1980 and earlier, quite a number of others within the disability community were saying the same thing that I said. I had picked up their message, adopted it, and perhaps put my own verbal polish or spin upon it. When I have appeared before legislative committees since that day, I have had chances to field-test arguments and select the punchiest turns of phrase used in earlier speeches, media interviews, and lectures to professional organizations. Other than this lead-off argument, I had not had a prior chance to field-test my other arguments in support of the disability amendment before I addressed the Joint Committee that day. The only earlier opportunity I had had was the paltry 5 minutes or less that I got to speak to the Special Parliamentary Committee on the Disabled and Handicapped 3 months earlier.

My strategy in December 1980 — namely, starting my argument by shaking up the audience with a paradigm shift when thinking about disability — is now deeply embedded in my advocacy. I summed it up for the Joint Committee:

> The biggest problem very often resulting from blindness or other handicap is the well-intentioned cruelty which many members of the public unintentionally or unknowingly impose upon us. The pity, the patronization, discriminatory attitudes and condescension which handicapped people know to be, unfortunately,

---

6 *Ibid* at 5.

> almost nonstop components of their life, is in fact the biggest problem they face.[7]

I did not candy-coat the barriers we faced in society. I attributed them to the prevailing public attitudes towards people with disabilities.[8] I argued that, for a majority of people with disabilities "the public is not often ready to accept us as equals, not by reason of malevolence, but because of uninformed or misinformed attitudes, underestimating our capabilities by fear of the handicapped person — you might call it the "freak syndrome," not perceiving a handicapped person as just a normal human being."[9] I explained that this has led to job discrimination against people with disabilities that, I said, "the public are only now becoming conscious of." The barrier we face is "the employer who cannot believe you can function" or a landlord who fears that a tenant with a disability may be "a health hazard."[10] I also said that education is only accessible "to a limited degree" to a student with disabilities.[11] I tied the pervasive attitude towards people with disabilities to the fact that most buildings are inaccessible "as we all know."[12]

I made a particular point that day that I continue to make in many of my speeches and lectures on disability issues four decades later, with only minor modifications to update my terminology: "These are functions of an attitude that the world simply does not contain handicapped people or that those handicapped people are not going to be out there trying to get job, trying to get into housing or buildings."[13] I explained that this attitude is most in need of action when it comes to legislation:

> Handicapped people in the struggle for equality and equality of opportunity find that not only do people discriminate in the access to jobs, buildings, facilities, services and housing, but that, in fact, legislators, persons passing laws have also experienced the same negative attitudes towards the handicapped and have passed laws which are in fact discriminatory. ... Here, we are

---

7 *Ibid.*

8 *Ibid.*

9 *Ibid* at 6.

10 *Ibid.*

11 *Ibid.*

12 *Ibid.*

13 *Ibid.*

> concerned with not just human conduct which is discriminatory, but legislation which discriminates.[14]

Rereading my presentation to the Joint Committee decades later, I almost cringe at the fact that so central a plank in my case in support of the disability amendment was that it was needed because of pervasive harmful attitudes towards people with disabilities.[15] I largely dropped that line of argument years ago. This is so even though I am keenly aware of the fact that problematic public attitudes towards people with disabilities persist to this day, though to a somewhat reduced degree or in a more gently expressed form. I have moved it to the back burner in no small part because politicians, who resist enacting or enforcing mandatory accessibility legislation, often argue that, because disability barriers arise from public attitudes, the solution is simply more public education on disability. Yet our overwhelming experience over these many decades shows that public education does not solve the problem. Our aim is to change actions that create or perpetuate barriers. Changes in attitudes will follow from those changes in actions.

## D. My Second Argument: Excluding People with Disabilities Contradicts the Government's Stated Goal of Equal Rights for All Minorities

Turning back to the Joint Committee, my second line of argument was that section 15's exclusion of disability contradicted the Trudeau government's stated purpose for the *Charter* as a whole.[16] I contended that it was in effect beyond dispute that section 15, as it was then worded, does not guarantee equality for people with disabilities.[17] I argued that this exclusion "perpetuates in our constitution an attitude which, as I have mentioned, is prevalent in society, some notion of handicapped people as second class citizens, people who need to be taken care of, not given independence, protected, not given the opportunity of equality."[18] I insisted that the only way for the *Charter* to live up to its own stated intent was to pass the disability amendment. To

---

14 *Ibid* at 6–7.

15 *Ibid* at 5, 14.

16 *Ibid* at 7.

17 *Ibid.*

18 *Ibid.*

support this, I contended that the government's stated intention was that the *Charter* would guarantee equality for all minorities.

In support, I referred to a statement by External Affairs Minister Mark MacGuigan.[19] In Chapter VIII, I described how I had questioned that minister weeks earlier when he spoke at Toronto's Holy Blossom Temple. I told the Joint Committee that section 15, as it was then written, only guaranteed equality for some, not equality for all: "In other words, it involves equality for some; and equality for some, I submit, really means equality for none. It means that there are two levels in society, one level of people who are entitled to equality and one level who are not. And when you have two distinct classes such as that the term 'equality' has been stripped of its meaning and rendered more of an illusion."[20] I told the committee that MacGuigan had said a couple of weeks earlier, on the government's behalf, that people with disabilities do not need a constitutional right to equality.[21] I described in Chapter VIII how he had said this at Holy Blossom Temple in response to my question to him about the disability amendment at a Sunday morning brunch event.

Having set my target in front of the Joint Committee, I launched into my counter-attack. I listed for the Joint Committee several laws that discriminate because of disability, some of which I learned of for the first time during my panicked Quicklaw search two nights earlier.[22] Referring to my earlier exchange with MacGuigan, I said: "[W]hen I pointed out certain things that I am about to point out to you, he explained that he had never heard of them before and would probably need to rethink the whole issue."[23] I gave six examples:

1. provincial minimum wage laws that let a government give an employer a license to pay people with disabilities less than the minimum wage, at times without requiring that government to give reasons;[24]

2. provincial jury legislation that categorically excludes blind persons from serving on a jury, whether or not vision is required to assess the

---

19 *Ibid.*

20 *Ibid.*

21 *Ibid* at 8.

22 *Ibid* at 8–9.

23 *Ibid* at 8.

24 *Ibid.*

case, even though "there are many cases where vision is not necessary and probably the lack of vision may be of benefit to a juror";[25]

3. Ontario social assistance legislation that lets the government, by executive order, pay social assistance owing to certain people with disabilities living in institutions, to the head of the institution (this is not limited to situations where the social assistance recipient was incapable of managing their own affairs);[26]

4. Ontario's education legislation that allows a student with a disability to be excluded from their local public school and provides only segregated education if the student cannot "profit from instruction";[27]

5. British Columbia's school legislation, which categorically provides that certain people with disabilities who are totally and permanently disabled cannot be employed by their school board until they lose their disability;[28] and

6. federal immigration legislation that imposes on a proposed immigrant with disabilities a higher burden to be allowed to immigrate to Canada. They must show that they will not present an excessive demand on health and social services.[29] Ten years later, I would author a chapter of a book, in which I show how such legislation violates section 15 of the *Charter*.[30]

I explained that each of these laws discriminates because of disability and that their very existence refutes MacGuigan's claims,[31] concluding: "This is evidence of how the legislatures have taken care of handicapped rights to equality."[32]

---

25 *Ibid.*

26 *Ibid* at 9.

27 *Ibid.*

28 *Ibid.*

29 *Ibid.*

30 David Lepofsky, "Equality Rights of Persons with Disabilities: Canadian and International Perspectives" in KE Mahoney & P Mahoney, eds, *Human Rights in the Twenty-first Century* (Dordrecht: Kluwer Academic Publishers, 1992) at 169.

31 *Minutes of Proceedings, 12 December 1980, supra* note 2 at 10.

32 *Ibid* at 10.

## E. My Third Argument: People with Disabilities Are a Large Minority

My third line of argument was that people with disabilities are a large minority. I argued that some say we comprise one in ten people.[33] That number seemed huge back then. Now, it is small compared to our present numbers, which are closer to one in five, based on government statistics.[34] In 1980, I did not use one of the strongest arguments I now use in virtually every speech I give on disability equality: people with disabilities are the minority of everyone! Everyone either has a disability now or gets one later as they age. That zinger would have strengthened my case before the Joint Committee.

## F. My Fourth Argument: Definitional Concerns Are No Reason to Reject the Disability Amendment

I then turned from making the case for the disability amendment to refuting the real or imagined arguments against us.[35] I always use this approach and strongly recommend it. I first take the high ground, showing why our position is right, before demonstrating why an opponent's contrary position is wrong. I always want my audience to immediately start to think through an issue in accordance with my approach to it. I then try to convince my audience that my opponent's reasoning is flawed. I do not want to let my opponent's arguments define the terms of the debate or to dominate how decision-makers think through an issue.

The first argument against us that I addressed was the claim that it was hard to define "disability" or "handicap." I told the Joint Committee that the government, and, possibly, Justice Minister Jean Chrétien, argued that we should not pass the disability amendment because it is hard to define disability. I said that the justice minister had argued that we should wait until we can formulate a disability definition and later ask for the *Charter* to be amended sometime in the future once the Constitution has been patriated.[36] I cannot remember how I had learned that the government was making this

---

33 *Ibid.*

34 See Statistics Canada, "New Data on Disability in Canada, 2017" (2018), online: *Statcan* <www150.statcan.gc.ca/n1/pub/11-627-m/11-627-m2018035-eng.htm>.

35 *Minutes of Proceedings, 12 December 1980*, *supra* note 2 at 10–12.

36 *Ibid* at 10.

argument. I countered with three points to refute that contention. First, I argued that some legislation had successfully defined disability and that other laws had not needed or "bothered" to include any definition of it. I offered to supply the committee with examples if they needed any. I felt very comfortable with this issue.[37] I had done volunteer work for the Ontario Coalition for Human Rights for the Handicapped earlier that year, drafting a proposed disability definition to incorporate into the Ontario *Human Rights Code*.

Second, I argued that the burdensome constitutional amending formula was not a practical option for people with disabilities, who often live below the poverty line, and for the limited resources of the non-profit charitable organizations that serve them.[38] Third, I contended that the Constitution as written and with the *Charter* added has any number of undefined and more vague terms. [39] I pointed to the term "religion" in section 15 and the term "reasonable limits" in section 1. Dredging up joyful memories of my first-year law school constitutional law course, I pointed to the amorphous term "criminal law" in section 91 of the *British North America Act 1867*, over which courts had wrestled for a century.[40]

## G. My Fifth Argument: Costs Are No Reason to Exclude Equality for People with Disabilities

My fifth line of argument was to refute any thought that the disability amendment should be rejected because it was too costly.[41] I did not attribute this argument to anyone, but I figured from all my experience to date that it was lurking somewhere out there. I questioned what those costs would be and whether they would be excessive. I was skeptical that there would be too many such costs.[42] I questioned whether the government had costed each of the other new rights in the *Charter*.[43] As I think now about that argument, I should have invited the Joint Committee to ponder more specifically the price tag for other *Charter* rights. A barrage of examples

37 *Ibid.*

38 *Ibid* at 10–11.

39 *Ibid* at 11.

40 *Ibid*; *British North America Act, 1867* (UK), 30–31 Vict, c 3.

41 *Minutes of Proceedings, 12 December 1980*, *supra* note 2 at 11.

42 *Ibid.*

43 *Ibid.*

would have driven my point home more effectively. For example, police and prosecutors have had to make major changes now that accused persons have a constitutional protection against unreasonable search and seizure.

I pushed back that to selectively hold cost against people with disabilities is inherently discriminatory.[44] I should have bluntly added that no one asked how much it would cost to guarantee equality to women, religious minorities, or racialized communities. Nor, of course, should they. This is simply the price of democracy. I argued that such a cost argument wrongly presupposes that equality for people with disabilities is the lowest of every governmental spending priority: "To say that the cost is too excessive is to assume that handicap inclusion is the absolute lowest priority of every government in Canada, that we have spent every last dollar of revenue we have taxed and collected and that there is no money left."[45]

I have learned over and over throughout my decades of disability advocacy that cost is often a major instinctive, knee-jerk, ill-reasoned, or unreasoned obstacle when one advocates for reforms to promote equality for people with disabilities. Too many still harbour a built-in stereotype that disability equality must cost a great deal. This assumes that we cannot do very much unless a lot of money is spent to enable us to fully participate. It tends to start from the presumption that spending that money to include us is just not worth it unless we can show otherwise. Since that day four decades ago, I have found that concerns about cost are raised even when it is transparently obvious that they are not relevant. For example, I had to fight a long battle and two human rights cases against the Toronto Transit Commission [TTC] between 1994 and 2007 to get the TTC to consistently and reliably announce each subway, bus, and streetcar stop so that blind people like me could know when we have arrived at our desired destination.[46] In the midst of that battle, a senior staff TTC lawyer once told me that their resistance was due to the cost of providing the stop announcements.

In fact, it costs absolutely nothing for a subway crew or a bus or streetcar driver to use their mouth and the pre-existing public address system to announce each route stop. Each driver has a mouth and, hopefully, knows where they are. The TTC never argued at the Human Rights Tribunal of

---

44 *Ibid.*

45 *Ibid* at 12.

46 *Lepofsky v Toronto Transit Commission*, 2007 HRTO 41; *Lepofsky v Toronto Transit Commission*, 2005 HRTO 20.

Ontario that costs were a reason for failing to consistently deliver route stop announcements. The TTC's piles of mandatory documentary disclosures did not show that cost was ever a factor in their decisions against me. Yet the senior TTC lawyer with whom I had been chatting no doubt just assumed that that was the case, exemplifying this deep-rooted and unfair stereotype. What did cost the TTC a great deal was the $450,000 of public money they wastefully spent on lawyers to fight against my two successful human rights claims.[47]

Were I before the Joint Committee today, I would make additional arguments to oppose the cost concern. I did not think of them in December 1980. I would add that the costs of removing and preventing barriers against people with disabilities have many collateral benefits. When a restaurant installs a ramp at its front entrance to replace a step or two, it makes the restaurant accessible to customers with disabilities. It also makes the restaurant accessible to customers with a baby stroller or shopping cart. The restaurant will make money as a result of installing that ramp. It will lose those customers' business if it does not fix that barrier. I would also add that we need equality for people with disabilities not only to remove existing barriers but also to prevent the creation of new ones. Preventing barriers costs little or nothing. To allow the creation of new barriers costs the public a great deal. That is because it triggers the entirely avoidable cost of later having to remove those barriers.

## H. My Sixth Argument: Do Not Strip from Section 15 Any List of Protected Grounds

I was alive to the serious problem, explained in Chapter XI that some organizations had called on the Joint Committee to strip from section 15 any list of prohibited grounds of discrimination so that the provision would simply guarantee a right to equality. I told the Joint Committee that this would be preferable to the original text of section 15 (which locked out people with disabilities).[48] However, we otherwise opposed that option because we had no assurance that the courts would interpret such a provision as including

47 David Lepofsky, "Waste of Public Funds to Oppose Accessibility," *Toronto Star* (22 November 2007), online: <www.thestar.com/opinion/2007/11/22/waste_of_public_funds_to_oppose_accessibility.html>.

48 *Minutes of Proceedings, 12 December 1980, supra* note 2 at 12.

equality for people with disabilities. I pointed to the courts' restrictive approach when it came to equality issues as well as disability issues.[49] I added that it would cost thousands of dollars to take the case all the way to the Supreme Court of Canada just to achieve this goal: "So the only way of guaranteeing our rights is by including us."[50]

At the Joint Committee, I did not present an additional argument about which I knew nothing at that time and which I discussed in Chapter XI. An open-ended section 15 that does not enumerate human rights-based grounds of discrimination upon which it is meant to focus could steer section 15 far away from egalitarian principles.

## I. My Seventh Argument: Make the List of Prohibited Grounds of Discrimination Non-Exhaustive

Beyond the disability amendment, I argued for four additional revisions to the *Charter*'s wording in section 15 and elsewhere. First, I asked for section 15(1) to be revised to guarantee equality before the law without unreasonable discrimination or without unreasonable distinction. I said it should provide "unreasonable discrimination meaning without restricting the generality of the foregoing" to be followed by a non-exhaustive list of prohibited grounds of discrimination.[51] This shows that I was alive to the need to expand section 15 so that its list of prohibited grounds could be judicially expanded, even if the disability amendment was explicitly incorporated into section 15. I argued: "[I]f an equality clause is truly to give us equality, it must give us equality with all others. And that is the way to do it."[52] I did not make the point during my presentation to the Joint Committee that my proposed wording was far preferable to the troubling hierarchical approach to equality that at least two women's organizations had requested, which I explored earlier in Chapter XI. I was aware of the danger that their argument posed for us. On the other hand, I was then oblivious to the fact that "unreasonable distinction" or "unreasonable discrimination" risked delivering protection that was too weak for equality of any sort. That understanding

---

49 *Ibid* at 12–13.

50 *Ibid* at 12.

51 *Ibid.*

52 *Ibid.*

would have to wait until my graduate law studies at Harvard in the following year, if not longer.

## J. My Eighth Argument: Strengthen the Guarantee of Equality in Section 15

I added the CNIB's voice to the other organizations that asked the Joint Committee to strengthen the way in which section 15 expresses the right to equality.[53] We all said one way or another that the *Charter*'s wording must deliver a loud, clear, and unmistakable message to Canada's courts if the courts are to overcome their reluctance to implement egalitarian principles.[54] However, I missed a good opportunity by not serving up to the Joint Committee a helping of specific wording to achieve this goal. What happened to my strong belief that, as a community advocate, you must do the detail work for decision-makers? We were all correct to worry in 1980 that Canada's courts were not prepared to vigorously enforce civil liberties guarantees. This concern has been reduced since then. We owe a huge debt of gratitude to the Supreme Court of Canada's Chief Justice Brian Dickson for his years of dedicated leadership during the years after the *Charter*'s enactment. He signalled in the earliest *Charter* decisions that the *Charter* is to be liberally and vigorously interpreted and enforced.[55]

## K. My Ninth Argument: Rein in the Sweeping Defence That Section 1 Affords Government

My ninth line of argument was to press the Joint Committee to reduce the overbroad defence that section 1 of the *Charter* gave governments.[56] It would let a government off the hook if it showed that a *Charter* violation was a reasonable limit on the *Charter* right, which is justified in a free and democratic society with a parliamentary system of government. I said that it "makes the rest of the *Charter of Rights* a virtually worthless and impotent

---

53 *Ibid.*

54 *Ibid* at 12–13.

55 See e.g. *Canada (Director of Investigation & Research, Combines Investigation Branch) v Southam Inc*, [1984] 2 SCR 145 at paras 1, 17–19, [1984] SCJ No 36; *R v Oakes*, [1986] 1 SCR 103 at paras 62–80, [1986] SCJ No 7; *R v Big M Drug Mart Ltd*, [1985] 1 SCR 295 at paras 137–143, [1985] SCJ No 17 (QL).

56 *Minutes of Proceedings, 12 December 1980*, *supra* note 2 at 13.

means of protecting civil liberties."[57] I, like others, called section 1 the "Mack truck" provision because it created a loophole that was so massive that a government could drive a Mack truck through it.[58] I argued that governments could well justify the discriminatory laws I had earlier outlined as "generally accepted," relying on the pervasive public belief that people with disabilities "are often not capable of taking care of themselves, not capable of maintaining a job, not capable of self-sufficiency."[59]

I proposed that section 1 should not apply to sections 14 or 15 of the *Charter*.[60] Section 14, as amended, ensures that a person involved in a legal proceeding has the right to an interpreter, if needed. The Joint Committee was later to amend section 14 to include deaf people.[61] I submitted: "[T]here should be no circumstances where the right to an interpreter, which a deaf-blind or just a deaf person may require in court, should ever be taken away. Why is it either in war or emergency that a deaf-blind person on trial should be denied an interpreter to know what the case is against them. It is too basic and a denial of natural justice."[62]

## L. My Tenth Argument: Do Not Delay Equality Rights

The original text of the *Charter* delayed section 15's equality rights from coming into force for 3 years.[63] I argued that there was no good reason for equality rights to be delayed: "If anything, they should be accelerated."[64] Looking back now, I understand why it made sense for me to pitch that argument. However, it was an unrealistic one. The federal government was correct to see that all governments would need 3 years to bring themselves into compliance with section 15. Sadly, however, governments did too little

---

57 *Ibid* at 13.

58 *Ibid.*

59 *Ibid.*

60 *Ibid.*

61 See *Canadian Charter of Rights and Freedoms*, Part 1 of the *Constitution Act, 1982*, being Schedule B to the *Canada Act 1982* (UK), 1982, c 11, s 14; Canada, Parliament, *Minutes of Proceedings and Evidence of the Special Joint Committee of the Senate and of the House of Commons on the Constitution of Canada*, 32nd Parl, 1st Sess, No 47 (28 January 1981) at 8.

62 *Minutes of Proceedings, 12 December 1980, supra* note 2 at 13.

63 Canada, Parliament, *The Canadian Constitution: 1980, Proposed Resolution Respecting the Constitution of Canada* (Ottawa: Government of Canada, 1980) at 20.

64 *Minutes of Proceedings, 12 December 1980, supra* note 2 at 13.

from 1982 to 1985 or since then to achieve this, insofar as things like equality rights for people with disabilities is concerned.

## M. My Closer

Winding up, I warned that, if the disability amendment was not passed, there would be two harms. It would be unfair to people with disabilities. It would also mislead the public into thinking that the *Charter* guarantees equality for all and protects all minorities when it did not.[65] I always aim to end an oral argument or speech on a strong, memorable note. Too often, I have not succeeded. On my daily walks home from the subway station earlier that month, spurred on by a nagging thought that we might get invited to present to the Joint Committee (no matter how long a long shot it was), I daydreamed about what I might argue. It was on one of those walks that I came up with the closing line that I used when addressing the Joint Committee. For years afterwards, I have used that closer to conclude speech after speech about equality for people with disabilities: "Finally, I would close by saying that there is an oft-stated adage that justice is blind; in fact, it is a cliché. Our concern — and the underlying concern of this presentation — is that while justice may have had the opportunity to experience blindness, we are asking for blind persons, as well as for other handicapped persons, to be given, at last, an opportunity to experience justice."[66]

## N. Fielding Three Questions from the Joint Committee

Once I finished, there was time for questions from the Joint Committee. I knew nothing about how legislative committee members conduct themselves during public hearings or how to use the process to advance my goals. When members of a legislative committee who are elected politicians ask questions, they can be posturing for the media and the public rather than making the kinds of inquiries you would expect from a judge grilling me in court. Often, members of a legislative committee are mainly trying to impress upon the presenters that they are genuinely listening and how deeply they do care. I have learned over the years since then, arguing many cases in court and presenting to legislative committees, that a question-and-answer exchange gives me a chance to see how much my audience has absorbed

---

65 *Ibid* at 14.

66 *Ibid.*

and understood my presentation. In the case of legislative committees, I never assume that their members have read my written brief that was filed with them in advance.

From the Joint Committee's three questions to me, my sense then and now is that the questioners barely understood many of the details that I had just tried to methodically present. They got the core message that there was something wrong with the proposed *Charter* from a disability perspective and that we had been left out. That alone was my core objective so whether they processed all the details in my argument was not as important. The audience I needed to convince that day went far beyond the Joint Committee members, whether or not I was aware of that as I was ploughing through my points. The Joint Committee was being carefully monitored by the three major political parties' officials in order to decide what their next moves would be in the political arena. No doubt, officials in the Department of Justice were also monitoring it so they could later brief their political masters on the options open to them and the arguments that would support those options. Those political masters were themselves thinking about how the television audience at home was reacting to what witnesses had to say. That would form part of their political calculation.

When I appear before a legislative committee now, I am keenly aware that party officials and senior public servants are the true audience whom I must convince. If the media covers the proceedings, I know that they are an additional important audience. In the case of a live broadcast of a legislative committee, I am laser-focused on the fact that I am also speaking to the television audience at home. Add to the mix the availability of live streaming, we can now use the video of my legislative committee presentation as a valuable social media weapon in our campaign.

The first question to me came from Senator Richard Donahoe. He told me that when he was a provincial attorney general, a blind person applied for a job as a crown attorney. Donahoe said he struggled with the decision but ended up hiring the person. The person worked out very well.[67] Donahoe asked me if I understood the difficulty he faced struggling with that decision. He asked me to highlight what would be the benefits to people with disabilities if we secured the amendment we sought.[68] I answered that I understood how difficult his deliberative process would

[67] *Ibid* at 15.

[68] *Ibid.*

have been since we people with disabilities must ourselves go through that process. I had to think it through before deciding to go to law school.[69] This question gave me an early chance to learn how to use such questions as a platform to drive home our argument. I explained that, if the disability amendment was passed, then we could take a case to court if a legislature had gone through such a deliberative process but gotten the result wrong. People with disabilities could challenge legislation that was discriminatory.[70]

I added that if the disability amendment were not added to the *Charter*, it would signal to people with disabilities that they are not entitled to equality before the law. It would constitutionally entrench the pervasive view of them that is inherent in the daily discrimination that people with disabilities face.[71] If it were adopted, then Canada would take the best possible move during the International Year of Disabled Persons to ensure equality for people with disabilities. It would tell Canadians that a new era has begun for those "who in the past have either been a forgotten minority or a lesser class of citizen."[72]

The second question to me came from Member of Parliament Victor Althouse. He asked whether the disability amendment would help address the problem of discrimination against blind people in employment.[73] I explained that this is principally the focus of human rights legislation, not the *Charter*. I said that the disability amendment would help educate the public that people with disabilities are entitled to equality.[74] I said that it might be argued that any province's *Human Rights Code* that does not ban discrimination because of disability might contravene the disability amendment. I tried to sound balanced by saying that I doubted that such an argument would succeed.[75] Ironically, my off-the-cuff legal judgment that day in December 1980 turned out to be incorrect. That argument, which I then doubted, has great merit.

In 1986, concern about this very kind of constitutional vulnerability under the disability amendment led the Ontario legislature to remove a

---

69 *Ibid*.

70 *Ibid* at 16.

71 *Ibid*.

72 *Ibid*.

73 *Ibid* at 16–17.

74 *Ibid* at 17.

75 *Ibid*.

problematic exemption from the Ontario *Human Rights Code*, which had hitherto unfairly limited protection for people with disabilities. In 1981, the Ontario legislature amended its *Human Rights Code* to prohibit discrimination because of disability in employment and access to goods, services, and facilities.[76] However, it created an unfair exemption that would not allow for a claim of disability discrimination if it were based solely on the fact that the premises were physically inaccessible. Section 16(1)(a) of the 1981 Code provided in material part:

> 16. (1) A right of a person under this Act is not infringed for the reason only
>
> (a) that the person does not have access to premises, services, goods, facilities or accommodation because of handicap, or that the premises, services, goods, facilities or accommodation lack the amenities that are appropriate for the person because of handicap.[77]

In 1986, the Ontario legislature repealed this exemption. It did so in an omnibus bill aimed at bringing provincial legislation in line with section 15 of the *Charter*.[78] The chain of reasoning that I largely dismissed in 1980 was the very chain of reasoning that led the Ontario legislature to helpfully expand human rights protections for people with disabilities in 1986. In the same vein, in 1988, the Supreme Court of Canada held that Alberta discriminated against LGBTQ2S+ people because it did not prohibit discrimination based on sexual orientation in Alberta's anti-discrimination legislation.[79] The Supreme Court's reasoning demonstrated that my thinking on the analogous disability issue in December 1980 was erroneous and far too cautious.

The third question to me, this time from Senator John Connolly, began with him telling me he thought I would make a good lawyer and hoped I might run for Parliament (which I have never wanted to do).[80] I will spare you from how that free unsolicited career advice landed with me, then and now. Connolly then asked whether it would be segregation against people who are blind or who have a disability if disability was included in section 15. His question read in material part:

---

[76] *Human Rights Code*, *supra* note 3, ss 1, 4(1).

[77] *Ibid*, s 16(1)(a).

[78] *Equality Rights Statute Law Amendment Act*, SO 1986, c 64, s 18(9)(1).

[79] *Vriend v Alberta*, [1998] 1 SCR 493, [1998] SCJ No 29 (QL).

[80] *Minutes of Proceedings, 12 December 1980*, *supra* note 2 at 18.

> You have been talking, and the other groups which have represented the handicapped have also been talking, about the importance of integrating the handicapped community into the normal stream of public life.
>
> I think great strides have been made as education has advanced, and as public education in this respect has improved. I do not ask you this as a trick question, but I wonder whether, by segregating the handicapped you are not, to use your own words, signaling to the disabled that they are forever a segregated group?
>
> Would your position not be stronger before the law, even before these provincial laws which you have criticized here, if a non-discriminatory clause applied equally to you, whether you are handicapped, equally to me, whether I do not happen to be physically handicapped, maybe mentally and so on; but would it not be better in the long run not to have a special category set out in a constitution which, presumably, is to last for a very long time?[81]

I did not understand, then or now, why a ban on discrimination against people with disabilities could constitute segregating people with disabilities. I responded to Connolly by explaining how the CNIB and other disability organizations were then advocating for the integration, not the segregation, of people with disabilities.[82] I then reiterated why it would be problematic for us if section 15 did not list some prohibited grounds of discrimination, including disability.[83] That latter answer was not responsive to the question. However, by luck, it ended up being a point worth making and was the point on which our presentation was to conclude. Our time had run out.

## O. A Surprise on the Way Out the Door

With my adrenaline pumping, we completed our presentation and started to leave the room. It was at that point, unexpectedly, that I was approached by a man who identified himself as Eddie Goldenberg. I had very briefly worked with him at a private law firm earlier that spring during my articling experience. Since that time, he had gotten a job working on Justice Minister Jean Chrétien's political staff. He would have a long career working for Chrétien after this time, ultimately becoming his chief of staff towards the end of Chrétien's later stint as Canada's prime minister.

He said hi to me as we were walking out of the Joint Committee's meeting room. I recall almost nothing of our inconsequential exchange. It

81 *Ibid* at 18–19.

82 *Ibid* at 19.

83 *Ibid*.

should have occurred to me on the spot that this was a golden opportunity at which I should immediately leap. I should have asked for his phone number so that we could have a follow-up conversation. In fact, I should have tried to schlep him out into the hall then and there to press him hard on getting the disability amendment approved: "What's the real hold-up? Who do we need to convince? Can we work together on this?" Foolishly, I did not. Instead, my preoccupation while leaving that meeting room was to get home as soon as possible to make up for my failing to be home that morning for the start of my mother's birthday. I did nothing whatsoever that day to celebrate the fact that I had just gotten a chance to tell Canada's Parliament to give people with disabilities a constitutional right to equality. It deserved a celebratory blowout but got none! It was time to get back to the endless boredom of studying for bar exams.

## P. Media Coverage the Next Day

On the same day that I appeared before the Joint Committee, the CNIB issued a news release. I have absolutely no recollection of anything about it, either working on its text or discussing its distribution. It too was excavated from my garage in preparation for this retrospective. It reads almost identically to the news release that the CNIB's Public Education and Advocacy Committee [PEA Committee] issued 5 weeks earlier. The CNIB staff must have thrown it together with lightning speed the day before our appearance in Parliament, drawing on the CNIB's brief to the Joint Committee and the PEA Committee's very similar earlier news release that I quoted in Chapter VI. The CNIB's news release on 12 December 1980 made this statement:

> "The exclusion of handicapped people from the right to equality under the proposed Constitutional *Charter of Rights* has made the *Charter* meaningless to hundreds of thousands of handicapped Canadians," stated CNIB spokesman David Lepofsky appearing before the Special Joint Committee on the Canadian Constitution in Ottawa on December 12.
>
> Mr. Lepofsky, a blind law student representing The Canadian National Institute for the Blind, recommended that "mental or physical handicap" be included in the nondiscrimination section of the *Charter*.
>
> The proposed wording provides for the right to equality before the law and to the equal protection of the law without discrimination because of race, national or ethnic origin, colour, age or sex. Because "mental or physical handicap" is not listed, handicapped persons remain disentitled to equality.

"The repudiation of handicapped persons' human rights is made all the more shocking because the *Charter* is proposed to be enacted in 1981, during the International Year of Disabled Persons."

Mr. Lepofsky also criticized the proposed exemption clause pointing out that exemption should not apply to certain rights such as protection from discrimination and the right to an interpreter for a deaf or a deaf-blind individual.

He said the proposed exemption clause could be interpreted by the courts as rendering constitutional virtually all legislation passed in Canada whether or not it infringed the fundamental rights listed in the *Charter*.[84]

Amazingly, the media briefly broke radio silence the next day on the campaign for the disability amendment. On 13 December 1980, the *Globe and Mail* included a Canadian press report on my presentation to the Joint Committee on page 12. I have no idea whether our 12 December 1980 news release played any part in triggering this article. The report incorrectly said I was a University of Toronto law student rather than a graduate of Osgoode Hall Law School. That mattered not a bit. The story read:

*Globe and Mail*, December 13, 1980, Page 12

Handicapped Require Help, Hearing Told
Saturday, December 13, 1980

Ottawa ONT — OTTAWA (CP) — Blind law student David Lepofsky told the parliamentary constitutional committee yesterday that handicapped people ought to be given constitutional guarantees against the discrimination many laws now inflict on them.

Reading his presentation in Braille before the committee, Mr. Lepofsky, a University of Toronto student, said that if the constitution is to guarantee equality before the law, "it must be equality for all and that must include the handicapped." He was speaking on behalf of a brief presented by the Canadian National Institute for the Blind.

He said that a section in a proposed charter of human rights that would prohibit discrimination on the grounds of race, national or ethnic origin, color, religion, age or sex should be amended to include "mental or physical handicap." This would make laws that discriminate against the handicapped unconstitutional.

He said provincial wage laws now shut out handicapped people from their protection, blind people are automatically excluded from juries when sight is not necessary in many trials, marriage laws discriminate against mentally

84 Canadian National Institute for the Blind, *CNIB Media Release* (12 December 1980) at 30.

> defective people and the *Family Benefits Act* of Ontario allows payments for handicapped people to be made to civil servants on their behalf.[85]

Supplementing that coverage were the reruns over that weekend of that Friday's proceedings on a cable television channel. I happened by luck to stumble upon the rerun of my testimony that Sunday while at home with my parents. What I did not then reflect upon, but now would be ecstatic about, is that such reruns provide a great chance for our message to reach a broader public, at least for the two or three other people across Canada who may watch that television channel! They also could play on the minds of political staffers in Ottawa who were sizing up what they needed to do to respond to the Joint Committee's public hearings.

## Q. Reflecting Back on That Day

Watching the video of my presentation to the Joint Committee is somewhat challenging for me. My voice sounds higher. My arguments at a technical level covered the ground I needed to cover. My repeated use of the term "handicap," common in those days but outdated now, makes me flinch. I got the chance to make points that the two prior disability organizations — the CAMR and COPOH — did not cover at all or in the same way, though I did not know at the time what they had said. My speaking style was far more reminiscent of a law student who is still trying too hard to sound like a lawyer. Years of public speaking since then have helped, I hope. If I had it to do again, I might be less deferential. I would try to hit home with zippier, readily quotable one-liners. A decade on Twitter has sharpened my pencil, as the outdated saying goes.

As I prepared and delivered my remarks, I incorrectly assumed that the only thing that could be challenged under section 15 was legislation that discriminates. I did not apply my mind to the fact that one could also challenge any government action that discriminated because of disability. Leaping to my own defence, I plead that, in the dreary federalism cases that we studied in first-year constitutional law, we focused virtually all the time on challenges to legislation and to nothing else. With decades of the *Charter* now under our collective belts, I am keenly aware of the fact that most discrimination that takes place against people with disabilities is not explicitly written into the text of legislation. It takes place in the application of

85 "Handicapped Require Help, Hearing Told," *Globe and Mail* (13 December 1980) at 12.

legislation or in the administration of government programs. Had I thought of this in 1980, my catalogue of disability discrimination that could be actionable under the disability amendment would have been longer and stronger.

If only I had known in advance that Goldenberg was in the room listening to me. I would have covertly directed my entire argument right at him, even though it would have been worded to sound like I was speaking to the Joint Committee members. In recent years, I have quite consciously done this sort of thing. If it is done correctly, even my chosen target should be left oblivious to this tactic. Today, with the miracle of live streaming in Parliament and YouTube, I have learned to get the video of a parliamentary committee presentation edited, captioned, and posted online as quickly as possible, sometimes within hours of the big event itself, as Chapter IV mentioned. Social media can do the rest, leading to hundreds or thousands of online views!

That is what we did when I addressed the House of Commons Standing Committee on Human Resources, Skills and Social Development and the Status of Persons with Disabilities on 14 November 2022 on the need to strengthen Bill C-22, the proposed *Canada Disability Benefit Act*.[86] My presentation was posted on our YouTube channel with captions, all within hours. Days later, it was sliced, diced, and posted in seven short videos on TikTok. In less than 2 months, it had been seen in whole or in part over 1500 times. It quickly became the tip of our advocacy spear on that bill. In contrast, the video of my presentation to the Joint Committee on 12 December 1980, posted about 10 years ago, has been seen on YouTube over 2000 times.

Finally, I always learn a great deal by taking a close and critical look at a speech, legislative committee presentation, or media interview that I have recorded. I always find that there is something I could have done better, and I hope each time to build on that reflection. I tell law students that we call the work of a lawyer "practising law" for a good reason. We should continue practising and practising, trying to eventually learn how to do it right, right up to the day when we take our final leave from the profession. The day you think you know it all and have nothing more to learn is the day

86 *Canada Disability Benefit Act*, SC 2023, c 17. See the "Video of David Lepofsky's Evidence at the House of Commons Standing Committee on Human Resources, Skills and Social Development and the Status of Persons with Disabilities" (14 November 2022), online: *YouTube* <www.youtube.com/watch?v=4Kq-DVtTu1s>.

you should immediately stop working as a lawyer because that misinformed arrogance will undermine your effectiveness, I warn students.

In the case of arguments made to support the disability amendment, we can all be proud that we collectively won and that we made a plausible case for it. We also need to be alive to positions that we advanced back then that were erroneous. I am certainly not exempt from this scrutiny! Fortunately, none of these turned out to matter one bit. Once again, no harm, no foul! Each of the three disability organizations that made presentations to the Joint Committee in support of the disability amendment made some remark or other that was, with hindsight, to say the least, not optimal! In Chapter X, I described how COPOH wrote the Joint Committee on 9 January 1981, urging that physical disability be added to section 15. This contradicted COPOH's earlier written and oral submissions that called for section 15 to ban discrimination based on all disabilities, not limiting it only to physical disabilities. Since then, the Council of Canadians with Disabilities, COPOH's revised name, has a proud history of strong inclusive cross-disability advocacy.

As I also explained earlier in Chapter X, the New Brunswick division of the CAMR took the lead position that section 15 should list no prohibited grounds of discrimination at all. This action, as I showed, would have created barriers and burdens for people with disabilities. However, thankfully, the CAMR's national leadership took a stronger position in favour of the disability amendment, pure and simple, while the New Brunswick division of the CAMR at least took the fall-back position that, if section 15 is to include a list of prohibited grounds of discrimination, disability should be added to that list.

For my part, I regret that I proposed that the Joint Committee use the term "unreasonable distinction" in section 15. Since then, I have come to understand that it has not been helpful for the cause of disability when judges, lawyers, and legal scholars talk about discrimination in terms of drawing "distinctions." In an article in the *Supreme Court Law Review*, which I mentioned in Chapter III entitled "A Professional Comedian's Fundamental Right to Publicly Bully a Child Because of His Disability? Scrutinizing *Ward v Quebec Human Rights Commission* through a Disability Lens," I summarized my thoughts on this terminology as follows:

> Ward is the latest in a long line of Supreme Court cases that assesses whether a person's equality rights were violated and whether they were subject to discrimination by asking if a distinction was drawn against them on protected

grounds such as disability. This erroneous "drawing distinctions" formulation has for years misdirected the equality/discrimination analysis.

People with disabilities do not experience discrimination as a government or private actor "drawing a distinction" against them. When the Toronto Transit Commission refused to reliably announce each bus or subway stop for the benefit of blind passengers like me, we did not decry: "TTC drew a distinction against me." This is instead experienced as a denial of a right or opportunity, as subjection to a burden, or as encountering a barrier to full participation and full benefit.

I am not being picky about wording. From a student's first week in law school, they learn about distinguishing cases, as they struggle to understand stare decisis. The drawing of distinctions is not what equality in Charter Section 15 or its Quebec Charter counterpart are about.[87]

[87] David Lepofsky, "A Professional Comedian's Fundamental Right to Publicly Bully a Child Because of His Disability? Scrutinizing *Ward v Quebec Human Rights Commission* through a Disability Lens" (2023) 108:2 SCLR 169 at 178–179.

# XIV. THE JOINT COMMITTEE ADOPTS THE DISABILITY AMENDMENT

## A. What Is a Clause-by-Clause Review of a Bill?

In January 1981, after the Constitution Committee's public hearings were finished, the time came for the Special Joint Committee of the Senate and the House of Commons on the Constitution of Canada's (Joint Committee) clause-by-clause review of the entire constitutional reform package, including the *Canadian Charter of Rights and Freedoms*.[1] Committee members review the package section by section and vote each section up or down. As each section of the package comes up for discussion, committee members can bring motions to amend that section. The Joint Committee debates a proposed motion, votes on it, and then votes on the section as a whole, with any approved amendments being part of that approval.

Clause-by-clause review began in earnest on 12 January 1981, with the justice minister delivering an all-important speech to the Joint Committee.[2] All politically obsessed eyes were on Ottawa that evening. After weeks of public hearings, this was the moment when the Trudeau government would respond. The justice minister was to announce which amendments to the constitutional reform package the government would introduce. Because the Liberals had a majority in the House of Commons, we knew that the Joint Committee would approve any amendments that the justice minister announced. The Liberals were eager to get as much public enthusiasm as possible for the *Charter*. It was their biggest selling point with the public in the patriation package and one of the biggest obstacles for the hold-out provincial premiers. The Liberals could help that effort by beefing up the *Charter* and responding favourably to a wide spectrum of community groups in this package of amendments.

---

1 *Canadian Charter of Rights and Freedoms*, Part 1 of the *Constitution Act, 1982*, being Schedule B to the *Canada Act 1982* (UK), 1982, c 11 [*Charter*].

2 Canada, Parliament, *Minutes of Proceedings and Evidence of the Special Joint Committee of the Senate and of the House of Commons on the Constitution of Canada*, 32nd Parl, 1st Sess, No 36 (12 January 1981) at 9–21.

Anyone seeking amendments to the proposed *Charter* was watching that night to see whether they won or lost. I was one of them, sitting in my bedroom with the television on while trying in vain to study for my next bar exam. We had not yet purchased a video cassette recorder to record live television broadcasts. I was left to simply listen and to react from memory. Two things are striking about this process, reading it with years of experience since then. First, it is fascinating to see how extemporaneous some of the justice minister's exchanges were with members of parliament and senators once he finished reading his prepared text. You could tell when he was going from pre-scripted talking points (with which he may not have agreed) to his folksy personal style. It is also striking how at least some fellow Liberals were prepared to show that they saw a need for the disability amendment. Years later, members of parliament on the government side are on a much tighter leash. Breaking ranks with the party line, even informally in such a public place, would now likely lead to some fast public backtracking for them. Second, I am delighted at how quickly and how often the issue of the disability amendment came up. It appears that the pro-disability amendments that the Joint Committee received from the CNIB, the Coalition of Provincial Organizations of the Handicapped [COPOH], and the Canadian Association for the Mentally Retarded [CAMR] sunk in.

## B. The Trudeau Government's Initial Response to the Public Hearings

Reading a carefully crafted speech, the justice minister commended the many presentations that the Joint Committee heard during its 175 hours of hearings. In response, he stated as a general starting point: "Today I want to announce that the government is prepared to make major changes to the draft resolution so as to strengthen the protection of human rights and freedoms in the *Charter*."[3] He announced an array of amendments.[4] They were aimed at strengthening the *Charter* in the face of critics who had argued at the public hearings that the *Charter* was too weak. Among these, he specifically said that the government was prepared to strengthen section 15.[5] However, from the perspective of those of us pressing for the disability

3 *Ibid* at 10.

4 *Ibid* at 11–21.

5 *Ibid* at 13–15.

amendment, Jean Chrétien's speech was a monumental let-down. He rejected the call for adding disability to the list of grounds of forbidden discrimination named in section 15, stating:

> Equality rights — There has been much discussion of the non-discrimination provisions of the Charter as found in Section 15. I want to deal with this in some detail. First, I want to state that I agree with the proposal made by the Advisory Council on the Status of Women and the National Association of Women and the Law that the section be entitled equality rights so as to stress the positive nature of this important part of the Charter of Rights.
>
> I want to take this opportunity to congratulate all of the witnesses who testified on this section. I want specifically to compliment the Advisory Council on the Status of Women for a particularly fine brief as well as for an impressive presentation before you. The work of the Council has greatly influenced the government as have the presentations of the many witnesses who have spoken on this subject on behalf of women's groups, the handicapped, and others.
>
> A provision on "equality rights" must demonstrate that there is a positive principle of equality in the general sense and, in addition, a right to laws which assure equal protection and equal benefits without discrimination. To ensure the foregoing and that equality relates to the substance as well as the administration of the law, I would be prepared to accept an amendment to Section 15(1) so that it would read: "Every individual is equal before and under the law and has the right to the equal protection and equal benefit of the law without discrimination and in particular without discrimination based on race, national or ethnic origin, colour, religion, sex or age." I know that many witnesses have recommended either that the grounds for non-discrimination be widened to include handicapped persons or others or that there be no specific enumeration and that more discretion be left in the hands of the courts. The government has studied these representations with great care.
>
> The position of the government is that certain grounds of discrimination have long been recognized as prohibited. Race, national or ethnic origin, colour, religion and sex are all found in the Canadian Bill of Rights and are capable of more ready definition than others.
>
> I want to make clear that the listing of specific grounds where discrimination is most prohibited does not mean that there are not other grounds where discrimination is prohibited. Indeed, as society evolves, values change and new grounds of discrimination become apparent. These should be left to be protected by ordinary human rights legislation where they can be defined, the qualifications spelled out and the measures for protective action specified by legislatures.

> For example, it was only four years ago that federal human rights legislation specifically provided protection for the handicapped in the area of employment.
>
> Recently the Special Parliamentary Task Force on the handicapped chaired by David Smith has recommended changes and improvements in the Human Rights Act with respect to the handicapped. The government will be acting on some of the recommendations of the Task Force. The government is also proposing to act on some of the recommendations made by the Canadian Human Rights Commission in this area and will propose amendments to the Human Rights Act.
>
> But if legislatures do not act, there should be room for the courts to move in. Therefore, the amendment which I mentioned does not list certain grounds of discrimination to the exclusion of all others. Rather, it is open-ended and meets the recommendations made by many witnesses before your Committee. Because of the difficulty of identifying legitimate new grounds of discrimination in a rapidly evolving area of the law, I prefer to be open-ended rather than adding some new categories with the risk of excluding others.
>
> Section 15(2) of the draft Resolution permits affirmative action programs to improve the conditions of disadvantaged persons or groups. I am proposing an amendment to read: "Subsection (1) does not preclude any law, program or activity that has as its object the amelioration of conditions of disadvantaged individuals or groups including those that are disadvantaged because of race, national or ethnic origin, colour, religion, sex or age." This section permits programs designed to achieve equality which might otherwise be precluded by the rules against discrimination in subsection 15(1).
>
> The amendment will not preclude other programs to assist the disadvantaged — be it on grounds such as handicap, marital status or other bases of discrimination identified by the courts. It is simply an assurance that an affirmative action program based on a recognized ground of non-discrimination will not be struck down only because it authorizes reverse discrimination for the purpose of achieving equality.[6]

Chrétien proposed a revised section 15 that would enable courts to add to that section additional grounds of discrimination on a case-by-case basis.[7] At the same time, he explicitly rejected the call for the disability amendment. He would not add disability now, but the courts were free to do so later. For us, this was better than the original wording of section 15 that had irremediably excluded us. However, it was certainly not as good as approving the disability amendment to guarantee from the start that

---

6 *Ibid.*

7 *Ibid* at 14–15.

disability discrimination was constitutionally forbidden. By this compromise amendment, the Trudeau government appeared to duck the controversy surrounding calls to include sexual orientation in section 15. It tossed that seemingly hot political potato to the courts.

I surmised back then that, in October 1980, the Trudeau government had deliberately offered up a weak first draft of the *Charter* so that the government could later come forward after public hearings with stronger amendments in order to look responsive to public input. To this day, I have absolutely no evidence to support this. Whether or not that was the government's strategy, it was helpful that the government expanded the wording of section 15(1) to include equality before and under the law and the equal protection and equal benefit of the law. This was clearly revised to deliver to the courts the constitutional battering ram that I and so many other presenters sought in order to convey to Canada's judiciary that equality really means egalitarian equality and nothing less.

Immediately after his speech, the Joint Committee got to question the justice minister. The need for the disability amendment was raised within minutes, thanks to the New Democratic Party [NDP]. NDP Member of Parliament Lorne Nystrom had this exchange with the minister:

> **Nystrom:** I would like to refer now to a couple of things in the Charter of Rights itself. You have said on page 7, for example, of your comments to the Committee tonight, and I quote:
>
> The work of the Council, and this is of course the Advisory Council on the Status of Women, the work of the council has greatly influenced the government as have the presentations of the many witnesses who have spoken on this subject on behalf of women's groups, the handicapped, and others.
>
> The government has been, as you say, greatly influenced by the groups that have appeared and you have moved some considerable distance in terms of women's rights, and I think the suggested amendment is very interesting, one we will take a very serious look at. You have moved some distance in some other areas.
>
> We have also had handicapped groups before the Committee and you said that the groups that have appeared have greatly influenced the government, and I would like to ask you why you do not include in the Charter of Rights any reference to the handicapped, to the physically disabled, to the mentally disabled in our country.
>
> We have had some groups before us who came and made some pretty good arguments, and you said you have been greatly influenced. I would like to know where the influence is.

**Chrétien:** The position is that the list enumerated there is not exclusive and any other rights on discrimination the court could intervene.

The problem is we say that these rights have to mature in the Canadian society. For example, we will still have a Human Rights Commission and we will still pass legislation on different groups to make sure that their rights are protected, but they have to mature and this list that I have enumerated, excluding the others, we have opened up that clause so that other types of discrimination can be taken care of by the courts, if Parliament and legislative assemblies do not intervene.

But to start to enumerate more in that category where their rights are starting to be protected by legislation and so on, and if there is discrimination against handicapped and so on, we say that the court can intervene even if we do not want to enumerate them at this time because many of those rights are difficult to define. It is in the process of maturing, that is why it is not there.

But before, the clause was limiting the element of discrimination. Now it is not limiting them; other types of discrimination can be covered by the courts too.

**Nystrom:** I remind you, Mr. Minister, that this year is the International Year of the handicapped, the year 1981, or the International Year of the disabled, rather, and I would like to know more of what you mean by rights have to mature. Why are the handicapped singled out? Why are the disabled singled out?

It seems to me that we should be enshrining some rights for them in our constitution. If you are not sure what kind of rights they are, perhaps the wording does not have to be as tight as in some other cases, but surely to goodness there can be some reference that we cannot discriminate against the handicapped.

**Chrétien:** I referred in my speech that we have enacted some legislation in relation to the handicapped in the last four years. There will be some more. We still have the Human Rights Commission working on that and we have to prepare some amendments.

But we have opened up the clause so that the clause is not limiting the type of discrimination to the enumeration of discrimination as mentioned.

Just to give you an example. In the Charter of Rights as presented by Mr. Diefenbaker, the word "age" was not there at that time, but over the years this has gained maturity and it is finding its place there, and the first enumeration we had was limiting the type of discrimination. We have opened up to other types of discrimination that can be covered by the courts if the Parliament or assemblies do not take care of the problem.

So I do think that it is a very important amendment but we do not want to have the problem of definition at this time because it was creating too many difficulties.

> **Nystrom:** In your personal opinion, Mr. Minister, has the right to enshrine the rights of the handicapped matured by this time?
>
> **Chrétien:** If there is positive discrimination against handicapped and nobody is acting, in my reading of that section, the courts could intervene.
>
> **Nystrom:** Why not enshrine it then if it has matured?
>
> **Chrétien:** They are, because the clause is open.[8]

After this, the first tiny crack in the government's armour started to appear in response to a question from Liberal Member of Parliament Bryce Mackasey.[9] The justice minister agreed that he might be open to further amendments coming from the Joint Committee beyond those that he had just announced, stating: "Of course, time is running short, but it is possible there are one or two amendments I might propose myself, and I will look at the discussions in this Committee, and I am a reasonably reasonable person, if I can use those two words, so I will be listening to the Committee."[10]

Mackasey adverted to the disability amendment issue that evening, a topic he would raise again days later, stating: "Now, I do think, Mr. Minister, that you have gone a long way. I would say to you that when we get to clause-by-clause I, too, have some reservations about Section 15, and perhaps rather than include handicapped people, just draw it even more terse and reflect nobody, but that would be truly open ended, but we can get into those details later."[11]

## C. A Partial Victory That Felt Like a Major Defeat

The Trudeau government's position regarding the disability amendment, announced on 12 January 1981, made no sense. It looked like they were talking out of both sides of their collective mouth. On the one hand, the government opposed including disability equality in the *Charter*, reiterating its earlier feeble reasons for this. On the other hand, Chrétien said the government's amended text of section 15 gave courts a power to add grounds like disability to section 15. If the government truly opposed the disability amendment and felt like it had good reasons for doing so, it made no sense to give courts the power to do the very thing that the government thought

8 *Ibid* at 30–32.

9 *Ibid* at 35–37.

10 *Ibid* at 35.

11 *Ibid* at 36–37.

was a bad idea. On the other hand, if it would be good enough for courts to later add disability to section 15, why not add it now?

The government kept intimating that some grounds like disability had not yet matured sufficiently to be written into section 15. Back in Chapter VIII when I first addressed this dubious line of argument, I asked (please superimpose a sarcastic tone of voice, if needed): what on earth a ground of discrimination must do "to mature" enough? The need for equality protection seems the strongest where society has not yet even acknowledged that the minority in question has been subjected to discrimination. What the Trudeau Liberals had devised was an unusual, if not unique, form of constitutional amendment by judiciary. For any other new constitutional right to be added to the *Charter*, it would be necessary to go through the long and winding constitutional-amending formula. A judge could not simply decide that some new right or liberty was "mature enough" and should be judicially written into the *Charter*. But, in the unique realm of equality rights, the justice minister proposed that a court could render a ruling that would operate in effect as a constitutional amendment, writing a new ground of discrimination into section 15, including one that Parliament had consciously declined to insert.

Looking back, it was open to us on the evening of 12 January 1981 to declare the justice minister's speech a partial victory. Chrétien and the Liberal government opened the door to our asking a court to write disability into section 15. On the initial wording of section 15, this would have been impossible so, undoubtedly, it was a clear step forward. Moreover, it was a major win for us that the government rejected the request by two leading women's organizations that a harmful hierarchical approach to section 15 protection be written into the provision (explored in Chapter XI). It was also far better for us than I realized at that time that the government did not heed the calls from several equality-focused organizations to strip out of section 15 any and all named grounds of discrimination. I explained in Chapter XI how that revision to section 15 would also have been problematic for us.

However, on 12 January 1981, it most assuredly did not feel to me like any kind of a victory. It seemed to me at the time that the federal government was simply passing the buck to the courts. They had no compelling reason for opposing the disability amendment, but they lacked the moral or political courage to approve it. It was also reasonable to infer that the government feared the perceived political ramifications of including sexual orientation in section 15. With superb 20/20 hindsight, I can now say with real confidence that, had the 12 January 1981 amendments gone through as then proposed, with no disability amendment, the Canadian courts would years later add disability to section 15 through judicial interpretation, just as they did with sexual orientation in the 1990s. However, I had no reason that day to think that our Canadian courts would be warmly receptive to adding disability to section 15 through judicial interpretation. The Supreme Court of Canada had not yet enunciated its major progressive principles for interpreting ordinary human rights legislation. That would not come until later that decade.[12]

As I discussed several times earlier in this retrospective, it was not then clear that courts would be committed to a broad, vigorous, and liberal interpretation of *Charter* rights. As well, in 1981, we were still in the throes of our long battle just to get the Ontario legislature to include disability protection to be added to the Ontario *Human Rights Code*.[13]

## D. Hitting the Media Jackpot!

As the justice minister spoke that wintery night, I did not undertake the detailed analysis of these developments that I have here laid out. I was just angry, frustrated, and determined. I knew the nub of the argument that we needed to make in response. I dropped my bar admissions studies on the spot and ran to the phone to call the *Globe and Mail*. It was after business hours. I wanted to get our story into the news before our issue got eclipsed by the many other topics that the justice minister's speech covered. I asked for the assignment desk. When I reached a reporter, I tried to steel myself to sound authoritative. I proclaimed that I was the constitutional spokesperson for the CNIB, and I wanted to offer our immediate response to the justice minister's speech on the *Charter*. I slammed the Trudeau government for leaving persons with disabilities out in the cold. I heard the reporter typing as I spoke. I forced myself to talk more slowly. I knew it was close to the newspaper's deadline. The Joint Committee's Hansard transcript states

---

12 See e.g. *Ontario Human Rights Commission v Etobicoke*, [1982] 1 SCR 202, [1982] SCJ No 2 (QL); *Ontario Human Rights Comm v Simpsons-Sears*, [1985] 2 SCR 536, [1985] SCJ No 74 (QL); *Central Okanagan School District No 23 v Renaud*, [1992] 2 SCR 970, [1992] SCJ No 75 (QL); *British Columbia (Public Service Employee Relations Commission) v BCGSEU*, [1999] 3 SCR 3, [1999] SCJ No 46 (QL).

13 *Human Rights Code*, RSO 1990, c H-19.

that the discussions began just after 10:00 p.m. It therefore must have been close to 11:00 p.m. when I called the *Globe and Mail*.

That night, I called only one news outlet. If only we then had the instant access that email provides, I could have written a news release in minutes and blasted it in nanoseconds to news outlets across Canada. My one short telephone interview that night yielded the best positioning of our story for which we could have hoped. It ran the next morning on 13 January 1981 on page 2 of the *Globe and Mail*, right by the text of the justice minister's speech. It read:

> Disabled Out in the Cold, Spokesman at CNIB Says
>
> Tuesday, January 13, 1981
>
> The Liberal Government's refusal to expand equality rights to include the handicapped makes a mockery of Canada's participation in the International Year of the Disabled, a spokesman for the Canadian National Institute for the Blind says.
>
> Rather than moving to protect the handicapped, Ottawa has decided to let discriminatory laws remain on the books, said David Lepofsky, a CNIB director who appeared before the parliamentary committee on the constitution last month.
>
> Mr. Lepofsky said Justice Minister Jean Chrétien's remarks in making the announcement "have absolutely no relation to reality. He's saying that the term 'handicapped' is too vague and that no one will know what it means. That's absolutely ridiculous — it's very clear what we're talking about." Mr. Lepofsky also criticized Mr. Chrétien for suggesting that entrenched protection for the physically and mentally disabled would only duplicate existing human rights legislation. On the contrary, he said, much of the current legislation is concerned only with discrimination in the workplace or in rental agreements.
>
> "Those provincial statutes don't address themselves to all the other provincial and federal laws which discriminate against the handicapped," Mr. Lepofsky said.
>
> He cited laws which prohibit blind people from sitting on juries in some provinces, deny minimum wage protection to some handicapped people and forbid some mentally handicapped couples from marrying.[14]

We hit the media jackpot! It rarely gets better than this. To have our reaction printed along with Chrétien's speech could not be better. I was not aware back then that it was very likely that almost every member of parliament,

---

14 "Disabled Out in the Cold, Spokesman at CNIB Says," *Globe and Mail* (13 January 1981) at 11.

every senior political staffer, and every senior Justice Department official working on the *Charter* project raced that morning to read the *Globe and Mail*. Top priority for them would have been to see the coverage of Chrétien's speech. Public servants and political staffers would have slaved for days formulating every word of his remarks, trying to calculate how to get the best reaction and what landmines loomed if they got it wrong.

In December 1980, we were nobodies with no media profile on the constitutional reform issue. Since then, I and other disability advocates have worked hard to create a greater media profile for our issues. Our gradual and intermittent progress has taken many years and innumerable interviews. I cannot count how many news releases I have written since December 1980, responding to a government's throne speech, budget, or other announcement. Most of the time, they have led to no media coverage whatsoever. Too often, many news organizations and some news reporters, reporting on a major government announcement, have not treated the response of people with disabilities as a priority. They routinely turn instead to their usual suspects in other sectors of society to solicit reactions to a government announcement.

Had we won this news coverage today, we would have immediately posted on our website, emailed it to our many supporters, and pumped it out on social media like Twitter and Facebook. A news release would quickly follow to get a second round of coverage of the issue. We would, for example, aim at public affairs radio and television programs that typically read today's newspapers to decide what should be on tomorrow's show. In contrast, I recall no media reaching out to us in response to that *Globe and Mail* article on Chrétien's speech with a view to follow-up coverage. To this day, it remains breathtaking that we secured that coverage in the *Globe and Mail* in 1981. At that late hour in the evening, the reporter could not do anything to verify my claim that I spoke for the CNIB. He could not phone the CNIB, whose offices were closed. There was no CNIB website that listed me as its constitutional spokesperson. For whatever reason, he trusted me. I will be forever grateful.

Were I to place a late night call to a newsroom today, a reporter could quickly check me out online. Their news databases would show that I have been interviewed by the media many times. Our advocacy efforts are plastered all over the website of the disability coalition I chair. A quick online search of Hansard reveals how often I and my coalition have been referred to or quoted in Parliament or the Ontario legislature.

## E. Never Give Up! Never Surrender!

Those advocating for the disability amendment kept up pressure after the justice minister's speech on 12 January 1981. I do not know what anyone else did at this point. For my part, I was pickled in studying for yet more bar exams. I briefly surfaced for air one cold Sunday evening that January. I was in my bedroom, desperately trying to get excited about studying real estate law. Those studies reinforced in my mind that I would absolutely never practice real estate law! The CBC radio was airing its weekly live 2-hour late afternoon phone-in program. That week's topic was the Trudeau constitutional reform package. The guest was a Trudeau cabinet minister, John Roberts.

I called CBC over and over on my now seemingly antique rotary dial phone. Repeatedly dialing was slow and hard on the index finger. I kept trying. At the same time, I did my level best to focus on the audiotape of my boring real estate course materials, droning on in the background. Finally, I got through. I was put in the queue of waiting calls. I stayed on hold for what seemed like an eternity. I held the phone up to one ear. Speaker phones were not yet on the consumer market. Through my other ear, the real estate audio tape prattled on about mortgages, liens on title, agreements of purchase and sale, and condominium law. The suspense grew. I impatiently listened to other callers ahead of me going on and on. I had no assurance that CBC would take my call before the radio program ended. At last, it was my turn. On national live radio, I roundly blasted the government for opposing the disability amendment. I do not recall Roberts' response.

I viewed this as just one more opportunity to try to bring our message to the public and to appeal to the government in a very public venue. Unknown to me at the time, it is quite likely that a cadre of political staffers and senior public servants were hanging on every call and every complaint during that program. Had this happened today, I would have been busy as I waited on hold, sending out a blizzard of tweets, Facebook posts, and other electronic notifications as well as encouraging people with disabilities to jam the CBC phone lines in an effort to get airtime to address our issue. I would also digitally record my few minutes on the air and use social media to repeatedly blitz it to as many people as I could. Sadly, I have no recording of my on-air exchange with that Trudeau cabinet minister.

Very late in this process, the CNIB Ontario division's Public Education and Advocacy Committee met again on 26 January 1981. It recommended that the CNIB publicly distribute its brief to the Joint Committee along with the correspondence that the CNIB had subsequently sent to members of the Joint Committee and the provincial premiers. I have no recollection or record of that correspondence. In an internal memo from 28 January 1981 that I have kept, the CNIB Ontario executive director Euclid Herie proposed that the CNIB ready itself to circulate this material publicly during its national publicity week, called White Cane Week. That annual week, regrettably, usually took place in February. That would have been after the Joint Committee had already voted on the disability amendment.[15]

## F. The Justice Minister is Prepared to Reconsider the Possibility of the Disability Amendment

Turning back to the Joint Committee, 2 days after the justice minister's 12 January 1981 speech at the Joint Committee, NDP Member of Parliament Svend Robinson again raised the disability amendment with the minister. Robinson pressed several arguments in support of the disability amendment that disability advocates had advanced at the public hearings.[16] Justice Minister Chrétien repeated the party line against the disability amendment.[17] However, in a dramatic move, he candidly acknowledged that he would like to make the disability amendment and did not feel good about opposing it. He said he had not agreed to it because he had received advice that the disability amendment would not be appropriate.[18] If accurate, this was a clear admission that senior public servants or political staffers were the barrier. Of course, it is not unheard of for a politician to deflect blame for something on their staffers or public servants. I have no way of knowing if there was an element of that here. In an incredible exchange, the justice minister agreed to Robinson's request that he go back to his officials and rethink the possibility of supporting the disability amendment:

---

15 Letter from EJ Herie, CNIB Executive Director, Ontario Division, to Cathy Browne, Acting Supervisor, Ontario Information Services, Children's Services, Re: Public Education and Advocacy Meeting (28 January 1981).

16 Canada, Parliament, *Minutes of Proceedings and Evidence of the Special Joint Committee of the Senate and of the House of Commons on the Constitution of Canada*, 32nd Parl, 1st Sess, No 37 (14 January 1981) at 21–24.

17 *Ibid* at 22.

18 *Ibid* at 23.

**Robinson:** Mr. Chairman, turning to another area of the proposed Charter of Rights and that is the question of the prescribed grounds of discrimination, Mr. Minister, I suggest to you that you have betrayed the hopes and the expectations of many, many Canadians in refusing to include as a prescribed ground of discrimination, disability. This Committee heard witness after witness appearing before us insisting that disabled Canadians, whether that be physically disabled or mentally disabled, should be entitled to protection from discrimination. This, Mr. Minister, is the International Year of the Handicapped.

Now, your justification, your rationale for not including the handicapped in your speech before this Committee was that there were difficulties in definition and that society is still evolving.

I would like to take up those two questions. Are you saying, Mr. Minister, are you suggesting that as of today, the day that you are proposing this Charter, that society has not evolved in Canada to the point that the handicapped deserve to be protected from discrimination?

**Chrétien:** We say that we have passed legislation on the subject. I just say that the problem is that there are many types of handicaps in this society. And this is the nature of the problem that we are faced with.

We all have handicaps. The way I speak English, some would say it is a handicap for me, others would say it is an asset, I do not know.

There are all sorts of handicaps that exist.

**Robinson:** Are you talking, Mr. Minister about substance or about ...

**Chrétien:** I am talking about a substance that is difficult to define satisfactorily, what is a handicap, to enshrine it in the constitution at this time.

There is legislation that has been passed. There have been recommendations, for example, by many of the Human Rights Commissions, making recommendations to improve the nature of our legislations on that. There is some legislation that has been passed and still is being passed in the different legislatures in Canada.

Of course I am not happy, personally it would have been much easier to just say yes to you because I am quite uncomfortable to be obliged to say that the best advice I am receiving is that it is not appropriate to put it here at this moment.

But in order to cope with this problem, if you look at Section 15, what we have done is we have tried in Section 15 to not limit the list. We have opened up. There was some recommendation, for example, that we should not list anything at all.

Some of the briefs that you have received said: take out all the lists you have in there and just talk in general terms, in terms of discrimination.

So we have opened it up, we have a descriptive list of the six items that are there and we say that the others will evolve and if there is evident cases of discrimination that the court could intervene because the list is not limiting the areas of discrimination. It is descriptive of areas of discrimination.

So in that way I am advised that the court could intervene. Now you say why do you not just use the word, and put after 6 as part of the description, the seventh one, that would be disabled.

**Robinson:** That is right.

**Chrétien:** I would like to do that. But I am told and the best advise I am receiving, is that it is premature at this time. I am willing to look again at it, if it could be done, but ...

**Robinson:** Mr. Minister I suggest that you look again at this particular section. I suggest you go back to your advisors. You yourself have indicated that the handicapped are dealt with in federal legislation. Well, if the handicapped are dealt with now, in federal legislation, there must be some definition. You must know in that legislation who it is you are talking about there. Why can we not apply the same kind of definition in this particular Charter.

Let me ask you at this point, are you prepared to go back to your advisors and at least to seriously consider, possibly adding this as a ground, an additional sixth ground, the question of disability following the advice of these many witnesses, listening to the concerns of disabled Canadians, listening to the Committee, the special committee on the handicapped, the chairman of whom appeared before our Committee asking that this be included.

**Chrétien:** You understand my problem. Yes, I will go back to my advisors, they are here. They are not such a big gang, they are all listening to this discussion. Of course there have been many members of the Parliament who have been on that committee; the chairman, David Smith, keeps talking to me about it and so on.

But at the same time we are not here just to do something that is pleasant to do. There is nothing that would please me more to add that word there. But I have at the same time to make sure that we are not creating a problem that will be very difficult for the administration of the law, the judgment of the court, the legislature and so on.

So, we say that this is an area of evolution in the law that has not attained the same maturity as other areas. We have opened up to make it possible for the court to intervene in obvious cases of discrimination to persons if they are handicapped, without having to put the word handicapped. Because after that I am told that, yes, there is a lot of types of handicaps, and this creates some problems for the court to make decisions.

Myself as a human, as a politician and as a man who has always been preoccupied with the disadvantaged groups in this society, I am not happy to give you that answer and I will look back again if I can but at the same time sometimes you do not do everything you want to do.

I admit very clearly that it is not perfect what I have here.

**Robinson:** One final question if I may, and naturally I appreciate the Minister's undertaking to have another look at this important question; and his recognition that while there may be problems for the courts that there are problems for hundreds of thousands of handicapped in this country as well that would be remedied by this kind of amendment, and they will be watching your response, Mr. Minister.

**Chrétien:** I intend to introduce legislation to that subject.

**Robinson:** Legislation that is given today can be taken away tomorrow, Mr. Minister.

**Chrétien:** I know, I know. It is better than nothing at all.

**Robinson:** Mr. Minister, we are not asking for nothing at all.[19]

Reading this exchange now, Chrétien's statement screams out for a news release, for a letter to the justice minister and the prime minister, and for immediate phone calls to any senior public servant I could reach. Of course, I did not do any of that since I had no idea that the justice minister had opened the door, even a crack, to the disability amendment.

Had I the technology now available to me, as well as my current level of experience, within seconds I would have tweeted news organizations and members of Parliament that the justice minister has admitted that he would like to make the disability amendment, that he has agreed to reconsider it, and that all that stands in the way are some unaccountable, faceless, foot-dragging nervous Nelly senior public officials. Within minutes, a letter would go by email to the minister, copied to the prime minister and all members of parliament and senators, asking for an urgent meeting with him and with his officials who advised against the disability amendment. This meeting could take place within hours or minutes on Zoom, without the delay and the cost of flying to Ottawa. A news release would spread that letter to the media. It would be quickly followed by an outreach to key opposition members of parliament, pressing them to issue similar news releases and to raise this issue in Question Period.

Even without all that technology, I wish I had built connections with the opposition parties in 1980 and 1981. We might have had the benefit of

---

19 *Ibid* at 21–24.

an opposition staffer calling us to let us know what the justice minister had just said. Fortunately, Robinson had already absorbed all the information he needed from listening to the presenters at the Joint Committee public hearings who supported the disability amendment.

## G. Sweetheart Questions to the Justice Minister from His Own Party

At the Joint Committee meeting on 14 January 1981, shortly after the telling exchange between the minister and Robinson, Liberal Member of Parliament Ronald Irwin (the minister's parliamentary secretary) had a friendly exchange with the minister, adorned with jabs at Robinson. In substance, he asked the minister whether it would be possible for the government to try to negotiate a disability amendment to the *Charter* after the Constitution is patriated, using the constitutional amending formula.[20] The minister said yes.[21] It is not unusual for a government to plant such friendly questions for a minister during such proceedings. These cheerleading questions give the minister a chance to reiterate his position in a friendly exchange, such as the following:

> **Irwin:** Apropos what you are saying Mr. Minister, it has been said that even a stopped clock is right twice every 24 hours.
>
> Now there are, Mr. Joint Chairman, three concerns I have: native rights, the handicapped; and language rights. I see Mr. Robinson wants perfection. I do not think he would ever have perfection.
>
> **Robinson:** I recognize it would not come from you.
>
> **Irwin:** Native rights, the handicapped, and language rights in Ontario. Will the government pursue negotiations with the provinces after patriation on these matters? Will there be continuing discussions?
>
> **Chrétien:** Yes; on the native rights, Mr. Trudeau and all the first ministers in February 1979 agreed that should be an item in the constitutional debate — natives in the constitution. It is a very difficult area. Requests of all members of this Committee have come with new language, confirming there are some native or aboriginal rights and that they are based upon the Royal Proclamation of 1763 — the Inuit, Tapirisat, the Order in Council regarding Rupert's Island.

---

20 *Ibid* at 26–27.

21 *Ibid* at 27.

> So we have made sure that these rights exist and are recognized and the negotiations as to the definition of these rights and how they can be implemented will come at a future constitutional conference, and in the first one it will be one of the items on the agenda. That was promised by Mr. Trudeau and all the first ministers agreed.
>
> Similarly, on the question of the disabled, when the law in this area evolves to maturity, it would be very nice then for the premiers and the national government to cause an amendment to the Canadian Constitution to include them precisely. I do not think that would be a problem. Every government, whatever its stripes, in Canada has always shown a lot of preoccupation for the disabled.[22]

A little later, the disability issue came up again:

> **Irwin:** On the handicapped, Mr. Minister, did I hear you to say that you will be introducing legislation to improve the federal human rights act with regard to the handicapped?
>
> **Chrétien:** There are some recommendations that were proposed by the Human Rights Commission on that. We are studying those recommendations and we intend to introduce legislation on the subject when the matter is ready.[23]

## H. The Conservatives Join the NDP in Supporting the Disability Amendment

Another powerful moment took place towards the end of that Joint Committee meeting on 14 January 1981. Conservative Member of Parliament David Crombie announced that the Conservatives would propose an amendment to add disability to section 15.[24] Again, I did not then hear about this at the time. This was enormous news. The NDP and Tories were now both on record supporting the disability amendment. The Joint Committee was inevitably going to have to hold a vote on the disability amendment. The ball would be in the Liberals' court. The Liberals would have to vote yes or no on the public record. Crombie stated:

22 *Ibid* at 26–27.

23 *Ibid* at 28.

24 *Ibid* at 47.

> On the question of substance, if I could, Mr. Chairman, I wanted to make an initial comment with respect to the questions raised by Mr. Robinson with respect to not including the handicapped and disabled, both physical and mental, the Minister's decision not to include them on the basis that there would be some difficulty with respect to definition.
>
> I would like to be able to return to that tomorrow because our party intends to move an amendment which will so include them and I would ask the Minister and his officials if they would please look at the recommendations which have been made in the past by the Human Rights Commissioner in that regard and before this Committee.[25]

What a torrential Twitter storm we would unleash if these events happened now. The opposition parties unanimously backed the Liberals into a corner. This put the government under incredible pressure to say yes to the disability amendment, even if they wanted to say no or simply lacked the courage to say yes. It turned up the heat on them to override the public servants' contrary advice. Social and conventional media would be a great way for us to try to turn that heat up even more. A somewhat similar dynamic would work to our incredible advantage almost 40 years later. In 2019, a number of disability advocates (of which I was one) got Canada's Senate to adopt some amendments to the proposed *Accessible Canada Act*, a weak bill that the House of Commons had passed at the end of 2018.[26] The federal government of Prime Minister Justin Trudeau had earlier rejected those amendments when the opposition tried to get them adopted in the House of Commons in 2018.

In 2019, the Senate's amendments to the proposed *Accessible Canada Act* had to go back to the House of Commons for a vote.[27] If Justin Trudeau's Liberals were to vote no, they would lose a bill that they had promised to pass, and this embarrassment was going to happen on the eve of a federal election. Our collective efforts succeeded in backing the Trudeau Liberals into saying yes to those Senate amendments to that bill, even though they wanted to say no (likely also on the advice of the federal public service).

---

25 *Ibid.*

26 *Accessible Canada Act*, SC 2019, c 10.

27 Canada, Parliament, *Debates of the Senate*, 42nd Parl, 1st Sess, Vol 150, No 287 (13 May 2019) at 8100.

## I. The Disability Amendment Kept Popping Up

There was yet another indication that the disability amendment was top of mind at the Joint Committee. On 15 January 1981, the justice minister got another sweetheart question from his parliamentary secretary, Irwin, to get the minister to explain how the controversial proposed new constitutional-amending formula would work.[28] Irwin asked what people with disabilities would have to do after patriation to get disability added to section 15:

> I want to put this question to you. If the referendum question said "Do you wish to include nondiscriminatory handicapped persons in Section 51 [sic: Section 15] with an amendment as follows" and then gave the amendment, it would seem to me that it would make it easier to pass such an amendment in the west, proposed by the federal government under the Constitution, of course, if we did not have to get 50 per cent of the population; we would only require, for instance, Manitoba and Saskatchewan 4 per cent each, to have it passed; whereas, Alberta is, I believe, around 9 per cent, and B.C. is around 11 or 12 per cent, or somewhat in that neighbourhood — or 8 per cent for Alberta. I am not sure of the exact amount.[29]

Chrétien responded with a long explanation of the amending formula.[30]

On 16 January 1981, the opposition again returned to the disability amendment.[31] Robinson, in an effective cross-examination of the justice minister, got him to agree that the moment that section 15 went into effect, it would be opened to the courts to interpret it as prohibiting disability discrimination:

> **Robinson:** [B]ut I would like now to turn to Section 15 of the proposed Charter of Rights, to return to Section 15 of the proposed *Charter of Rights* and to deal with an argument that has been made and a statement that you made in your statement on Monday night to this Committee.
>
> You indicated that you have responded to some of the concerns of various groups and that rather than restricting the proposed grounds of discrimination to those originally set out in the Charter of Rights, that you are leaving this

---

28 Canada, Parliament, *Minutes of Proceedings and Evidence of the Special Joint Committee of the Senate and of the House of Commons on the Constitution of Canada*, 32nd Parl, 1st Sess, No 38 (15 January 1981) at 52.

29 *Ibid* at 52.

30 *Ibid* at 52–55.

31 Canada, Parliament, *Minutes of Proceedings and Evidence of the Special Joint Committee of the Senate and of the House of Commons on the Constitution of Canada*, 32nd Parl, 1st Sess, No 39 (16 January 1981) at 16.

open ended, that you are allowing for the possibility that the courts might interpret this to include additional grounds of discrimination.

Am I paraphrasing what you said accurately, Mr. Minister?

**Chrétien:** Yes, you are reading my text.

**Robinson:** No, I am not reading your text. If that is the case, are you then saying that immediately following the passage of this Charter, when it becomes law in Canada, not sometime in the future but immediately following that, that it is your intention and your understanding that a court might interpret this Charter in such a way as to include a prohibition of discrimination on the grounds of disability.

**Chrétien:** If it is an obvious case, yes.

**Robinson:** So you think that immediately following the passage, that that is a possibility?

**Chrétien:** No, Mr. Robinson, because there are three years after on that, on this section. We have said that on a nondiscrimination clause, we have agreed that there would be three years lapse between the passage of it here and approving it, being proclaimed after it had been passed in London there would be a lapse of three years, but yes, at the end of three years.

**Robinson:** But at that point it is your intention in making this proposal that at least the courts would have that opportunity to interpret this more broadly to include discrimination on the basis of disability?

**Chrétien:** Yes. I say it is broad. There are other types of discrimination. The courts then look ...

**Robinson:** But specifically disability you say yes?

**Chrétien:** If it is discrimination because of disability, I would say yes.[32]

Then came another important exchange, one that I caught on television either as it was happening or during a rerun later that day. I undoubtedly did not want to admit to my friends that, when taking breaks from law studies, my choice for television watching was the Joint Committee's clause-by-clause drama. In a friendly exchange with the justice minister, liberal Member of Parliament Bryce Mackasey asked the minister if he was open to reconsider the inclusion of people with disabilities in the *Charter*. From the tenor of the exchange, it sounded to me as if this issue was troubling Mackasey. The justice minister said that he was open to reconsidering it. When I saw this at

---

32 *Ibid* at 16–17.

the time, it gave me a sense of optimism, even though I still felt that the battle was an extremely uphill one:

> **Mackasey:** Finally, there is the possibility, Mr. Minister, of adding the category of disability, and can you be persuaded to reconsider and is there a possibility because of the work going on by the particular Committee of the Commons and the fact that there is international recognition of the problems of disabled people; you have mentioned some groups in particular, leaving the rest open — would you reconsider with your officials all the ramifications of adding to Section 15 some recognition of the particular problems that this category of Canadians has to face, a fact which the public are now only beginning to realize? it would fall into the category of — it could almost be classified as a fundamental freedom.
>
> **Chrétien:** I am willing to review that and see if it can be added. But I cannot give you any answer.
>
> **Mackasey:** But there is still a possibility? You are still open-minded on it?
>
> **Chrétien:** Bryce, you know I am a very open-minded man.[33]

There were sound tactical steps I could and should have taken at the time to jump on this new development, even without the invention of Twitter. Had we issued a news release or even phoned the two reporters who had earlier written articles on this, set out in full in Chapters XIII and XIV, it would have both helped our momentum and alerted the disability community that hope was not lost. On 20 January 1981, Robinson again returned to section 15. At this point, he was questioning a Mr. Kaplan, possibly Liberal Member of Parliament Robert Kaplan and not the minister.[34] He again asked if it would be open to a court to interpret the amended section 15 as protecting against disability discrimination. Kaplan answered in the positive. This was a point that the justice minister had already agreed to, days earlier. The exchange continued as follows:

> **Robinson:** Secondly, is it your intention or that of the drafters of the *Charter* that it would be open to a court to proscribe discrimination on the grounds of marital status, political belief, sexual orientation and disability.
>
> Could you deal with each of those in turn?

---

33 *Ibid* at 18.

34 Canada, Parliament, *Minutes of Proceedings and Evidence of the Special Joint Committee of the Senate and of the House of Commons on the Constitution of Canada*, 32nd Parl, 1st Sess, No 41 (20 January 1981) at 14.

> **Kaplan:** I would deal with each of them all together and say it would be open indeed to a court to do that. I do not see any particular advantage of the expression that you have proposed over the one which is proposed in the bill.[35]

## J. Conservatives and NDP Table Their Proposals for the Disability Amendment

On 20 January 1981, Conservative Member of Parliament Jake Epp made a major speech before the Joint Committee. He outlined a series of amendments that the Conservative Party planned to propose.[36] Among them, he proposed adding deaf persons to section 14 of the *Charter*, entitling them to an interpreter in legal proceedings. He also repeated that the Conservative Party would propose an amendment to include people with disabilities in section 15 of the *Charter*.[37] Add this to the growing list of earlier events that I should have resoundingly trumpeted to the world and celebrated. Epp stated:

> Clause 14: The deaf deserve equal treatment accorded to all other citizens. Thus, we propose that Clause 14 should be amended to read as follows:
>
> > A party or a witness in any proceedings who does not understand or speak the language in which the proceedings are conducted or who is deaf has the right to the assistance of an interpreter.
>
> This is but a recognition, Mr. Chairman, not only of one group of handicapped, but I believe more importantly that sign language is another language form and should be included as well.
>
> Clause 15(1): We feel that the rights of persons with mental or physical disabilities should be protected. The so-called handicapped clause. Accordingly we are proposing an amendment to meet that objective:
>
> > Every individual is equal before and under the law and has the right to the equal protection and equal benefit of the law without discrimination and, in particular, without discrimination based on race, national or ethnic origin, colour, religion, sex, age, or mental or physical disability.
>
> It is the last four words we are adding.[38]

---

35 *Ibid* at 22.

36 *Ibid* at 93–103.

37 *Ibid* at 99.

38 *Ibid* at 99.

Discussing the conservative proposals that day, Mackasey reiterated his own clear support for the disability amendment: "Mr. Epp, you have divided the package, and secondly, there has been a refinement to the Charter of Human Rights and other features, and many of your amendments I think are commendable and positive and I happen to share your views on handicapped people as an individual."[39]

On 21 January 1981, Robinson announced the text of amendments to section 15 that his party would table.[40] Neither opposition party consulted us on the wording of the disability amendment that we would prefer. Since then, I have learned a great deal from extensively working with opposition parties at the federal and provincial levels on proposing amendments to legislation. Several times, though not always, we have gotten them to consult us in advance on the legislative wording that they were going to propose in order to ensure that we are happy with them. Looking now at the wording that the NDP proposed, it was extremely troubling. It proposed a hierarchical approach to equality that I critiqued in Chapter XI. This would have been better than having no constitutional protection at all for people with disabilities. However, it could have been worse than simply going with the wording that the justice minister had tabled on 12 January 1981. Mr. Robinson stated:

> Finally, Mr. Chairman, at this point, with respect to Clause 15, the proposed equality rights, I think it might be in order if I were to read our proposal on this so that members would be well aware of what we are proposing. As I say, you will be receiving a written copy of this, and with that, Mr. Chairman, I will conclude.
>
> We proposed a new Clause 15 with three subclauses as follows:
>
>> 15(a) Every person is equal in, before, and under the law and has the right to equal protection and equal benefit of the law, and to access to employment, accommodation and public services without unreasonable distinction on grounds, including race, national or ethnic origin, colour, religion, sex, age, marital status, sexual orientation, political belief, physical or mental disability or lack of means.

---

39 *Ibid* at 115.

40 Canada, Parliament, *Minutes of Proceedings and Evidence of the Special Joint Committee of the Senate and of the House of Commons on the Constitution of Canada*, 32nd Parl, 1st Sess, No 42 (21 January 1981) at 5–9.

> And there will be a Clause 15(b) to the effect that sex, race, colour, religion, national or ethnic origin shall never constitute a reasonable distinction for the purposes of Clause 15(a); and finally Clause 15(c) the affirmative action subsection, that Clause 15(a) does not preclude any law, program or activity which has as its object the amelioration of conditions of disadvantaged groups, including those who are disadvantaged because of grounds specified therein.
>
> Mr. Chairman, as I say, I apologize for not having these in writing, and they will be forwarded very shortly in both French and English and certainly at the time the amendments are moved there will be elaboration on the objectives that we attempt to achieve on these amendments.[41]

## K. Justice Minister's Parliamentary Secretary Evidently Needed Some Venting of Spleen

On 22 January 1981, as various amendments unrelated to section 15 were being debated, Irwin vented his spleen at the opposition and at community groups for seeking so many amendments to the *Charter*.[42] He complained about how infrequently he had gotten to see his wife.[43] He used the disability amendment as one of his illustrations for his complaint:

> Now, what has happened is in fact from a very simple concept; we have had groups come from across Canada, hundreds of them, and wanting to add on, add on, add on, and I quite agree with many of the things that the NDP Party has done and especially on aboriginal rights. But there are certain things that are not ready to go into that charter.
>
> We cannot enshrine everything in Canada. Today we heard "God," "union," "citizenship" as if we were opposed to those things. If we were opposed to those things, we would not be with our back up against the wall trying to get these rights through. …
>
> do not think that we are prepared to keep throwing more and more and more things in because they smack of apple pie and motherhood. I think our charter is a good charter now and it has your support and I think we should get it on and over with and then start dealing with many of these things that have been espoused, the marital status, the handicapped, the Section 133 provisions in Ontario. We just cannot put every good thing, as you can conceive, like a

---

41 *Ibid* at 8.

42 Canada, Parliament, *Minutes of Proceedings and Evidence of the Special Joint Committee of the Senate and of the House of Commons on the Constitution of Canada*, 32nd Parl, 1st Sess, No 43 (22 January 1981) at 118–119.

43 *Ibid* at 118.

> shopping list because that is what it is at this late stage, a shopping list, this particular Charter, no matter how well intentioned your motives are.[44]

## L. David, the Disability Amendment Will Pass Today, but Don't Tell Anyone!

Then came the historic day, 28 January 1981. For reasons I cannot explain, it was only on that morning that I finally decided to call Chrétien's political staffer, Eddie Goldenberg. As explained earlier, he knew me from the law firm where I had articled the year before, and he had come over to say hello to me at the end of my presentation to the Joint Committee on 12 December 1980. On the morning of 28 January 1981, a leisurely month and a half after I spoke with him at the Joint Committee, I gave him a call to try to talk him into supporting the disability amendment. Before I could launch into my spiel, he told me that the disability amendment would be passing and that it would happen that very day!

I was not at all expecting to hear this. I was overjoyed but decided that I would only believe that the government would support the disability amendment when it actually happened. I could not celebrate this news that day for three reasons. (Must I always have three reasons for things?) First, Goldenberg told me that morning not to tell anyone this news before it happened. I had to keep that to myself. Unbelievable! Second, I was still swamped, filling my skull full of mush in preparation for the next bar exam (a weak reference to the 1973 movie *Paper Chase* about studying law). Third, I was not plugged in with any network of other disability advocates around Canada who were fighting for the disability amendment.

## M. Prequel to the Disability Amendment: Amending Section 14 of the *Charter* to Entitle Deaf Persons in Court to an Interpreter

Later that day, I watched the proceedings live on television, eager to see if the disability amendment was actually going to be adopted. Before the Joint Committee got to section 15, it addressed the need to add people with

---

44 *Ibid* at 118–119.

hearing loss to section 14.[45] The Joint Committee voted to amend section 14 to include the right to an interpreter for deaf people involved in legal proceedings. The original text of section 14, introduced into Parliament in October 1980, provided: "14. A party or witness in any proceedings who does not understand or speak the language in which the proceedings are conducted has the right to the assistance of an interpreter."[46] As amended, it now read: "14. A party or witness in any proceedings who does not understand or speak the language in which the proceedings are conducted or who is deaf has the right to the assistance of an interpreter."[47]

The Hansard transcript of the Joint Committee's discussion of this issue, which is no page turner, is included in Appendix 3. The Joint Committee first considered an amendment to section 14 proposed by Robinson.[48] The Liberals shot it down because it was considered too broadly worded.[49] The Joint Committee then considered a narrower amendment proposed by Conservative Member of Parliament James McGrath.[50] Chrétien said that the government would support it. It was quickly and unanimously passed.[51]

## N. Reaching a Historic Moment

When the big moment came, the justice minister announced that he was prepared to accept the amendment to include disability.[52] He also acknowledged that there was some sort of event that was expected the next day.[53] From this, I gathered that there might have been some kind of disability demonstration plan. I had no idea about that then or now. Once again, had we the technology then that we have now, I can imagine having been very involved in that. In Appendix 4, there are the key pages of the Hansard transcript of the Joint Committee's proceedings on 28 January 1981 where

45 Canada, Parliament, *Minutes of Proceedings and Evidence of the Special Joint Committee of the Senate and of the House of Commons on the Constitution of Canada*, 32nd Parl, 1st Sess, No 47 (28 January 1981) at 86–88 [*Minutes of Proceedings, 28 January 1981*].

46 Canada, Parliament, *The Canadian Constitution: 1980, Proposed Resolution Respecting the Constitution of Canada* (Ottawa: Government of Canada, 1980), s 14.

47 See *Charter*, *supra* note 1, s 14.

48 *Minutes of Proceedings, 28 January 1981*, *supra* note 45 at 84–86.

49 *Ibid* at 85–86.

50 *Ibid* at 87.

51 *Ibid* at 88.

52 *Ibid* at 91.

53 *Ibid*.

the committee amended section 15 to add mental and physical disability as prohibited grounds of discrimination. First, Robinson proposed the major rewrite of section 15 that he had earlier announced to the Joint Committee. Adding disability was one part of it.[54] Following that, Crombie proposed a narrower amendment to section 15. It would simply add mental or physical disability as prohibited grounds of discrimination, without the other changes that the NDP sought.[55] Crombie's historic words were:

> Thank you, Mr. Chairman.
>
> Mr. Chairman, dealing with Clause 15 and our amendment to it, which is numbered CP-8(1) on the sheet, I wish to move that the proposed amendment to Clause 15 of the proposed constitution act, 1980, be amended by striking out the words "or age" in Clause 15(1) thereof and substituting therefor [*sic*] the following words:
>
> > age or mental or physical disability.[56]

He provided the French translation that he was proposing[57] and then explained:

> Mr. Chairman, speaking to the motion, my understanding is that the government is willing to accept our amendment.
>
> Now, I am not sure we can continue to take this prosperity any longer!
>
> However, on behalf of those groups, organizations and individuals who find themselves physically and mentally disabled in this country, I would like, on their behalf, since I am the spokesman on their behalf at this point, to offer my thanks to the government for their acceptance of the amendment.[58]

Chrétien had a bit of light-hearted banter with the other members of parliament and then said:

> It is with great pleasure that I accept the amendment on behalf of the Government.
>
> I do not think we should debate it. There was a great deal of debate. I was very anxious that we should proceed tonight. They were preparing to have a big group tomorrow.

---

54 *Ibid* at 89–90.

55 *Ibid* at 90–91.

56 *Ibid* at 90.

57 *Ibid*.

58 *Ibid* at 90–91.

> You can have lots of beer on my health.[59]

Finally, the Joint Committee's presiding co-chair, Serge Joyal, obviously happy at all the events, said these historic words that 3 months ago seemed so manifestly impossible:

> So the amendment is carried, I should say wholeheartedly with unanimous consent.
>
> Amendment agreed to.[60]

The Joint Committee turned to Robinson to present the case for his proposed broader wording for section 15.[61] The committee eventually voted it down. However, at the start of that discussion was a brief exchange involving both Robinson and Chrétien that acknowledged the fact that Canada had just reached a historic milestone. As Robinson responded, "[o]nce again, Mr. Chairman, I know that the Minister will listen carefully to the representations made on the amendment which we will be proposing, just as he has listened with care to the representations of the groups representing the physically and mentally disabled."[62] The next day on 29 January 1981, the NDP continued to present its series of amendments to section 15, which would have constitutionally entrenched lesser protection from discrimination for some equality-seeking groups, including people with disabilities.[63] These were not passed.[64] The NDP proposed that the word "discrimination" should not be used in section 15 at all and that, instead, it should refer to unreasonable distinction.[65] It is exceedingly fortunate that this terminology was rejected and that the term "discrimination" is the core term that is operative in section 15 to this day.

---

59 *Ibid* at 91.

60 *Ibid.*

61 *Ibid* at 91–92.

62 *Ibid* at 92.

63 *Ibid* at 17–22.

64 *Ibid* at 34.

65 *Ibid* at 20.

## O. The Importance of the Joint Committee's Unanimity on the Disability Amendment

I did not then give a thought to the fact that the disability amendment passed unanimously. I was just thrilled that it passed at all. However, this unanimity foreshadowed important future events in our non-partisan campaign for equality and accessibility for people with disabilities. In 2005, the Ontario legislature unanimously passed the *AODA*.[66] The same has been the case for the federal *Accessible Canada Act*[67] and for most provincial accessibility legislation. I cannot tell from Hansard transcripts whether anyone voted against the accessibility legislation passed in British Columbia, Nova Scotia, and Newfoundland and Labrador.[68] I would expect that no one voted nay.

There is only one exception of which I am aware. It is an understandable one. In 2001, the extremely weak *Ontarians with Disabilities Act*,[69] brought in by the provincial Conservative government of Mike Harris, passed but not unanimously.[70] The opposition Liberals and NDP voted against it because the bill was so weak as to be insulting to people with disabilities. It has since been repealed and superseded by the stronger *AODA*, which, as noted above, was unanimously passed. Even Cam Jackson, the Ontario Conservative cabinet minister who had introduced the weak *Ontarians with Disabilities Act*, when later in opposition, conceded that it was too weak. He voted along with his party for its repeal and for the Ontario Liberals' stronger *AODA*.[71]

---

66 Legislative Assembly of Ontario, *Hansard Transcripts*, 38th Parl, 1st Sess (10 May 2005) at 6961. See also *Accessibility for Ontarians with Disabilities Act*, SO 2005, c 11.

67 Canada, Parliament, *House of Commons Debates*, 42nd Parl, 1st Sess, Vol 148, No 359 (27 November 2018) at 24071; Canada, Parliament, *House of Commons Debates*, 42nd Parl, 1st Sess, Vol 148, No 422 (29 May 2019) at 28255. See also *Accessible Canada Act*, SC 2019, c 10.

68 Legislative Assembly of British Columbia, *Debates of the Legislative Assembly (Hansard)*, 42nd Parl, 2nd Sess (3 June 2021) at 2494; Province of Newfoundland and Labrador, *Hansard, House of Assembly Proceedings*, 50th General Assembly, 1st Sess, Vol L, No 26 (25 October 2021) at 1266; Nova Scotia House of Assembly, 62nd Assembly, 3rd Sess (27 April 2017) at 2640.

69 *Ontarians with Disabilities Act*, SO 2001, c 32.

70 Legislative Assembly of Ontario, *Hansard Transcripts*, 37th Parl, 2nd Sess (13 December 2001) at 4589–4590.

71 Legislative Assembly of Ontario, *Hansard Transcripts*, 38th Parl, 1st Sess (10 May 2005) at 6955.

## P. There's Got to Be a Morning After!

For people with disabilities in Canada, 28 January 1981 was truly historic. However, at the time, it barely merited a footnote, if that, in the daily news. The only exception to this media silence that I recall took place early on 29 January 1981, the morning after the disability amendment passed. I awoke very early to the ringing of my bedside telephone. CBC's national morning radio program *This Country in the Morning* (later renamed *Morningside*, and now called *The Current*) wanted to interview me in a few minutes on the significance of the disability amendment. The journalist who woke me up begged me to go and down some coffee so that I would wake up. I was interviewed by the legendary enthusiastic host Don Harron. In the interview, I spoke about my hopes and aspirations for the disability amendment, which were the same then as they are today. Appendix 5 includes a transcript of the interview.[72]

I began the interview by emphasizing that the disability amendment did not give people with disabilities special rights. This had been a major public relations concern on our minds — something that seems hard to believe so many years later. In the interview, I continued to use the term "handicapped." I explained that the original draft of section 15 guaranteed equality to only a small number of minorities. I emphasized that this amendment to the *Charter* was aimed at laws that discriminate. As noted earlier, I was oblivious to the idea of the *Charter* restricting the constitutionality of government action in addition to legislation. I emphasized that, as originally written, section 15 would grant equality only for some and that equality for some is not equality.

CBC asked me to recite the reasons why the justice minister initially opposed including disability in section 15. I recited his three reasons given on 12 January 1981, condemning them as "absurd." I argued, incorrectly, that the 12 January change in the wording of section 15 that was meant to open up the provision would not in fact do so. I argued that courts would act on discrimination based only on the grounds that were enumerated in the provision. I claimed that the justice minister's contrary argument was "absurd." In fact, regrettably, I see that it was my argument during this part of the radio interview that was absurd. By this time, I had substantially

---

72 Interview, 29 January 1981, online: *YouTube* <www.youtube.com/watch?v=PnqNpeGhWP0>.

sharpened my arguments as compared to my presentation a month earlier when addressing the Joint Committee. I also added a new line of argument during this interview.

In outlining the justice minister's earlier reasons for rejecting the disability amendment, I explained that he had said that our rights to equality are best protected through legislation and not through the *Charter*. I noted that once the justice minister had rejected the disability amendment on 12 January 1981, both opposition parties said that they would support the disability amendment. I argued that, if the rights of people with disabilities are best protected through the vehicle of legislation, then why does the same not go for the rights of anyone else identified in the *Charter*? I questioned: "Why are we going through this constitutional exercise in the first place?" Making the case for the disability amendment, I emphasized that both opposition parties supported it. I highlighted that 1981 was the International Year of Disabled Persons with the theme of equality for people with disabilities. I capped this off with the fact that the Special Parliamentary Committee on the Disabled and Handicapped had supported the disability amendment.

As the interview reached its last minutes, I was asked to reflect on what the disability amendment would mean for people with disabilities in the future. I had a real sense that this was an important question deserving a thoughtful answer. I had not prepared an answer for this. In fact, I had not prepared for this interview at all. I was lying on my bed, phone in hand, still in my pajamas. I said that the disability amendment would mean three things. First, assuming that the patriation package actually gets enacted, any law that discriminates against people with disabilities would be unconstitutional. I gave the example of a categorical ban on blind people ever serving on a jury, even in a case where eyesight is not needed to effectively serve. A second example I gave was provincial legislation that gives a public official the authority to license an employer to pay handicapped employees less than the minimum wage.

According to the second long-term benefit, I predicted that the *Charter* would be widely publicized, posted all over the place and taught to children in schools. This would reinforce for the public that people with disabilities have the right to equality. I said that the biggest problem facing blind people, the focus of the CNIB, is public misunderstanding of us and the discrimination that results. Our Constitution will signal a new message across Canada, which is that this public stereotype is inaccurate. The third benefit I predicted derives from the fact that some people with disabilities at times were then somewhat passive in promoting their rights. I said that this was changing, as illustrated by the disability groups that advocated for the disability amendment. Then, for me, it was back to the bar admissions course!

# XV. WHY DID WE WIN?

## A. Will We Ever Know Why?

What led the Trudeau Liberals to agree to the disability amendment? I still don't know. It may be impossible to find out unless someone were to unearth the paper trail that may be buried in federal government archives, if those records were retained. If only we could penetrate the Byzantine morass of the federal government to unearth where the real decision took place. Who was it within the federal government that finally gave the yes to overturn the no. Sometimes it can be a politician who is favourable to a position doing it for the right reason. It might be a politician who simply sees its political value or who does not want to fight against the issue. It might be a politician or public servant who is horse trading one issue for another with their colleagues. It could even be a politician who hears from a senior public servant who is supportive despite the public service's collective corporate opposition.

The person in the best position to know why the government finally agreed to the disability amendment is Justice Minister Jean Chrétien. I got the extraordinary opportunity to ask him a mere 5 years after these events. His answer for the ages? He did not remember! Sigh! In Chapter XIX, I will describe how that came about! What do I think drove the Liberals to see it our way? Here is my informed assessment. It is perhaps more accurately labelled as my unsubstantiated speculation.

## B. Will We Ever Know When?

I have never pinned down when it was that the Trudeau Liberals internally decided to agree to the disability amendment. We know that they were still not agreeable when Chrétien addressed the Special Joint Committee of the Senate and the House of Commons on the Constitution of Canada (Joint Committee) on 12 January 1981.[1] By 16 January, he indicated to the Joint

---

1 Canada, Parliament, *Minutes of Proceedings and Evidence of the Special Joint Committee of the Senate and of the House of Commons on the Constitution of Canada*, 32nd Parl, 1st Sess, No 36 (12 January 1981) at 14–15.

Committee that he was prepared to reconsider this issue but had still not said that the government would agree to the disability amendment.[2] From the narrative in the book *The National Deal* by Robert Sheppard and Michael Valpy, an investigative journalists' account of the constitutional patriation saga, the Liberals must have reached this decision by 25 January 1981, 3 days before it was announced at the Joint Committee.[3] As of 25 January, there was high-level secret bargaining between the federal Liberals and Saskatchewan Premier Alan Blakeney (one of the hold-out premiers). Blakeney was vacationing in Hawaii.

Prime Minister Pierre Trudeau sent representatives to Hawaii to present a proposed deal to Blakeney. Trudeau's delegation gave Blakeney a briefing on the forthcoming changes to the *Canadian Charter of Rights and Freedoms* that were about to be made.[4] He was told that among the changes would be adding rights for people with physical disabilities. I wonder if Sheppard and Valpy got the details right — that this was only to cover physical disabilities — or if the Liberals were already agreeable to adding protection for both people with mental or physical disabilities. As detailed in *The National Deal*,

> [t]he agreed-upon format was that Blakeney and Trudeau would exchange letters setting down what each side was prepared to give. If the deal fell through, all letters and documentation — draft paragraphs for amendments, and so on — were to be returned. Gibson and the Saskatchewan trio began the Monday meeting by going over every piece of paper. The federal side presented a small change: rights for the physically handicapped were to be inserted in the charter. The Saskatchewan people did not object to rights for the physically handicapped; but the change itself made them nervous.
>
> One of the conditions on which there had been concurrence in Toronto was that no more amendments could be accepted after the consummation of their deal — with the understanding, of course, that the federal government was unable to tie the hands of Parliament (a caveat that Leeson and Romanow feared Ottawa might use as a ruse to sneak something by them, such is the paranoia of federal-provincial relations). The no-more-changes agreement was discarded

---

2 Canada, Parliament, *Minutes of Proceedings and Evidence of the Special Joint Committee of the Senate and of the House of Commons on the Constitution of Canada*, 32nd Parl, 1st Sess, No 39 (16 January 1981) at 18.

3 See Robert Sheppard & Michael Valpy, *The National Deal: The Fight for a Canadian Constitution* (Toronto: Fleet Books, 1982) at 128–129.

4 *Canadian Charter of Rights and Freedoms*, Part 1 of the *Constitution Act, 1982*, being Schedule B to the *Canada Act 1982* (UK), 1982, c 11.

> as politically unworkable, but the Saskatchewan team was left with the impression that the federal government was gradually losing control of its own resolution. Chrétien, having returned to work, was negotiating with the senators, and could not make a deal, and he was negotiating with Saskatchewan about the Senate and could not make a deal — there was still nothing on paper about the Senate — and suddenly up pops rights for the physically handicapped.[5]

## C. What Makes for a Good Social Justice Argument?

The policy arguments in favour of the disability amendment were as strong as we could have ever wanted. I have presented zillions of arguments in my career. Few were ever any stronger than this one. No one could dispute in 1980 that people with disabilities were a large, worthy, and substantially disadvantaged minority. No one could deny that people with disabilities suffered from unequal treatment. There was no public animus against people with disabilities as a minority group to fuel hostility to the disability amendment. We faced no community-based organized opposition to the disability amendment.

What makes an argument for a new policy or law strong? Several ingredients can go into the stew. As you add good ingredients, they combine to reinforce and strengthen each other. To begin, it helps when your cause has compelling public appeal and the people who need this new policy or law engage public support and no antipathy. If there are any legal issues that underpin your argument, it makes things much easier when those points are easy to understand and are all clearly and decisively in your favour. It is no fun to get mired in a spat over whose position on a contested legal question is the right one. Things get better when your "ask" and the arguments supporting it are clear, convincing, and easy to explain in a single sentence that could fit into a headline or a 280-character tweet. Life is simplified even more if there are no good arguments raised against you or if the arguments advanced in opposition to you sound like they came from some cold bureaucrat who long ago ran out of good ideas.

If we do have an opponent who publicly argues against us, it helps if their position involves a long complicated, labyrinthian, and unsympathetic argument. The stars are shining down on us when an opponent is frankly squirming because they would rather be anywhere else but opposing our position. The recipe gets even more flavourful when the disability community

---

5 Sheppard & Valpy, *supra* note 3 at 128–129 [footnotes omitted].

is united behind our argument or, at the very least, when there is no public divisiveness over it. Unanimity is typically impossible to achieve. My goal is to attain harmony. Finally, the stew is most tasty when it readily lends itself to a good news story; if it looks, smells, and tastes like something that a news editor would rush to include in their newspaper or broadcast. I have developed something of an intuitive nose for this over the years, though this is nothing to brag about. It is not rocket science. In the best of all possible worlds, you have all these features going for you. In 1980, we came as close as I have ever come in my years advocating on disability issues.

## D. An Undisputable Legal Foundation

The legal argument that lay at the foundation of our case for the disability amendment was simple and uncontestable. As a matter of legal interpretation, no one did or could disagree with us that the initial wording of section 15, introduced into Parliament in October 1980, provided equality for some equality-seeking minorities but not for people with disabilities. Our legal starting point was that we had been left out.

## E. A Simply Appealing Argument: The Strong, Simple, Straightforward Claim for Equality

What we sought cut to the very core of equality itself — the very essence of section 15 of the proposed *Charter*. Could Canada enact a constitutional provision, stated to guarantee equality to people in Canada, if it did not entitle people with disabilities to equality? No one could argue that people with disabilities enjoyed full equality in Canada in 1980 and that they needed no protection from discrimination. No one could deny that we faced barriers. No one could claim that legislators were magically immune or exempt from the discriminatory practices that people with disabilities faced in access to jobs, goods, services, and housing.

## F. Blistering Hypocrisy to Say No to the Disability Amendment in 1981, the International Year of Disabled Persons

It never hurts if your opponent's contrary position looks hypocritical, even without our ever having to use that nasty word. As has been repeated in these pages, how could people with disabilities be denied equality in Canada's brand-new *Charter* in 1981, the very year internationally recognized as being dedicated to advancing equality for people with disabilities? Hypocrisy was doubly amplified by the fact that the theme for 1981, the International Year of Disabled Persons, was equality and full participation and that Canada was one of the sponsors for this United Nations [UN] designation.

## G. No Good Argument against the Disability Amendment

Our stew was thickened by the fact that the federal government's contrary argument was so weak and smelled like the product of bureaucrats trying to find any excuse they could. I question whether Chrétien felt comfortable even making the arguments against us that public servants had scripted for him. He showed no enthusiasm for them at the Joint Committee. As a public policy debate, there was only one side to this issue. No constituency in society publicly campaigned against us. The only witness before the Joint Committee who might possibly be read as questioning whether to add mental disability to section 15, the Saskatchewan Human Rights Commission's chief commissioner Ken Norman, only took that position (if he did at all, which is entirely unclear) in answer to a question from a member of the Joint Committee. His confusing submissions ended up being a momentary blip. I doubt the media noticed it. It quickly fizzled into oblivion. Had I not stumbled upon it and spent time trying to figure out exactly what his position was while preparing this retrospective, it would likely have remained lost and forgotten. Those women's organizations that sought harmful hierarchical wording in section 15, described in Chapter XI, which would have diluted protection that people with disabilities and some other equality-seeking groups would receive, were not against disability equality *per se*.

## H. Support for the Disability Amendment from the Disability Community

Another important factor that could only have helped get the disability amendment over the finish line was that it was broadly supported by disability organizations that appeared before the Special Parliamentary Committee on the Disabled and Handicapped (Smith Committee) and the Joint Committee. Further buttressing this was the strong support for the disability amendment that the Joint Committee's public hearings received. As described earlier in Chapters X and XIII, this included the presentations by the COPOH, the CAMR, and the CNIB, endorsed at the hearings by some other equality-seeking organizations.

Beyond those formal deputations, and without the availability of community organizing and advocacy tools like the Internet and social media, plain old disability advocacy had to play an indispensable role in our eventual collective success. I will never know how many unsung heroes there were who made this possible. I have no way to track them down. I do not want to leave an impression that people with disabilities were flocking to the streets *en masse* to demand the disability amendment. I have earlier indicated that it is reasonable to conclude that, back then, the vast majority of people with disabilities did not know about this issue at all. However, among enough of those who did know, sufficient action was taken to help us move forward on this cause.

In contrast with my experience during the fight for the disability amendment, I have encountered in recent years the troubling situation of some disability organizations that actively oppose amendments that would strengthen a disability-related statute. I ran into this when we and others went to the Senate in 2019 to get amendments to Bill C-81, the proposed *Accessible Canada Act*, and when we went to the House of Commons in the fall of 2022 and to the Senate in the spring of 2023 to seek amendments to Bill C-22, the proposed *Canada Disability Benefit Act*.[6] In both cases, there was significant grassroots support for the amendments we sought. In both instances, we and others together succeeded in getting some of the amendments we wanted. However, those disability organizations that opposed any amendments (no doubt, at the request of the government) made it harder for us to make progress. This never deters me. Fortunately, in 1980 and 1981, we did not have that obstacle.

For her part, in her published book chapter that describes COPOH's efforts on the disability amendment, disability rights advocate, colleague, and COPOH co-presenter at the Joint Committee Yvonne Peters summarized some of the grassroots disability advocacy efforts about which she knew a great deal and about which I knew nothing. She wrote:

> **The Committee Vigil**
>
> According to Jim Derksen, a small group of Ottawa-based people with disabilities made a concerted effort to be in attendance at all deliberations of the

---

6 *Accessible Canada Act*, SC 2019, c 10; *Canada Disability Benefit Act*, SC 2023, c 17.

Parliamentary Committee. As the Committee hearings were televised, their purpose was to provide a constant, visible disability presence to demonstrate to both the Committee and the Canadian public that people with disabilities were serious about their demands for inclusion.

To this end, Derksen recollects that individuals with disabilities would situate themselves behind the person presenting to the Committee to ensure that they would be in the vicinity of the television camera and thus visible to the viewing public.

Apparently, their vigilant tactics extended beyond the Committee room. At the lunch break, this same persistent group would follow Committee members to the Parliamentary dining room and choose a table near them. They would then engage in a boisterous dialogue about their desire for equality recognition and about what they might do if their hopes were not realized. For example, one version of the story suggests that one of the men who used a power chair indicated that one day he just might accidentally knock over a couple of tables and chairs when leaving the Committee room.

Even the privacy rights of Committee members were occasionally compromised by zealous disability rights activists. One story suggests that one day Allan Simpson, National Chair of COPOH, never wanting to miss an opportunity, noticed Mr. Chrétien leaving the Committee room. Simpson followed and the unsuspecting Chrétien found himself being lobbied for Charter inclusion in the men's washroom at the urinal.

It is possible that the government buckled under the tenacious pressure of people with disabilities.

**The Threat of Busloads of People with Disabilities**

John Rae, an Ontario disability rights activist, recalls that, after making many cogent presentations to the Joint Parliamentary Committee, and after sending hundreds of letters and telegrams to government officials and politicians, including the Prime Minister, "we were still hitting our heads against a brick wall." In a January 1981 news article, this frustration was noted, and it was hinted that busloads of people with disabilities were prepared to descend on Ottawa to protest their lack of inclusion in the Charter.

Rae confesses that there was some truth to this suggestion. Discussions were underway regarding the possibility of chartering buses and taking folks to Ottawa. What isn't so clear is how many people might have participated. Nevertheless, the rumour was fuelled, and circulated widely throughout Ottawa.

It is possible that the government buckled at the thought of busloads of people with varying disabilities descending on Ottawa to protest their lack of inclusion in the Charter, particularly as it prepared to launch the International Year of Disabled Persons. In fact there may be some truth to this suggestion. In his remarks supporting the amendment to include people with disabilities in

> the Charter, Chrétien states: "I was very anxious that we should proceed tonight. They were preparing to have a big group tomorrow."[7]

In *The National Deal*, Sheppard and Valpy talked about how much advocacy on the constitutional reform package took place in the hallway during the Joint Committee proceedings, including advocacy on disability issues:

> More often than not, the hearings went on late into the night, the debates careening wildly between shrill partisan rhetoric and sincere collegiality, sometimes with the mood changing eerily on the spur of the moment when the government conceded a hard-fought-for point.
>
> But much of the wheeling and dealing took place in the corridors and cloakrooms outside, where officials huddled to discuss drafting changes, and politicians negotiated feverishly with lobbyists. It was here that Jean Chrétien jollied along groups of francophones from Manitoba, Saskatchewan and Ontario, or sipped coffee quietly with handicapped persons in wheelchairs.[8]

As I noted in Chapter XIV, on 28 January 1981, when Chrétien agreed to the disability amendment on behalf of the Trudeau government, he mentioned his desire to avert some sort of demonstration.[9] The vast majority of protests and demonstrations in Canada likely get no media or public attention. Yet, in my experience, a fear of such grassroots political action can be as potent a tool as the event itself. I had nothing to do with any discussions back then about disability advocates going to the UK Parliament to lobby in support of the disability amendment if Canada's Parliament did not incorporate it into section 15. However, I referred to rumours about the possibility of some advocates going to approach the British Parliament during my interview on the CBC radio on 26 November 1981. In the next section of this retrospective, I have more to say about that radio interview.

Beyond these accounts, there is likely lost to us the paper trail of other efforts by people and organizations within the disability community to get the disability amendment passed. When I applied to Canada's National

7 Yvonne Peters, "From Charity to Equality: Canadians with Disabilities Take Their Rightful Place in Canada's Constitution" in Deborah Stienstra & Aileen Wight-Felske, with Colleen Watters, eds, *Making Equality: History of Advocacy and Persons with Disabilities in Canada* (Concord, ON: Captus Press 2003) 119 at 132–133 [citations omitted].

8 Sheppard & Valpy, *supra* note 3 at 137.

9 Canada, Parliament, *Minutes of Proceedings and Evidence of the Special Joint Committee of the Senate and of the House of Commons on the Constitution of Canada*, 32nd Parl, 1st Sess, No 47 (28 January 1981) at 91.

Archive to get COPOH's, the CAMR's, and the CNIB's briefs to the Joint Committee, I was also given letters to the Joint Committee from those three organizations.

## I. Internal Championing by Liberal Member of Parliament David Smith and the Smith Committee

An absolutely pivotal reason for our winning the disability amendment was the leadership of Liberal Member of Parliament David Smith and the members of the Smith Committee. I earlier described how they supported the disability amendment in their committee's interim report on 30 October 1980. Members of the Smith Committee voiced this enthusiasm at Joint Committee meetings. Fortifying this, Smith mounted a tenacious internal lobbying campaign within the Liberal caucus for the disability amendment. In her book chapter that focuses on COPOH's advocacy in support of the disability amendment, Peters wrote:

> According to Mr. Derksen, the members of the Obstacles Committee played a pivotal role in convincing their colleagues to support the position of people with disabilities and ultimately, our eventual inclusion in the Charter. Members of the Conservative and NDP parties exerted pressure on the government by asking questions in the House and raising the issue with the Parliamentary Committee.[10]

Sheppard and Valpy elaborated, suggesting that the government expanded section 15 to include people with disabilities in order to also help secure backbench Liberal support within the federal caucus. Sheppard and Valpy wrote:

> At the start of the marathon cabinet meetings, Trudeau set down two imperatives. He would not use Westminster to transfer powers from the provincial sphere to the federal government ("There would be a revolution if we did that"); and he would not impose obligations on provincial legislatures. This ruled out enforcing official bilingualism on the courts and legislature of Ontario, as many in his party were demanding. But Trudeau's injunction was later broken when the resolution was being scrutinized by a joint parliamentary committee in the winter of 1980-81: increased language and non-discrimination rights for the disabled and native people — cutting directly into provincial legislation — were included to secure federal NDP [New Democratic Party] and backbench Liberal support.[11]

---

10 Peters, *supra* note 7 at 128 [footnotes omitted].

11 Sheppard & Valpy, *supra* note 3 at 68 [footnotes omitted].

Elsewhere in their book, Sheppard and Valpy added:

> The only addition to the list was the specific reference to the mentally and physically disabled, whose cause both the Tories and NDP took up in earnest. The handicapped also had influential champions in the Liberal caucus, including Dr. Peter Lang and David Smith, a Toronto MP who headed a special task force on handicapped rights, and cabinet ministers from Toronto and Winnipeg, where the main lobby groups were located.[12]

## J. Opposition Parties' Support for the Disability Amendment

We also owe a major debt of gratitude to the federal Progressive Conservative Party and the NDP of 1980–1981. They helped raise this issue with witnesses at the Joint Committee and pressed Chrétien to explain why we were left out of the *Charter*'s equality rights guarantee. Governments always closely watch the opposition parties to see if they will take up an issue or let it slide. If no opposition party will take up our cause, our uphill battle gets closer to a vertical climb. As I explained earlier, once the opposition parties announced that they would move an amendment to section 15, the Trudeau Liberals were cornered. Did the Liberals want to be the only party in the House of Commons that went on the record, voting against equality for people with disabilities? If the opposition parties did not bring such a motion, the Liberals could have entirely ducked this issue during the clause-by-clause review by not bringing any motion of their own. The disability amendment issue would simply never have come up for a debate and vote at that point in the Joint Committee's work. With all the controversy swirling around Trudeau's constitutional patriation package, the last thing the Liberals needed was for them to look like the least supportive party on an important equality question, on which the Conservatives on the right and the NDP on the left had united.

## K. The Trudeau Liberals' Unending Negotiations with Hold-Out Provincial Premiers

In January 1981, the Trudeau Liberals were locked in a headline-grabbing, protracted, and seemingly unsolvable political battle with eight of the ten provincial governments and with the opposition federal Conservative Party

12 *Ibid* at 154 [footnotes omitted].

over its entire constitutional patriation package. The federal government was busy trying to bring them on side but was running into stiff, tenacious resistance. Trudeau desperately wanted public support for his reforms. The only part of the Constitution reform package that looked to stir any public interest was the proposed *Charter*. Most Canadians lost no sleep over whether Canada's Constitution resided in the UK Parliament or in Canada. Adrenaline did not get pumping over how the constitutional-amending formula was going to be designed. However, Canadians, who watched tons of American television, might be more interested in the fact that our Constitution is nothing like the US *Bill of Rights*.[13]

It is no brilliant insight on my part to suggest that the Trudeau Liberals were looking to see what amendments they could make to the *Charter* to maximize public support for it. The disability amendment stuck out as an issue that needed to be addressed. It did not help the Liberals for us to be telling the public that the *Charter*'s equality rights provision did not guarantee equality to people with disabilities. The public had historically been favourably disposed towards people with disabilities, though too often out of feelings of pity and charity. It was fortuitous in the extreme when, on 13 January 1981, the *Globe and Mail* prominently reported on my criticism of Chrétien's opposition to the disability amendment on the previous day. I did not then know that Chrétien was trying to use arguments like focusing on the rights of people with disabilities in his efforts to persuade the hold-out premiers to drop their opposition to the patriation package. Sheppard and Valpy wrote:

> The charter was in very high favour in Metro Toronto, particularly among the so-called ethnic communities which form the base of Liberal support in the city; private discussions with the Davis government revealed that they too saw the same political advantage in emphasizing the charter. Perhaps it could even be the Liberals' wedge into barren western Canada, some ministers argued; after all, the idea had been championed in Saskatchewan by both John Diefenbaker and Tommy Douglas in the 1940s and 1950s. The charter of rights was thought to be an invincible political tool, a modern-day Excalibur. As Chrétien often said later to his provincial opponents during the protracted negotiations: "You come out against the rights of Indians and women and the handicapped, and I'm going to cut you into little pieces."[14]

---

13 *Bill of Rights*, 1791, *General Records of the United States Government*, RG 11, National Archives.

14 *Ibid* at 68.

Were I waging this campaign today, that line of argument, I hope, would have leapt out at me (though using somewhat more elegant wording)! I would want to use it in the media and to prod the federal government to use it in its hard bargaining with the hold-out premiers. Why did I not think of it back then?

The Joint Committee's public hearings had received a deluge of demands on an extraordinary range of issues. Amidst that blizzard, the disability amendment may have emerged as a targeted compelling aspirational measure, rising amidst the fray. In *The National Deal*, Sheppard and Valpy catalogued the outpouring of different requests but then contrasted them as follows:

> But, in marked contrast, there was the serene dignity of the Nishgas, the small west coast band whose persistence led to a landmark court decision in 1973, opening the door to the acceptance of the concept of aboriginal rights by governments. Their presence added a certain poignancy to the deliberations, as did the bright spirited arguments from blind law student David Lepofsky on rights for the handicapped.[15]

## L. Helpful Political Chemistry When All Parties Raise an Issue in Parliament

Wind is added to the sails of a law reform campaign if it keeps coming up in Parliament. It especially helps when politicians from more than one party raise it. When politicians from all the parties chime in, that is even better. That gives it the optimal badge of a non-partisan or bipartisan issue. It was therefore a boost for the disability amendment in October 1980 when several members of parliament raised the lack of protection for people with disabilities in section 15 during debates in Parliament. This took place even before the patriation package was referred to the Joint Committee for public hearings.

The first rather oblique reference to disability concerns came from Liberal Member of Parliament Jim Fleming, the minister of state for multiculturalism, during the House of Commons debates over the constitutional reform package.[16] He was not there pressing for the disability amendment. Rather, he was arguing against one of the most intransigent

---

15 *Ibid* at 138 [footnotes omitted].

16 Canada, Parliament, *House of Commons Debates*, 32nd Parl, 1st Sess, Vol III (8 October 1980) at 3407.

hold-out premiers, Manitoba Premier Sterling Lyon.[17] Fleming argued that Lyon was wrong to suggest that the proposed *Charter* would somehow hurt people with disabilities, among others. He contended:

> The constitutional bill would place minority and individual rights beyond the reach of majority opinion, and beyond the reach of political expediency. Rather than lessen, it would increase legislative responsibility, since the constitution would force us to exercise more care in delegating power to administrators. Premier Lyon has tried to turn the virtue of entrenchment into a defect. Opinions change, as he points out, and new rights emerge — rights for children, homosexuals, the handicapped-and entrenchment would prevent further progress. History gives us no grounds for such fears. It has certainly not prevented the growth of liberty in the United States.[18]

On 15 October 1980, during debates over the patriation package, NDP Member of Parliament Bill Blaikie became the first member of parliament to identify the need for the disability amendment in the House of Commons.[19] It is clear from this and later exchanges that there lurked in the background an ongoing debate over which items should be included in this round of constitutional reform and what items might be deferred to a future second round. Blakey argued:

> In this context I wish to reinforce what my leader has already said about our demand that an amendment reinforcing and clarifying provincial ownership and control of resources be accepted in order for us to be able to support the entire constitutional package. This is because we believe that in order for this constitutional watershed to be a positive one and not a negative one, the felt priorities of western Canada must be addressed. It is true there are many other things left to work on, from the Supreme Court to the Senate to family law to communications, and so on.
>
> This, we hope to God, is not the final constitutional word. There is plenty of work to be done after patriation. Much remains to be done, for instance, in terms of guaranteeing the rights of women, of native people and of the handicapped. We will be offering amendments in these areas as well and we trust the government will be open to these very important areas of concern. Perhaps some changes might even be made before the constitution is patriated.[20]

---

17 *Ibid* at 3406.

18 *Ibid* at 3407.

19 Canada, Parliament, *House of Commons Debates*, 32nd Parl, 1st Sess, Vol IV (15 October 1980) at 3708.

20 *Ibid* at 3711.

A unique moment in this unfolding series of events took place 5 days later on 20 October 1980. During Question Period in the House of Commons, Prime Minister Pierre Trudeau was directly asked whether he would agree to the disability amendment. His answer left the door open, but he made no commitments. He referred to the possibility of it being considered in a second round of constitutional reforms once the Constitution was patriated. He did not address the merits of the disability amendment. What makes this question of the prime minister stand out even more is the fact that it came from a Liberal member of parliament, Peter Lang. Usually, a governing party only lets its own members of parliament ask carefully scripted friendly questions of their own ministers and, especially, of their own prime minister. Lang's question would be unimaginable today unless the government had already decided to approve the disability amendment and had then staged this question during Question Period as a platform to announce it while the media are looking on. Lang had this exchange with Trudeau:

> **Peter Lang (Kitchener):** Madam Speaker, my question is for the Prime Minister. In view of the fact that many persons with disabilities are presently suffering from discrimination and have voiced their desire to be protected in any new constitution, I would like to ask the Prime Minister if non-discrimination rights for persons with disabilities could be incorporated by amendment into the proposed constitution act of 1980?
>
> **An Honorary Member:** And women?
>
> **An Honorary Member:** And natives?
>
> **Right Honorary Pierre Trudeau (Prime Minister):** Madam Speaker, I hear, along with this constructive suggestion from the member for Kitchener, members of the official opposition saying we should also include other factors in this bill of rights, and they have suggested women and natives. I am very happy that at last we have the support of the Tory party for our action.
>
> **Some Honorary Members:** Hear, hear!
>
> **Right Honorary Pierre Trudeau (Prime Minister):** I am grateful to the member from Kitchener for having at last brought forth this honest support of our action in protecting the basic rights of Canadians. I am prepared to examine any amendments which can improve the status of the resolution before the House. In some cases I have indicated it would be useful to carry on the discussion so that in the second phase of negotiations, once we have a constitution in Canada, amendable in Canada, we could indeed improve in

> many ways the bill of rights, including the way suggested by the hon. member from Kitchener.[21]

The disability amendment came up again an impressive three times on 22 October 1980. Liberal Member of Parliament Marie Thérèse Rollande Killens called for the disability amendment, saying:

> Mr. Speaker, my time is running out, but before closing I would like to tell members on both sides of the House about a point that I find very important. It concerns Section 15 of the proposed resolution, which deals with the right to non-discrimination. That article lists various categories of people who should be protected, but I note that the handicapped had been omitted. I draw that omission to the attention of all hon. members and take this opportunity to ask for their support when the special committee of the House tables its preliminary report, in the very near future, and recommends that the handicapped be included in the bill of rights.[22]

Later that day, Smith, chair of the Smith Committee added his voice to the call for the disability amendment:

> There is one final point I should like to make, and that is that I for one happen to-think it is possible to make some improvements to the charter. I think that is the function of the committee. Some hon. members might be aware of the fact that I am chairman of the committee on the handicapped and disabled. I happen to believe that the charter would be improved if a specific reference to them were included in it. I have spoken on this before and I intend to carry on with this idea and hope to address the committee on that. It would not be a new thing which would open the floodgates to many minority groups because, in fact, a precedent has already been established in the Human Rights Act. The reference in it to the rights of the handicapped and disabled would improve even further what I believe to be a sound and good charter.
>
> After having had the opportunity to travel across the country with the committee and to listen to people speak, I can assure you that Canadians from coast to coast, particularly disabled Canadians, feel very strongly about their rights. They do not really feel certain about them being guaranteed by the various provincial governments of this land. We heard over 600 briefs and many of them spoke to this issue. Without exception they support the concept of a charter enshrining rights. I hope it will ultimately be expanded and made clear that those rights refer specifically to disabled Canadians.[23]

21 *Ibid* at 3821.

22 *Ibid* at 3957.

23 *Ibid at 4003.*

Still later that day, legendary NDP Member of Parliament Stanley Knowles (who coincidentally was the keynote speaker 1 year earlier at my graduation from the Osgoode Hall Law School) joined in the call for the disability amendment:

> I was pleased a moment ago to hear the hon. member for Don Valley East (Mr. Smith) raise a point, which was one of the three that I intended to deal with in this portion of my remarks, namely, the rights of the handicapped people of this country. They feel very upset that nothing seems to be done for them in this constitution. Again, I would like to see that done.[24]

On 3 November 1980, NDP Member of Parliament Neil Young brought forward a motion in the House of Commons calling for the disability amendment. It appeared to need unanimous consent to be debated. That consent was not forthcoming. The Hansard transcript does not give any details on who or how many voted for or against this motion. The brief proceedings on point were as follows:

> **Madam Speaker:** I rise under the provisions of Standing Order 43. Whereas the special committee on the disabled and handicapped has recommended in its interim report that any charter of rights include provisions to prohibit discrimination against the disabled and the handicapped, I move, seconded by the hon. member for Kamloops-Shuswap (Mr. Ruis):
>
> That the Minister of Justice be instructed to bring forward amendments the proposed charter of rights to include the disabled and to prohibit discrimination against the disabled and the handicapped in all areas, not just in the area of employment.
>
> **Madam Speaker:** For presentation, this motion requires the unanimous consent of the House. Is there unanimous consent?
>
> **Some Honorary Members:** Agreed.
>
> **Some Honorary Members:** No.[25]

After those parliamentary exchanges, and once the Joint Committee was holding its public hearings and then conducting a clause-by-clause review of the package, individual members of parliament on that committee from each of the three parties in Parliament spoke up in sympathy with the disability amendment at different times, as Chapter XIV documents. Some members of parliament went out of their way to raise the call for the

---

24 *Ibid* at 4005.
25 *Ibid* at 3517.

disability amendment, with some deputants who had not themselves raised the disability amendment in their presentations to the Joint Committee. After Chrétien gave reasons why the Trudeau government would not agree to the disability amendment on 12 January 1981, NDP Members of Parliament Svend Robinson and Lorne Nystrom went right at him with a series of questions, pressing him to agree to talk to his officials and reconsider the disability amendment afresh.[26]

Finally, on 22 January 1981, Conservative Member of Parliament Bill Clarke jabbed at the Trudeau government about the fact that people with disabilities were ignored in the proposed constitutional reform package. He was speaking in the House of Commons while the Joint Committee was still in the midst of its clause-by-clause review. By this point, the Trudeau government was on the verge of deciding to support the disability amendment, which the Joint Committee was to approve 6 days later. Clarke poked at the government as follows:

> On the constitution, the government brought in the resolution which still has not been reported back to this House. The plight of women and other women's issues were ignored in the proposals put forward by the government. When the Advisory Council on the Status of Women was finally invited to appear before the constitutional committee, it stated it had not been asked, until the second round of meetings, to have any input into the constitutional proposals.
>
> The members of the advisory council were not the only ones to be ignored; there were other groups such as the handicapped. In fact, many groups appeared before that committee and complained that they had been ignored.[27]

## M. A Defining Moment When Politicians Override the Advice of Public Service?

Federal Liberal politicians, such as Chrétien, who were committed to the ideas embedded in the *Charter*, would have found the disability amendment to be intuitively appealing had they had the time and opportunity to think about it. The contrary advice of public servants must have been frustrating. I think it was a possible moment of candor when Chrétien made it sound like he would like to approve the disability amendment but was being advised against it by his officials. Of course, that could be self-serving political

---

[26] See section XIV.

[27] Canada, Parliament, *House of Commons Debates*, 32nd Parl, 1st Sess, Vol VI (22 January 1981) at 6475.

blarney. As I said earlier, it is easy for a politician to blame public servants for their decisions. Those public servants typically cannot speak out to set the record straight if a politician publicly misrepresents their advice.

In my experience, some cabinet ministers are policy wonks who get down and dirty into the details of policy issues. Others do not. They leave that all to their political staff and public service officials. Chrétien was not known to be a detail person. He may have played a marginal role in this decision, deferring to his officials along the way from beginning to end. He tried to portray himself as more proactively involved in his memoir *Straight from the Heart*, published before he ran for prime minister. He said this about his involvement in answering questions at the Joint Committee generally: "Though I occasionally let my officials handle the more technical issues, I answered most of the questions from my study of the briefs and my own experiences during the summer."[28] Whether or not Chrétien was much of a detail person, there are moments — too rare I suspect — when politicians will flex their political muscle, thank their officials for their nervous doom-and-gloom advice, and decide, despite that advice, to go bold. That could have played a part in our victory.

## N. What Was My Role?

How much of a difference did I make? I am decidedly the wrong person to answer this question. I do not have access to the information I would need if I even wanted to take a strong position on this question. As I explained in Chapter I, I have been flustered a few times over the years when a well-meaning person introduces me to an audience before I am to give a speech, claiming that I was largely responsible for winning the disability amendment to the *Charter*. I feel it is very important for me to immediately and firmly set the record straight. Each time, I explain that I was one of many people who fought for the disability amendment and that our victory was the result of the combined efforts of all of us, converging at the right time and place.

---

[28] Jean Chrétien, *Straight from the Heart*, rev ed (Toronto: Key Porter Books, 1994) at 178–179.

I hope it was helpful to the cause for me to get the *CNIB* to take action on the disability amendment and for me to deliver one of the three presentations at the Joint Committee in support of the disability amendment. It was fortuitous that my presentation came third, after COPOH and the CAMR. It is exactly where I would want to appear in the line-up. Let me reinforce something I said in Chapter X. When I have appeared in court as crown counsel on a case where there are multiple interveners and parties on our side, I always try to arrange to speak last, if possible. That lets me watch the other arguments unfold. Being "closer," I can drill right into the major issues that others did not cover and that cry out for some attention.

In 1980, I sadly got no opportunity to review COPOH's and the CAMR's presentations to the Joint Committee public hearings before it was my turn at bat. I was not thinking in those strategic terms on 12 December 1980. I was desperately struggling to cobble together the points to make, without the luxury of such tactical nuances. Even without my thinking about those tactical considerations, my going third gave me a golden opportunity to drive home once again a message that the Joint Committee had already heard twice, with my own spin on it (another baseball metaphor, but with no *Star Trek*). This perhaps could help keep the disability amendment alive in the minds of the Joint Committee members as they grappled with so many other issues. It was also incredibly fortuitous timing that my deputation came very late in the hearings. You want your arguments to be the freshest in the minds of those making the decision when it comes time for them to decide.

When I give talks on community organizing and activism, I often use the metaphor of trying to chop down a tree (at the risk of offending some of my environmentalist friends). I explain that winning the enactment of something like new legislation is like chopping down a tree. If you put your hands on some big, tall tree and try to push it over yourself, you will accomplish nothing, except maybe straining your arm muscles. You will not budge the tree one millimetre. If you pick up an axe and swing it once as hard as you can at the base of the tree, you will make a tiny dent in it. That too will make no difference at all. However, we know that if you swing that axe enough times at the tree and aim it at the right spot, you can chop down the tree. If someone else takes turns with you, you will succeed more quickly. If you both swing axes at the tree at the same time and carefully coordinate your efforts and your aim, you will succeed even more quickly. If you do not coordinate these efforts, you could injure each other instead of speeding up the progress. We know with certainty that if you work long enough and hard enough at it and get enough help then, together, you can chop down that tree. When the tree comes down, every swing has contributed to the ultimate result. No one can say which swing made more of a difference. A final swing may come just before the tree falls. However, that swing, like the first one, would have made no difference had it not been for all the other swings.

When we try to get a new law passed, each person who writes a politician, gives a media interview or newspaper guest column, attends a public rally, or sends a tweet is making a swing of the axe. Each of these individual swings may feel like it makes no difference at all. However, without all of them in combination, the result will not be possible. No one specific letter, interview, email, tweet, or other swing of the axe can be isolated objectively as the decisive knockout punch. There may be no knockout punch at all. However, each swing contributes. I hope that my appearance on behalf of the CNIB at the Joint Committee was one of the swings of the axe. My interviews in the media, few as they turned out to be, were swings of the axe. They contributed. I am proud of that. I cannot evaluate the size of their impact any further than that.

## O. The Yvonne Peters Perspective

Like myself, disability advocate Yvonne Peters tried to figure out why we won. As she wrote,

> [n]o one seems to know for certain exactly what sparked the Committee to make this eleventh hour decision. Clearly, much of the credit must be attributed to the hard work of the members of the Obstacles Committee, who were relentless in their efforts to convince their political colleagues to accept the amendment. But additional stories have circulated throughout the disability rights movement as to how the scales were tipped in favour of people with disabilities. Below is a summary of some of these stories, which may or may not have played a vital role in bringing about a successful conclusion to the Charter lobby.
>
> **International Year of Disabled Persons**
>
> The year 1981 was designated by the UN the International Year of Disabled Persons (IYDP), based on the themes of "full participation and equality." Canada was one of the co-movers of the UN resolution that established the IYDP. COPOH argued that including disability in the proposed *Charter* "would be a good demonstration that our domestic actions are in line with the policies we are promoting in the world."[38] Other groups such as the CNIB argued that, "[f]or Canada to entrench in its Constitution in the Year of Disabled Persons

a Charter of Rights that expressly denies its handicapped citizens the same right to equality before the law which is to be enjoyed by the majority of Canadians would be travesty and would make a mockery of Canada's commitment at the U.N. to equality for the handicapped." It is possible that the government buckled under the prospect of having to reconcile its decision to exclude people with disabilities from the equality guarantee of the *Charter*, with its support for the IYDP's goals of full participation and equality.[29]

---

29 Peters, *supra* note 7 at 131–132.

# XVI. "IT AIN'T OVER TIL IT'S OVER": FIGHTING TO PRESERVE OUR VICTORY

## A. The Late Arrival of the *Charter*'s Infamous "Notwithstanding Clause"

When the Special Joint Committee of the Senate and the House of Commons on the Constitution of Canada (Joint Committee) passed the disability amendment in January 1981, it seemed that for us the battle was over. However, I foreshadowed in my CBC radio interview on 29 January 1981 that this was conditional on Parliament passing the constitutional package. That outcome remained uncertain, despite the Trudeau Liberals' majority in Parliament. In the winter of 1981, the Joint Committee finished its work and sent the constitutional reform package back to the House of Commons for debate and vote on third reading.[1] A huge parliamentary battle ensued between the Trudeau government and the opposition over procedural manoeuvres that blocked the House of Commons from being able to do any business at all.[2] In the face of that stalemate, Prime Minister Pierre Trudeau agreed to refer a case to the Supreme Court of Canada for a ruling on the question of whether the UK Parliament was constitutionally permitted to amend Canada's Constitution (then a British statute) with the consent of only Ontario and New Brunswick.[3]

Gallons of ink has since been spilled, which I will not repeat here, on the Supreme Court of Canada's patriation reference decision on 28 September 1981 and the ensuing wrangling between the Trudeau government and the provinces to work out an agreement.[4] I shall zero in on the part of that saga that is important for the story of the disability amendment. On 8 October 1981, the Canadian National Institute for the Blind's [CNIB]

---

[1] Canada, Parliament, *Minutes of Proceedings and Evidence of the Special Joint Committee of the Senate and of the House of Commons on the Constitution of Canada*, 32nd Parl, 1st Sess, No 57 (13 February 1981) at 42.

[2] Robert Sheppard & Michael Valpy, *The National Deal: The Fight for a Canadian Constitution* (Toronto: Fleet Books, 1982) at 109, 345.

[3] *Ibid* at 109, 345.

[4] *Ibid* at 136–159.

managing director Robert Mercer sent a telegram to Trudeau, calling for swift enactment of the disability amendment. This telegram, which reads like something I must have written, reiterated key arguments that we had been pressing for the past year:

> ON BEHALF OF THE CANADIAN NATIONAL INSTITUTE FOR THE BLIND, I WISH TO REITERATE OUR STRONG SUPPORT FOR THE FEDERAL GOVERNMENT'S PLAN TO INCLUDE THE PHYSICALLY AND MENTALLY HANDICAPPED WITHIN THE EQUAL RIGHTS SECTION OF THE PROPOSED CHARTER OF RIGHTS. THE CNIB, ALONG WITH OTHER ORGANIZATIONS OF, AND FOR, THE HANDICAPPED, ACTIVELY PURSUED THE AMENDMENT TO THE CHARTER OF RIGHTS, ULTIMATELY APPROVED LAST WINTER, WHICH WILL ENTITLE THE 10% OF CANADA'S POPULATION WHO ARE DISABLED TO "EQUALITY BEFORE AND UNDER THE LAW AND TO THE EQUAL PROTECTION AND EQUAL BENEFIT OF THE LAW WITHOUT DISCRIMINATION". THE PLAN OF THE FEDERAL GOVERNMENT IS HIGHLY APPROPRIATE FOR 1981, THE INTERNATIONAL YEAR OF DISABLED PERSONS, WHOSE THEME IS "EQUALITY AND FULL PARTICIPATION FOR THE HANDICAPPED". WITH LEGAL OBSTACLES NO LONGER PRESENT, WE HOPE AND TRUST THAT THE FEDERAL GOVERNMENT'S PROPOSAL REGARDING THE HANDICAPPED WILL BE SPEEDILY FULFILLED.[5]

In November 1981, over a month after the Supreme Court of Canada's ruling, the federal government cut a deal with nine of Canada's ten provinces, all of them except Quebec.[6] Those nine provinces agreed to support the Trudeau constitutional reform package. One of the conditions of that deal was that a new section would be added to the *Canadian Charter of Rights and Freedoms*, the controversial section 33.[7] It provided that the federal Parliament or a provincial legislature could immunize a statute from being challenged under certain *Charter* provisions, including section 15, among others, if the enacting legislature included a "notwithstanding clause" stating

---

5 Telegram from Robert F Mercer, Managing Director, the Canadian National Institute for the Blind, to Pierre Elliot Trudeau, Prime Minister of Canada (8 October 1981). Note that the use of all caps was a common style for telegrams and should not be construed as shouting.

6 Sheppard & Valpy, *supra* note 2 at 144, 297–299, 346.

7 *Canadian Charter of Rights and Freedoms*, Part 1 of the *Constitution Act, 1982*, being Schedule B to the *Canada Act 1982* (UK), 1982, c 11 [*Charter*].

that the legislation operates notwithstanding the *Charter*.[8] If a provincial legislature or Canada's Parliament included a notwithstanding clause in a piece of legislation, that exemption from certain attacks under the *Charter* would last for only 5 years before expiring. Extending it would require its re-enactment for another 5 years.[9]

The notwithstanding clause, which is also called a legislative override, could not apply to some rights guaranteed in the *Charter*. It only overrode rights in sections 2 and 7–15, which encompass the fundamental freedoms of conscience, religion, expression, press, peaceful assembly, and association.[10] It also includes the right not to be deprived of life, liberty, or security of the person except in accordance with the principles of fundamental justice, the right not to be arbitrarily detained or subjected to unreasonable search and seizure, and a selection of other rights for people charged with offences. Of direct concern here, it also let Parliament, or a provincial legislature, override equality rights that are guaranteed by section 15 of the *Charter*. This federal-provincial political compromise tried to bridge the divide between the federal government and the hold-out provinces. The federal government wanted courts to have the final say on whether a government had violated the *Charter*. The hold-out provinces wanted their legislatures to have the final say, even if a court ruled against them.[11]

## B. Joining the Growing Opposition to the Notwithstanding Clause

When the political deal was made public, it triggered opposition, particularly from women's organizations and advocates for Canada's Indigenous peoples. They argued that Parliament or a provincial legislature should not be able to violate their constitutional rights and then insulate this from a challenge in court by using a section 33 notwithstanding clause.[12] As these events were unfolding, I was living in Cambridge, Massachusetts, up to my ears in graduate law studies at the Harvard Law School. I had no way to closely track the daily news in Canada. What little information I sporadically received

8 Sheppard & Valpy, *supra* note 2.

9 See *Charter*, *supra* note 7, s 33.

10 *Ibid*, s 2.

11 Sheppard & Valpy, *supra* note 2 at 38–64, 65–77, 109, 144, 297–299, 345–346.

12 Penney Kome, *The Taking of Twenty-Eight: Women Challenge the Constitution* (Toronto: Women's Educational Press, 1983) at 87–95.

was by word of mouth. I heard nothing about anyone organizing to stop the new section 33 notwithstanding clause from overriding the equality rights guaranteed by section 15. If others within the disability community were actively concerned about, or taking action on, the new notwithstanding clause, I did not know about it. I was very unlikely to hear anything about it because I was so buried in my studies.

There was one very memorable exception. One day that fall, I received a blistering phone call from the highly authoritative source of much of the early wise advice I received over the years on how to stand up for myself — my beloved mother. "All I hear about in the news are objections from the women and Native groups about this constitutional thing," she remonstrated. "Where are people with disabilities? Why the heck aren't they fighting about this? This is ridiculous." I pleaded with her that I really had no time to deal with this because my exams were quickly coming up. How futile of me! Spurred on by maternally induced guilt of the first order, I took action. I have no idea how I managed it, but I lined up another interview with CBC's national morning program *This Country in the Morning*, on which I had appeared the previous January to discuss our winning the disability amendment.[13]

I spoke by phone to the program's new host, the legendary Peter Gzowski. I was somewhere in New Jersey, enjoying the American Thanksgiving weekend before the fall term exams crunch. Pumped up with studies in US constitutional law, my tighter and less wordy delivery was a real improvement on my wordier and less punchy presentation a year earlier to the Joint Committee. I wish I could have travelled back in time to use that new, clearer delivery back when I was speaking to the Joint Committee. A comparison of the transcript of my presentation to the Joint Committee on 12 December 1980, provided in Appendix 1, with the transcript of my CBC radio interview on 26 November 1981, provided in Appendix 6, shows what I mean!

At the start of the CBC interview, I was asked what the *Charter* will give people with disabilities. My answer, I regret, was a real overstatement. I said that section 15 was going to give us a lot, but, in light of the recent developments (that is, the addition of section 33's notwithstanding clause), the *Charter* would give people with disabilities "virtually nothing." I once

---

13 Interview, 26 November 1981, online: *YouTube* <www.youtube.com/watch?v=rcn6mZcJeLc>.

again felt it necessary to go out of my way to make it clear right at the top of the interview that we were not seeking special rights. I was still driven by fear of irrational backlash. I explained how people with disabilities were left out of the original draft of section 15 and how we and other disability groups had to fight very hard to get the disability amendment passed. I said we won inclusion in the *Charter* as an "equal rights minority" (a new turn of phrase for me, which I have long since dropped from my repertoire). I objected to the fact that the new legislative override would potentially apply to the equality rights guaranteed in section 15. I summed this up as a "colossal setback": "What that basically means is rather disconcerting. It means that Section 15 guarantees our inalienable right to equality, except when the Government takes it away. It makes the Charter into an umbrella that protects us from rain, but which is taken away once the rain starts falling."

I cannot claim credit for that clever turn of phrase. I confess that I shamelessly stole this sizzling turn of phrase from Abba Eban, Israel's dazzlingly articulate ambassador to the United Nations [UN] in 1967 (when I was 10 years old). He was defending Israel's actions during the Six Day War against its neighbours. Since 1957, the UN had an emergency force in the Gaza Strip to protect a free flow of shipping in the Gulf of Aqaba. In May 1967, the UN pulled that peace force out at the request of Egyptian President Gamal Abdel Nasser. Egypt massed its army on the border with Israel that was no longer occupied by the UN peacekeeping force. Military buildups were thereby triggered by Israel, Egypt, Jordan, and Syria on their respective borders, leading to a breakout of war within days. When I gave that 1981 CBC radio interview, I vividly remembered Eban in 1967, telling the UN that its peacekeeping force between Egypt and Israel, having been withdrawn on the Egyptian president's unilateral request, was like an umbrella that is taken away when the rain starts to fall.

In my CBC interview, I tried to shoot down the arguments that had been made in support of the notwithstanding clause. Canadians had been told that this notwithstanding clause was necessary to protect provincial rights. Yet I argued that the notwithstanding clause could also be invoked by the federal Parliament, not just the provinces. We were told not to worry about the notwithstanding clause. It would be "political suicide" for them to use it. In response, I argued that the provinces would not have refused to agree to the adoption of the *Charter* unless the notwithstanding clause was added to it if, indeed, they had no desire to use it. I once again explained why we needed the disability amendment. I listed examples of legislation that violated disability equality. I said that our *Criminal Code* makes it an offence to have sex with a feeble-minded person.[14] Ontario's marriage legislation does not allow a person to get a marriage license who is mentally defective. I pointed to the federal and provincial minimum wage legislation that permits employers under some circumstances to pay employees with disabilities less than minimum wage.

I voiced my worry about the possibility of governments feeling free to invoke the notwithstanding clause without political consequences. Events since then unfortunately proved that I was correct about that. I told CBC radio:

> And when we're told that it would be political suicide to add an override to a statute like that, that conjures up the following hypothetical. Could you imagine one of the provincial premiers being turfed out of office during an election campaign because they enacted a law that discriminated against the disabled? Can you see people making their votes in an election determined based on how a particular innocuous statute affecting disabled rights was phrased?[15]

I argued that, initially, the disability amendment would serve as a monument during the International Year of Disabled Persons. However, for the government to now make it subject to this legislative override during that same year was "farcical."

Gzowski described how there had been major demonstrations that were quite effective by Indigenous groups and the women's movement. He asked me if we would see the same from the disability community. I had no idea as I sat there in New Jersey speaking to a national Canadian radio audience. I did my best to answer, invigorated by my US constitutional studies:

> The purpose of an equal protection section is to protect the right of a minority who cannot get the ear of the public, and therefore can't get a fair shake out of the political process. We're going to try our best. I've heard some vague rumours about London England (meaning going to England to lobby the UK Parliament, as some other sectors had threatened to do) if Ottawa doesn't listen. I don't know about that myself.[16]

---

14 *Criminal Code*, RSC 1985, c C-46.

15 Interview, 26 November 1981, online: *YouTube* <www.youtube.com/watch?v=rcn6mZcJeLc>.

16 Interview, 26 November 1981, online: *YouTube* <www.youtube.com/watch?v=rcn6mZcJeLc>.

I urged CBC's listeners to contact their member of parliament to oppose the legislative override being permitted to apply to the *Charter*'s equal rights guarantee.

I got to slip one final point into this interview that was not in response to any particular question. I explained that one of the most important equal rights decisions under the US *Bill of Rights* was the 1954 ruling that desegregated the racially segregated schools.[17] I argued that if the United States had had a legislative override, it is extremely unlikely that schools would have been desegregated. Gzowski said that this was a good point. I concluded: "So if the Charter is going to mean anything when it's protecting the minorities who can't get the ear of the majority, can't get the ear of the political process, of the political system, then it's got to protect rights from precisely actions like a legislative override."[18]

## C. Trying to Contact Well-Placed Liberal Members of Parliament

In addition to doing that interview, I made two other phone calls from my dorm room at Harvard in an effort to stop the legislative override from applying to Section 15. I somehow got the nerve up to call the office of Justice Minister Jean Chrétien, whom I had never met. Unsurprisingly, I did not get put through to him personally. I was connected with one of his political staffers. I clearly remember two things about this call. First, the political staffer listened patiently as I explained to her why the legislative override should not apply to equality rights, such as the rights of people with disabilities. Second, I recall how elated I was when she thanked me for my call and told me that she was going to immediately go right down the hall to tell the minister of justice what I had had to say. I was bouncing off my dorm room walls with excitement: Chrétien himself is going to hear exactly what my concerns are, right from one of his staffers. That is amazing. Over the years since then, I have had innumerable conversations with ministerial political staffers. I know only too well that a standard practice is to say such things to callers to make them feel important and to get them

---

17 *Brown v Board of Education of Topeka*, 347 US 483 (1954); *Bill of Rights*, 1791, *General Records of the United States Government*, RG 11, National Archives.

18 Interview, 26 November 1981, online: *YouTube* <www.youtube.com/watch?v=rcn6mZcJeLc>.

to believe that they were being heard. Older and wiser, I do not fall for such nonsense. Back then, I fell for it hook, line, and sinker. How embarrassing!

I also tried to call Liberal Member of Parliament David Smith. I somehow actually reached him. He remembered me from my appearance before the Special Parliamentary Committee on the Disabled and Handicapped (Smith Committee) over a year earlier. All I remember from this phone call was his bemoaning the provincial pushback against the *Charter*, including from Saskatchewan's left-leaning NDP Premier Alan Blakeney. On 20 November 1981, the CNIB sent a telegram to Smith from its chief executive officer Robert Mercer and me. In it, we objected to the new notwithstanding clause applying to equality rights guaranteed by section 15 of the *Charter*. I have no recollection of this telegram and have not been able to find it. However, I figure I must have been the impetus behind it and likely was its author. I only know about it because, while preparing this retrospective, I unearthed from my garage Smith's letter to Mercer and me from 18 January 1982, which he wrote in response to that telegram. He wrote as the chair of the House of Commons Special Committee on the Disabled and Handicapped, which by then, may or may not have still been in operation. Here is what he said to us:

> Thank you for your telegram of November 20, 1981 expressing your concern about the "notwithstanding clause" in the Charter of Rights and Freedoms.
>
> As you may recall our Special Committee has been actively working for the inclusion of protection of the human rights of disabled persons. In October 1980 our first report stressed the importance of including full and equal protection for disabled persons in any proposed *Charter of Rights*. When the Special Joint Committee of the Senate and the House of Commons was studying the constitutional resolution, members of the Special Committee on the Disabled and the Handicapped and the House of Commons lobbied both publicly, and in caucus, for the inclusion of protection for disabled persons. Finally, in January 1981, protection from discrimination on the basis of physical or mental disability was included in the constitutional resolution.
>
> With respect to your concern about the "notwithstanding clause", I must note that this agreement was reached in consultation with the provinces, and unfortunately, the provinces were not prepared to accept the constitutional resolution unless this clause was included. In any negotiations each side must compromise, otherwise the entire effort may be lost. I should point out however, that it will be particularly difficult for a province to use the "notwithstanding clause".

> The political consequences and the ill-will that would result from actually invoking this clause will discourage a province from considering such an action.
>
> Once again, thank you for bringing this matter to my attention.[19]

## D. The Campaign by Women's Rights Organizations in Response to the Notwithstanding Clause in Section 33 of the *Charter*

Throughout the fall of 1980 and the winter of 1981, women's organizations came together to mount an amazing lobbying blitz to strengthen the *Charter*'s guarantees for women. These led Justice Minister Chrétien to agree to beef up section 15 on 12 January 1981 in order to strengthen the wording of its guarantee of equality. That would benefit all of the equality-seeking groups that this provision protects. In Chapter XI, I described how some other proposals by some women's rights organizations worked against our goal of securing full equality rights for people with disabilities in the *Charter*. They asked the Joint Committee to amend section 15 in a way that would create a harmful hierarchical approach to equality. Under it, some equality-seeking groups, such as women, would get stronger constitutional protection from discrimination. Other equality-seeking groups, such as people with disabilities, would get weaker constitutional protection from discrimination. Fortunately, in January 1981, the Joint Committee rejected those proposed amendments to the wording of section 15.

When the Joint Committee finished its clause-by-clause review of the *Charter*, those women's organizations kept up the pressure.[20] They wanted the *Charter* to be expanded to include a new section that provided a categorical guarantee of equality for women. On 23 April 1981, they succeeded in convincing the Trudeau government to amend the *Charter* in the House of Commons by adding a new section 28. As originally worded, it provided: "28. Notwithstanding anything in this Charter, the rights and freedoms referred to in it are guaranteed equally to male and female persons."[21] This was an attempt to secure the enactment of a transcendent

---

19 Letter from David Smith, Member of Parliament, Chairman of the Special Committee on the Disabled and the Handicapped, to Robert F Mercer and David Lepofsky, Canadian National Institute for the Blind (18 January 1982).

20 Kome, *supra* note 12 at 57–71.

21 Canada, Parliament, *House of Commons Debates*, 32nd Parl, 1st Sess, Vol IX (23 April 1981) at 9470.

guarantee of sex equality in the *Charter*. It was inspired by the American women's rights movement's campaign around that time to secure the enactment of an "Equal Rights Amendment" [ERA] to the US Constitution. The ERA was sought to create a stronger constitutional right to sex equality than had been judicially recognized in the equal protection clause of the US Constitution's 14th Amendment.[22]

At that point, I was not following these developments regarding section 28 very closely, if at all. It did not then occur to me that this new provision would create a two-tier guarantee of equality in the *Charter*, in which other equality-seeking groups would be relegated to the lower tier. I did nothing at the time in response to it. Fast-forward to November 1981, when the Trudeau government cut its deal with nine provinces to add section 33 and the "notwithstanding clause" to the *Charter*. Those activists for women's rights who had rejoiced over the addition of section 28 to the *Charter* half a year earlier quite understandably felt like the rug had subsequently been unceremoniously yanked out from under them. They worried that the new section 33 could override their win in section 28.[23] Don't try to get your head around how to interpret two provisions — section 33 and section 28 — that each say they operate "notwithstanding" certain other parts of the *Charter*!

In November 1981, the women's rights movement rapidly unleashed another incredible nation-wide blitz. They objected to the new section 33 if it applied to equality for women. They wanted to be sure that section 28 was exempted from section 33.[24] Their incredibly impressive advocacy efforts across Canada under breathtakingly tight time pressures led the federal government and the provinces to agree to a last-minute amendment to section 28, so that it would ultimately read: "28. Notwithstanding anything in this *Charter*, the rights and freedoms referred to in it are guaranteed equally to male and female persons."[25] Does the wording of section 28 achieve the goal that those women's rights organizations sought — of ensuring that the *Charter*'s guarantee of sex equality cannot be legislatively overridden by section 33's notwithstanding clause? Section 28's wording, read in the context of the entire *Charter*, is something of a mess. In this

---

22 US Constitution, 14th Amendment, § 2.

23 Kome, *supra* note 12 at 82–83.

24 *Ibid* at 87–95.

25 Sheppard & Valpy, *supra* note 2 at 329.

retrospective, I will not debate this brainteaser of constitutional interpretation. I shall proceed on the assumption that it does do what those tenacious women's organizations sought.

In November 1981, I was not aware of any other concerted efforts from within the disability community to block the notwithstanding clause from applying to the equality rights guaranteed by section 15 of the *Charter*. However, in *The National Deal*, Robert Sheppard and Michael Valpy wrote:

> Under these kinds of pressures, the provincial governments folded like omelettes. A compromise wording from Lougheed on the aboriginal rights clause — which guaranteed to protect *existing* rights — was agreed to by the provincial and federal governments. The sexual equality clause was restored. The provinces then urged Trudeau to hurry up and get the resolution through Parliament before other protest forces could gather strength (a coalition of women's groups and handicapped organizations, supported by the formidable former senator, Eugene Forsey, already was petitioning MPs to remove the *non obstante* clause.[26]

Sheppard and Valpy characterized the notwithstanding clause as a breach of faith with people with disabilities and others who had successfully fought at the Joint Committee to strengthen the *Charter*. They wrote the following, which incorrectly makes it sound like disability equality was somehow eliminated from the *Charter* at the last minute:

> In the spring of 1981, the charter's guarantees went far beyond anything envisioned by Diefenbaker in the 1950s or Trudeau at Victoria (the prime minister referred glowingly to the new bill as a model for the rest of the world) but it was subsequently gelded in a shabby breach of faith with those groups that had been given an unexpected opening to fight for its improvement. The native peoples, women and the handicapped were a significant contributory stream in the development of the constitutional proposals but they were muscled out in the end.[27]

In the end, of course, the *Charter* was enacted. It went into effect on 17 April 1982. Its equality provision — section 15 — went into force on 17 April 1985, 3 years after Queen Elizabeth signed the patriation package into law on Parliament Hill in Ottawa. The *Charter* includes equality rights for people with disabilities in section 15. That was a monumental step forward for people with disabilities in Canada. However, the *Charter* also includes section 28. If it exempts sex equality claims but no other equality claims

---

26 *Ibid* at 307.

27 *Ibid* at 143.

from the *Charter*'s notorious notwithstanding clause, then it creates a hierarchical treatment of equality-seeking groups. To repeat a concern that I have raised at different points in this saga, it would make Canada a place where some people are more equal than others.

Although an exploration of this is beyond the scope of this retrospective, I feel that I should mention another equality rights concern with section 28. Section 28's reference to "male and female persons" threatens to exclude from the gender equality at which it is aimed, any non-binary persons who do not self-identify as male or female. If so, that illustrates another way that section 28 produces a hierarchical approach to equality rights. Although I believe that this impact was entirely unintentional, it does not eliminate or reduce its impact. How do I now react to those women's rights advocates who pressed for an amendment to section 15 that would create a hierarchy among equality-seeking groups and who succeeded in winning the enactment of section 28, which gives a preferred status to sex equality over all other equality-seeking groups? My reactions are mixed.

On the one hand, I admire their magnificent efforts at community organizing and advocacy. There is much for social justice advocates to learn from their campaign. Having myself spent many hours since then on community organizing and advocacy over the years within the disability community, I can only dream of the kind of campaign that they pulled off, especially considering how limited the advocacy tools were in 1980, as Chapter IV explains. There has been amply justified pride within Canada's women's movement about the gains for which they fought during the patriation debate. We have those women's rights advocates to thank for playing a central role in getting the general wording of section 15 strengthened, so that it is as clear as could be that it protects egalitarian rights. They took on and effectively stared down an overwhelmingly male-dominated cadre of political leaders and senior public servants. Back then and today, I have looked on with envy and admiration on their dedication, tenacity, inventiveness, and moxie. On the other hand, I respectfully disagree with their proposed wording changes to section 15, described in Chapter XI, which would have given more protection to some equality-seeking groups like women and less protection to others like people with disabilities. I similarly am troubled by section 28's hierarchy among equality-seeking groups when it comes to vulnerability to the legislative override in section 33 of the *Charter*.

Is it fair for me to characterize some of their proposals to be hierarchical ones? After all, the entire focus of the women's equality movement during the patriation debate was equality, was it not? Those women's rights advocates no doubt correctly saw themselves as the victims of a male-dominated hierarchy, one that they sought to replace with a level playing field. My characterization of some of their positions appears discordant with their core message. I stand by my characterization of the proposed amendments to the *Charter* with which I disagreed. That those women's advocates were commendably trying to tear down a gender-based hierarchy (that very much needed to be eliminated) does not alter the fact that their proposals with which I disagree would end up creating other kinds of objectionable hierarchies.

Some publications written by key players in that movement document that their goal and core focus was sex equality for women in order to improve the disadvantaged status of women in Canada. That was a laudable goal, of course, with which I fully agree.[28] In an informative retrospective on the women's rights movement's efforts during the patriation debate, Chaviva Hosek made it clear that, in the fall of 1981, they wanted to get the section 33's "notwithstanding clause" removed from section 15's equality rights provision as well as for the specific sex equality guarantee in section 28. I agree whole-heartedly with their desire to exempt section 15 in its entirety from the legislative override in section 33 of the *Charter*. However, Hosek explains that they made the tactical decision instead to focus their efforts on getting section 28 exempted from the legislative override in section 33. I regret that I do not understand their reasoning for that tactical decision. She wrote:

> The ad-hoc committee and women's groups wished to remove the override from both the general equality provisions and section 28. However, since section 28 was the only one dealing exclusively with sex, the strongest push was made there. In effect, the federal government's statement on November 9 that the override did apply to section 28 narrowed the protest of women's

---

28 Kerri A Froc "Shouting into the Constitutional Void: Section 28 and Bill 21" (2019) 28:4 Constitutional Forum constitutionnel 19; Beverley Baines "Constitutionalizing Women's Equality Rights: There Is Always Room for Improvement" (2016) 37:2 Atlantis 112; Marilou McPhedran "The Fight for the Charter" (2007) 26:2 Canadian Woman Studies 80; Marilou McPhedran "Creating Trialogue: Woman's Constitutional Activism in Canada" (2006) 25:3–4 Canadian Woman Studies 6; Sandra Burt "The Charter of Rights and the Ad Hoc Lobby: The Limits of Success" (1988) 14:1 Atlantis 75.

> groups. If section 28 had been declared at the outset to be outside the scope of the override, women's groups would have focussed on section 15(1) and might have succeeded, together with other interest groups, in removing the override from equality rights as a whole.[29]

It might be argued in response to my assessment that their proposals were not meant to create any new hierarchies in equality rights protection. Yet few people who create disability barriers ever consciously intend to make things harder for people with disabilities. Whatever was their motive or intent, the results are what matters and with what we must live. Four decades later, the organized women's rights movement and the disability rights movement have both come a long way. In both, there is an increased acknowledgement about the importance of intersectionality. Yet, as Chapter XI notes, subsequent efforts such as some employment equity programs, and, more recently, some equity, diversity and inclusion [EDI] efforts, have replicated a harmful hierarchical approach to equality that can hurt people with disabilities. We need to proactively prevent this from happening again without in any way undermining or weakening employment equity or EDI efforts. There is ample room for strategies, programs, and initiatives that focus on progress for one disadvantaged equality-seeking group, such as women, racialized persons, or people with disabilities. However, it is important to make sure that this does not have the collateral harm of disadvantaging other equality-seeking groups.

I myself have advocated for years for a disability-specific strategy — namely, the enactment and effective implementation of disability accessibility legislation. In so doing, I want such legislation to fully benefit all people with disabilities, whatever their gender, racialized status, or other equality-seeking identity. Just as I here critique the position espoused by the 1980 leadership of some of Canada's women's rights organizations, I fully expect and invite others to hold up to critical scrutiny the positions for which I advocate. It goes with the equality advocacy territory! In this retrospective, I have not hesitated to take a critical look at things I did in support of the disability amendment so that others can learn from my actions, including my mistakes.

---

29 Chaviva Hosek, "Women and the Constitutional Process" in Keith Banting & Richard Simeon, eds, *And No One Cheered* (Toronto: Methuen, 1983) 280 at 293.

# XVII. REFLECTING ON THE ROLE OF THE MEDIA IN OUR FIGHT FOR THE DISABILITY AMENDMENT

Let me reflect on the role that the conventional media played, or failed to play, in the campaign for the disability amendment, a theme that pops up several times in this retrospective. Four decades later, it is impossible to assemble every media report that covered the fight for the disability amendment. I have only the four reports in which I was directly involved. In 1980, the conventional media — radio, television and newspapers — had a monopoly on conduits for an individual, community organization or organized equality-seeking community to get a message to the public. We had no Internet, World Wide Web, social media, YouTube, or podcasts. I have used all of those alternative media since then, with some success. It is staggering to ponder the overwhelming power that conventional news organizations enjoyed over public discourse on the constitutional patriation issue.

As discussed earlier, I recall there being scant coverage of the question of whether disability should be added to section 15 of the *Canadian Charter of Rights and Freedoms*.[1] The vast majority of the public would not have known that this was an issue or that the Trudeau Liberals had left disability rights out of section 15, that the government's arguments to justify this were transparently bogus, that people with disabilities and disability organizations were pressing for the disability amendment, or that the federal opposition parties were eventually on our side. All of these points were obviously newsworthy. They were immediate, important, and interesting. Disability affects millions of people in Canada. It related to the top political subject of the day — the patriation debate. It even had conflict between parties to give it some sizzle.

How different it would have been had the media given our issue more coverage and perhaps a little less attention to the personality battles between opposing political leaders. Imagine if a reporter had pointedly asked the prime minister or justice minister why the government is opposing the

1 *Canadian Charter of Rights and Freedoms*, Part 1 of the *Constitution Act, 1982*, being Schedule B to the *Canada Act 1982* (UK), 1982, c 11.

disability amendment on the grounds that "disability" is hard to define, when the same could easily be said about *Charter* terms like "freedom of religion," "the principles of fundamental justice," and "freedom of belief"? Imagine if the *Toronto Star*, *Globe and Mail*, *Montreal Gazette*, or *Winnipeg Free Press* had editorialized against the government's refusing to entrench equality for people with disabilities in the *Charter* in the very year that the United Nations declared the International Year of Disabled Person. We would have been in a much stronger position. It might potentially have deterred some public servants from trying to get the federal government not to support the disability amendment. It might have even been possible to get the last-minute section 28 expanded to insulate all equality claims from the notwithstanding clause rather than protecting only the right to gender equality.

Mainstream media organizations speak of their public role, holding public officials accountable, shining the spotlight on important issues, and fulfilling what they call the "public's right to know." They proudly claim credit when their coverage triggers improvements in public policy. Judged against their own rhetoric, the media's performance in 1980 to 1982 on the issue of the disability amendment was terribly poor. However, it was better than nothing. We eked out a bit of coverage. However, it was far less coverage than the issue deserved. News organizations could hardly claim that they did not have any more airtime or newspaper space available for this issue. The media devoted ample time and space to the patriation issue. For significant stretches, there was little or nothing new on which to report, insofar as the overall constitutional reform initiative was concerned.

Here is one illustration. The day when the Special Joint Committee of the Senate and the House of Commons on the Constitution of Canada (Joint Committee) united to unanimously pass the disability amendment was truly historic for Canada. Amidst all the other issues over which politicians were wrangling, here was an issue that united them. Here was a demand for a change to the *Charter* that emanated from the public, not from the powerful, the pundit class, or the politicians. Here was the only new constitutional right to be added to the *Charter* during the entire 18-month saga of the patriation battle. Yet, on that momentous day — 28 January 1981 — the disability amendment got no coverage on one prime source of news, CBC's nightly national newscast. It deserved at least a single sentence, if not more. Neither was it covered in the CBC television news the next day. This is so even though CBC radio commendably interviewed me on

*This Country in the Morning* on 29 January 1981. On that same day, a CBC television reporter shot an interview with me, standing in front of the CNIB Toronto headquarters, commenting on the disability amendment that we had collectively won. Neither the story nor any part of that interview made it onto the airwaves.

You would be right to think that this is inexcusable. As a result, I was happily surprised when I found out in 1982 that there was any reference to the disability amendment in the major publication about the patriation debate, *The National Deal*, by Robert Sheppard and Michael Valpy.[2] Do I sound a wee bit frustrated? I have lived this same story over and over, in a manner rivalling the Groundhog Day movie. Over my four decades of volunteer disability rights advocacy, most decisive transformative moments in the fight for equality, accessibility, and inclusion for people with disabilities have garnered no media attention at all, despite our valiant efforts. For example, on 29 October 1998, the Ontario legislature unanimously passed a landmark resolution calling for the enactment of a strong Ontario disability accessibility law that embodied 11 key principles that disability advocates had formulated.[3] Right afterwards, the Ontario opposition leader at the time and future Ontario premier Dalton McGuinty sat beside me in the Ontario legislature's Media Studio. He promised in public for the first time that, if the Conservative Ontario government did not fulfill that resolution, he would. That was a monumental turning point in our decade-long campaign for the enactment of the *AODA*.[4] Media coverage? Nada.

As another example, when I appeared before the House of Commons in October 2018 and the Senate in April 2019 to press for amendments to the weak proposed *Accessible Canada Act*, we had the advantage of email, the Internet, and social media to alert the media.[5] This led to not a word of media coverage. When we collectively got the Senate to amend that bill to strengthen it over the objections of the Liberal government and then got the Liberals in the House of Commons to ratify those improvements —

2 Robert Sheppard & Michael Valpy, *The National Deal: The Fight for a Canadian Constitution* (Toronto: Fleet Books, 1982).

3 Legislative Assembly of Ontario, *Hansard Transcripts*, 36th Parl, 2nd Sess (29 October 1998), online: <www.ola.org/en/legislative-business/house-documents/parliament-36/session-2/1998-10-29/hansard#P7_177> (see the eleven principles discussed at 10:04 a.m).

4 *Accessibility for Ontarians with Disabilities Act*, SO 2005, c 11, s 41 [*AODA*].

5 *Accessible Canada Act*, SC 2019, c 10.

another swim up Niagara Falls to be sure — the media said not a syllable. In fact, the audience of CBC, Canada's national public broadcaster, would not even know that Parliament ever passed the *Accessible Canada Act* after years of disability community advocacy.

I have learned through all of this to keep up our efforts whether or not the media covers our issues. I have also learned the importance of social media as an effective alternative to conventional media. Despite this frustration, a dramatic difference between now and four decades ago is that more reporters are now alive to disability issues than ever was the case, even compared to a few years ago. Some reporters even come to me and the Accessibility for Ontarians with Disabilities Alliance, which I chair, with a disability story, seeking our comment, when we have not initiated that story. On the other hand, too many reporters, including too many senior pundits, still show little or no interest in covering many of our issues and stories.

I am certainly not alone in my critique of the media's failure to give more coverage to disability issues. Under the *AODA*, the Ontario government must appoint an independent review of that legislation every few years on a timetable spelled out in the *AODA*.[6] The interim report of the fourth such independent review was released on 1 March 2023, just as I was putting the finishing touches on this retrospective. The review, conducted by Rich Donovan, found that Ontario was lagging miserably behind in becoming accessible to people with disabilities. Among the causes for this was poor government leadership, with the media failing to hold the government to account. The interim report includes:

> A key reason for the lack of leadership on accessibility is there has been little perceived incentive for potential leaders to prioritize it. Lacking "breaking news" stories, accessibility rarely enters the media cycle in a sustained way. This has helped keep accessibility off the social or political agenda in Ontario.
>
> The absence of disability in the news cycle reflects a failure of Ontario and Canada's major media outlets. The reality is that People with Disabilities regularly face discrimination not just in attitudes, but in the physical and digital environments in which businesses and government operate. People with Disabilities are over one fifth of the population and reflect a larger

---

6 *AODA*, *supra* note 4.

> population than many other equity-deserving groups whose (rightful) challenges are far more prominent in news cycles.[7]

Should I be at all surprised that despite our news release, publicizing that report, the media has done extremely little to cover the Donovan report.

---

7 Rich Donovan, *Independent Fourth Review of the Accessibility for Ontarians with Disabilities Act, 2005 (AODA)*, Interim Report (March 2023) at 21–22.

# XVIII. THE AFTERMATH: HAS THE DISABILITY AMENDMENT LIVED UP TO ITS POTENTIAL?

## A. The Bottom Line

Has the *Canadian Charter of Rights and Freedoms*' guarantee of disability equality lived up to my hopes for it?[1] My overall conclusion is that it has unquestionably helped. Things would clearly be worse had Parliament never passed the disability amendment. However, it still has a long way to go to fully realize its full potential. This retrospective does not offer a comprehensive assessment of the record of Canada's courts under the disability amendment since section 15 went into effect on 17 April 1985. Legal scholars and disability rights advocates can and should size up how much of a difference the disability amendment has made. I here offer a personal perspective.

## B. My Original Aspirations for the Disability Amendment's Impact

In Chapter XIV, I described my initial hopes for the disability amendment, which I shared with a national radio audience on the morning after the Special Joint Committee of the Senate and the House of Commons on the Constitution of Canada (Joint Committee) amended section 15 to include disability equality. A full transcript of my interview on 29 January 1981 on CBC radio's *This Country in the Morning* can be found in Appendix 5.

Let me expand on those comments. First, I hoped that the disability amendment to the *Charter* would lead courts to tear down major barriers in the public sector, including disability barriers, that have been impeding people with disabilities from fully participating in Canadian life on a footing of equality. Because disability equality was the only right added to the *Charter* during the patriation debate, I hoped that courts and legal academics would get a loud and clear message that this important new constitutional right needs to be liberally construed and effectively implemented. Second,

1 *Canadian Charter of Rights and Freedoms*, Part 1 of the *Constitution Act, 1982*, being Schedule B to the *Canada Act 1982* (UK), 1982, c 11.

I hoped that the disability amendment would significantly raise the profile and attention of disability issues in Canada beyond the narrow microcosm of courtroom constitutional combat. It could propel our issues onto the broader agenda of governments, the media, and the public, making it easier for us to raise these issues.

I expanded on this second hope months after the constitutional dust had settled and 1 year after that early morning CBC radio interview. On 4 January 1982, I gathered my post-mortem thoughts on the successful fight to get disability equality added to the *Charter* and to the Ontario *Human Rights Code* in a 20-page memo to the CNIB (a memo that gathered dust in my garage).[2] I anticipated that these new constitutional and human rights protections could lead the public to have a more positive attitude towards, and perception of, people with disabilities. I cautioned that "the only long range, effective way for ensuring that visually handicapped persons will form an active integrated part of Canadian society, is by reshaping Canada's educational system."[3] I wrote:

> The final, and most important use for the Charter concerns not government, but the people of Canada. In the long run, the most significant impact a Charter of Rights can have, as illustrated by the American experience, is not by influencing the decision of judges and politicians directly but by educating the public as to the kinds of things they should tolerate and expect from their government and from each other. If the Charter is taught in schools and posted in public buildings, then the message that blind and other disabled persons are entitled to equal rights will be relayed across Canada. If Canadians are educated to expect that disabled persons have a right of equality, then actual instances of discrimination against handicapped persons will be less tolerated than at present. The message of Section 15 of the Charter will not be taught in schools and posted in public places, in a manner most likely to effect the consciousness of Canadians, unless CNIB takes action to ensure that this happens.[4]

For me, this was no remote abstract idea. In my own life, that pejorative perception of us had shockingly come home to roost back in 1974 when that stranger who saw me on the Toronto subway handed me a dollar and told me to buy myself a coffee.

---

2 *Human Rights Code*, RSO 1990, c H-19.

3 M David Lepofsky, *A Final Report on CNIB Lobbying Work in the Human Rights Area, with a view to Future Advocacy Endeavors* (4 January 1982) at 2 [Lepofsky, *Final Report*].

4 *Ibid* at 4–5.

When I wrote those words, I had no clue how this strategy for all people with disabilities and not just people with vision loss would pervade my efforts in the ensuing years. For example, in the 2007 Ontario election, as part of my work with the AODA Alliance, I led our blitz to get Ontario's Premier Dalton McGuinty to pledge to embed a disability accessibility/inclusion component in our publicly funded schools' curriculum. Sadly, that promise was never kept.[5] In my 4 January 1982 memo, I forecasted that it would take some time for Canada's courts to start to effectively implement the *Charter*. I urged the CNIB to make good use of the *Charter* in the meantime, recommending: "[The] CNIB should use the equal rights provision of the Charter of Rights as a tool in its advocacy for new laws and social programs vis à vis all levels of government."[6] I explained: "When discussing new programs and legislative proposals with MPs and MLAs, CNIB can hold out Section 15 as a command to the lawmakers of Canada to ensure that disabled people achieve social and economic equality in Canadian society."[7]

My third hope for the disability amendment to the *Charter* was that it would positively improve how people with disabilities saw themselves. Historically, Canadians with disabilities too often were made to feel powerless, isolated, and marginalized. The most important services that they needed to get by were for the most part delivered by charitable community organizations. This signalled to the public and to people with disabilities themselves that we were principally the objects of charity, not the bearers of a fundamental right to equality. I hoped that, with the disability amendment enshrined in Canada's Constitution, a new generation of people with disabilities would grow up with a very different self-image — one in which they saw the opportunity to fully participate in society as a birthright to be insisted upon, not a charitable privilege to be graciously bestowed upon them as an act of societal kindness or pity.

One year after I told CBC radio, back on 29 January 1981, how I anticipated that the disability amendment could change how people with disabilities perceived themselves, I concluded that the CNIB had to

---

5 Letter from Premier Dalton McGuinty, Leader of the Ontario Liberal Party, to Doreen Winkler, Acting Chair, Accessibility for Ontarians with Disabilities Act Alliance (14 September 2007), online: *AODA Alliance* <www.aodaalliance.org/whats-new/newsub2011/what-the-liberal-party-promises/>.

6 Lepofsky, *Final Report*, *supra* note 3 at 4.

7 *Ibid.*

take proactive action if we are to extract this benefit from the disability amendment. In my reflective memo to the CNIB on 4 January 1982, I explained that, regarding people with disabilities such as people with vision loss,

> [t]raditional passivity in the face of widespread discriminatory practices in Canadian society should give way to a new reasonable assertiveness. This cannot occur unless disabled persons are informed of their new rights in the context of their adjustment to a new disability, and as part of job-training. The benefits of these new rights in this context can be substantial, since the new status of disabled persons in Ontario helps generate a more positive goal towards which a newly disabled person can strive.[8]

This led me to recommend the following to the CNIB in that memo (which should have also included references to the disability amendment to the *Charter* at this point and not just to the new disability provisions of the Ontario *Human Rights Code*):

> All CNIB staff engaged in direct work with clients, especially employment and vocational counsellors, adjustment to blindness and mobility instructors, and caseworkers, should be thoroughly briefed about the new provisions of the Ontario *Human Rights Code*, with a view to passing this information along to clients as part of professional provision of services. Formal training programs in Ontario, such as the Adjustment to Blindness course, should incorporate a Human Rights counselling component, which could integrate the notion of equality into the rehabilitation and training process.[9]

Beyond those three hopes on which I was then focused — the winning of both the disability amendment to the *Charter* and Ontario's *Human Rights Code* protections against disability discrimination — together led me to urge in my reflective memo that the CNIB reimagine what rehabilitation services mean. The CNIB historically saw its role narrowly as a rehabilitation agency that gives people with vision loss training in the skills they need to live independently. I wrote:

> Until now, CNIB has viewed the rehabilitation process as a measure which starts when the client enters a CNIB office and ends when the adjustment to blindness and employment counselling has been completed. This has resulted in well-trained, well-adjusted visually handicapped individuals being sent into a hostile, unreceptive and unaccommodating world. For CNIB to add advocacy for social and legal reform as a part of its service provision is to recognize

---

8 *Ibid* at 11.

9 *Ibid.*

> that rehabilitation and adjustment to the conditions of visual impairment do not end when the client departs from the place of his/her adjustment training. The visually handicapped person must be trained to function with his disability. The world must be trained to adjust to his disability as well. Without both measures being taken concurrently, either is an exercise in futility.[10]

## C. The Disability Amendment's First Decade in Court

In a law journal article published a quarter of a century ago, I offered an academic commentary on the first decade of disability equality court rulings from 1985 to 1995. I summarized my conclusions as follows:

> Canada's justice system deserves a "C minus" on its implementation of the equality guarantee in disability cases during s. 15's first decade. As this article documents, the Supreme Court of Canada initially fashioned appropriate general principles for all equality cases which offered persons with disabilities great promise. Section 15's first decade had some bright moments for persons with disabilities, the most salient of which is the Ontario Court of Appeal's *Eaton* decision on the right to equal educational opportunities for children with disabilities. *Eaton*'s result and analysis comes far closer to s. 15's core aims than has any other disability equality ruling.
>
> However, apart from *Eaton* and a small number of other cases, most courts, including the Supreme Court of Canada, often failed to implement proper equality principles in disability cases. There were many lost opportunities and much judicial reasoning which is discordant with fundamental equality principles. Among the worst of these is the only case in which the Supreme Court of Canada granted leave and considered a *Charter* disability equality case as such, namely the *Rodriguez* assisted suicide challenge. That case's aberrational, if not "sui generis" legal issue led a majority of justices to disregard or misapply the basic equality analysis which the Court had previously approved.
>
> After s. 15's first decade, many old barriers still impede Canadians with disabilities contrary to s. 15's equality guarantee and related statutory human rights provisions. Canadian courts have ample jurisprudential tools to tackle these barriers and to require their rectification during s. 15's second decade. These tools can be fine-tuned in accordance with this article's recommendations.
>
> For example, many public government buildings and facilities, including many courts, schools, public transit services and government office buildings, remain either totally or partially inaccessible to persons with mobility impairments. Where persons without disabilities have access to comprehensive local bus and subway services in major municipal centres, persons with mobility disabilities

---

10 *Ibid* at 17.

often have access, at most, only to separate, under-funded, over-utilized and inferior disability parallel transit services. Public sidewalks too often have full curbs at corners which impede wheelchair passage. It is better and can even be cheaper to have ramped "curb-cuts" at street corners which allow for wheelchair access while having a sufficient ridge to enable a blind person's white cane to locate the road's edge.

Augmenting these physical impediments are numerous legal barriers. In the face of often inaccessible inter-city bus services, it can be difficult to find a wheelchair-accessible taxi. Once found, it may not be possible for the taxi to drive its patron from one municipal jurisdiction to another. This is due to the myriad of unharmonized local legal restrictions on where a taxi can go.

The educational programs offered in many, if not most, public schools are still designed on the unfair premise that they are to serve students without disabilities. This usually relegates students with disabilities to attending either special education programs or segregated schools or fighting to obtain assistance in the mainstream classroom to overcome barriers resulting from the program's non-disability design.

Very little government information is available in accessible formats for persons with print handicaps, even though the transcription of print information into formats such as Braille has become cheaper and easier than ever before. Efforts at stream-lining public government services to make them more "user-friendly" often involve the introduction of computer equipment which does not accommodate disability access needs.

Federal, provincial and other public sector workplaces are still replete with systemic employment barriers, including public sector collective agreement provisions governing areas such as job security, impeding equal access to public sector employment by persons with disabilities. This has led to reductions in the representation of persons with disabilities among the federal and Ontario workplaces in the late 1980's and early 1990's, at a time when both governments had a stated employment equity commitment to increase the representation of persons with disabilities in their workforces.

Our criminal justice system remains replete with legal and practical barriers barring equal access to justice for persons with disabilities. For example, *Criminal Code* provisions establishing accommodations for children to alleviate the hardship of testifying have not uniformly been extended to persons with similar needs due to developmental disabilities. Open justice principles do not fully accommodate the disproportionate impact that public attendance at court and unrestrained media coverage has on highly vulnerable persons with disabilities. Typical processes for evaluating a witness' evidence are largely premised on the unfair, implicit assumption that the most credible witness is the one who has no disability, be it visual, psychological, auditory or otherwise.

As well, our civil justice system is replete with barriers impeding access to justice for persons with disabilities. As but one example, a litigant may ordinarily choose to represent him — or herself in civil proceedings if he or she wishes — an especially important choice in light of the increasing cost of hiring a lawyer. Yet Rule 15.01(1) of Ontario's *Rules of Civil Procedure* imposes the mandatory requirement that a party to civil litigation who is "under a disability" must be represented by a lawyer. A plaintiff with a mental disability thus cannot bring or defend a civil claim unless he or she has a lawyer. People with disabilities frequently cannot afford lawyers. This rule, combined with government cuts to Legal Aid that reduce access to legal services, result in an unconstitutional disability-based bar to access to civil justice.

Canada's health care system, in which governments are so inextricably involved, is replete with disability barriers and other inequalities. The *Eldridge* case so poignantly illustrates this, in the case of deaf persons who need a sign language interpreter to be able to receive health care. As well, much of the law across Canada governing the civil commitment of persons on grounds of mental disability, limiting their right to consent to or refuse medical treatment, and regulating their control over their financial holdings, has yet to be subjected to meaningful s. 15 scrutiny.

Many new, eminently preventable barriers are now being erected contrary to s. 15. These pose at least as great a threat to the future equality rights of persons with disabilities as do the old barriers which our courts have yet to order removed. For example, a great deal of government effort and money is being pumped into the research, development and construction of the future "information super-highway" intended to link all homes, businesses, governments and schools. Yet little regulatory or other effort is being devoted to ensure that this new public information highway will be accessible to and fully usable by all persons with disabilities. If it is accessible, this will contribute dramatically to the goal of full participation for persons with disabilities in Canadian society. If, as is now reasonably feared, the public information highway, like much of modern computer innovation, is designed without regard to disability needs, there will be a new set of serious though now-preventable barriers impeding persons with disabilities when they seek to participate in work, education, and the enjoyment of public and government services.

Governments are now looking to implement new on-line ways of delivering government services. Schools are also increasingly acquiring new computers and software for educating students. If these new systems include "touchscreen" technology or graphics-driven software, they will freeze out many persons with disabilities unless they are designed to allow for disability access.

Governments are also creating new yet preventable barriers in the important area of public transit services. Every year, new buses are purchased to replace old ones. If governments purchase only accessible buses in the future, the entire fleet would eventually be disability accessible. Yet governments often

> do not take this approach. Every time a municipal government or transit service purchases a new bus that is not accessible to wheelchairs, a new obstacle is created.[11]

I felt compelled to add an epilogue to that extensive law journal article because the Supreme Court of Canada got a very poor start to section 15's second decade. The Court harmfully overturned the most important gain that people with disabilities had won under the disability amendment in its first decade. In *Eaton v Brant County Board of Education* (discussed in Chapter XI), the Ontario Court of Appeal had wisely ruled that students with disabilities have a presumptive constitutional right under section 15 to be educated with students without disabilities.[12] If a school board was to segregate a student with disabilities into a special education classroom over the objection of the child and their family, it could do so only if it justified this action under section 1 of the *Charter* as a reasonable limit on the student's constitutional rights. That seemed obvious to me. The Ontario Court of Appeal did not ban segregated special education classes. It merely decided that a student cannot be forced to attend such a segregated class over their objection unless the school board can constitutionally justify it.

Resisting progress, the Brant County Board of Education appealed that Ontario Court of Appeal ruling to the Supreme Court of Canada. An organization of Ontario's other public school boards and the Ontario government all appeared at the Supreme Court to collectively oppose Emily Eaton's claim. This exemplifies the enormous institutional might that people with disabilities, like other equality-seeking groups, too often have amassed against them when they try to enforce their basic constitutional rights. In a crushing blow to the cause of equality for people with disabilities, the Supreme Court speedily overturned the Ontario Court of Appeal's decision in less than 24 hours after the oral argument.[13] The epilogue to my report card on the first decade of court decisions under the disability amendment identified some parts of the reasoning of the Supreme Court in the *Eaton* decision that could support a positive impact for people with disabilities in

---

11 M David Lepofsky, "A Report Card on the Charter's Guarantee of Equality to Persons with Disabilities after 10 Years: What Progress? What Prospects?" (1997) 7:3 NJCL 263 at 402–406 [Lepofsky, "Report Card"].

12 *Eaton v Brant County Board of Education*, [1995] OJ No 315, 123 DLR (4th) 43 (QL).

13 *Eaton v Brant County Board of Education*, [1997] 1 SCR 241, [1996] SCJ No 98 (QL).

other contexts. However, I roundly blasted a series of severe errors in the court's equality rights reasoning.

In the end, I concluded in substance that disability equality could survive the Supreme Court of Canada's *Eaton* decision in the long run, but Emily Eaton's right to equal education did not. The Supreme Court ruled that it was constitutionally permissible for the Brant County Board of Education to segregate Emily Eaton in a special education class over her family's objection. It is a cruel irony that Emily's family had eventually found a Catholic school board that would place her in a mainstream class. That stunning fact undermines the entire Supreme Court ruling.[14] In a later law journal publication, I highlighted an especially stark moment in the Supreme Court's oral argument in the Eaton case:

> [C]ounsel for the intervener Ontario Public School Boards Association, speaking for all of Ontario's public schools, was defending the public school's segregation of Eaton. In her oral argument she explicitly distinguished between students with disabilities on the one hand and "normal" students on the other. This transparently offensive and grossly outdated term drew no response from the bench. She argued: Our system is set up on the basis of pupil needs, even those of non-exceptional pupils. The materials you have before you indicate that every pupil, whether exceptional or non-exceptional, must be approached as an individual. The Ministry of Education mandates that is what school boards do. They approach each child and its determination is made with respect to the needs of each child. One child may need a little bit more work in reading and writing. In the case of an exceptional child, the needs are much, much different, much greater than the needs of a normal child in a regular class.
>
> Imagine if in the employment context, one referred to "normal employees" on the one hand, and female employees or non-white employees on the other. For counsel representing all Ontario's public schools during oral argument in Canada's highest court on a major disability equality case to refer to people with disabilities as not being "normal" is emblematic of wrenching discriminatory attitudes that have held back people with disabilities for so long.[15]

When I wrote my reflective memo to the CNIB on 4 January 1982, referred to earlier in this chapter, I saw the potential for the disability amendment to help expand inclusive and non-segregated educational opportunities for

---

[14] Lepofsky, "Report Card," *supra* note 11 at 407–431.

[15] David Lepofsky, "*Carter v Canada (Attorney General)*: The Constitutional Attack on Canada's Ban on Assisted Dying: Missing an Obvious Chance to Rule on the Charter's Disability Equality Guarantee" (2016) 76:5 SCLR 94 [citations omitted].

students with vision loss. I predicted that it would be some time before Canadian courts were as effective as the US courts at implementing a constitutional right to equality. I take no joy or pride in having thereby essentially forecasted the Supreme Court of Canada's failure to effectively implement equality rights for students with disabilities 15 years later in its problematic *Eaton* decision. In my 4 January 1982 memo, I wrote:

> We might see some hint of the usefulness that this equal rights provision offers from American experience under the "equal protection" clause of the 14th amendment of the U.S. Constitution. Disabled groups in the U.S. challenged the constitutionality of state education programs which summarily hustled learning-disabled children into separate segregated school facilities, inferior in quality to the ordinary school system. The U.S. Supreme court over a decade ago ruled that this wholesale segregation without regard to the needs of individual handicapped children was an unconstitutional violation of these children's right to "equal protection of the law." As a result, in the mid 70s, Congressional legislation was passed guaranteeing disabled children the right to an education in the "least restrictive environment," based on an individual assessment of their needs. One can see the potential for this kind of challenge to the Canadian education system in the future. Because our courts are less aggressive than their American counterparts in protecting the civil rights of individuals, I expect that it will be several years before the Canadian judiciary actively implements the *Charter of Rights*.[16]

In 1954, the US Supreme Court was visionary in courageously ruling against racially segregated schools in *Brown v Board of Education*.[17] In 1997, the Supreme Court of Canada lacked any such vision. It did a disservice to vulnerable students with disabilities when it ruled against Emily Eaton. So many years later, the presumption in favour of inclusive education in Ontario schools that the Supreme Court of Canada feared constitutionally mandating is now supposed to be core Ontario education policy. Sadly, there is ample room to debate how effectively it is implemented. Three long decades would have to pass after the Joint Committee adopted the disability amendment before the Supreme Court of Canada would take a more principled and effective approach to equal educational opportunities for students with disabilities. In *Moore v British Columbia*, the Court undid most, if not all, of the damage to the right to an equal education for students with disabilities that the *Eaton* decision had caused. It based that decision on human rights

---

16 Lepofsky, *Final Report*, *supra* note 3 at 3–4.

17 *Brown v Board of Education of Topeka*, 347 US 483 (1954).

legislation and not on the disability amendment to the *Charter*.[18] Neither the disability amendment to the *Charter* nor the *Eaton* case were even mentioned in the Court's reasons.

## D. A Major Judicial Stride Forward in 1997

Since the Supreme Court of Canada's 1997 *Eaton* ruling, there have been some major jurisprudential breakthroughs and some real letdowns in court. If only the daily pressures of our ongoing disability advocacy battles would let up long enough for me to write another comprehensive progress report on the courts' implementation of the disability amendment! Here, I offer a few reflections. The high-water mark in the courts' application of the disability amendment remains the Supreme Court of Canada's unanimous 1997 ruling in *Eldridge v British Columbia (Attorney General)*.[19] The Court held that British Columbia has a constitutional duty to provide sign language interpretation in hospital emergency rooms when deaf patients need this to effectively communicate with healthcare providers.

The Court's reasons, read as a whole, go far beyond the four walls of hospital emergency rooms. In pursuit of a barrier-free society for people with disabilities, section 15 of the *Charter* imposes a constitutional duty to accommodate the disability-related needs of all people with disabilities. As a matter of general principle, the government has a duty to take into account the needs of people with disabilities when it designs or implements a law, program, or policy.[20] If the government fails to fulfill this duty, it must justify that failure. The decision recognizes the core goal of section 15 as being the achievement of the barrier-free society for people with disabilities. It recognizes the importance of full inclusion for people with disabilities. It looks askance at government attempts to justify a failure to accommodate deaf patients because, if they provide sign language interpreters for deaf people, they will also have to provide interpretation for people who speak languages other than French or English.[21]

The *Eldridge* decision extends the *Charter*'s reach well beyond the parameters that the Supreme Court of Canada earlier recognized. Previously,

---

18 *Moore v British Columbia (Education)*, 2012 SCC 61, [2012] 3 SCR 360.

19 *Eldridge v British Columbia (Attorney General)*, [1997] 3 SCR 624, [1997] SCJ No 86 (QL) [*Eldridge*].

20 *Ibid* at paras 42–44.

21 *Ibid* at paras 90–92.

it was settled that the *Charter* applies only to legislation or programs that the government directly operates.[22] *Eldridge* goes further. It also extends the *Charter*'s reach to programs that a government funds but which it delivers through private parties.[23] For example, governments fund healthcare services, but those services are very often delivered by private hospitals and private doctors. Before *Eldridge*, those private hospitals and private doctors would be judicially treated as being outside the *Charter*'s reach. They were not government actors. In a dramatic new approach to the *Charter*'s reach, *Eldridge* held that the *Charter* applies to them in their delivery of government-funded health services. This is because health services constitute a major government program, albeit one that is so often delivered at the frontlines by private actors.[24]

## E. *Charter* Litigation Too Often Remains a Remote Untenable Option for People with Disabilities

Most pre-existing disability barriers that are within the *Charter*'s reach remain in place to this day. New barriers continue to be created despite the disability amendment. Yet there has been far too little disability equality constitutional litigation. This is due to several factors. First and foremost, people with disabilities in Canada are for the most part in no position to launch a major barrage of costly and lengthy constitutional litigation against federal, provincial, or municipal governments or other entities that are bound to comply with the *Charter*. Far too many people with disabilities continue to languish in poverty. They are over-represented among those receiving systemically inadequate social assistance benefits. They remain perennially under-represented among those who enjoy gainful employment. If people with disabilities launch a *Charter* case, they are very likely to run up against a relentless defence team including salaried government lawyers, financed by the taxpayer, armed with fulsome legal briefs and well-credentialled expert witnesses. Our legal profession has yet to ensure that it effectively serves the disability community's substantially unmet legal needs.[25] Chronic underfunding of provincial legal aid programs only

---

22 *McKinney v University of Guelph*, [1990] 3 SCR 229, [1990] SCJ No 122 at paras 22–24.

23 *Eldridge*, *supra* note 19 at paras 41–43.

24 *Ibid* at paras 49–50.

25 Rosalie Silberman Abella, *Access to Legal Services by the Disabled: Report of a Study* (Toronto: Government of Ontario, 1983).

makes things worse. Compounding this, our court system continues to be replete with substantial disability accessibility barriers that impede court participants with disabilities despite some uneven recent progress.

Second, the Supreme Court's vague, confused, unpredictable, and fluid legal test for assessing equality rights claims is likely to deter some potential *Charter* claimants.[26] I cannot fault a potential *Charter* claimant from shying away from bringing a disability equality claim under the *Charter*, due to the troubling unpredictability of court outcomes under that sand trap of a legal test. Third, a resounding win under the disability amendment does not necessarily trigger the prompt, comprehensive corrective government action that a court ruling's clear language warrants. The best (or worst) illustration of this is the Supreme Court's landmark *Eldridge* decision. In *Eldridge*, the Supreme Court of Canada gave the BC government 6 months to fix the problem.[27] Even though *Eldridge* was about hospital emergency room services, it obviously extends to all healthcare services delivered in a hospital and, without much imagination, to those delivered anywhere in the publicly funded healthcare system. Despite that, the Ontario government took years to allocate any additional funding for sign language interpretation services in the healthcare system. Our healthcare system remains chock full of disability barriers over a quarter century after the *Eldridge* decision, as was fully documented in 2022 by the Health Care Standards Development Committee, which the Ontario government appointed to study the problem.[28]

What is the bottom line? As an instrument of change, the *Charter*'s disability equality provision is for the most part a de facto voluntary constitutional requirement. By that I mean that government bodies may choose voluntarily to comply with it, but, if they don't, their risk of being forced to do so is not as great as we need it to be. Too many lawyers still have little specific knowledge about the *Charter*'s guarantee of equality to persons with disabilities, the barriers facing persons with disabilities, and the steps needed to provide barrier-free, accessible services to clients with

---

26 See e.g. *Law v Canada (Minister of Employment and Immigration)*, [1999] 1 SCR 497, [1999] SCJ No 12 (QL); *R v Kapp*, 2008 SCC 41, [2008] 2 SCR 483; *Withler v Canada (Attorney General)*, 2011 SCC 12, [2011] 1 SCR 396.

27 *Eldridge*, *supra* note 19 at para 96.

28 Health Care Standards Development Committee, *Development of Health Care Standards: Final Recommendations Report 2022* (February 2022), online: <www.ontario.ca/page/development-health-care-standards-final-recommendations-report-2022>.

disabilities. Ontario's lawyer-licensing body, the Law Society of Ontario, has sadly cancelled training for bar admissions law students on this topic several times over the past decades and now provides no focused training on this subject to those students. Without effective access to legal services, *Charter* equality rights will largely remain a phenomenon of academic study much more than a practical reality for most persons with disabilities. Many will be reluctant to invest time and resources in a long court battle whose outcome is very uncertain and whose practical results, as in *Eldridge*, may be spotty and incomplete, even after a resounding victory.

## F. The Ongoing Unmet Need for All Governments to Review Their Laws and Programs to Bring Them into Full Compliance with the Disability Amendment

*Eldridge*'s powerful words go far beyond the constitutional rights of deaf patients in the healthcare system. It breathed substantially more content into section 15's disability equality guarantee than had any earlier court decision. In the face of such a powerful, unanimous, resounding Supreme Court of Canada decision, it is natural to expect that governments across Canada would launch reviews of their laws and programs to make them *Eldridge* compliant. Yet the only time that the Ontario government undertook a comprehensive review of all its laws to bring them into compliance with section 15 was just before 1985, when section 15 was about to come into force. It screened for possible legislative discrimination contrary to section 15 on any ground that the provision identified, including disability. That internal government review was conducted before the Supreme Court of Canada had issued its major early rulings that enunciated how the *Charter* was to be interpreted. That was also more than a decade before the Supreme Court's *Eldridge* ruling substantially expanded section 15's reach.

Regrettably, I am not aware of any government undertaking a comprehensive *Eldridge* analysis of their legislation, programs, or policies. In dramatic contrast, some levels of government undertook major reviews of their legislation to ensure it complied with a Supreme Court of Canada's ruling extending constitutional protection for same-sex couples under section 15 of the *Charter*. That legislative review led to the enactment of omnibus legislation in Ontario on the issue of entitlements for same-sex couples.[29] There is nothing constitutionally different between the Supreme Court of Canada's same-sex rulings, on the one hand, and its *Eldridge* ruling on disability equality, on the other, that would justify such a radically different legislative response.

When a standing committee of the Ontario legislature was reviewing Bill 118 in 2005, the proposed *AODA*, I proposed on behalf of the Ontarians with Disabilities Act Committee (predecessor to the Accessibility for Ontarians with Disabilities Alliance [AODA Alliance], which I now chair) that the bill be amended to require the Ontario government and municipal governments to review their legislation for disability accessibility barriers.[30] Such a review naturally flows from the *Eldridge* decision. An opposition motion proposed this amendment at our request. Ontario Premier Dalton McGuinty's governing Liberal government used its majority to defeat that amendment.[31] By enacting the *AODA*, the McGuinty government genuinely sought to advance the cause of disability equality across Ontario. It was committing Ontario to becoming fully accessible within 20 years through the enactment of the *AODA*. It was bizarre that that same government actively opposed an amendment to that bill requiring a systematic review to ensure that its own legislation and regulations complied with section 15 of the *Charter*.

We did not give up on this. Two years later, in the 2007 Ontario election, I got the AODA Alliance to ask each political party to pledge that, if elected, they would review all Ontario laws for disability accessibility barriers. That was another way to express a request for a review of all laws for *Eldridge* compliance. All three political parties responded favourably. Each agreed that, if elected, they would undertake the legislative review that we sought. Perhaps the Liberals had forgotten their "no" vote 2 years earlier. McGuinty's letter to the AODA Alliance on 14 September 2007, setting out the Ontario Liberals' commitments on disability accessibility in the 2007 Ontario election, made this very positive pledge, stating:

> The Ontario Liberal government believes this is the next step toward our goal of a fully accessible Ontario. Building on our work of the past four years, we will continue to be a leader in Canada on accessibility issues. For Ontario to

---

29 See *Modernization of Benefits and Obligations Act*, SC 2000, c 12.

30 *Accessibility for Ontarians with Disabilities Act*, SO 2005, c 11, s 41 [*AODA*].

31 Legislative Assembly of Ontario, Standing Committee on Social Policy, *Committee Transcript*, 38th Parl, 1st Sess (12 April 2005) at 936–937, 939.

> be fully accessible, we must ensure no law directly or indirectly discriminates against those with disabilities. To make that happen, we commit to reviewing all Ontario laws to find any disability barriers that need to be removed.[32]

Sadly, the Ontario Liberals' action on that 2007 election pledge was, stated gently, pathetic. They took over 4 years just to start seriously talking about the conduct of the promised legislative review. It took even more years for them to decide to first look at a mere 51 of Ontario's 750 or more statutes. They initially assigned the project to a team of public servants that included no lawyers at all, much less lawyers with constitutional expertise.[33]

On behalf of the AODA Alliance, I spent a great deal of time over those years pressing the Ontario government at the highest levels to conduct McGuinty's promised review of all Ontario statutes and regulations for disability barriers. I realized that there was a real possibility that those public servants who might be assigned to conduct this review would not know what to do. I took several steps to help. With my friend and colleague Randal Graham, I co-wrote a law journal article that laid out a total roadmap for reviewing legislation for disability barriers entitled "Universal Design in Legislation: Eliminating Barriers for People with Disabilities."[34] In September 2008, 1 year after McGuinty's promise, I gave a lecture on this topic at a national conference of lawyers who draft legislation for governments across Canada. In the audience, among others, were a number of Ontario public servants who draft legislation.

The Ontario Public Service commendably held a government-wide conference on 4 April 2011 to train public servants from across the government on how to conduct this legislative review. I was honoured to be invited to give the keynote address at that event. While it had been

---

32 Letter from Premier Dalton McGuinty to the AODA Alliance (14 September 2007), online: <www.aodaalliance.org/whats-new/newsub2011/liberal-party-writes-aoda-alliance-with-election-commitments-regarding-disability-accessibility/>.

33 See Brief from the AODA Alliance to the first phase of the Rich Donovan Fourth Independent Review of the Accessibility for Ontarians with Disabilities Act (6 February 2023), online: <www.aodaalliance.org/whats-new/feb-6-2023-finalized-aoda-alliance-rich-donovan-assessment-brief/>. See also Brief from the AODA Alliance to the Third Independent Review of the Accessibility for Ontarians with Disabilities Act, conducted by David Onley (15 January 2019), ch 8, online: <www.aodaalliance.org/whats-new/please-support-the-aoda-alliances-finalized-brief-to-the-david-onley-independent-review-of-the-aodas-implementation-and-enforcement/> [Brief from the AODA Alliance].

34 M David Lepofsky & Randal NM Graham, "Universal Design in Legislation: Eliminating Barriers for People with Disabilities" (2009) 30:2 Statute L Rev 97.

an inexcusable delay of 4 years before the government got started, this conference gave me a glimmer of hope, which was to be resoundingly dashed over the following years. Later in 2011, I delivered two training sessions on this topic to the Ontario legislature's Office of Legislative Counsel. That is the all-important expert team of Ontario public servants who draft legislation and regulations for the Ontario legislature and government. I was delighted at their receptiveness to this training, which I had proactively offered to them. I was appalled at the fact that this was the first time they had received any training on this topic. Had the law books not contained the *Charter*, replete with the disability amendment since 1982, not to mention the Ontario *Human Rights Code*, the 2001 *Ontarians with Disabilities Act*, and the 2005 *Accessibility for Ontarians with Disabilities Act*?[35]

Two years later, I presented at least one additional training session on this topic for lawyers in the Ontario Ministry of the Attorney General's Policy Division when this legislative review was shuffled to them. By then, the Ontario Public Service had developed a tool for reviewing legislation for disability barriers that was distilled directly from the law journal article on point that Graham and I had written. Thus, all the pieces were in place for real progress. Sadly, this never translated into major results. When Kathleen Wynne ran for leadership of the Ontario Liberal Party in late 2012, she pledged that she would honour all the commitments on disability accessibility that McGuinty had earlier made.[36] Yet, under her leadership, we faced more years of delay on the 2007 promise to review all Ontario laws for accessibility barriers. In 2016, 9 years after McGuinty's election pledge, the Liberals passed a paltry omnibus bill that made only minor amendments to a meager eleven statutes. That bill disregarded major disability barriers in the 51 supposedly high-impact Ontario statutes that the Ontario Public Service had reviewed. It fixed none of the barriers in the remaining 90 percent of Ontario statutes that public servants had not even cracked open during this review.

We ultimately discovered that some faceless, unnamed bureaucrats had called off the rest of the legislative review. That meant that 90 percent of Ontario's statutes and all its regulations were never reviewed as part of

[35] *Ontarians with Disabilities Act*, SO 2001, c 32.

[36] See letter from Kathleen Wynne to the AODA Alliance (3 December 2012), online: <www.aodaalliance.org/whats-new/on-this-international-day-for-people-with-disabilities-we-look-back-at-kathleen-wynnes-written-promises-to-1-8-million-ontarians-with-disabilities-made-four-years-ago-today-on-what-shed-do-on-d/>.

this effort over a decade after McGuinty made his 2007 election pledge to us. This issue was shuffled from ministry to ministry over a dozen years, under a series of deputy ministers. Premier Doug Ford's Conservative Ontario government that has been in power since June 2018 has done nothing about this and has not even answered our written inquiries about it.[37] Having learned from this bitter experience, on the AODA Alliance's behalf, I called on Parliament to legislatively require the federal government to review all its laws for accessibility barriers. This was part of the package of amendments we sought from the House of Commons in 2018 when it was debating Bill C-81, the proposed *Accessible Canada Act*.[38] The Liberals under Prime Minister Justin Trudeau rejected this request, without giving any reasons.[39]

## G. An Example Illustrates the Disability Amendment's Potential Legislative Reform Power

When a government takes the disability amendment seriously, it can lead to significant legislative reforms. One case in point about which I have a great deal of knowledge is the troubling original section 16(1)(a) of the Ontario *Human Rights Code*, enacted in 1981.[40] The good news was that it

---

[37] See Brief from the AODA Alliance, *supra* note 33, ch 8.

[38] *Accessible Canada Act*, SC 2019, c 10. See Brief from the AODA Alliance to the House of Commons of Canada on Bill C-81, the Proposed Accessible Canada Act (27 September 2018), online: <www.aodaalliance.org/whats-new/click-here-to-download-in-ms-word-format-the-aoda-alliances-finalized-september-27-2018-brief-to-the-parliament-of-canada-requesting-amendments-to-bill-c-81-the-proposed-bill-c-81/> [Brief from the AODA Alliance, 27 September 2018].

[39] The Brief from the AODA Alliance, 27 September 2018, *supra* note 38, included:

> We therefore recommend that:
>
> The bill should be amended to require the Federal Government to:
>
> a) Conduct a review of all federal statutes and regulations for accessibility barriers, including any provisions that authorize or require the creation or perpetuation of accessibility barriers, including among all laws, the Criminal Code, and immigration legislation.
>
> b) Set deadlines for the start and for the completion of this review.
>
> c) Mandate which cabinet minister should bring forward an omnibus bill, and timelines for that bill, to correct any accessibility barriers that this internal review finds, and that require correcting legislation.
>
> d) Require periodic public reporting on the progress of this review of federal laws.

[40] *Human Rights Code*, SO 1981, c 53, s 16(1)(a).

made it illegal in Ontario, for the first time, to discriminate because of disability in activities such as employment and access to goods, services, and facilities. The bad news was that it initially included a provision that categorically said that a disability claim could not be based solely on the physical inaccessibility of premises. It provided: "16. (1) A right of a person under this Act is not infringed for the reason only, (a) that the person does not have access to premises, services, goods, facilities or accommodation because of handicap, or that the premises, services, goods, facilities or accommodation lack the amenities that are appropriate for the person because of handicap."[41] In 1986, the Ontario legislature commendably repealed that provision in its omnibus Bill 7, the *Equality Rights Statute Law Amendment Act*, which aimed to bring Ontario legislation into compliance with section 15 of the *Charter*.[42] Had it not been repealed, it would have been an easy target for constitutional challenge as violating the disability amendment to the *Charter*.

## H. The Disability Amendment Helped Drive the Enactment of Comprehensive Accessibility Legislation

One of the disability amendment's largest impacts for people with disabilities has been its role in spurring on the enactment of several accessibility laws across Canada. This movement began in 1994 in Ontario as a handful of disability advocates, including me, kicked off a decade-long campaign. It first led to the enactment in 2001 of the weak *Ontarians with Disabilities Act*[43] and 4 years later to the passage in 2005 of the stronger *AODA*.[44] I have written a detailed account of the first 8 years of that grassroots effort.[45] We conceived of, and fought for, the *AODA* as a legislative measure to effectively implement the rights that section 15 of the *Charter* and the Ontario *Human Rights Code* confer on people with disabilities. We wanted to avoid the need for people with disabilities to litigate one barrier at a time to enforce their rights.

41 *Ibid.*

42 *Equality Rights Statute Law Amendment Act*, SO 1986, c 64, s 18(9)(1).

43 *Ontarians with Disabilities Act*, *supra* note 35.

44 *AODA*, *supra* note 30.

45 M David Lepofsky, "The Long, Arduous Road to a Barrier-Free Ontario for People with Disabilities: The History of the *Ontarians with Disabilities Act* — the First Chapter" (2004) 15:2 NJCL 125.

This new wave in the disability rights movement spread to several other parts of Canada. It led Manitoba to pass the *Accessibility for Manitobans Act* in 2013,[46] Nova Scotia to pass its *Accessibility Act* in 2017,[47] Newfoundland and Labrador to pass their *Accessibility Act* in 2021,[48] British Columbia to pass the *Accessible British Columbia Act* in 2021,[49] and Parliament to pass the *Accessible Canada Act* in 2019.[50] In 2022, it led the government of Saskatchewan to introduce the *Accessible Saskatchewan Act* into its legislature for debate.[51] These statutes provide for the enactment of detailed accessibility standards on a sector-by-sector basis. An accessibility standard is a regulation that spells out in detail what an obligated organization must do, and by when, to remove and prevent disability barriers. When people with disabilities give feedback on what these accessibility standards should include, we can and do emphasize that they must live up to the *Charter*'s guarantee of equality to people with disabilities to the extent that organizations must comply with the *Charter*.

Are these laws helping? So far, the *AODA* has fallen miles short of its potential. Since 2009, I have led the AODA Alliance's campaign to get the Ontario government to do better. In the final report of the third independent review of the *AODA* on 31 January 2019, David Onley found that the pace of change since 2005 for people with disabilities "has been glacial."[52] With under 6 years left before 2025, the report found that "the promised accessible Ontario is nowhere in sight." Progress on accessibility under this law "has been highly selective and barely detectable."[53] Onley concluded: "[T]his province is mostly inaccessible."[54] The Onley report correctly found: "For most disabled persons, Ontario is not a place of opportunity but one of

46 *Accessibility for Manitobans Act*, CCSM 2013, c A1.7.

47 *Accessibility Act*, SNS 2017, c 2.

48 *Accessibility Act*, SNL 2021, c A-1.001.

49 *Accessible British Columbia Act*, SBC 2021, c 19.

50 *Accessible Canada Act*, *supra* note 38.

51 See *Accessible Saskatchewan Act*, introduced in 2022.

52 See David C Onley, *Report of the Third Review of the Accessibility for Ontarians with Disabilities Act 2005* (2019), online: <www.aodaalliance.org/whats-new/click-here-to-download-in-ms-word-format-the-final-report-of-the-david-onley-independent-review-of-the-implementation-and-enforcement-of-the-accessibility-for-ontarians-with-disabilities-act/>.

53 *Ibid* at 1.

54 *Ibid*.

countless, dispiriting, soul-crushing barriers."[55] The fourth independent review of the *AODA*, conducted by Rich Donovan, delivered an interim report to the Ontario government on 1 March 2023. Its scathing findings make the earlier Onley report sound mild and gentle.[56]

Despite this, people with disabilities are better off with the *AODA* than without it. Similarly, progress so far under the *Accessible Canada Act* has been far too slow and very disappointing. This means that persons with disabilities will have to keep fighting disability barriers one at a time via individual human rights complaints or *Charter* claims. We tenaciously soldier on!

## I. Changing How People with Disabilities See Themselves

Has the disability amendment helped people with disabilities see themselves as entitled to equality rather than mere recipients of charity? I would love to present comparative, externally validated, scientifically gathered public opinion survey data contrasting 1980 and the present. I have none to offer. Yet I do not want to let the absence of valid data get in the way of a juicy opinion! It is my strong sense that the disability amendment, guarantees of equality in all human rights codes across Canada, and the enactment of accessibility statutes federally and in five of Canada's ten provinces have combined to help transform how people with disabilities see themselves. It is not that millions of people with disabilities are ploughing through law books, discovering all these laws, and then experiencing a cleansing moment of self-realization. Many of them may not even know about some or all of these laws and what they mean, that disability was added to the *Charter* after our collective fight in 1980, or that it was even added to the *Charter* at all. I see this as a far more subtle process.

I have now been immersed for many years in volunteer, grassroots disability community organizing and advocacy. I have attended and spoken at hundreds of public events, received tens of thousands of emails and social media posts, and had innumerable individual exchanges with a seemingly endless number of people with different disabilities as well as their families, friends, and supporters. Reporters have called me hundreds of times about

55 *Ibid.*

56 *Ibid*; Rich Donovan, *Independent Fourth Review of the Accessibility for Ontarians with Disabilities Act, 2005 (AODA)*, Interim Report (March 2023).

different wrenching disability-related stories on which they are working. From all this, I have seen the trend demonstrated over and over. So many are determined to fully participate in society and consider this as their right (in the lay utilization of that word). They relentlessly feel this way about themselves no matter how many barriers they continue to face, no matter how isolated they feel, and no matter how uphill the battle against those barriers appears to be. More and more, I hear anger and determination from people who, decades ago, would have been resigned to passively, if not gratefully, accept the unfair status quo, feeling that they are entitled to nothing better.

In this way, the disability amendment has played an important role below the radar in helping energize the decade-long movement I led in Ontario for the enactment of comprehensive disability accessibility legislation. It will continue to serve as a centrepiece in making the case for the effective implementation of that legislation. Each time we win another seemingly impossible uphill battle, each time we succeed in swimming up Niagara Falls, starting with winning the disability amendment, it fuels optimism and determination for the next round!

## J. The Failure of the 1992 Charlottetown Accord

Known to extremely few, the disability amendment directly or indirectly helped mobilize some disability activists during the failed attempt to pass yet another constitutional reform package in 1992, the so-called Charlottetown Accord. An outgrowth of the failed 1987 Meech Lake Accord, the Charlottetown Accord sought to engineer a formula to get the Quebec government to formally ratify the 1982 Trudeau constitutional patriation package. To reconcile a myriad of conflicting demands for this reform package, the federal government proposed, among other things, to add a "Canada clause" to the Constitution. It would list certain fundamental characteristics of Canada.

To many this was a rather dubious exercise in constitutional symbolism, far removed from the day-to-day life of Canadians. However, some within the disability rights community became concerned, myself among them, because this Canada clause was proposed to enumerate equality for women and racial minorities. It thereby would have enshrined a rather narrow vision of equality that left out the disability equality rights for which we fought and won in 1980. The disability advocacy effort on the Canada clause was rather small and last minute. I was not then involved in any public disability law reform efforts. Any efforts by people with disabilities regarding the proposed Canada clause did not form a significant part of the visible public battle over the Charlottetown Accord. When that accord was put to a national referendum, it failed for a matrix of reasons, of which this was at best a microscopic one, I surmise. However, the fact that anyone from the disability community felt any compulsion to raise this issue at all is traceable back to the disability amendment of 12 years earlier.

## K. Contrasting Gains under the *Charter* by People with Disabilities with Those of the LGBTQ2S+ Community

I want to again focus on what I discussed in Chapter VIII. In my view, Canada's LGBTQ2S+ community has reaped far more substantial gains under section 15 of the *Charter*, both in court and in legislatures, than has Canada's disability community. This result is quite ironic. In Chapter VIII, I explained how the two most vocal equality-seeking groups that tried to get added to section 15 in 1980 were people with disabilities and the LGBTQ2S+ community. Back then, regrettably, the LGBTQ2S+ community did not have much of a chance given the politics and perceived level of public acceptance at that time. In contrast, it was then seen as politically feasible to include disability. The equality-seeking group that could not even get in the door by explicit amendment in 1981 turned out to benefit more from the progress under the *Charter* than has the disability community, which was openly allowed in through that constitutional door. Moreover, there have been those in society who mounted organized opposition to equal rights for the LGBTQ2S+ community. The same is not so for people with disabilities.

The differential degrees of progress under the *Charter* for the disability community, on the one hand, and the LGBTQ2S+ community, on the other, cannot be explained by a suggestion that disability equality engages cost concerns, whereas LGBTQ2S+ rights do not. Each can engage cost factors in some cases and not in others.

## L. Final Thoughts

It is impossible to totally measure the disability amendment's impact. Some constitutional law scholars have erroneously used the raw number or outcomes of the Supreme Court of Canada's *Charter* rulings, under one *Charter* provision or another, as an informative measure of the *Charter*'s impact. That, however, is only the tiny tip of the iceberg that sits atop a glacier. Much of the disability amendment's impact happens behind closed government doors and is protected from public disclosure by lawyer-client privilege. The public will never know when a government lawyer has nixed a proposed new law or policy because it would be indefensible under the disability amendment as unconstitutional disability discrimination.

One compelling way to assess the disability amendment's impact is to try to project an alternative timeline for Canada. Imagine that Parliament had defeated the disability amendment on 28 January 1981. How different would Canada look today? Even without the disability amendment, people with disabilities could have gone to court to argue that disability should be "read into" section 15, just as courts eventually recognized grounds like citizenship and sexual orientation. Government lawyers might have argued that a court should not overturn a Joint Committee decision not to include disability. The applicant, on the other hand, would argue that the justice minister had made it clear to the Joint Committee that judges could add such grounds to section 15 over time. As I earlier suggested, we would likely have won the day, though it could have taken years. The costly litigation road to that result could easily have had ugly jurisprudential bumps along the way. The need for the cash-strapped disability community to pull together scarce advocacy resources for this legal fight would have diverted us from other worthy causes. Federal and provincial governments would in the interim have been even less active in taking steps to modify their legislation, policies, and programs than has been the case over the past four decades.

The message to people with disabilities from a failure to pass the disability amendment would have been a loud, sad, and negative one. Canada's political leaders would have declared at a pivotal moment in history that persons with disabilities remain second class citizens and that their quest for equality remains unrecognized even at the level of constitutional symbolism, much less at the level of constitutional action. I am confident that the disability amendment was an implicit contributing force in the pivotal Royal Commission report on equality in employment by then Judge Rosalie Abella.[57] It laid the groundwork for including persons with disabilities among the regularly recognized target groups for employment

57 Rosalie Silberman Abella, *Equality in Employment: A Royal Commission Report* (Ottawa: Commission on Equality in Employment, 1984), online: <equalpaycoalition.org/wp-content/uploads/2017/07/Equality-in-Employment-A-Royal-Commission-Report-Abella-Complete-Report.pdf>.

equity programs. Even then, we have still had to battle our way into equality-seeking strategies such as employment equity and, more recently, equity, diversity, and inclusion. Without the disability amendment and its consequential impacts, that battle would have been even more difficult.

# XIX. THE AFTERMATH: HOW THE DISABILITY AMENDMENT HAS PERVADED MY LIFE AND CAREER

## A. A Day Job in Anything but Disability Rights

You might think that, with the fight for the disability amendment and a Harvard graduate law degree under my belt, I was itching to get started in a career dedicated to practising disability rights law. The opposite was the case! I wanted to be a courtroom lawyer, but I resolutely did not want to be a courtroom disability rights lawyer. Anything but that! As early as the day when I graduated from Osgoode with my Bachelor of Laws degree, I had firmly decided that I was not going to specialize in disability rights in my day-to-day law practice. This is because I feared being typecast from the start of my career as the blind guy who only represents blind people. My fear of that stereotype was well founded as I discovered on the brutally hot June afternoon in 1979 when I received my law degree at an outdoor Osgoode Hall Law School graduation ceremony. With my beaming parents in the audience, I proudly strode across the stage under the hot sun and shook hands with the university's chancellor. The moment I stepped off the stage, a CBC television reporter stuck a microphone in front of me and asked if I planned to dedicate my career to representing blind clients. I looked at him like he was from Mars. I quipped that I did not plan to choose my clients based on how little they could see.

In the fall of 1982, armed with my degree from Osgoode and a Master of Laws from Harvard, I faced a depressing uphill struggle getting my first job as a lawyer. Even getting a job interview was a discouraging battle. I remember trying to mask my sense of utter insult when a senior litigation partner at one major Toronto law firm ended an interview by declaring that he was satisfied that I could work as a lawyer. Heck, I was a lawyer! By the way, years later, that lawyer, who was actually quite a nice fellow, met me in combat in court. I guess I really could work as a lawyer. I won the case. He lost! In the fall of 1982, I was offered a job at the ARCH Disability Law Centre. I turned it down. I consciously opted to endure a longer stretch of unemployment rather than risk being typecast.

After deploying in my job search the lobbying skills I had been developing over the previous year, I landed a job in December 1982 with Ontario's Ministry of the Attorney General. That job lasted for a third of a century up to my retirement from the Ontario Public Service at the end of 2015. The architect of my success in getting that first job was the attorney general for Ontario, Roy McMurtry, who had the year before been one of the architects of the national deal that brought Canada its reformed and patriated Constitution. I spent my first 10 years arguing civil and constitutional cases for the Ontario government. I then spent 23 years arguing criminal appeals for the Crown in the Ontario Court of Appeal and, occasionally, in the Supreme Court of Canada. During those years, I avoided arguing disability rights cases, with only one early exception that I recall.[1]

## B. Teaching and Writing about Equality for People with Disabilities

That early career choice did not stop the disability amendment from pervading my life in so many ways. Starting very early in my career, I have given many, many talks that revolve around the topic of equality for people with disabilities, whether guaranteed by the *Canadian Charter of Rights and Freedoms*, the Ontario *Human Rights Code*, or both.[2] Over the years, I have authored a number of law journal articles and book chapters that address this topic. Many of the key ones are referenced in this retrospective.

## C. Training Judges about Equality for People with Disabilities

Judges who decide *Charter* cases play a pivotal role in the implementation of Canada's Constitution. Yet to be appointed to serve as a judge, a person need not know anything about the constitutional right to equality for people with disabilities. Starting almost three decades ago, I began to train judges on equality for people with disabilities. The disability amendment is a major foundation for that training. Since the mid-1990s, I have annually delivered a lecture on accommodating people with disabilities in the

1 *Cameron v Nel-Gor Castle Nursing Home*, 1984 5054 ON HRT, 5 CHRR 2170.

2 *Canadian Charter of Rights and Freedoms*, Part 1 of the *Constitution Act, 1982*, being Schedule B to the *Canada Act 1982* (UK), 1982, c 11; *Human Rights Code*, RSO 1990, c H-19.

courtroom to new federally appointed judges as part of the boot camp for new judges. I have also been invited to present on equality for people with disabilities at a number of other judicial education programs around Canada. To assist with that training, I authored a law journal article 15 years after the disability amendment was adopted, entitled "Equal Access to Canada's Judicial System for Persons with Disabilities: A Time for Reform."[3]

In 2005, this effort substantially expanded when the legendary Roy McMurtry, then the chief justice of Ontario, appointed a committee on which I served comprising members from the bench, bar, and Ontario government to recommend actions to make Ontario's courts accessible to court participants with disabilities. Under the able leadership of its chair, Justice Karen Weiler, the ensuing Weiler report that we collectively wrote provided a comprehensive roadmap for reform.[4] That report led the chief justice of Ontario and the attorney general of Ontario to appoint a permanent Ontario Courts Accessibility Committee, on which I have sat as a member since 2007. That influential committee oversees the implementation of the Weiler report. All these efforts trace themselves back to the disability amendment.

## D. Community Organizing and Advocacy for the Enactment and Effective Implementation of Strong Accessibility Legislation

As mentioned earlier, section 15's guarantee of equality for people with disabilities has been a central launching pad for my volunteer efforts since 1994 to advocate for the enactment and implementation of strong accessibility legislation in Ontario. I have also been invited to give input and advice on this in some of the other provinces that have headed in that direction. In the most recent phase of these efforts, starting in 2015, I, along with others, joined together to advocate for the enactment of Bill C-81, the *Accessible Canada Act*, a federal statute that aims to implement the disability amendment.[5] It has made me quite nostalgic about the early days when we fought for the disability amendment. 38 years after my appearance before

---

3 M David Lepofsky, "Equal Access to Canada's Judicial System for Persons with Disabilities: A Time for Reform" (1995) 5:1 NJCL 183.

4 See Courts Disabilities Committee, *Making Ontario's Courts Fully Accessible to Persons with Disabilities* (2006), online: <www.ontariocourts.ca/coa/about-the-court/publications-speeches/reports-courts-disabilities/>.

5 *Accessible Canada Act*, SC 2019, c 10.

the Special Joint Committee of the Senate and the House of Commons on the Constitution of Canada (Joint Committee), it was front and centre in my mind when I addressed the House of Commons Standing Committee on Human Resources, Skills and Social Development and the Status of Persons with Disabilities on 25 October 2018 to call for amendments to strengthen the proposed *Accessible Canada Act*. I concluded my presentation:

> In conclusion, I have a real strong sense of personal history today, because 38 years ago, when the *Charter of Rights* was only a proposal, it did not include equality for people with disabilities. And I had the privilege of being one of the many people that came here to argue that the Charter be amended to include equality for people with disabilities.
>
> Working together, we succeeded then. Working together now, we can succeed to make this bill — which is strong on intention but weak on enforcement and implementation — we now have the opportunity to again work together with you, to create a strong law that will make the victory of 38 years ago, equality for people with disabilities, not only a legal guarantee, but a reality in the lives of all of us.[6]

Six months later, I returned to that theme when I appeared before the Senate's Standing Committee on Social Development on 11 April 2019 in another effort to get Bill C-81 strengthened. I wound up my opening remarks:

> I conclude by saying this: I'm speaking for my coalition, but as an individual, I first came before Parliament 39 years ago as a much younger individual — my wife said I had hair back then when she saw the video — to appear before the standing committee considering the *Charter of Rights*. At that time, the *Charter* proposed to guarantee equality but not to people with disabilities. I and a number of other folks argued and succeeded in getting the *Charter* amended to include that right.
>
> I leave you with two thoughts. First, the amendments we seek are aimed at making that right become a reality, not just as a matter of good intention but as effective implementation.[7]

---

6 Canada, Parliament, *Standing Committee on Human Resources, Skills and Social Development and the Status of Persons with Disabilities*, 1st Sess, 42nd Parl, No 119 (25 October 2018) at 3.

7 Senate of Canada, *Proceedings of the Standing Senate Committee on Social Affairs, Science and Technology*, 1st Sess, 42nd Parl, No 57 (11 April 2019) at 78.

## E. Battling to Make Our Education System Accessible to Students with Disabilities

In December 1980, to convince the Joint Committee to adopt the disability amendment, one example of disability discrimination I listed was our education system's failure to fully include students with disabilities on a footing of equality. This issue had been a passion of mine ever since my mother successfully battled our school system in 1971 to let me remain in a regular classroom at my neighbourhood school, a story I described in Chapter IV. In Chapter XVIII, I explained how I initially hoped that the disability amendment would spur on reforms in our school system to ensure equal educational opportunities for students with disabilities. For me, that passion burns as strongly today as it did in 1980. Starting in 2009, it led me to lead the AODA Alliance's campaign to get the Ontario government to enact an Education Accessibility Standard under the *AODA*. This regulation is needed to remove and prevent disability barriers in Ontario's education system. It would implement the disability amendment.

It took seven exhausting years of campaigning just to get the Ontario government to agree in 2016 to develop an Education Accessibility Standard. After that, in 2018, I managed to get the Ontario government to appoint me to the Kindergarten–Grade 12 Education Standards Development Committee, created under the *AODA*. It is an advisory committee, half of whose members came from the disability community and half from the community of educators. In early 2022, the Kindergarten–Grade 12 Education Standards Development Committee submitted a major final report to the Ontario government that recommends what the Education Accessibility Standard should include.[8] Ours was the first comprehensive review of Ontario's education system in more than a generation from the perspective of students with disabilities. That report, if implemented, would make the disability amendment become a reality for hundreds of thousands of students with disabilities in Ontario. I played an active role in the crafting of that committee's recommendations.

---

8 See Kindergarten–Grade 12 Education Standards Development Committee, *Development of Proposed Kindergarten to Grade 12 (K-12) Education Standards — 2022 Final Recommendations* (2022), online: <www.aodaalliance.org/whats-new/download-in-an-accessible-ms-word-format-the-final-report-of-the-k-12-education-standards-development-committee-on-what-the-promised-education-accessibility-standardshould-include/>.

The commands of the disability amendment also underlie my volunteer work since early 2015 as a member of the Special Education Advisory Committee of Canada's largest school board, the Toronto District School Board [TDSB]. We are mandated to make recommendations to the school board on what is needed to improve education for students with special education needs. I served as that committee's chair in 2016 and 2017. Over those 2 years, I spearheaded a major review of the board's offerings and supports for students with special education needs. Our recommendations to the TDSB, which it has largely ignored, did make their way into the 2022 final report of the Kindergarten–Grade 12 Education Standards Development Committee.

## F. Embedding Disability Equality in Law School Curriculum

The disability amendment lies at the core of my ongoing efforts, described in Chapter IV, to expand legal education in Canada so that it effectively trains law students how to serve the legal needs of clients with disabilities. This includes teaching law students how to scrutinize any area of law through a disability lens. How do family law principles play out when applying them to parents or children with disabilities in the midst of a family law dispute? How do these legal principles need to be adapted to accommodate their needs and rights as guaranteed by both section 15 of the *Charter* and human rights legislation? I lectured on this at the Osgoode Hall Law School from 2016 to June 2023 and at the Faculty of Law of the University of Western Ontario since the fall of 2023. The disability amendment is the vital foundation of my recent law journal article to which I referred in Chapter IV, entitled "People with Disabilities Need Lawyers Too! A Ready-to-Use Plan for Law Schools to Educate Law Students to Effectively Serve the Legal Needs of Clients with Disabilities as well as Clients without Disabilities."[9] It gives law faculties a roadmap on how to include disability content in their curriculum.

---

[9] David Lepofsky "People with Disabilities Need Lawyers Too! A Ready-to-Use Plan for Law Schools to Educate Law Students to Effectively Serve the Legal Needs of Clients with Disabilities as Well as Clients without Disabilities" (2022) 38 Windsor YB Access Justice 148.

## G. See You in Court

### *1.* Lepofsky v Toronto Transit Commission

From 1994 to 2007, I waged a legal battle to get the Toronto Transit Commission [TTC], Canada's largest municipal public transit provider, to consistently and reliably make audible announcements for each subway, bus, and streetcar stop so that blind passengers like me can know when we have reached our destination. I fought and won this battle by arguing two successive cases at the Ontario Human Rights Tribunal. I invoked the Ontario *Human Rights Code* and not the *Charter*. I first fought and won a case that held that the TTC must reliably announce all subway stops.[10] Despite that victory, the TTC refused to agree to require its bus and streetcar drivers to announce all stops on their routes. I therefore had to bring a second case against the TTC where I won the right to have all bus and streetcar stops consistently announced.[11] Through a Freedom of Information application, I revealed that the TTC spent $450,000 on lawyers to oppose my two cases, presenting a defence that was obviously doomed to fail.[12]

Public transit authorities like the TTC are part of municipal government. They must obey the *Charter*. I would certainly have won if I had chosen to go to court to invoke the *Charter* rather than going to the Ontario Human Rights Commission under the Ontario *Human Rights Code*. I opted to bring it under the *Human Rights Code* because I would have the benefit of the Human Rights Commission's public investigation and public prosecution powers. As well, had I lost, I would not face the risk of being ordered to pay the TTC's legal costs.

### *2.* Lepofsky v the Ontario Minister of Health

Amazing as it may sound, it was not until January 2022 that I would bring a claim of my own under the disability amendment. This absurd story began at the start of the COVID-19 pandemic. The Ontario government wisely decided to let Ontarians continue to receive publicly insured

10 *Lepofsky v Toronto Transit Commission*, 2005 HRTO 20.

11 *Lepofsky v Toronto Transit Commission*, 2007 HRTO 41.

12 David Lepofsky "Waste of Public Funds to Oppose Accessibility," *Toronto Star* (22 November 2007), online: <www.thestar.com/opinion/2007/11/22/waste_of_public_funds_to_oppose_accessibility.html>.

healthcare services, even if their official Ontario health card had expired. Before the pandemic, an expired health card had to be renewed at an official Service Ontario office. In March 2020, the government prudently suspended the requirement to renew an expired health card to avoid the risk of exposure to the virus on a visit to Service Ontario.

The problem began in September 2021 when the government announced a decision to end its moratorium on renewing expired health cards by 28 February 2022. After that date, a person could not get health services insured by the government unless they had a valid Ontario health card and not an expired one. My health card had expired in the summer of 2020. A person had to go to Service Ontario in person by 28 February 2022 to renew their expired health card, risking exposure to the virus, unless they qualified to renew their health card online. Here's the catch. You had to have a valid driver's license to renew a health card online.

We blind people don't seem to qualify for a driver's license for some reason. This obvious disability barrier contravened the guarantee of equality to people with disabilities in section 15 of the *Charter* and in the Ontario *Human Rights Code*. It gets worse! Years earlier, the Ontario government commendably established an official Ontario photo identification card. I had an official Ontario photo identification card. It is supposed to be equivalent to a driver's license as government-approved photo identification for those of us who do not have a driver's license. However, the Ontario government did not let a person renew an expired Ontario health card online by using the official Ontario photo identification card. Only an Ontario driver's license would do. Capping off this Kafkaesque absurdity, the same Ontario ministry manages both the Ontario photo identification card and the Ontario driver's license.

In the fall of 2021, I described this barrier in great detail to a cadre of senior Ontario government officials. Nobody disputed these facts. Nevertheless, I could not get the problem fixed. By late January 2022, the deadline was fast approaching to get an expired Ontario health card renewed. I asked the government to extend its moratorium if it needed more time to set up the technology to let members of the public renew their Ontario health card online using an official Ontario photo identification card. I kept slamming into brick walls. The disability amendment beckoned to me. With the help of pro bono counsel and a team of volunteer Osgoode law students, I filed an application for urgency-based judicial review in Ontario's

Superior Court. I invoked the *Charter*'s guarantee of equality to people with disabilities and comparable protections in the Ontario *Human Rights Code*.

After my media blitz and Twitter storm, the Ontario government fell on its sword within 2 weeks. I had alerted the government lawyer assigned to oppose me that I aimed to drag him in front of a judge as quickly as I could on any piddly point of procedure if necessary. Any judge was very likely to ask some extremely tough questions of the government lawyer. My pro bono lawyer helped me book a rapid scheduling motion in Civil Practice Court to ask for an urgent hearing of my *Charter* challenge. 20 minutes before that Civil Practice Court's virtual session, the government rushed out a news release. It gave me everything I had demanded. The government committed to let people renew an expired health card online using the Ontario photo identification card. The government extended its moratorium on renewing an expired health card until the end of September 2022 to give the government time to set this all up. My record so far is one to zero under the disability amendment.

## H. Crossing Paths with Several Key Public Figures in the Disability Amendment Story

It is quite amazing how many of the key public figures in the disability amendment story happened to cross paths with me over the years after Canada patriated our Constitution. I never set out to meet each of them. Sadly, with two exceptions — Barry Strayer and Jean Chrétien — I did not probe them on what arguments won the day for us.

### *1. Meeting Barry Strayer, One of the Charter's Authors*

As recounted in Chapter VIII, the first of these incidents took place in the fall of 1981 in Cambridge, Massachusetts. I had lunch at Harvard with Barry Strayer, a senior Department of Justice lawyer who had been heavily involved in the crafting of the *Charter*. He is the one who told me that disability was originally left out of section 15 because it had been a battle within the federal government just to get any degree of disability protection included in the *Canadian Human Rights Act* in 1977.[13]

[13] *Canadian Human Rights Act*, RSC 1985, c H-6.

## 2. *Meeting Jean Chrétien*

Second, in October 1986, I crossed paths with Jean Chrétien himself, 5 years after the events recounted in this retrospective. He had left federal politics but was expected to eventually re-enter the fray to take a second run at the leadership of the federal Liberal Party. The ARCH Disability Law Centre decided to give him, as a private citizen, an award for agreeing in 1981 to pass the disability amendment at a well-attended public event on 30 October 1986. I was honoured to be asked to introduce him at the formal award presentation. The media flocked to this event because, earlier that day, a new public opinion poll suggested that Chrétien would fare better in an election than federal Liberal leader John Turner. Reporters wanted to grill Chrétien about a possible return to politics, not about the award he was there to receive.

Before the event started, a small group was invited to meet Chrétien. This was the only time I have ever met him. I enthusiastically asked him what the argument was that got him to agree to the disability amendment. I anticipated that he would have given that question some advance thought since he came to Toronto for the very purpose of publicly receiving an award for the disability amendment. I clearly recall his response. He said that he did not really remember.

## 3. *Meeting Former Prime Minister Pierre Trudeau*

In 1991, I became a part-time adjunct member of the Faculty of Law at the University of Toronto, launching a stretch of over three decades teaching an upper-year constitutional seminar on the freedom of expression and press. In 1991, I attended a ceremony at which Pierre Trudeau received an honorary doctorate at the University of Toronto. At the reception afterwards, I was introduced to him as he made the rounds and shook his hand. You would think I would have capitalized on this opportunity to say something about the disability amendment. I was frankly too overwhelmed by meeting such a historic figure. I am sure he had no idea that I had been one of the advocates for the disability amendment a decade earlier.

## 4. *Meeting the Next Generation of Senator Richard Donahoe and the Blind Lawyer He Hired*

Here is an amazing moment of constitutional serendipity. In Chapter XIII, I described a question that Donahoe, one of the Joint Committee members, asked me when I addressed that committee in 1980. He began by telling me that when he was a provincial attorney general, a blind person applied for a job as a crown attorney. Donahoe said he wrestled with the decision but decided to hire that individual. The blind lawyer, he said, did a good job. That exchange with Donahoe instantly flashed back in my memory 13 years later in the most unlikely circumstances. In 1993, I appeared as counsel on behalf of the attorney general for Ontario in the Supreme Court of Canada. The Court was hearing a case that considered whether the Nova Scotia legislature violated the freedom of expression and press guarantee in section 2(b) of the *Charter* because it did not allow the media to deploy television cameras in the legislature to broadcast its proceedings.[14] That case had absolutely nothing to do with disability rights.

After the oral argument in the Supreme Court, I went out for a drink with several lawyers who had argued the case on one side or the other. A lawyer representing CBC told me that his father was blind and was a lawyer. When this CBC lawyer was a teenager, he had to read his father's tedious law books aloud to his dad. His father was then studying in law school. I connected the dots on the spot that his father must have been the blind lawyer to whom Donahoe had referred back in 1980 in his question to me. It gets even better! I also figured out that Donahoe's son later became the speaker of the Nova Scotia legislature. It was Donahoe's son who brought the appeal to the Supreme Court of Canada that we had just argued. I believe that, earlier that day, I said a brief hello to the younger Donahoe in the Supreme Court, not yet having pieced together my previous encounter with his father. This was an incredible convergence of the next generations of both Senator Donahoe and that blind lawyer whom that senator told me about in 1980.

## 5. *Meeting Ronald Irwin, Justice Minister Chrétien's Former Parliamentary Secretary*

In the early 1990s, I had another extraordinary encounter with a character in this narrative. I flew to Sault Ste. Marie, Ontario, to appear as counsel for the Ontario Human Rights Commission at a hearing on a racial discrimination case. The case's issues are not relevant here. During a break in the proceedings, I exchanged pleasant small talk with the defence counsel

---

14 *New Brunswick Broadcasting Co v Nova Scotia (Speaker of the House of Assembly)*, [1993] 1 SCR 319, [1993] SCJ No 2 (QL).

who was arguing the other side of the case. I learned that this lawyer, Ronald Irwin, had been a Liberal member of parliament and Justice Minister Chrétien's parliamentary secretary back in 1980. A quick look back at Chapter XV will reveal some of Irwin's remarks during the clause-by-clause debates.

During our chit chat, I told Irwin that I had appeared before the Joint Committee on behalf of the CNIB. He then told me something utterly jaw dropping. He explained that after the *Charter* was enacted, he had gotten his hands on a copy of the CNIB's Braille brief. He got it autographed by the three federal party leaders at the centre of the patriation battle, Prime Minister Pierre Trudeau, Conservative leader Joe Clark and New Democratic Party [NDP] leader Ed Broadbent. Irwin had earlier presented this autographed copy of our Braille brief to the CNIB's Sault Ste. Marie office. No one at the CNIB had told me about this constitutional gem. After we finished the human rights hearing, I raced over to the CNIB's Sault Ste. Marie office. Our brief was hanging on the wall there.

This otherwise amazing incident has a sorry ending. Years later, I heard through the grapevine that the CNIB had closed some of its regional offices, reportedly including the one in Sault Ste. Marie. I contacted the CNIB's chief executive officer and told this story. He launched a search of their archives. It never turned up. In 2022, as I prepared this retrospective, I reached out to the CNIB again. Once again, no one has found it. That wonderful and irreplaceable artefact from this piece of Canadian disability rights advocacy history appears to have been lost.

## 6. *Meeting a Fierce Opponent of the Charter, Former Alberta Premier Peter Loughheed*

In early June 1999, I had the privilege of receiving an honorary doctorate from Queens University in Kingston, Ontario. After the graduation ceremony, my guests and I enjoyed a sumptuous lunch at the university. At lunch, I sat next to the university's chancellor, Peter Loughheed. In 1980, he was Alberta's premier and one of Pierre Trudeau's most tenacious opponents during negotiations over the Constitution's patriation. He had staunchly opposed the *Charter*. I had a captive audience! What a chance to ask juicy questions about the disability amendment. Once again, I lost a golden opportunity.

## *7. Meeting a Charter Opponent, Former Manitoba Premier Sterling Lyon*

Earlier in this chapter, I described how, starting sometime in the 1990s, I began to annually teach new federally appointed judges about disability issues as part of a New Judges course. In one of my sessions, my students included Manitoba Court of Appeal Justice Sterling Lyon. In 1980, he had been the premier of Manitoba. He too was a major opponent to entrenching the *Charter*. I would love to have debated that with him. Instead, he had to listen to me teach him about the importance of the constitutional right to equality that we had won for people with disabilities, a right that he, as a judge, must now vigorously enforce.

## *8. Meeting Former Conservative Member of Parliament David Crombie*

As if all those encounters were not more than I could have hoped for, I got to share a public stage for a few minutes in 2004 with the very person who brought the motion at the Joint Committee to pass the disability amendment, former Conservative Member of Parliament David Crombie. This is the only time our paths had crossed since the December 1980 Joint Committee hearings. An organization called the Canadian Foundation for the Physically Disabled holds an annual event to induct people into the Terry Fox Hall of Fame (which has since been renamed the Canadian Disability Hall of Fame). In 2004, I was one of the four individuals inducted into that body. Crombie was the master of ceremony of the lovely luncheon where I received that award. He was the one who presented the award to me, making it all the more meaningful. In his remarks, he commented in a flattering way on my deputation before the Joint Committee those many years earlier.

## *9. Meeting Other Key Players*

During the summer of 1991, I had the privilege of attending and chairing a panel at the Cambridge Lectures, one of the pre-eminent Canadian law conferences. Organized in Canada, the conference is held in facilities rented at Cambridge University in the United Kingdom. My panel was entitled "Choosing the Road to Equality." I grilled panellists on which was the most effective avenue for advancing equality: human rights legislation, the *Charter*, or political action. Speaking about the strengths of using the political process was former NDP Member of Parliament Lorne Nystrom, who had actively pressed Justice Minister Chrétien to support the disability amendment during the Joint Committee's clause-by-clause debates.

Almost two decades later, I rounded out my plethora of encounters with major actors on the disability amendment's sound stage when I was invited to speak at an event in 2010 to honour the 25th anniversary of section 15 of the *Charter*'s going into effect. In my speech, I reflected on some of the themes expanded upon in this retrospective. Attending this conference was an impressive list of key players from the heady days of the patriation debates. Among those I got to meet, albeit briefly, were former Saskatchewan Attorney General Roy Romano (who was a central player in negotiating the final deal that led to the Constitution's patriation, along with Chrétien and McMurtry), former Conservative leader Joe Clark, former NDP leader Ed Broadbent, and one of the Joint Committee members who pressed for the disability amendment especially vigorously, former NDP Member of Parliament Svend Robinson.

### *10. Meeting Time and Again with Former Ontario Attorney General Roy McMurtry*

I cannot conclude this list without an honourable mention for McMurtry. I have met him innumerable times over the years and consider him a valued friend and my guardian angel! Had he not played a key role in the patriation deal's final compromise, I might not have had a retrospective to write. Had he not played a critical role in my getting my first job, I have no idea how my career would have unfolded.

## I. Epilogue or Prologue?

It is my fondest hope that young, inexperienced, untrained people with disabilities will grab any opportunities they can to aim to achieve the impossible. Any number of people with disabilities in Canada tried that four decades ago, with too little time and, in my case, as an example, while oblivious to what others were doing at the same time. I hope this epilogue might serve as a prologue to disability advocacy to come! I was able in this retrospective to name just some of the figures involved in this saga, like David Smith, Dayton Foreman, Robert Mercer, Yvonne Peters, Jim Derksen, Orville Endicott, David Vickers, David Crombie, Svend Robinson, and Barry Strayer. I am saddened that too many of them as well as others involved in these events are no longer alive to know that this story is documented here.

Thankfully, some are still with us. Canada is indebted to them and to all the other people with disabilities, buttressed by their supporters and community organizations, who in one way or another helped make the impossible possible. I am so fortunate that circumstances conspired to give me a chance to contribute to this history. On 10 May 2005, a quarter of a century after we won the disability amendment, I received sacred advice from, of all places, a fortune cookie that I was served at lunch in a Chinese restaurant in downtown Toronto. That afternoon, the Ontario legislature was about to pass the *AODA*, for which I led the campaign throughout the preceding decade.[15] As I earlier described, it is legislation that is aimed at implementing the disability amendment and its companion guarantees in the Ontario *Human Rights Code*. That visionary fortune cookie's wise advice resoundingly speaks to the disability amendment to the *Charter* in 1981 as well as to the enactment of the *AODA* a quarter of a century later. The cookie's fortune read: "Every great accomplishment is at first impossible."

[15] *Accessibility for Ontarians with Disabilities Act*, SO 2005, c 11, s 41.

# APPENDIX 1: HANSARD OF THE PRESENTATION BY THE CANADIAN NATIONAL INSTITUTE FOR THE BLIND TO THE MEETING OF THE SPECIAL JOINT COMMITTEE OF THE SENATE AND THE HOUSE OF COMMONS ON THE CONSTITUTION OF CANADA, 12 DECEMBER 1980

SENATE
HOUSE OF COMMONS
**Issue no. 25**
Friday, December 12, 1980

*Minutes of Proceedings and Evidence of the Special Joint Committee of the Senate and of the House of Commons on the*

**Constitution of Canada**

RESPECTING:

The document entitled "Proposed Resolution for a Joint Address to Her Majesty the Queen respecting the Constitution of Canada" published by the Government on October 2, 1980

First Session of the Thirty-second Parliament, 1980

*Representing the Senate:*
Senators Austin, Connolly, Cottreau, Donahoe, Lamontagne, Lapointe, Lucier, Murray, Tremblay - (10)

*Representing the House of Commons:*
Messrs. Allmand, Bockstael, Campbell (Miss) (*Southwest Nova*), Corbin, Dantzer, Epp, Fraser, Hawkes, Irwin, Lapierre, Mackasey, McGrath, Nystrom, Ogle - (15)

(Quorum 12)

Richard Prégent
Paul Bélisle

*Joint Clerks of the Committee*

Pursuant to S.O. 65(4)(b) of the House of Commons:

On Friday, December 12, 1980:

Mr. Corbin replaced Mr. Henderson;
Mr. Althouse replaced Mr. Robinson (Burnaby);
Mr. Allmand replaced Mrs. Côté;
Mr. Ogle replaced Mr. Althouse.

Pursuant to an order of the Senate adopted November 5, 1980:

On Friday, December 12, 1980:

Senator Connolly replaced Senator Cottreau;
Senator Cottreau replaced Senator Wood;
Senator Muir replaced Senator Tremblay.

MINUTES OF PROCEEDINGS

FRIDAY, DECEMBER 12, 1980

(45)

[Translation]

The Special Joint Committee on the Constitution of Canada met this day at 9:35 o'clock am., the Joint Chairman, Senator Hays, presiding.

*Members of the Committee present:*

*Representing the Senate:* The Honourable Senators Austin, Connolly, Cottreau, Donahoe, Hays, Lamontagne, Lapointe, Lucier, Muir and Murray.

*Representing the House of Commons:* Messrs. Allmand, Althouse, Bockstael, Corbin, Dantzer, Epp, Fraser. Hargrave, Hawkes, Irwin, Joyal, Lapierre, Nystrom and Ogle.

*Other Member present:* Mr. Robinson (*Burnaby*).

*In attendance: From the Parliamentary Centre:* Mr. Peter Dobell, Director. *From the Research Branch of the Library of Parliament: Mr. Louis* Massicotte, Researcher.

*Witnesses: From the Canadian National Institute for the Blind:* Mr. Robert Mercer, National Managing Director; Dr. Dayton Foreman, National Vice-President; Mr. David Lepofsky, Member of the Ontario Board of Directors. *From the World Federalists of Canada — Operation Dismantle:* Dr. Francis

Leddy, National President of World Federalists of Canada; Mr. T. James Stark, Director, Operation Dismantle.

The Committee resumed consideration of its Order of Reference from the Senate dated November 3, 1980 and its Order of Reference from the House of Commons dated October 23, 1980, both relating to the document entitled "Proposed Resolution for a Joint Address to Her Majesty the Queen respecting the Constitution of Canada" published by the Government on October 2, 1980. (*See Minutes of Proceedings, Thursday, November 6, 1980, Issue No. 1.*)

The witnesses of the Canadian National Institute for the Blind made statements and answered questions.

The witnesses of the World Federalists of Canada, Operation Dismantle, made statements and answered questions.

Friday, December 12, 1980

**The Joint Chairman (Senator Hays): May I call the meeting to order.**

We are honoured this morning to have with us the Canadian National Institute for the Blind, represented by Mr. Robert Mercer, Doctor Dayton Foreman, and Mr. David Lepofsky.

As you know, the procedure is that you would make an opening statement, then members should like to question you.

You may proceed.

**Dr. Dayton Foreman (Vice-President, National Council. Canadian National Institute for the Blind):** Mr. Chairman and members of the Senate, House of Commons Committee, as Vice-President of the Canadian National Institute for the Blind's National Council, its volunteer Board of Directors, I am privileged to be, once again, a part of a group coming to assist in deliberations of this government and Parliament and also to field your questions.

Our group today consists of the fifth Managing Director of the Institute, Mr, Robert Mercer, who was appointed by National Council on September 1, 1980. He is the chief executive officer of this National Institute and will outline some concerns that he has.

Our third speaker is a fellow-volunteer, Mr. Lepofsky, who will speak on some points in our brief which have been submitted.

In advance, I would like to thank you for your time and hope we can answer some of the questions you will be asking.

**The Joint Chairman (Senator Hays): Mr. Mercer.**

**Mr. Robert Mercer (Fifth Managing Director, Canadian National Institute for the Blind):** Mr. Chairman, members of the Committee, the Canadian National Institute for the Blind was incorporated federally in 1918 with the dual purpose of providing services in this country to people who were blind as well as to prevent blindness in Canada.

We are a service agency, and as such we would like to make the point this morning that we do not profess to represent the views in Canada of all people who are blind, particularly on a major issue which will be addressed by Mr. Lepofsky a little later.

However, we would like to indicate that, as a service agency, working with blind people in this country, we are the largest and have a long history of involvement with blind people and generally with the community.

We have taken a great deal of time on this matter of human rights to listen carefully to what blind people have been saying and to what other handicapped people have said as well, and in putting forward our position this morning, we say, with some assurance. that what we have to say represents in fact the view of many people who are handicapped in this country, and we trust that this Committee will take most seriously the concerns that handicapped people have in this Canada in your later deliberations.

I would like to call on David Lepofsky, who is a member of the Ontario Division Board of Management of the Canadian National Institute for the Blind to present the position of CNIB on the subject of human rights.

**The Joint Chairman (Senator Hays):** Mr. Lepofsky.

**Mr. David Lepofsky (Member, Ontario Division Board of Management, Canadian National Institute for the Blind):** Mr. Chairman, I would like to begin with my thanking you both as a volunteer member of CNIB Ontario Board and as a blind individual for this opportunity to speak to you on what is a crucial issue in our view.

I would indicate at the outset two things, the first of which is I believe all the members of the committee have a letter from the Committee addressed to me from the Ontario Federation of the Physically Handicapped, a federation of some 37 organizations which deal with various kinds of disabilities, a letter endorsing the position articulated in our written brief. I would ask in pursuance of what Mr. Mercer has just said, that this is indicative of the kind of support for all of you which exists amongst all kinds of disabled persons and not merely persons with a visual handicap.

I would ask at this time, Mr. Chairman, that in the spirit of the equality which we are promoting here, the clerk to pass around to the various members — if they prefer not to read our brief in print, they have the choice of reading it on a cassette or in Braille; I would ask the clerk to pass them around, and I apologize that there will not be enough for absolutely everyone, but we would be pleased to provide you with extras if they are needed in the future.

**The Joint Chairman (Senator Hays):** Thank you very much; they are being passed around.

**Mr. Lepofsky:** As I say, it is demonstrative of our efforts towards equality and our concern about the equality of blind and other handicapped persons.

Mr. Chairman, to begin, I would like to mention a point which may come as a surprise to some. The biggest problem very often with being handicapped — and so far as CNIB are concerned — is not blindness or the handicap. Blindness, visual handicap or other kinds of disability, are frequently conditions which one can learn to adjust to through training, with which one can learn to cope and ultimately achieve some substantial, if not total, degree of independence, self sufficiency and self worth.

The biggest problem very often resulting from blindness or other handicap is the well intentioned cruelty which many members of the public unintentionally or unknowingly impose upon us. The pity the patronization, discriminatory attitudes and condescension which handicapped people know to be, unfortunately, almost nonstop components of their life, is in fact the biggest problem they face.

A handicapped person, in the case we are discussing today, namely that of a blind person, can learn through specific training to overcome the limitations imposed by their blindness, so that blindness no longer functions in most cases as "a handicap"; in fact it can become at times merely a marginal aspect of one's life, compelling one to read in Braille rather than from print or to use a guide dog or cane to get from point A to B, rather than using one's eyes, but nonetheless accomplishing substantially the same things as a sighted person would.

Once one has achieved this degree of independence, however, the problem that is confronted by the majority of handicapped persons is the fact that the public is not often ready to accept us as equals, not by reason of malevolence, but because of uninformed or misinformed attitudes, underestimating our capabilities by fear of the handicapped person — you might call it the "freak syndrome," not perceiving a handicapped person as just a normal human being. This is manifested in several ways, many of which are frightening and harmful.

Job discrimination against the disabled is something which the public are only now becoming conscious of; the fact that once you have learned to do a job, the fact that you are ready to go out into the market and be competitive, you will find the only barrier you have is not your blindness or other handicap, but the employer who cannot believe you can function.

Housing and other facilities a landlord may not be permitted to rent because a blind person might be considered a health hazard and people do not want to look at someone who has cerebral palsy because it might be somehow unpalatable to look at in the opinion of some.

Educational systems are accessible primarily to nondisabled persons, but only to a limited degree to disabled persons, and, of course, as we all know, most buildings are not accessible.

These are functions of an attitude that the world simply does not contain handicapped people or that those handicapped people are not going to be out there trying to get job, trying to get into housing or buildings.

Our concern is generally with this attitude, and CNIB as well as other organizations have taken many steps, both with public education and also lobbying, to change this. Where this kind of problem with attitudes becomes perhaps most frightening and most requiring of action, is something which is addressed in the Charter of Rights which is before you.

Handicapped people in the struggle for equality and equality of opportunity find that not only do people discriminate in the access to jobs, buildings, facilities, services and housing, but that, in fact, legislators, persons passing laws have also experienced the same negative attitudes towards the handicapped and have passed laws which are in fact discriminatory.

Accordingly, the major thrust of our presentation is that it is necessary that they should be included in Section 15 of the Charter of Rights, the so-called equality or nondiscrimination clause, and be referred to as a protected class, mentally or physically handicapped persons.

We are not looking at this as a means of getting jobs or housing, because that is something which is done at the federal or provincial Human Rights Code level, and we are actually lobbying for that.

Here, we are concerned with not just human conduct which is discriminatory, but legislation which discriminates,

Why should we be included in Section 15? Why are handicapped people entitled to equality before the law and to the equal protection of the law?

To begin with, I am sure you have all come to the conclusion yourselves and you have heard from other groups, as the clause is presently drafted it is unarguable, unquestionable that handicapped persons are not entitled to equality before the law.

By this exclusion, it perpetuates in our Constitution an attitude which, as I have mentioned, is prevalent in society, some notion of handicapped people as second class citizens, people who need to be taken care of, not given independence, protected, not given the opportunity of equality.

Inclusion in Section 15 for the handicapped would be consistent with what is the stated intention of the government with respect to the Charter of Rights. I refer to a statement made by the Minister of External Affairs, Mr. Mark MacGuigan, in speaking at a public forum on the constitution some weeks ago in Toronto, when I asked him about the handicapped issue. He had said that the Charter of Rights was central to the government's package of reforms and that equality for all minorities is central to the Charter of Rights.

If that is the intention, then that intention is thwarted by the present proposed Section 15 because equality for all minorities is not provided. Equality for some is the rubric or the essence of Section 15 as it stands, and it is a respectful submission of the Canadian National Institute for the Blind that, if the intention of the government is to, in fact, give equality to all minorities and is, given the fact that there are some hundreds of thousands or millions of handicapped persons in Canada all told, there is a minority that requires protection. That is not disputed. So the government's intention must only be manifested, it is our view, if we are included.

Moreover, if the purpose of the equality clause is truly to grant equality, one must look at its wording. It provides equality for certain minorities: in other words, it involves equality for some; and equality for some, I submit really means equality for none. It means that there are two levels in society, one level of people who are entitled to equality and one level who are not. And when you have two distinct classes such as that the term "equality" has been stripped of its meaning and rendered more of an illusion.

Accordingly, if equality is the goal, then it must be equality for all and "all" must include, we submit, handicapped. Now, as I said previously, Mr. MacGuigan in his statement, in answer to certain questions I put to him about the handicapped issue, acknowledged that the handicapped are not included and raised the question whether handicapped people need protection in a bill of rights, whether they need egalitarian liberties. His statement was that what the handicapped need are jobs and access to buildings, and these are economic not political or egalitarian liberties, and are not the kinds of things that are required in a constitution.

Now, in a world that was not our own, where economic liberties were generally being entrenched, I would be prepared to address issues such as jobs and architectural access in the constitution; but we are not going to address that today because we recognize the constraints under which Canada and the Parliament are operating. However, I would like to address the statement that Mr. MacGuigan made, speaking at that time on behalf of the government on the Constitution. He said that what handicapped people need is not constitutional protection for equality, and it is our submission that Mr. MacGuigan's view is inaccurate. In fact, when I pointed out certain things that I am about to point out to you, he explained that he had never heard of them before and would probably need to rethink the whole issue.

Legislation, as I said, in many instances discriminates against the disabled. You have heard this before, but I believe that we will be the first handicapped group that will in fact itemize examples. Many statutes across Canada, both federally and provincially, which provide that everyone is entitled to a minimum wage when they are in the employment situation provide exemptions for handicapped persons. That is discrimination under or in law with respect to a legal right to a certain minimum wage.

Certain statutes explain when that right is to be administered and when not; certain do not. They merely say that the government has or a Minister has the power to give a licence to allow an employer to pay less than minimum wage, without giving reasons. This is not equality, this is discrimination, in our view.

Many statutes across Canada dealing with eligibility to sit on juries exclude blind persons from the right to serve on juries. Now, there are times when vision may be needed to serve as a juror. It is not our view that every trial should always be open for a blind person to sit on a jury; however, there are, and as a law student and soon to be a lawyer, I can speak with some limited knowledge of this, there are many cases where vision is not necessary and probably the lack of vision may be of benefit to a juror. So, legislation which just blanketly excludes blind persons without reference to their ability or inability to function as a juror, is discriminatory. The marriage legislation in Ontario provides in Section 7 that a marriage licence cannot be granted to someone who is mentally defective. It does not refer to whether their mental limitation is so serious that it would impede their ability to understand or consent to a marriage agreement. It merely excludes someone who is mentally defective from the right to be married. Such, in our submission, is discriminatory.

The Family Benefits Act in Ontario, a piece of welfare legislation, provides in one section that certain handicapped persons who are in institutions and entitled to certain welfare payments may, by executive order, have those payments paid to a civil servant, a director of the institution or whatever — I do not have the details here, unfortunately — rather than to the handicapped persons themselves. It does not ever require that a handicapped person's right to receive welfare can be impeded only if that person is incapable of managing their own affairs. It merely says any handicapped person, so that if it is a person who is perfectly capable of handling that money capably, nonetheless their right can be taken away by executive action, perfectly legally under a statute of the province of Ontario. Such is legislation which discriminates.

The Education Act in Ontario, Mr. Chairman, provides that a handicapped person, whether physically or mentally handicapped, can be excluded from the right to go to their local elementary school if they are "incapable of profiting by instruction." And then a separate school system is established to deal with those situations. Now education is a big and serious issue and

I do not intend to address it in its totality here, but I think it is fair to say that a provision that says that only where handicapped people cannot profit from instruction, only those people are excluded from the right to go to their local schools. If it is a nonhandicapped person who for some other reason is incapable of profiting from instruction, the statue does not exclude them from the right to go to their local schools. Such is unequal treatment; such is discriminatory, at least prima facie, in our submission.

Other legislation, and I will only deal with other legislation briefly, British Columbia schools legislation, Section 107(5) provides, Mr. Chairman, in certain circumstances that an employee of a board of education who is totally and permanently disabled — and I could not find a definition in the act of that term — cannot be hired by the board until they lose their disability. Now, certain disabled persons cannot function in a teaching environment, but others can. So, such a blanket exemption, if applied against any person with any disability, would be, in fact, discriminatory; and I bring to your attention that blind persons are functioning both in Canada and the United States in the teaching profession.

I am not sure if that act would include blind people within their definition of total and permanent disability, but there is the risk, and that is discriminatory legislation with which we are concerned.

The Immigration Act passed by the government some couple of years ago in Section 19(1) provides a higher burden on a handicapped person who proposes to immigrate to Canada. If that handicapped person can meet all the requirements required of a non-handicapped person, able to support themselves, finding a job, et cetera, et cetera, they still must prove to a medical officer that they will not be an excessive demand on health and social services. There is not requirement that other persons wanting to immigrate have to prove that they will not provide such a demand on health and social services. Such separate treatment not applied to all immigrants is discriminatory in our view.

I would submit that there are other laws that do discriminate but I think that these are sufficiently illustrative to respond to the suggestion that we need no constitutional protection, the legislatures can take care of it themselves. This is evidence of how the legislatures have taken care of handicapped rights to equality and moreover, Mr. Chairman, I think that it rebuts the suggestion made by Mr. MacGuigan a couple of weeks ago in response to my question, that handicapped people simply need rights to jobs; they can be provided by statutes, they do not need constitutional rights.

Moving on, Mr. Chairman, I would say that there are other reasons why we need to be included in the clause providing for equality. We are a substantial minority. We are not talking about a very small number of people. We have 30,000 clients registered at CNIB and Dr. Foremen can provide you with information of how many other visually handicapped people, as well as other handicapped people, may well be out in the community. Some have suggested that there are one in ten persons in Canada handicapped in some way and therefore would benefit from the kind of constitutional protection we are talking about.

There are a couple of arguments that have been raised primarily by spokesmen for the government — in one instance, I think it is the Minister of Justice, Mr. Chrétien — against handicapped inclusion. One argument that he made is that we should not include it now because it is hard to define the term handicapped. We should wait until we can come up with a definition and put it in through an amending formula. Well, with respect to the Minister of Justice, I do not believe that position is tenable.

Firstly, if this Committee requires information on how to define handicapped, having looked over most Canadian statutes that contain the word and have various definitions over the past few days, I have found that some statutes do not even bother defining it but those that do have been able to effectively, and having done some research on this particular issue myself, I am more than happy to supply you with information to show that definition of handicapped would be no problem.

Secondly, leaving it to an amending formula is not a realistic proposition, because the process of amendment which requires a lot of lobbying, a lot of time, a lot of money, would not be in our view, probably manageable by handicapped persons being for the most part served by not altogether wealthy, non-profit organizations who live off of charity donations in many cases, and handicapped people themselves often living at or below the poverty line.

So the amendment process will simply not be open to us as a practical matter, I submit. But more importantly, definitional arguments I do not think are persuasive in saying that handicapped persons not be included. Many terms are included, both in this Charter of Rights as proposed and in the British North America Act, 1867, which are much more vague than is the word handicapped, or mental or physical handicap. We note that in Section 15 they refer to discrimination on the grounds of religion. Mr. Chairman, I would invite anyone to define what religion means in a comprehensive manner. I think that that term, while we know that certain religions, Judaism, Christianity, Buddhism are religions, there will be many borderline cases where we do not know if those groups are religions or not. But that has not precluded the drafters of this Charter form including religion.

You will note in the British North America Act that under Section 91, criminal law is given to the federal government. We have had 100 years of litigation over what criminal law means in the constitution but that never stopped the framers of the BNA Act from including the words "criminal law" within that constitutional document.

And finally, in Section I, of the proposed Charter, the words "reasonable limits" are used, which I would submit are incredibly harder to define, if not impossible to define, than are the words "mental or physical handicap." Accordingly, I do not think one can simply avoid the issue or duck the issue because of definitional problems.

The final reason that I would like to articulate for including handicapped in Section 15 concerns an argument that some have raised against it: namely, that the costs occasioned by including the handicapped would be excessive. I have several responses to that argument.

Number one, I would ask what those costs would be. I am not altogether clear and I would submit that there probably are not that many. Intuitively nothing really comes to mind as being excessively costly.

Secondly, I would submit that unless this Committee is going to go through the process of looking at every liberty enumerated in the Charter of Rights and say how much will this one cost, should we include it, is it too expensive?

Unless we are to do that with every single liberty then there is a certain inequality to simply looking at one group, namely the handicapped, and say that they will be excluded on the basis of a cost argument. And so, if that argument is presented before this Committee, I would ask that your bear that in mind. And finally, if that argument is presented before this Committee, that is that including handicapped would be too costly, I would ask you to bear the following argument in mind, or the following point in mind.

To say that the cost is too excessive is to assume that handicap inclusion is the absolute lowest priority of every government in Canada, that we have spent every last dollar of revenue we have taxed and collected and that there is no money left. If you were to look at the priorities of the various governments, provincial and federal, of spending, you might find that there are others that are lower priority than handicapped equality and you might find that it might be worth including the handicapped in the constitution and perhaps let some more inconsequential programs go by the board.

I do not think it is fair to simply say it costs too much, therefore we cannot do it.

Moving very quickly through the other points of ours, because the other points we have made are ones which other groups have made as well, we recommend not only that handicapped be included in the Charter, Section 15, but we would prefer it if the Charter read something like equality before the law without unreasonable discrimination or without unreasonable distinction. Unreasonable discrimination meaning without restricting the generality of the foregoing, and then you can put a list of protected classes and include mental or physical handicap.

The reason we suggest this is because if an equality clause is truly to give us equality, it must give us equality with all others. And that is the way to do it.

It has been suggested before this Committee that perhaps it would be best to simply say equality before the law without discrimination, period, no reference to a list of protected classes. Now, that would be preferable to what is proposed in the present bill, but in our view, it is not desirable for the following reasons.

Firstly, it would mean that some thousands and thousands of dollars would be required going to court, appealing up to the Supreme Court of Canada, in order to get a precedent that decides whether handicapped is a class protected by the clause. To avoid that kind of cost, delay and uncertainty, it could be easily included now without any such costs.

And secondly, Mr. Chairman, the fact of the matter is, if we have to go to court and argue it, there is no guarantee that we will be included by the courts. The courts take a very restrictive view of civil liberties in general, and handicapped civil liberties is a new area in Canadian law and therefore the risk is that we may never get in, even after an appeal process. So the only way of guaranteeing our rights is by including us.

Briefly, Mr. Chairman, we recommend, as is mentioned in our brief, that the words "equality before the law" and "equal protection of the law" are far too weak a means of protecting egalitarian liberties. You have heard this from other groups and we endorse the views that have been presented namely that the courts under the present bill have interpreted those words to not provide egalitarian liberties, and they have done it in an unequivocal way. And these words, even though there is one word that is different, these words are far too close, far too close to the existing Bill of Rights to ensure anyone that the courts will use this as a strong lever to nullify discriminatory laws. It is our concern that, once again the same amendment argument goes, if we get bad precedent, we have to go through the amending process, and we have seen in the State with the ERA battle how many years and at what cost that fight is and that there is no certainty of success.

More importantly, it is our view that the courts have a tradition of taking a very restrictive view of civil liberties. Now, that is not by way of criticism or by way of anything less than respect for the members of the judiciary, but it is something which is, nonetheless, true, I think that it will be necessary, and it is our submission that it will be necessary for strong direction to be given to the courts through very specific wording directing them to invalidate discriminatory legislation.

Moving to the end of my presentation, Mr. Chairman, it is our submission, as you will see in our brief, that Section I should not govern either Section 14 or Section 15. It is our view that there should be no circumstances where the right to an interpreter, which a deaf-blind or just a deaf person may require in court, should ever be taken away. Why is it either in war or emergency that a deaf-blind person on trial should be denied an interpreter to know what the case is against them. It is too basic and a denial of natural justice.

Moreover, when should unwarranted discrimination be permitted? At wartime? At peacetime? In the case of an emergency? It is hard to imagine a situation where it is justifiable, and therefore we have recommended, as have other groups, that Section 14 and Section 15 be absolute rights, rights not subject to Section 1.

Alternatively, if that point of view is not acceptable to the Committee, it is our submission that the wording in Section I is far, far too broad. You have heard all the arguments before, we can only reiterate them, that Section 1 — labelled by some as the Mack truck provision — will in fact make the rest of the Charter of Rights a virtually worthless and impotent means of protecting civil liberties,

In particular, the generally accepted view of the public with respect to handicapped persons is that they are often not capable of taking care of themselves, not capable of maintaining a job, not capable of self-sufficiency, and therefore the kinds of laws that I have discussed previously that are discriminatory would be under Section I generally accepted in a free and democratic society, passed by these kinds of Parliaments. And accordingly, if Section 1 remains, and if Section 15 is still subject to it, it is our view that Section 1 must be very narrowly constrained to protect minority rights and in particular, handicapped rights.

Finally, it is our submission that Section 29(2), which provides that the equality clause will go into effect later than all other parts of the bill should be repealed, simply because there is no good reason in our view why egalitarian liberties should be delayed. If anything, they should be accelerated.

In conclusion, I would like to make the following points. Our concern is that there is a danger of misleading people if the Charter does not include the handicapped. There is the danger that people will believe that in Canada under such a provision, egalitarian liberties are truly safeguarded, there is equality for all. Without handicapped inclusion such is not the case. And it is not only unfair to handicapped persons to deny them equality, but it is a risky venture for the public to be misled into believing that all minorities are protected when they are in fact not.

Our concern, as I said at the outset, is dealing with public attitudes. Public attitudes are something which we must battle at various levels. At the constitutional level we are battling public attitudes as they are manifested through legislation, and this is a battle which is both serious and crucial.

Finally, I would close by saying that there is an oft stated adage that justice is blind; in fact it is a cliché.

Our concern — and the underlying concern of this presentation — is that while justice may have had the opportunity to experience blindness, we are asking for blind persons, as well as for other handicapped persons, to be given at last an opportunity to experience justice.

**The Joint Chairman (Senator Hays):** Thank you very much, Mr. Lepofsky.

Inasmuch as Mr. Lepofsky and his group have given us a thorough understanding of their brief, we have a few minutes left.

We have another group scheduled to be here at 10.15 this morning and the House sits at 11 o'clock, I am wondering if I could have some agreement that we have three questions on it and that we could probably terminate at 10:20 or 10:25 and have our time as five minutes rather than the 10-minute round?

Mr. Epp.

**Mr. Epp:** Mr. Chairman, I was going to make the recommendation and Mr. Lepofsky has been excellent in the presentation and on this topic; and there are just two points: one, he kindly offered us to make information available re definition of the handicapped. I hope I have stated that correctly, but I would ask the Committee to request of Mr. Lepofsky that he make that information available to us, though it does not necessarily have to be appended to the minutes of this hearing, but that the information be circulated.

Secondly, I would recommend, Mr. Chairman, instead of the 10-minute round for the witnesses this morning, that you reduce it to five minutes, and if there are any questions after that first round we will leave that with the Chair.

**The Joint Chairman (Senator Hays):** Thank you very much. Is that agreed?

**Some hon. Members:** Agreed.

**The Joint Chairman (Senator Hays):** I see that is agreed.

Senator Donahoe.

**Senator Donahoe:** Thank you, Mr. Chairman.

Gentlemen, I am very happy that good fortune presented me this morning with the opportunity of sitting in on this Committee as a substitute for one of the regular members, because I am very pleased to have had the opportunity of hearing the very excellent presentation made by Mr. Lepofsky.

I was interested to hear the illustration that was given of discrimination possibly against an unsighted juror, because in my experience as an Attorney General for many years, I was once faced with the application for appointment as a Crown Prosecutor by a blind person.

He was an excellent lawyer, a good student and so on; but he was asking to be made a Crown prosecutor to conduct criminal prosecutions.

I would ask you to believe that it was a matter of real difficulty for me to determine whether or not that handicap, in fact, was of a nature which detracted from his ability to do the fullest and most complete job in that particular capacity.

I want to say that I did, in fact, appoint the gentlemen and that he conducted himself with great credit for a number of years.

But I wonder if the person who suffers the handicap can appreciate the difficulty that a person in the position in which I was at that time might have had in determining whether they are in fact discriminating against that person because of the handicap or whether they are in fact merely endeavouring to see that their obligations and responsibilities are discharged in the best possible manner.

However, I do not wish to say or to ask too much, because I think your presentation was, indeed, excellent and from the point of view of the organization for which you are speaking and the people whom it represents, it has been exceedingly well put here this morning.

I would like to ask this simple question. Do you believe that the position of the handicapped will be substantially improved or enhanced if this procedure is followed? The procedure that is suggested is to entrench certain rights.

You have indicated that you find the suggestions inadequate, insufficient and in need of substantial amendment, and that those amendments should be specifically directed towards the class of person for whom you are speaking here this morning.

Do you feel that the position of the handicapped is going to be very much improved and very much enhanced if this procedure is followed with or without your suggested amendments?

**Mr. Lepofsky:** Mr. Chairman, to answer both your points, understanding the fact that an employer or service must go through a very difficult analysis and thought process to decide what one is capable of, is something which is only too well understood by any handicapped person, because before someone like myself decided to go into law school I had to make that same analysis.

So it is something which not only I have thought about, but I would think about it before any of my potential employers have thought about it.

It is a very difficult process. The equality clause, if it included the disabled, would give us a right, in the instance where a legislature had gone through that thought process and in fact had made a wrong decision in the passage of laws which end up discriminating, would give us a right to appeal that to the court and to argue that it is an unreasonable distinction which is being drawn against handicapped persons.

My first point would be, Mr. Chairman, that this would provide a means or mechanism for handicapped persons and other interested groups, to challenge legislation which is discriminatory. If these provisions are not put in, then it would signal to the disabled that it is the prevailing view in Canada that handicapped people are not entitled to equality before the law and that the kinds of discrimination that are experienced by any handicapped person in their everyday life are in fact representing a pervasive view which in fact has been articulated through the actions of the framers of the new constitution.

On the other hand, if this provision is included as we have proposed, several benefits would accrue, I would submit. The first is that next year being the International Year of the Disabled Person, it would show Canada as doing what could be the best possible move to ensure disabled persons equality, which is to pass a constitution enshrining their rights; secondly, it would be a signal to the Canadian people that as regards handicapped persons, who in the past have either been a forgotten minority or a lesser class of citizen — and I say this was not intentional or out of malevolence; but it has happened nonetheless — that a new era has dawned and that as deeply felt a concern is being presented to Canada as can be expressed through a Charter of fundamental rights as acknowledging this liberty.

As I say, some of the more odious legislation, some of which I have already enumerated, would be amenable to attack. I know that certain lobbying has succeeded in Ontario, and lobbying by certain groups have inspired the

Ontario legislature, after 100 years of having similar legislation to finally change it, and it is now about to get the Royal Assent, but the process of getting the reform has taken a long time. Had we an equality clause we could have had it adjudicated upon and probably won the matter possibly much more quickly. It was only, frankly, out of luck, that in our view this amendment ever came through.

**The Joint Chairman (Senator Hays):** Thank you very much.

We have Mr. Althouse followed by Senator Connolly.

Mr. Althouse.

**Mr. Althouse:** Thank you, Mr. Joint Chairman.

Other evidence seems to suggest that the disabled and handicapped people suffer an unemployment rate of between 70 per cent and 80 per cent. I note in your remarks this morning that you mentioned employers who do not believe you can function as one of the big handicaps you are facing.

Is that the greatest difficulty faced by blind people, for instance, access to opportunity to function? Will the proposed amendment encourage this access to opportunity in your opinion?

**Mr. Lepofsky:** I would agree that the access to jobs and other facilities is perhaps the greatest problem. As I said, it is the attitude to the public that is the greatest problem and perhaps is the worst manifestation of it, aside from the other manifestation I have mentioned, namely the legislative discrimination.

Our proposals would not require employers to hire a handicapped person who can do the job. That is something which is dealt with by the Human Rights Code. I would say that we are involved in lobbying along with many other organizations for amendments to such laws. I am personally involved in that and could give you a lot of information on the subject if necessary.

It would, however, have two beneficial effects on the employment situation. The first is that, by entrenching this in a charter of rights, as I have said before, it would be a signal to the Canadian public that handicapped people are entitled to equality. That is an educational effect which would be of profound importance and help.

Secondly, there is the possibility and I did not mention this in my list of discriminatory legislation, because a good law student is told that you should use your weakest argument at the end or drop them altogether; but the federal Human Rights Code provides protection for the handicapped in the area of employment, but does not refer to them in the area of access to services or goods. I would say that is a form of discrimination. As you know, the Canadian Human Rights Commission has recommended amendments to cover that.

I would be interested to know if we could build a case that we are getting unequal treatment under the Human Rights Code, since in certain provinces we are not included at all in the code, and in other provinces we are only given partial protection.

But that is a case as to which, while I would like to argue it personally, I am not overwhelmed by the fact that it would be successful. But the most important point is the educational effect on the public and that laws which are a barrier to education, a barrier to equal opportunity, and signals second-class citizenship for the handicapped to the public, would be attackable by us.

**Mr. Althouse:** In this regard, the slow movement towards access to jobs and equal access to buildings and services, I note one of the supporting groups, the Federation of the Physically Handicapped for Ontario, has mentioned in supporting documents which were passed out along with your brief, that Section 29, they make the point — in the proposal before us places a restriction on the implementation of such rights; under Section 29 it is stated that there will be a three-year waiting period, and they would not come into effect any sooner than the amending formula.

What is the reaction of your group to this waiting period? Your group of handicapped individuals seem to be the only group that have been singled out for this by subsection (2).

**Mr. Lepofsky:** I would say it is a concern of ours. The delay, if anything, is undesirable; and we would prefer to have seen an equality provision protecting us in effect ten years ago. However, I am bound to confess it is not our major concern. Our principal concern is getting into the bill in one form or another at all.

**The Joint Chairman (Senator Hays):** Thank you very much.

Senator Connolly.

**Senator Connolly:** Thank you, Mr. Chairman.

First of all, we are all very happy indeed to have the CNIB here, because over the years this organization has done a tremendous amount, and I think perhaps the witnesses might agree that the important feature of that work is the fact that they have helped so much to promote the integration particularly of blind people into the community, into society and all phases of Canadian life. This is a great achievement on the part of the CNIB and of the people who work with them.

But may I also, on a personal basis, congratulate Mr. Lepofsky for the very lucid, very comprehensive statement that he has made. I predict that he is going to be a very good lawyer. I would hope that he might become a member of Parliament, but I would tell him immediately that he will not be the first person who is without sight who has been in the House of Commons. I do not say that as a joke. There are lots there who perhaps physically see, but perhaps mentally do not. That does not, of course, apply to the Senate. We have had people without sight in Parliament: Trevor Morgan was here in the early 1970's on the Conservative side.

**The Joint Chairman (Senator Hays):** Senator Connolly, I think Doctor Foreman would like to ask you a question.

**Mr. Foreman:** I was just going to thank the Senator for his kind remarks about the Institute and about Mr. Lepofsky. I would also like to thank the Committee from the point of view of letting my guide dog in.

**Senator Connolly:** Good, good. I think I can remember a man — I believe his name was Estey or something of that nature, but whatever his name was, I think he may have been the first in Parliament, this man whose name escapes me; and for this I apologize. There is a great story of an exchange between Mackenzie King, R. B. Bennett and this man at one time over the Doukhobors — one of the great stories on the record of Parliament.

But I would like to ask Mr. Lepofsky this. You have been talking, and the other groups which have represented the handicapped have also been talking, about the importance of integrating the handicapped community into the normal stream of public life.

I think great strides have been made as education has advanced, and as public education in this respect has improved. I do not ask you this as a trick question, but I wonder whether, by segregating the handicapped you are not, to use your own words, signalling to the disabled that they are forever a segregated group?

Would your position not be stronger before the law, even before these provincial laws which you have criticized here, if a nondiscriminatory clause applied equally to you, whether you are handicapped, equally to me, whether I do not happen to be physically handicapped, maybe mentally and so on; but would it not be better in the long run not to have a special category set out in a constitution which, presumably, is to last for a very long time?

**Mr. Lepofsky:** I can answer that question, Mr. Chairman, briefly. First, I thank you for your compliments with respect to my potential future in Parliament; but my immediate concern, perhaps a little myopic, is that I have another four bar examinations to write and I will continue to be a law student for a lot longer.

On the question of integration generally, I must say, particularly under the leadership of the new management of the CNIB with Mr. Mercer, among other things, CNIB as well as other organizations are becoming much more active in adopting integration of handicapped people into society as a goal, phasing down and phasing out segregationist programming and lobbying for equal rights legislation; this is demonstrative of our kind of work.

While there has been segregation, in fact somewhat imposed by handicapped organizations over the years, this is something which is changing, and I would say that the three gentlemen in front of you representing the CNIB are hoping and striving to see that change continue and accelerate.

As to whether it is somewhat discriminatory or special treatment to mention us expressly in the equality clause, I have two answers or brief points to make to that. First, is that, as I have mentioned in my general remarks, if you do not put us in expressly, and merely say equality before the law without discrimination period; then, you are leaving it to us to have to litigate and go to court and spend thousands of dollars and try our luck.

First of all, I do not think we could afford it too readily, and secondly, we are at risk that we would lose. Frankly, having read a good deal of civil liberties case law, which is a particular area of law which interests me, in Canada our courts have a restrictive or very narrow approach to the treatment of civil liberties and only enforce them, as evidenced by the treatment of the 1960 Bill of Rights, when there is no way out: and even then they do not.

So that my concern is that we may well not win such a case, no matter what the intention is of the Senate, no matter what the intention is of the House of Commons in passing this bill. The only way we could be sure to be in, speaking from a legal point of view, is to put us in. Saves us money and improves our chances.

**The Joint Chairman (Senator Hays):** Thank you very much, Mr. Lepofsky.

At this time, I would like to thank you on behalf of the Committee. Mr. Mercer, Dr. Foreman, I want you to know that your dog is most welcome in here. I was going to say something and I thought better of it after. I have great respect for dogs.

In your brief you have raised some problems that I am sure none of the Committee had heard before, at least I had not, and we appreciate your being here.

Thank you very much.

**Mr. Lepofsky:** Thank you.

**The Joint Chairman (Senator Hays):** Mr. Mercer, did you have something you wished to say?

**Mr. Mercer:** Yes, Mr. Chairman.

I know that our president, Mr. Dick Smith from Winnipeg, would like me to express thanks and appreciation from CNIB for all of you today for taking the time to listen to our point of view, so thank you very much.

**The Joint Chairman (Senator Hays):** Thank you.

# APPENDIX 2: DAVID LEPOFSKY'S GUEST COLUMN IN THE *TORONTO STAR*, 2 MARCH 2020

Canada mourns the passing of Sen. David Smith, who dedicated decades to public service as a municipal and federal politician. Let's ensure that his eulogies recognize his enduring and incredible achievement for millions of Canadians with disabilities.

It is known to far too few that he played a decisive role in the successful grassroots battle to get Parliament to include equality for people with disabilities in Canada's proposed Charter of Rights. He championed that cause not on the front pages of newspapers, but where we needed help the most, in the backrooms of the halls of federal political power.

Forty years ago, Prime Minister Pierre Trudeau proposed to add a Charter of Rights to Canada's Constitution. His proposed Charter of Rights included a guarantee of equality rights, to protect against discrimination by laws and governments. However, that proposed equality clause left out equality for people with disabilities.

A number of us in the disability community rushed to campaign to get Parliament to add disability equality rights to the Charter. We contended that otherwise, the Charter would only guarantee equality for some. Equality for some means equality for none.

It was a near hopeless uphill battle. Trudeau was racing to blitz his constitutional reforms through Parliament. We had no internet, email, social media or other such campaigning tools. The media gave us scant attention.

Thankfully, along came a new Liberal backbench MP David Smith. Entirely unconnected to our campaign, earlier in 1980 he had been appointed to chair an all-party Parliamentary committee to hold public hearings on disability issues, because the UN had declared 1981 to be the International Year of Disabled Persons. Those hearings were undoubtedly a Government PR gesture, of which we people with disabilities have seen many.

Yet those hearings galvanized Smith. He learned about the pressing need to amend the proposed Charter of Rights to protect equality for people with disabilities, before Parliament passed the Charter. With no public fanfare, and known only to a few, he took it on himself to work the backrooms on his own impetus, buttonholing MP after MP, pressing our case.

The result of all these efforts? On Jan. 28, 1981, another Parliamentary Committee (of which Smith was not a member) was debating the Trudeau constitutional reforms when it held a historic vote. It unanimously voted to amend the proposed Charter of Rights to entrench equality for people with disabilities as a constitutional right.

Smith was likely not even in the room where that committee was meeting. Yet he was arguably the most important MP, relentlessly and successfully advocating for our cause behind-the-scenes. Equality for people with disabilities was the only right that was added to the Charter during those debates.

To my knowledge, Smith sought no limelight for this achievement. Yet as we look back on his life of accomplishments, this should rank very high among them.

Decades later, the grassroots campaign across Canada to win strong disability accessibility legislation at the federal and provincial levels traces itself back to that historic amendment to the proposed Charter of Rights. It spawned accessibility laws enacted in Ontario, Manitoba, Nova Scotia and federally. Other provinces are now playing catch up.

Rest in peace David Smith, with our undying gratitude for what you have done for everyone in Canada for generations to come.

# APPENDIX 3: PROCEEDINGS OF THE JOINT COMMITTEE AMENDING SECTION 14 OF THE CHARTER OF RIGHTS TO ENTITLE DEAF PEOPLE IN COURT PROCEEDINGS TO AN INTERPRETER, 28 JANUARY 1981

The proceedings of the Special Joint Committee of the Senate and the House of Commons on the Constitution of Canada on January 28, 1981, included the following:

**The Joint Chairman (Mr. Joyal):** I would invite honourable members to take the next amendment related to Clause 14.

On Clause 14 — *Interpreter*

**The Joint Chairman (Mr. Joyal):** There are two amendments in relation to Clause 14, the first one is the amendment identified N-20, Clause 14, page 5. It is an amendment moved by the New Democratic Party and I would like to invite Mr. Robinson.

**Mr. Robinson:** Mr. Chairman, we are on N-20, are we?

**The Joint Chairman (Mr. Joyal):** I have already called the amendment identified as N-20, Clause 14, page 5.

**Mr. Robinson:** Thank you, Mr. Chairman.

I would then move this amendment as follows, that Clause 14 of the proposed Constitution Act, 1980 be amended by striking out lines 40 to 44 on page 5 and substituting the following:

14. Every person has the right to the assistance of an interpreter in any proceedings before a court, tribunal, commission, board or other authority in which the person is involved or is a party or a witness if the person does not understand or speak the language in which the proceedings are conducted, or is subject to a hearing impairment.

Et en français, il est proposé

Que l'article 14 du projet de Loi constitutionnelle de 1980 soit modifié par substitution, aux lignes 40 à 43, de ce qui suit:

«14. Les personnes qui ne comprennent pas ou ne parlent pas la langue dans laquelle se déroulent des procédures devant une instance judiciaire, quasi-judiciaire, administrative ou autre, ont droit à l'assistance d'un interprète; les personnes atteintes de déficiences auditives ont également ce droit dans les mêmes circonstances.»

**The Joint Chairman (Mr. Joyal):** Before I invite you to give an explanation, Mr. Robinson, the honourable James McGrath on a point of order.

**Mr. McGrath:** I am just wondering, Mr. Chairman, at first glance it would seem that our amendment, which is CP-7, Clause 14, page 5 should come first.

**The Joint Chairman (Mr. Joyal):** The only reason I have called the amendment proposed by the New Democratic Party, I refer to you the previous indication that the Chair would call in order the amendments, and so far as the New Democratic Party amendment deals with line 40 and your amendment deals with line 43, that is why I have to call according to the previous procedure, I have to call the New Democratic Party amendment first even though the Chair realizes that if the New Democratic Party amendment is accepted by this Committee, the amendment identified CP-7 is already included in the previous amendment, but if the amendment by the New Democratic Party is not accepted that does not prevent you from moving the amendment identified as CP-7.

**Mr. Chrétien:** Mr. Chairman, for a matter of clarification, you gave the background of the discussion on Clause 14. We cannot accept the amendment of Mr. Robinson and I will explain why, but we can accept the amendment of the Conservative Party and so perhaps we should deal with the two and I can give the explanation to Mr. Robinson so that it will not — the intention is all the same but the way of drafting one is better than the drafting of the other, and the Robinson amendment, if I can use that term, the 150th amendment, it is too vague and could create all sorts of problems.

I am informed, for example …

**Mr. Robinson:** Mr. Chairman, on a point of order. Mr. Chairman, with great respect to the Minister, if I might have an opportunity to at least explain the amendment before it is shot down by the Minister. That is, I believe the normal procedure.

**The Joint Chairman (Mr. Joyal):** I will invite Mr. Robinson to present his amendment in the usual way.

**Mr. Robinson:** Thank you, Mr. Chairman.

I know that the Minister still has an open mind on the subject and will be listening with great interest and will not be subject to any impairment involving hearing. it is one thing not to listen, Mr. Chairman, it is another thing to be subjected to a hearing impairment.

Mr. Chairman, the purpose of this amendment is to expand the protection presently accorded in Clause 14 to an interpreter, and it is not something which is unusual or vague or difficult to apply, as the Minister suggested, because with respect, Mr. Minister, through you, Mr. Chairman, the wording is taken precisely from the terms of Bill C-60.

Now, once again, Mr. Minister, I would have assumed that the same people who advised you on Bill C-60 would be advising you today and I am sure that they would not have wished to advise you at that time to accept something which was vague or impossible to interpret.

Mr. Chairman, it is not a question of vagueness, it is a question of scope. In Clause 14, as the amendment would read, we would be going beyond proceedings in which a person was a party or witness, but we would be going to proceedings in which a person was involved, to use the words of the proposed amendment, and we would also be expanding the words to deal with other authorities.

As I say, this is the proposal in Bill C-60, it was accepted by the MacGuigan-Lamontagne Committee, it was not considered by the government two years ago to be vague or difficult to interpret. I suggest that the amendment was reasonable and that it should be accepted. I would hope that it would be accepted by the government.

I would also say that I am pleased to hear that the government is prepared to accept the amendment with respect to deafness which is being proposed both by the Conservative Party and the New Democratic Party, but I would hope that the government would recognize the desirability of expanding this in terms which it was presented in Bill C-60.

Thank you, Mr. Chairman.

**The Joint Chairman (Mr. Joyal):** Thank you very much, Mr. Robinson.

**Mr. Chrétien:** I will ask my advisor to give the explanation but the fact that it was accepted in Bill C-60, the deputy minister is not the same, perhaps he is a judge now, so we have a different troop and to explain why we feel after reflection what is better.

**Mr. Ewaschuk:** Obviously in relation to the proceedings the administration of justice is conducted by provincial authorities. The expression in which the person is involved means more than the party or the witness so you can have all kinds of interested parties come to court and this would in fact give them a constitutional right to have interpreters so they could understand the proceedings.

Now, oftentimes that is so. If it is a language problem, the interpreter is there, and there is translation that goes on and there is certain accommodation, but if you were to do that for everybody who came in, who is somehow involved, they may be in fact a relative or so who does not understand the language but they are not a witness, they are not the accused and such, it could have certain important ramifications for the administration of justice and I think that the position we take is that, yes, we are not opposed to that but we would let the provincial try to work that out rather than saying that they have to in fact do it.

We say the minimal, yes, it should be for the witness, it should be for the party, extended to the deaf, but that is as far as we are willing to go at this particular time.

**The Joint Chairman (Mr. Joyal):** Thank you very much.

Mr. Robinson to conclude.

**Mr. Robinson:** Just a question, Mr. Chairman, if I may, to the officials or to the Minister.

Is it my understanding that Clause 14 as the government is proposing now would not cover the right to an interpreter of a person who is, let us say, arrested or detained; if they are being questioned, that they would not be protected by this right to an interpreter, that is my reading at least of Clause 14. Whereas, under the proposed amendment, because of the insertion of the words "or other authority" in which the person is involved, they would be protected in those circumstances?

**Mr. Ewaschuk:** Well, I kind of doubt that. When you are talking about proceedings before another authority, I doubt that you would get a court characterizing that as being police interrogating somebody.

You must keep in mind again, and we have gone over this before, that the Crown has to prove a statement as voluntary, so if you have two English policemen who were in fact interrogating somebody who did not understand English, it is very unlikely that the judge is going to find that that statement is voluntary.

So rather than say that the police have to bring in, anytime there is a question on whether or not somebody was being interrogated can understand English, they will do that as a matter of course if they want to get that statement in, but it would not be an absolute right in relation to proceedings because I just do not see that as being characterized as proceedings.

**The Joint Chairman (Mr. Joyal):** Mr. Robinson to conclude.

**Mr. Robinson:** Yes, Mr. Chairman.

Just to conclude, I would remind the Minister through you, Mr. Chairman, of the recent case in Toronto in which this very point was canvassed and raised in connection with an East Indian who was questioned under circumstances in which it was alleged that he did not understand the language in which he was being questioned.

I would also suggest that the words "other authority" have been interpreted by our courts to include circumstances in which a person is being questioned by the police, that the person is an authority figure, when we are dealing, for example, with confessions, and that is the way Canadian jurisprudence has interpreted those words.

I think, Mr. Chairman, with great respect to the present deputy minister, that the advice which was given in 1978 was very sound advice and I would suggest that this Committee should accept that advice.

**The Joint Chairman (Mr. Joyal):** Thank you, Mr. Robinson.

Amendment negatived.

**The Joint Chairman (Mr. Joyal):** I would like then to invite the motion identified as CP-7, Clause 14, page 5, the motion proposed by the Conservative Party to be moved and invite the Honourable James McGrath to so do.

**Mr. McGrath:** Mr. Chairman, before I read the amendment there is a slight change. The amendment should read "ed or who is deaf" to make it conform technically with the page.

Mr. Chairman, the amendment is as follows, I move that Clause 14 of the proposed constitution act, 1980, be amended by striking out line 43 on page 5 and substituting the following:

ed or who is deaf has the right to the assistance of an"

I will ask my colleague, Senator Tremblay, if he will read it en français, s'il vous plait.

[Translation]

**Senator Tremblay:** Just to please my colleague who could very well read it himself.

[Text]

Il est proposé

Que le projet de Loi constitutionnelle de 1981 …

j'imagine soit modifié par substitution …

Il faut continuer à dire 1980, n'est-ce pas? Merci, monsieur le président, de cette indication.

… soit modifié par substitution, à l'article 14, de ce qui suit:

«14. La partie ou le témoin qui ne peuvent suivre les procédures, soit parce qu'ils ne comprennent pas ou ne parlent pas la langue employée, soit parce qu'ils sont atteints de surdité, ont droit à l'assistance d'un interprète.»

[Translation]

**The Joint Chairman (Mr. Joyal):** Thank you, Senator Tremblay.

[Text]

Mr. McGrath, to propose the motion in the usual way?

**Mr. McGrath:** Thank you very much, Mr. Chairman.

I must be getting overtired or perhaps I must be developing a hearing impediment because I thought I heard the Minister say he was going to accept our amendment.

**Mr. Chrétien:** Yes. Yes.

**Mr. McGrath:** Well, Mr. Chairman, now that that fact has been so dramatically verified I expect any minute to ask the Minister to give consent to have the amendment withdrawn to be moved on a subsequent amendment. It would be more in keeping with the experience we have had here.

However, Mr. Chairman, this is a serious amendment and I am very, very encouraged by the fact that the government has seen fit to accept it because there are a number of people in this country who have a serious hearing handicap. Indeed, I stand to be corrected on this, but there are over 200,000 Canadians who are deaf or have a hearing disability to the point where they are clinically or legally deaf, and it is a serious problem because their handicap is not apparent and it becomes compounded when they are party to legal proceedings. That is why this amendment is so important.

It is not without interest to note that we are moving in the direction of recognizing the rights of these people, for example in broadcasting they have mechanical devices now in the public broadcasting system in the United States for the hard of hearing or the deaf. I understand that we are moving in that direction in Canada as well.

Mr. Chairman, I am gratified that the government has accepted our amendment and, as a matter of fact, I am speechless.

**Mr. Crombie:** Two good events on one motion. Two!

**The Joint Chairman (Mr. Joyal):** I will not speak on behalf of the government, of course, honourable James McGrath, but you might wonder why the government has changed its mind about that and I told you last week that some see the light because they found their hearts and some change their mind because they hear the voices, and that is probably what happened in the present case.

**An hon. Member:** I am sure they heard footsteps.

**The Joint Chairman (Mr. Joyal):** I see that the honourable members are ready for the vote.

Amendment agreed to.

Clause 14 as amended agreed to.

# APPENDIX 4: PROCEEDINGS OF THE JOINT COMMITTEE AMENDING SECTION 15 OF THE CHARTER OF RIGHTS TO INCLUDE DISABILITY AS A PROTECTED GROUNDS, 28 JANUARY 1981

The proceedings of the Special Joint Committee of the Senate and the House of Commons on the Constitution of Canada on January 28, 1981, included the following:

On Clause 15 — *Equality before the law and equal protection of the law.*

**The Joint Chairman (Mr. Joyal):** I will invite, then, honourable members to take the amendments in relation to Clause 15. There are a certain number of amendments dealing with Clause 15, especially taking into account that very clause of the proposed motion has two subclauses, Clause 15(1) and Clause 15(2), and in order to deal with the two subclauses in order I would like to invite honourable members to take the amendment identified G-20, Clause 15(1) page 6.

There are two subamendments to that amendment. The first subamendment that the Chair will invite honourable members to take is the one identified N-21, Clause 15(1), page 6, revised, that is the one with the word "revised" on it, and the next subamendment in relation to the same main amendment is the one identified as CP-8(1), Clause 15, page 6.

So it means that the first subamendment we will be dealing with is the last one that I have mentioned, CP-8(1), Clause 15, page 6, but before we deal with that second subamendment I would like to invite Mr. Irwin to move, or Monsieur Corbin, to move the one identified G-20, subclause 15(1), Page 6.

Monsieur Corbin.

**M. Corbin:** Merci, monsieur le president.

Or, je propose

Que le paragraphe 15(1) du projet de Loi constitutionnelle de 1980 soit modifié par substitution, à la rubrique qui précède la ligne 1, et aux lignes 1 à 5, page 6, de ce qui suit:

«Droits à l'égalité

15. (1) La Loi ne fait acception de person ne et s'applique également à tous et tous ont droit à la même protection et au même bénéfice de la loi, indépendamment de toute discrimination, notamment des discriminations fondées sur la race, l'origine nationale ou ethnique, la couleur, la religion, le sexe ou l'âge.»

Mr. Chairman, I would like to move that the heading preceding Clause 15 and Clause 15(1) of the proposed Constitution Act, 1980, be amended by striking out the heading immediately preceding line 1 and lines 1 to 5 on page 6 and substituting the following:

"Equality Rights

15. (1) Every individual is equal before and under the law and has the right to the equal protection and equal benefit of the law without discrimination and in particular, without discrimination based on race, national or ethnic origin, colour, religion, sex or age."

[Translation]

Thank you, Mr. Chairman.

**Le coprésident (M. Joyal):** Thank you, Mr. Corbin.

[Text]

I would like to invite Mr. Robinson on behalf of the New Democratic Party to introduce the subamendment revised N-21, Clause 15(1), page 6.

**Mr. Robinson:** Thank you, Mr. Chairman. I am very pleased to move the subamendment as follows …

**Mr. Epp:** Just a point of order, Mr. Chairman.

I must have misunderstood you. I take it now that you are going to ask for the New Democratic subamendment first and then call for our subamendment to the subamendment?

**The Joint Chairman (Mr. Joyal):** Yes. That is what I have already stated, Mr. Epp.

**Mr. Epp:** I did not understand it that way. I thought you asked for our subamendment to the amendment.

**The Joint Chairman (Mr. Joyal):** No, that is not the way.

Go on, Mr. Robinson.

**Mr. Robinson:** Thank you, Mr. Chairman.

The amendment is as follows, first of all in English, this is to the proposal of the government, I move that the proposed amendment to Clause 15(1) of the proposed constitution act 1980, be amended by (a) striking out everything immediately following the words "Every individual is equal" and substituting the following:

in, before and under the law and has the right to equal protection and equal benefit of the law, and to access to employment, accommodation and public services, without unreasonable distinction on grounds including sex, race, national or ethnic origin, colour, religion or age.

And then, Mr. Chairman, there are six additional subsections. The first is: (b) adding to Clause 15(1) the following: "physical or mental disability,"; (c) adding to Clause 15(1) the following: "marital status,"; (d) adding to Clause 15(1) the following: "sexual orientation,"; (e) adding to Clause 15(1) the following: "political belief,"; (f) adding to Clause 15(1) the following: "lack of means"; and (g) moving the word "or" so that it appears immediately after the penultimate proscribed ground of discrimination.

Mr. Chairman, those are our proposed amendments to Clause 15(1) to recognize some very fundamental and important grounds of discrimination which are not recognized in the government's proposal.

In French, Mr. Chairman, if you would like me to read this in French.

Il est proposé

Que le projet de modification du paragraphe 15 (1) du projet de Loi constitutionnelle de 1980 soit modifié par:

a) substitution, à ce qui suit le membre de phrase «La loi ne fait exception de personne», de ce qui suit:

«Tous ont droit à la même protection et au même bénéfice de la loi, ainsi qu'à l'accès aux emplois, au logement et aux services publics, indépendamment de toute distinction abusive fondee notamment sur le sexe, la race, l'origine nationale ou ethnique, la couleur, la religion ou l'âge.»

b) adjonction, au paragraphe 15 (1), de ce qui suit: «les déficiences physiques ou mentales,»

c) adjonction, au paragraphe 15 (1), de ce qui suit: «la situation familiale,»

d) adjonction, au paragraphe 15 (1), de ce qui suit: «l'inclination sexuelle,»

e) adjonction, au paragraphe 15 (1), de ce qui suit: «les croyances politiques,»

f) adjonction, au paragraphe 15 (1), de ce qui suit: «l'insuffisance de moyens.»

g) insertion de la conjonction «or» avant la dernière distinction discriminatoire énoncée au paragraphe 15 (1) tel que modifié.

Monsieur le president, je crois que cela doit etre «ou» et non' pas «or».

Mr. Chairman, again these are proposed additions and changes to Clause 15(1) and I am very pleased to note that the Conservative Party will also be proposing the addition of physical and mental disability, supporting our amendment on that particular subclause.

**The Joint Chairman (Mr. Joyal):** Thank you, Mr. Robinson.

I would like to invite the honourable James McCrath to move the amendment on behalf of the Conservative Party.

**Mr. McGrath:** Mr. Chairman, my colleague, Mr. Crombie will do so.

**The Joint Chairman (Mr. Joyal):** The honourable David Crombie.

**Mr. Crombie:** Thank you, Mr. Chairman.

Mr. Chairman, dealing with Clause 15 and our amendment to it, which is numbered CP-8(1) on the sheet, I wish to move that the proposed amendment to Clause 15 of the proposed constitution act, 1980, be amended by striking out the words "or age" in Clause 15(1) thereof and substituting therefor the following words:

age or mental or physical disability.

En français, il est proposé

Que le projet de modification de l'article 15 du projet de loi constitutionnel de 1980 soit modifie par la substitution, a «ou l'âge», au paragraphe (1), de «l'âge ou les déficiences mentales ou physiques.»

Mr. Chairman, speaking to the motion, my understanding is that the government is willing to accept our amendment.

Now, I am not sure we can continue to take this prosperity any longer!

However, on behalf of those groups, organizations and individuals who find themselves physically and mentally disabled in this country, I would like, on their behalf, since I am the spokesman on their behalf at this point, to offer my thanks to the government for their acceptance of the amendment.

Thank you very much.

**The Joint Chairman (Mr. Joyal):** Thank you, the honourable David Crombie.

**Mr. Chrétien:** But who told you that I have accepted the amendment. I have not yet spoken. I think it was a good put on.

**Mr. Crombie:** I have already spoken to Bob Kaplan and he has said it is okay!

**Mr. Chrétien:** If I can have five minutes, I will call the Prime Minister.

It is with great pleasure that I accept the amendment on behalf of the Government.

I do not think we should debate it. There was a great deal of debate. I was very anxious that we should proceed tonight. They were preparing to have a big group tomorrow.

You can have lots of beer on my health.

Thank you for your good representation.

**The Joint Chairman (Mr. Joyal):** So the amendment is carried, I should say wholeheartedly with unanimous consent.

Amendment agreed to.

**The Joint Chairman (Mr. Joyal):** I would like, then, to invite honourable members to come back to the first subamendment and to invite Mr. Robinson to introduce the amendment in the usual way.

**Mr. Robinson:** Thank you, Mr. Chairman.

I certainly would like to express my sincere gratitude to the Minister for listening to the concerns of both the physically and mentally disabled.

I know the Minister will recognize that this is in many ways unprecedented and a historic occasion, because it is a right which has not yet been recognized in many international covenants and charters; I think the Minister and the government deserves full credit for accepting the recommendations of the subcommittee and of many other Canadians.

Certainly, I want to join with my colleague and friend, Mr. Crombie, in thanking you, Mr. Minister, for accepting this very important amendment.

**Mr. Chrétien:** I forgot to mention, with your permission, Mr. Chairman, that I think we should thank all the members of the special committee, presided over by Mr. David Smith, who has worked very hard indeed.

I would like to thank Mr. Smith and all members of the Committee who have worked all summer very hard on the problem.

We are entering a new field, and quite properly breaking good ground. I think we should be careful that we should not take it to the extent of opening the door to a list that would be meaningless. It is on the list as an amendment which will be accepted.

**Mr. Robinson:** Once again, Mr. Chairman, I know that the Minister will listen carefully to the representations made on the amendment which we will be proposing, just as he has listened with care to the representations of the groups representing the physically and mentally disabled.

Mr. Chairman, I also cannot resist pointing out that this fundamental right to protection from discrimination on grounds of physical and mental disability is surely one which should be accorded to all Canadians right across Canada, in every province in Canada, and that no provincial government should be permitted to opt out of providing basic and fundamental rights and freedoms to the handicapped.

Mr. Chairman, perhaps my Conservative colleagues would pay particular attention to that point, that the effect of their proposed amending formula, would grant rights to the handicapped in some provinces and not to the handicapped in other provinces which chose to opt out.

**The Joint Chairman (Mr. Joyal):** Mr. Robinson, I regret to interrupt, but as I have already expressed on other occasions, I think you should address yourself to the content of the proposed amendment.

The amending formula will come later on in our discussions; but at this point we are dealing on a clause which does not have any reference to the amending formula as such.

I would invite you to restrict your remarks to the contents of the proposed amendment.

**Mr. Robinson:** Thank you, Mr. Chairman.

I wonder if I could seek some guidance from the Chair, in that this is a rather substantive amendment and there are a number of major areas which will be touched upon in the course of the amendment and in that on each clause I will be proposing that they be voted upon separately, I wonder whether we might call it 10:30 p.m. and I might explain to you the purpose of the proposed amendment immediately upon starting tomorrow morning, rather than giving an explanation, then adjourning and having to explain again tomorrow morning?

**The Joint Chairman (Mr. Joyal):** The Chair is in the hands of honourable members of this Committee, and I would invite the honourable Jake Epp on the very suggestion as expressed by Mr. Robinson.

**Mr. Epp:** Mr. Chairman, I have no comment.

But I want to comment on his amendment.

**The Joint Chairman (Mr. Joyal):** I am sorry.

Mr. Corbin, I repeat that Mr. Robinson has invited honourable members to adjourn at this point instead of cutting him short.

..."

# APPENDIX 5: DAVID LEPOFSKY'S INTERVIEW ON CBC RADIO'S *THIS COUNTRY IN THE MORNING* PROGRAM, 29 JANUARY 1981

### Host: Don Harron

**Don Harron:** A change of heart last night by Justice Minister Jean Chrétien, allowed the Constitutional Committee to include the handicapped, so called, under the proposed Charter of Human Rights. The amendment will give the disabled equal rights and protection under Canadian laws. To comment, David Lepofsky, a Toronto law student and official constitutional spokesman for the Canadian National Institute for the Blind. He's on the phone from his home in Toronto. Good morning, David.

**David Lepofsky:** Good morning.

**Don Harron:** Is that right? It's disabled not handicapped.

**David Lepofsky:** The term that's been included is mental or physical disability.

**Don Harron:** Ah. Now what has the position of the three federal parties been on the inclusion of the handicapped in the Charter of human rights before this?

**David Lepofsky:** To begin, just so people don't get confused on this issue, we're not talking about special rights for the handicapped, we're talking about a section of the Charter of Rights which is to guarantee all persons in Canada the right to equality before the law, and to the equal protection and the equal benefit of the law without discrimination. The section was aimed at laws which discriminate, which give different and unequal and unfair treatment to certain minority groups.

**Don Harron:** So, all the disabled really want is equality?

**David Lepofsky:** That's what were talking about. Now the original proposed Charter, which the government brought forward last fall, was written in such a way that only a few minority groups were entitled to protection, the legal language that was utilized guaranteed minority rights only for certain minorities such as racial minorities and religious minorities. It did not protect the handicapped, and this led to a rather absurd situation. It proposed that some minorities were entitled to equality, while others weren't.

**Don Harron:** You mean some minorities were more equal than others, to quote George Orwell?

**David Lepofsky:** Even worse, it suggested that there would only be minority for some and in our view, minority for some really means privileges for some.

**Don Harron:** Well David what were Mr. Chrétien's arguments against accepting the proposed amendment?

**David Lepofsky:** Well, after I appeared before the Constitution Committee, the justice minister as everyone will recall, proposed wide-ranging amendments to a package of proposals to the Constitution. And he expressly two weeks ago stated that the handicapped were not to be included. He gave us about three reasons why the handicapped should not be included, all of which were absurd, and all of which I think were ultimately the cause for the government changing its views, because their arguments were so devoid of any content.

**Don Harron:** What were the arguments anyways?

**David Lepofsky:** The first argument was that the wording that he was offering would in fact somehow provide protection for the handicapped, that it was open-ended enough so that even though all minorities weren't listed, other minorities could go to court and argue the issue. Any first year law student has learned basic rules of how to interpret a law, and one of the rules that you learn is that when they give you a checklist like this, unless very specialized wording was implemented, and this specialized wording was not offered in this case, that on a checklist such as the six or seven minorities that were offered, would be the only list of protected minorities. So he was suggesting that even though we weren't mentioned, somehow we were still protected. And as a matter of very basic law this was an absurdity.

The second argument they utilized is that we shouldn't include the mentally and physically handicapped because somehow the concept of handicap is too difficult to define. Now the government has utilized vague language in this Charter, it's talked about not being denied unreasonable bail, it's talked about "freedom of expression," and these are all terms which have a certain amount of fluidity, there is certain innate vagueness in them, and the nature of constitutional rights as we've learned from 200 years of experience of constitutional civil rights in the U.S., is that you have to employ language that has a certain amount of fluidity or ambiguity, as long as there's certain basic certainty, the courts will sort out whether blindness is a physical or mental handicap. Whether deafness is a physical or mental handicap. And so, for the justice minister to have argued that the term is too vague, or it was too difficult to define, was frankly contradictory with other language that he was using that was equally or more vague in the Charter, and it was simply an invalid argument. It suggested the courts did not have the expertise to define what is a handicap, and I think they do, and I believe the government has come to that opinion itself.

**Don Harron:** Now —

**David Lepofsky:** The final argument that they utilized it that somehow handicapped right to constitutional equality would be best guaranteed by legislation and not in the Constitution. Well, if our rights are best protected by legislation, why are the rest of Canadians' rights not protected best by legislation as well? Why are we going through this constitutional exercise in the first place? Either we need a Constitution to protect our rights, and if so make sure everybody's protected, or we don't need a Constitution to protect our rights, and make sure everybody's right are protected by legislation.

**Don Harron:** Now were you supported by any political party in your proposals?

**David Lepofsky:** Our proposals, and I should add that while I'm speaking on behalf of the Canadian National Institute for the Blind, and we have been acting very actively on this issue, that other handicapped groups as well have been pushing this issue, and non-handicapped groups, including the Canadian Human Rights Commission, the Canadian Jewish Congress, the various status of women groups, have all been promoting this, so I don't want anyone to believe we are the only people promoting this,

**Don Harron:** Does this include the Native peoples too?

**David Lepofsky:** I don't recall — that is to say, the proposal that we're discussing?

**Don Harron:** They're being left out of the Constitution I understand.

**David Lepofsky:** Well, their claims are being argued and are being very, very strongly argued within the committee from my understanding. As to how that's going to be resolved, unfortunately, my studies for my Bar Exam haven't allowed me the time to follow that particular issue.

**Don Harron:** But you have heard the news that last night Mr. Chrétien was applauded by the Conservative members of the constitutional committee?

**David Lepofsky:** On the handicapped issue and that's because as soon as the package of the Chrétien amendments were tabled two weeks ago, which again left us out, both the Conservatives and the NDP came up with platforms totally in support of handicapped rights to equality being included in the Constitution. So, the government was faced with a very difficult situation. Its arguments were absurd, both opposition parties were sympathetic to us, this is the international Year of the Disabled Person, whose theme is equality for the handicapped, so it would have been kind of embarrassing to go ahead with this. And the ultimate embarrassment for the government, frankly, was that the government appointed a special Committee, a parliamentary Committee on the handicapped last summer. It was chaired by David Smith who's a very bright and capable Liberal member of Parliament from the Toronto area. It was an all-party Committee, it had hearings right across the country last summer on the interests of the handicapped, and in its interim report this fall, one of its first and most strong recommendations was that the handicapped should be included in the right to equality section of the Constitution. So not only did the government face this issue from the opposition, but its own government spokesperson who was appointed to look into this issue of the handicapped rights, had been promoting this issue publicly for some time now.

**Don Harron:** Now what will the inclusion of the disabled in the proposed Charter of Human Rights mean in the future?

**David Lepofsky:** it will mean three things. The first and most directly is that, once this Charter is entrenched in the Constitution, and once it's patriated, assuming that the government goes ahead with its present plans and that there is no legal or political way or cause for it being changed, assuming that all of this happens, what it means is that any law passed in Canada which discriminates against the handicapped will be rendered unconstitutional. For example, there are various provincial statutes which deny blind people the right to sit on a jury even if, even if they don't need eyesight to adjudicate on the trial. Now, there are some trials where eyesight is needed, but I myself am blind and going into the practice of law, and I can tell you that there are a lot of times in a courtroom situation where vision is not needed to be able to know what's going on. And believe me, the job of a lawyer is as difficult if not more difficult than that of a juror, and yet there are many blind practicing lawyers in Canada and the U.S. and hopefully I'll be joining their ranks. So that's an example of a law that discriminates.

Another example is the fact that certain provincial and federal minimum wage laws say that everyone is entitled in employment to being paid a minimum wage. But it then says that certain government officials can license an employer to pay a handicapped employee less than the minimum wage, under certain circumstances, not under all circumstances, under certain circumstances. And there are times when this would be patently discriminatory and that the law would promote it. So, the first effect of these amendments, if this all becomes a real live actual Constitution, is that laws which discriminate unfairly against a person, against the handicapped, will be unconstitutional.

The second goal, and this is very important, this Charter of Rights, once it's enacted, will be something which will be posted up all over the place, will be read by people and children in school, will be discussed publicly, and the notion that will be clearly written on its face — that handicapped are entitled to equality — is something which will be very actively promoted. The biggest problem facing many handicapped persons, specifically in the area that CNIB is experienced, in the area of blind and partially sighted people, is public misunderstanding and discrimination and an unwillingness to perceive a blind person, or other handicapped person, as an equal, and our Constitution will be signaling a new message across Canada, which is that this public stereotype is inaccurate.

And the final effect that this amendment will have is that handicapped people unfortunately, or at least some, have tended to be a little passive, when it comes to promoting their rights. This is changing and this is evidenced by the lobbying by handicapped groups on this particular issue.

**Don Harron:** Thank you David, good luck on the Bar Exams.

**David Lepofsky:** Thanks a lot.

**Don Harron:** I've been speaking to David Lepofsky, a law student and official constitutional spokesman, for the Canadian National Institute for the Blind. He spoke to us from Toronto.

# APPENDIX 6: DAVID LEPOFSKY'S INTERVIEW ON CBC RADIO'S *THIS COUNTRY IN THE MORNING* PROGRAM, 26 NOVEMBER 1981

**Host: Peter Gzowski**

**Peter Gzowski:** In Ottawa, the House of Commons is about to consider the new revised version of the Charter of Rights. In the flurry of anguish and self-congratulation on women and on native people, disabled people have been almost forgotten. My next guest is David Lepofsky, a lawyer who is himself blind, and who is specialized in law affecting the disabled. He's on the line now. Good morning Mr. Lepofsky.

**David Lepofsky:** Good morning.

**Peter Gzowski:** Could you spell out exactly what the Charter of Rights will give disabled Canadians?

**David Lepofsky:** Well up until about a week ago it was going to give us a lot. Unfortunately, with the latest draft that they're offering us, it's going to give us virtually nothing. Section 15 of the Charter, the equality rights section, was supposed to guarantee equality status for all minorities in Canada. It provided that every individual is equal before and under the law and has the right to the equal protection and equal benefit of the law without discrimination on such bases as race, national or ethnic origin, colour, religion, age, sex and particularly of concern to us, physical or mental disability. You see what we're seeking is not some special status for disabled people, but to be recognized as a minority who is entitled to equal rights like all other minorities.

Originally, the Charter did not include the words "physical or mental disability," and we fought very hard, I on behalf of the Canadian National Institute for the Blind, testified before the Constitution Committee seeking the inclusion of the disabled, and many other disabled groups and nondisabled groups pushed, resulting in what we thought to be a major victory last spring. The government agreed to include the disabled as an equal rights minority. Unfortunately, we had a colossal setback in the past few days, one which people aren't really all too aware of and one which is extremely distressing.

You see, the equal rights section, Section 15, is going to be subject to what we've all been hearing called as the legislative override.

**Peter Gzowski:** Mh-hm.

**David Lepofsky:** What that basically means is rather disconcerting, it means that Section 15 guarantees our inalienable right to equality, except when the government takes it away. It makes the Charter into an umbrella that protects us from rain but which is taken away once the rain starts falling.

**Peter Gzowski:** When override was the core of the argument about women's rights, there was a position that one could take that said the override could be a good thing. People could put in discriminatory clauses that would give extra rights to women, on behalf of women. That was that argument. Is there any similar argument about the disabled?

**David Lepofsky:** That argument is totally and utterly false. Section 15(2) allows laws to be passed which are discriminatory in favour of a minority when their objective, or where their aim, is the amelioration of the conditions of a disadvantaged group. So that for example a law could be passed providing some technical aids or Braille typewriters or whatever for disabled people, without it being accused of being discriminatory, as long as its aim was to give an extra helping hand to a disadvantaged minority. So Section 15(2) automatically protects that sort of thing. The override is absolutely unnecessary in that connection.

**Peter Gzowski:** I know you're the last person in the world of whom I ought to ask this question, but why would they take that out, that phrase out. Why have you lost what you appeared to have gained?

**David Lepofsky:** Well, the reason that the override, there's a nice little quiet move going on that the people have not understood and that the media has not really covered. You see, Trudeau originally offered to entrench a Charter to have inalienable rights in the Constitution.

**Peter Gzowski:** Right.

**David Lepofsky:** Okay, and that was what he was offering, and it would bind the federal government and federal power areas and provincial government and provincial power areas. So what happened? The provinces said, "no we don't want it," and they held out and they fought for a year and they went to the Supreme Court of Canada, and they bargained, and they called each other names and all that sort of thing. So, the provinces finally entered into a settlement a couple of weeks ago. What did it say? It said that the provinces would get the Charter, it would bind the provinces, but then they could override it when they used one of these override clauses. And we were told that the provinces would probably not use it, because after all, it would be politically embarrassing, and they even used the term political suicide for them to use it.

Well, there are two very interesting things going on. Firstly, I don't believe that the provinces would fight for a year to get an override section put in the Charter unless they really wanted to have it. I can't believe they'd go through all that effort for something they don't really want to use. I also think that it's rather surprising, we were told that it was thrown in to protect provincial rights, and we can understand that, may agree with it, may disagree with it, but we can understand that. Interestingly, the override section of the Charter adds into it an override in the hands of the federal government. What that means is the federal government can make laws which violate the Charter, and in the case of Section 15, which discriminate against minorities, whether religious, racial, sex or handicap or other minorities, and they can use an override to basically make the charter not apply.

**Peter Gzowski:** So, this is the unchangeable the law unless we decide to change it.

**David Lepofsky:** Not only that, but why, I mean that's bad enough, that's basically making the Charter substantially meaningless. I mean what are inalienable rights when they're not inalienable? But more importantly, the federal government claims that the override is there to protect the provinces, but they've slipped in this federal override which protects the federal government. I've talked to justice ministry officials, and they've given me such answers as, you know, "we won't use it" or "it would be political suicide to use it."

**Peter Gzowski:** And is that whole a question of, if they don't want to use it, why have they got it there? Could you give me, I guess it's a hypothetical question, but it's real to you, something specific that could happen with the override that would be of damage to the disabled.

**David Lepofsky:** There are several laws on the books across Canada today which discriminate against the disabled. There is a crime in the federal Criminal Code for having sexual relations with a feeble-minded person. Now I don't care whether people have been charged under that lately or not, it's on the books. The Ontario marriage legislation provides you cannot get a marriage license if you're mentally defective. There are various provincial, and under the Canada Labour Code, federal laws which permits employers under certain circumstances, sometimes vaguely defined, sometimes specifically defined, to permit employers to pay handicapped people less than minimum wage.

**Peter Gzowski:** There is such a law?

**David Lepofsky:** Yeah, it's not blanket across the board, and they have to get a government license, but sometimes those licenses could be handed out in a rather discretionary manner. This is discrimination which is clearly intended. It may be intended to be beneficial or whatever, albeit with a paternalistic attitude underlying it, but nonetheless it is discriminatory. And, you know, when we're told that it would be political suicide to add an override to a statute like that, that's conscious of the following hypothetical. Could you imagine one of the provincial premiers being turfed out of office during an election campaign, because they enacted a law that discriminated against the disabled, can you see people making their votes in an election to turn, determined at least, based on how a particular innocuous statute affecting disabled rights was phrased.

**Peter Gzowski:** I'm still left with the question that troubled me right from the beginning. Particularly, this is 1981, it's the year of the disabled, and we have here some forces at work which are arguing that the law or the legal situation you're describing, where it's okay to discriminate against the handicap, people are supporting that.

**David Lepofsky:** It's pretty distressing that the year of the handicapped, whose theme is equality, was originally the year in which we thought we got our most substantial breakthrough, our inclusion in the Charter like all other minorities. And I have to emphasize we are not talking about special rights. We want to be treated as an equal rights minority like all other minorities. Unfortunately, what we thought was our major breakthrough, what would be the lasting monument to the year of the disabled, has in fact been subjected to this legislative override. And as a result, will make it quite farcical.

**Peter Gzowski:** And Mr. Lepofsky I got kind of a final question for you. We have seen active demonstrations and effective demonstrations on behalf of similar situations, if I can say that, with women and with native rights.

Those things got into the Constitution largely because of demonstrations not only from within those communicates but from the population at large. Are we going to see the same thing with the disabled?

**David Lepofsky:** The purpose of an equal protection section is to protect the rights of the minority who cannot get the ear of the public, and therefore can't get a fair shake out of the political process. We're going to try our best, I've heard some vague rumours about, you know, London England, if Ottawa doesn't listen, you know, I don't know about that myself. We're going to do our best, we would urge people to contact their MPs and say that they think that equal rights minority section, Section 15, should not be subject to any provincial override, or more importantly, any federal override. You should know, by the way, that one of the most important decisions under the equal rights section in the U.S. Supreme Court, in the entire American experience with equal rights, was the decision to desegregate schools, saying that you can't have separate schools for blacks or for whites. Had there been a legislative override in the United States in 1954 when that case was decided, the chances are, and the likelihood is, that the schools would never have been desegregated in the United States.

**Peter Gzowski:** Nice point.

**David Lepofsky:** So, if a Charter is going to mean anything, when it's protecting the minorities who can't get the ear of the majority, can't get the ear of the political process, of the political system, then it's got to protect rights from precisely actions like a legislative override.

**Peter Gzowski:** Thank you very much.

**David Lepofsky:** Thank you.

**Peter Gzowski:** I've been speaking this morning with David Lepofsky, a lawyer specializing in the law of the disabled. He's at the Harvard Law School this year and studying civil liberties and constitutional law.

## ABOUT THE AUTHOR

David Lepofsky is a retired lawyer, volunteer disability rights community organizer and advocate, and part-time law professor. He graduated with honours from Osgoode Hall Law School with a Bachelor of Laws in 1979 and received a Master of Law from Harvard in 1982. He was admitted to Ontario's Bar in 1981.

From 1982 to 2016, he practised law in Toronto with the Ontario Ministry of the Attorney General in constitutional, civil, administrative and criminal law. For over three decades, he has been an adjunct member of the University of Toronto's Law Faculty. From 2016 to 2023, he was a visiting professor at the Osgoode Hall Law School. Currently, he is a visiting research professor of disability rights at the University of Western Ontario's Law Faculty.

Since the late 1970s, he has advocated for new laws to protect disability rights. From 1994 to 2005, he led the Ontarians with Disabilities Act Committee, winning enactment of the *Accessibility for Ontarians with Disabilities Act*. Since 2009, he has chaired the Accessibility for Ontarians with Disabilities Act Alliance, campaigning to get that legislation effectively implemented. He has also brought test cases in his own name to advance disability rights.

Awards include investiture in the Order of Canada, the Order of Ontario, and the Terry Fox Hall of Fame, honorary doctorates from Queen's University, the University of Western Ontario, the Law Society of Ontario, and Brock University, and awards from other organizations such as the City of Toronto, the Law Society of Upper Canada, the Ontario Bar Association Public Lawyers Section, the Advocates Society, the Ontario Crown Attorneys Association, the American College of Trial Lawyers, the Ontario March of Dimes, and Community Living Ontario.

When *Canadian Lawyer Magazine* listed him among Canada's 25 most influential lawyers in 2010, he was left wondering: "If I am so influential, why doesn't anyone listen to me?"

He is the author of one law book and the author or co-author of over 30 law journal articles and book chapters on topics including constitutional law, criminal law, administrative law, human rights, and the rights of persons with disabilities. His publications have been cited by courts across Canada including several Supreme Court of Canada decisions. He has lectured on a wide variety of legal topics across Canada, and in the U.S., Israel, the Republic of Ireland, Denmark, Belgium, and New Zealand. He has created an extensive online series of videos on disability rights and advocacy, which has garnered over 100,000 views.

He lives in Toronto with his wife and daughter.

Twitter: @davidlepofsky

Jean Chrétien and David Lepofsky. *Photo by Gillian Kearney. Ontario March of Dimes.*

Made in United States
Orlando, FL
04 November 2026

90203413R00238